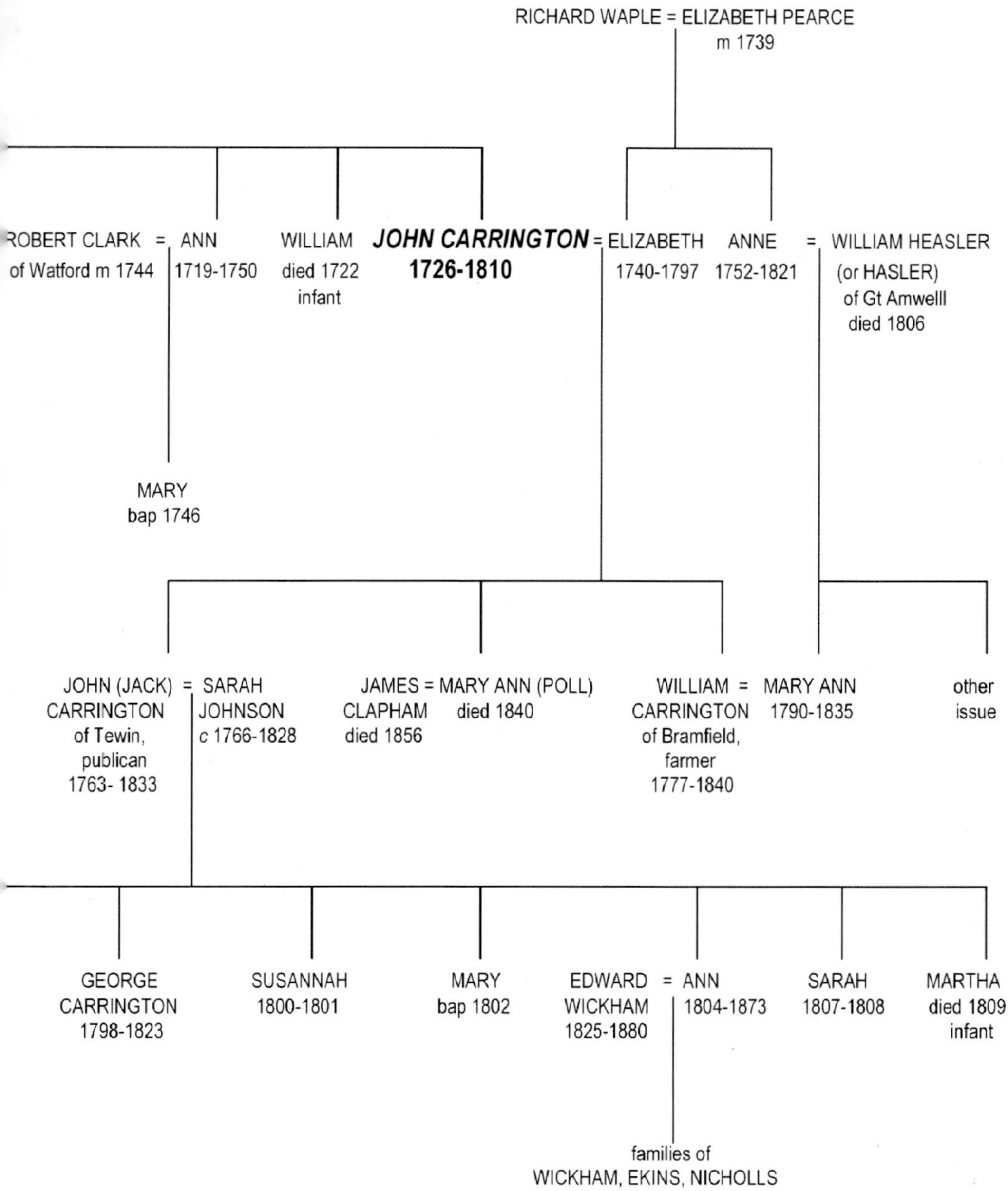
RICHARD WAPLE = ELIZABETH PEARCE
m 1739
ROBERT CLARK = ANN
of Watford m 1744
1719-1750
WILLIAM
died 1722
infant
JOHN CARRINGTON = ELIZABETH
1726-1810
1740-1797
ANNE = WILLIAM HEASLER
1752-1821
(or HASLER)
of Gt Amwelll
died 1806
MARY
bap 1746
JOHN (JACK) = SARAH
CARRINGTON
of Tewin,
publican
1763- 1833
JOHNSON
c 1766-1828
JAMES = MARY ANN (POLL)
CLAPHAM
died 1856
died 1840
WILLIAM = MARY ANN
CARRINGTON
of Bramfield,
farmer
1777-1840
1790-1835
other
issue
GEORGE
CARRINGTON
1798-1823
SUSANNAH
1800-1801
MARY
bap 1802
EDWARD = ANN
WICKHAM
1825-1880
1804-1873
SARAH
1807-1808
MARTHA
died 1809
infant
families of
WICKHAM, EKINS, NICHOLLS

Bacons Farm, Bramfield, from a watercolour traditionally attributed to William, the 13-year-old son of Joseph Strutt, *c*1790

Hertfordshire Record Publications Volume 26

THE DIARY OF

JOHN CARRINGTON, FARMER OF BRAMFIELD,

1798-1810

Volume 1, 1798-1804

Edited and with an Introduction by Susan Flood

Hertfordshire Record Society
Volume for the membership year
2010/11

Hertfordshire Record Society

The publication of this volume has
been assisted by generous grants from:
The Scouloudi Foundation in association with
the Institute of Historical Research
Mr and Mrs Keith Childs
Mr and Mrs Nicholas Collingridge
Mr and Mrs Arthur Mead
Hertford and Ware Local History Society
Hertford Oral History Group

ISBN 978-0-9547561-9-2

Printed and bound in the UK
by Stephen Austin Ltd,
Caxton Hill, Hertford, England

Contents

Illustrations

Foreword

John Carrington's diary offers us a fascinating insight to the many aspects of his long life and times and the society in which he lived. The diaries deserve to be better known both locally and further afield for a unique record of a rural life during the Napoleonic Wars coupled with Carrington's public duties.

The diaries had been deposited in the Hertfordshire Record Office in 1943 (Accession 125 now with the reference DE/X3) by Miss Hilda Wickham, a descendant of Carrington through his granddaughter Anne. The original volumes were in reality a collection of scraps of paper – old auctioneers' sales particulars, accounts, bills, official instructions, assize calendars, navy lists and anything else that came to hand. At some time they had been roughly bound together. They were later conserved and re-bound by County Record Office staff. Any suggestion that Carrington wrote for posterity is easily dispelled. The papers can be divided into two parts – the diary proper opens in 1798 soon after his wife's death and continues until a few days before his own death in 1810. The rest being a collection of notes contained in a vellum bound quarto volume known by the family as the 'Arithmetic Book'. One of the earliest entries describes the 'terable storme' of 1738, and together with notes on local personages, reports of accidents, memories of floods and fires and a cure for lice in cattle they continue until 1802, showing that Carrington still used this volume after he began his main diary.

In the early 1950s Miss Eileen Lynch, a member of staff at Hertfordshire Record Office, heroically typed out the transcript made of the original manuscripts by W Branch Johnson. In 1956 and 1970 Branch Johnson published two popular accounts of the diary. Then finally in 1973 came a publication reproducing some three quarters of the diary and extracts from the Arithmetic Book – '*Memorandoms For' ...The Diary between 1798 and 1810 of John Carrington, Farmer, Chief Constable, Tax Assessor, Surveyor of the Highways and Overseer of the Poor, of Bramfield in Hertfordshire* also edited by Branch Johnson. These works have been long out of print.

To commemorate John Carrington's death in 1810, a small group of local historians led by the County Archivist agreed to republish the diaries in their entirety by returning to the original manuscript and its transcript. The first volume includes the diary from 1798 to 1804 and the Arithmetic Book, the second will include, not only the remaining years of John's diary (1805-1810) but his son's also, taking the Carrington story to 1812. Only some minor repetitions will be omitted. John Carrington's punctuation and spelling were erratic but as editors we have attempted to regulate these solely to make the diary flow in a more readable form for the modern reader. Maps, footnotes and illustrations have been added to enhance the volume's interest.

We acknowledge our grateful thanks to all at Hertfordshire Archives and Local Studies (HALS) for their support. Others include Hertford Museum, Hertford and Ware Local History Society, Hertford Oral History Group, the Tewin Society, Ken Griffin for invaluable information on the criminal cases mentioned by Carrington, and Philip Sheil and Jane Walker for their expertise in drawing the maps and family tree. We have been unable to trace W Branch Johnson's family but are grateful to Phillimore Publishing for permission to use his material. We thank the Hertfordshire Record Society for agreeing to publish the diary and the members and others who gave generously in subscriptions and sponsorship. In addition we record a warm tribute to Eve Sangster who died suddenly in 2008. She was a member of our small team and is greatly missed.

Dorothy Abel Smith, Jill Cordingley, Susan Flood, Graham Irwin, Jean Riddell.

Introduction

The Carrington Family

John Carrington was baptised at Tewin parish church, Hertfordshire, on 2 August 1726, the youngest child of John Carrington of Tewin, gardener, and his wife Mary, née Piggott. An older brother William died as an infant in 1722. The remainder of his siblings were girls, all of whom married and had children of their own. Members of this extended family, including Piggott relatives of his mother, and Pearce and Hasler relatives of his wife Elizabeth, feature prominently in his diary.

Following in his father's footsteps, John became a gardener and was employed as an under gardener by Lady Cathcart of Tewin Water, when 'about 15 years of age in 1743, and lived with her until [she was] taken away to Irland'. He relates at length the story of Lady Cathcart's disastrous fourth marriage to Colonel Hugh Macquire as her abduction presumably put him out of work.[1] However, by the 1750s, he was working for Richard Warren of Marden Hill, Tewin, who soon after 1760 gave him the tenancy of Bacons Farm, held by Warren from the manor of Bramfield. Carrington refers to Richard Warren as 'my good old master' and was a witness to his will.[2]

John married Elizabeth Waple, whose family originally came from Watton at Stone. The couple had three children: John (sometimes known as Jack) baptised at Bramfield on 16 October 1763, Mary Ann (also known affectionately as Poll) born *c*1769, and William baptised at Bramfield on 21 January 1777. A baptism entry for Mary Ann has not been found. Branch Johnson relates that at the back of the diary transcript lent to him by Mrs Rosanna Ekins there was a copy of a certificate, dated 1769, stating that the marriage (of John and Elizabeth) was celebrated by licence at St Paul's Shadwell, London on the 15 February 1760 'by me Jeremy Griffith curate of the s[ai]d parish'.[3] This transcript was not subsequently deposited at

---

[1] See extra items at the end of the Arithmetic Book in Appendix One.

[2] Proved Prerogative Court of Canterbury, May 1768 [A J Camp, *An index to the wills proved in the Prerogative Court of Canterbury, 1750-1800* 6 vols (1992)].

[3] W Branch Johnson, '*Memorandoms For…*', *The Diary between 1798 and 1810 of John Carrington Farmer, Chief Constable, Tax Assessor, Surveyor of Highways and Overseer of the Poor, of Bramfield in Hertfordshire* (Chichester, 1973), p20].

Hertfordshire Archives. In his research Branch Johnson failed to discover the entry referred to in the original St Paul's marriage register. An internet search in *Ancestry* has now revealed that John Carrington, of Tewin, Hertfordshire, actually married Elizabeth Waple 'of this parish' at St Paul's Shadwell by licence on 15 February 1767.[4] The ceremony was performed by Jeremy Griffith, curate, and there were two witnesses: Joseph Liversidge and Thomas Street. The date given for the ceremony on the photograph of the parish register page on *Ancestry* is very clear, as it is written in words. The baptism of John junior was definitely recorded in the Bramfield parish register in 1763, so perhaps this wedding, by licence in London, quietly legalised their situation. They certainly appear to have had a very happy marriage. John refers to Elizabeth as 'my Dame' and composed the epitaph for her tombstone himself. Elizabeth died in January 1797 aged 58 when John was 71 and was buried in Tewin. It was only a year later that he began to write his diary which he continued until just before his own death in 1810.

Jack married Sarah (or Sall) Johnson at St Albans Abbey on 25 January 1791 and seems to have become the landlord of the Rose and Crown Inn at Tewin, also owned by the Marden estate, around this date. The couple had 10 children but sadly only four lived into adulthood. Carrington was called upon to help out Sarah's brother Billy in November 1798 after he had been recruited into the Light Horse regiment which had gone to Ireland. Mary Ann kept house for John after the death of her mother. She married James Clapham of Tewin, bachelor, at Christ Church in Greyfriars, Newgate, on 14 December 1814.[5] In his will her father left her the Eagle public house at Amwell End, Ware, which was run by his cousins the Haslers. William married Mary Ann, a Hasler cousin, and helped to run Bacons Farm in his father's later years, holding the tenancy for some time after John's death.

Farmer at Bacons Farm

The parish of Bramfield, with a total of 1,609 acres and a population of 214 in 1801, has a gently rolling landscape no more than 100 metres above sea level. The soils are freely draining, slightly acid with underlying chalk. The chalk was used to manure the fields and at the end of 1802 Carrington records using

[4] LMA: marriage register for St Paul's Shadwell [Accessed through *Ancestry*].
[5] LMA: marriage register for Christ Church, Greyfriars, Newgate [Accessed through *Ancestry*].

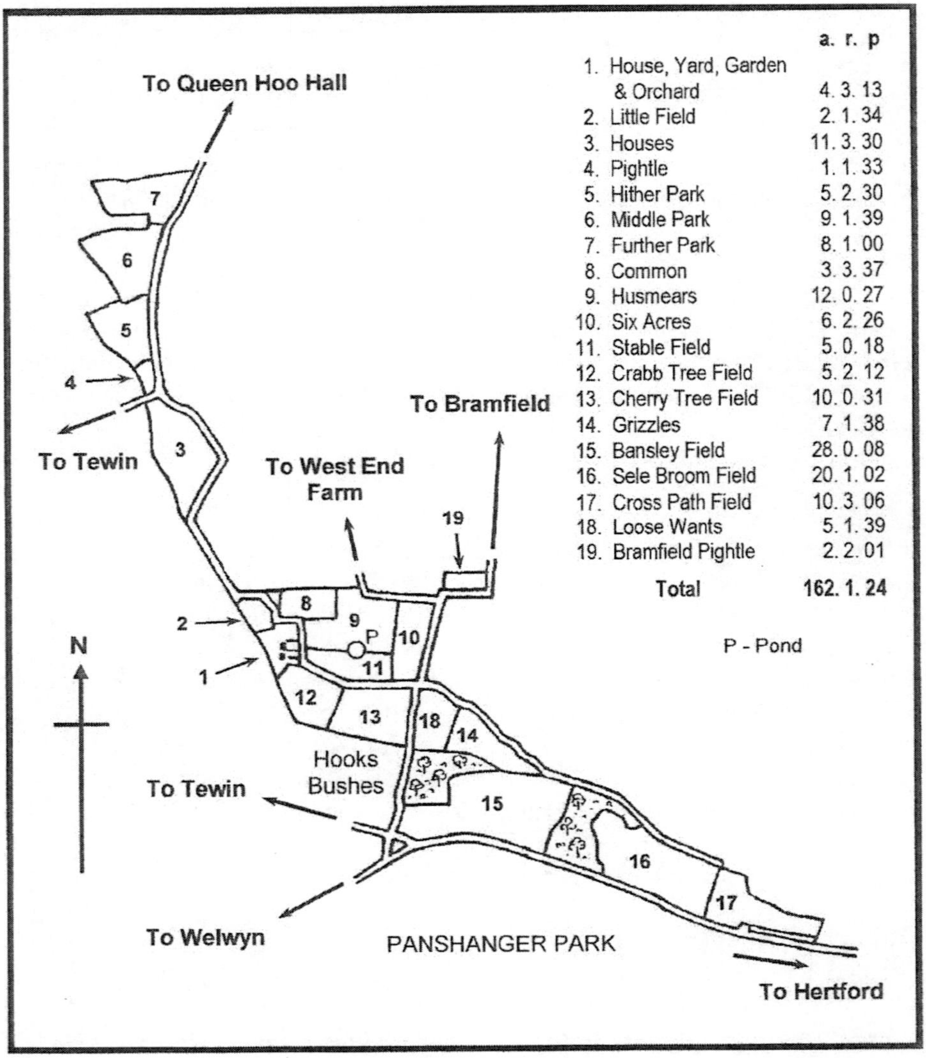

Plan of Bacons Farm, Bramfield based on the Cowper estate survey of 1810 (*HALS: DE/P/P38*)

local labour to dig the pits in order to extract chalk for this purpose at considerable expense.

Bacons Farm lies about 2½ miles north-west of Hertford, half a mile south of Bramfield village and about the same distance east of Tewin. *Hertfordshire Place Names* suggests its name derives from the family of John Bakyn listed on the 1545 Hertfordshire Lay Subsidy roll.[6] The farmhouse Carrington knew may well have been built in the sixteenth century. A substantial building of two storeys, with two gabled cross wings, it suffered extensive damage by a fire in the 1850s and had to be largely rebuilt. There were also timber barns and smaller outbuildings associated with it, one of which Carrington may have used as a brewhouse.[7] The 1810 survey prepared by the Cowper estate steward shows the farm to be about 160 acres, comprising a total of 18 fields of varying shapes and sizes (see plan on previous page based on this survey). Two patches of woodland between Grizzles, Bansley and Sele Broom Field did not belong to the farm and Carrington records paying Earl Cowper's steward for wood taken from there.

Carrington ran his farm with a mixture of arable crops and livestock. He regularly bought and sold cattle, sheep and horses both in private sales and at the local markets and fairs. In December 1802 he negotiated for his flock of sheep to be pastured at Essendon. Sheep dung was a useful manure, so this was something of a reciprocal arrangement as the Essendon farmer would benefit as well as John. Turnips and tares were grown to feed animals but the main crops were barley, oats and wheat. Carrington regularly reports on the quality of the crops in his local area as well as the prices achieved in the markets. Hertfordshire already had an excellent reputation for its barley grown for its flourishing malting industry, centred on Ware and Hertford.[8]

Several factors were at work during this period that affected both the quality of the produce and their sale prices. The weather played a large part in both the quality and quantity of the yield from arable crops. In April 1799 Carrington reports:

---

[6] J E B Gover, A Mawer and F M Stenton, *The Place-Names of Hertfordshire* (Cambridge 1938), p109.
[7] A diary entry at the end of Dec 1803 mentions brewing with water taken from the river at Poplar Green.
[8] P Mathias, *The Brewing Industry in England, 1700-1830* (Cambridge, 1959).

> No grass. No vigetables. No turnops. Occaisond by the long winter and the wather still continues wet and cold. The farmers in general, except some few on the light lands, has not sowd half their barley yet. I have not sowd half mine this 22 of April. Obliged to feed the sheep with hay and oates, maltdust, brann, chaff &c &c.

As a farmer he was interested in the extremes of weather conditions particularly as they affected his business. He reports great storms and floods and the happenings associated with them. The lack of rain in the summer and autumn of 1803 caused other problems as water supplies dried up, and he was forced to fetch water from the River Mimram at Poplar Green. Carrington took all the fish out of his Husmear Pond so that he could clean it out – the first time he had ever done this.

If crop yields were low then prices would remain high in the markets, but the high price would cause some distress to the local population – something that Carrington was all too well aware of as Chief Constable and overseer of the poor. Added to this, England was at war with France, which occasioned some disruption in supplies of grain usually sourced from the Continent. Prices remained high even though 'guaranteed minimum import prices had been raised sufficiently to attract supplies from the continent, even from the enemy'.[9] The government's intervention may well have ensured that supplies of grain would be forthcoming but did little to lower the price.

In December 1799, and again in January and February 1800, Carrington states that he sold his wheat at below the market price for the benefit of the poor of Bayford. This practice got him into real trouble in September 1800:

> **Saturday 27** Markets rather dearer, best wheat about £4 8s 0d. There was a great to do in the market today, for a fortnight back I sold a load to the Association of Poor Men held at Cambells the Green Dragon for 10s per bushell & promisd them some more. Therefore they got a great cheair into the market with a mobb to cheair me but I hid myself, but it had an affect on some of the great dealers, and they was forsd to fly.

---

[9] Cited in J Broad, 'John Carrington and the crisis of 1800-01: ambiguity in the face of the "moral economy"', paper given in Glasgow in April 2012, quoting J Bohsted, *Food Riots, Moral Economy, and Market Transition in England c1550-1850* (Farnham, 2010) p206.

Prices became slightly lower as riots in several towns and cities were reported. Local philanthropy took over in an attempt to ward off the very real threat of civil disturbance. The scale of the crisis was recognised by the government, but their attempts to cut the price of bread by forcing wheat to be mixed with cheaper grains for bread making proved abortive. The disastrous effects of this practice are reported by Carrington in January 1800:

> **Saturday 25** Jorney to the Town Hall, St Albans as a meeting of the Justices and the bakers in the Hund[red] of Cashio being sumond to appear about baking but one sort of flower (*flour*), the wheat to be dresed so as to leave all in but the bran. Went on Dimon, and so it was done, but it was so corse & bad, & did not agree with the constitutions. Maney was hurt & some died & it was orderd to be made againe as usuall.

A year later, in February 1801, when prices had risen even further the situation had not improved:

> **Saturday 7th** Marketts much the same, best wheat about £5 11s 0d per load or 5 bushell. There is an order by Act to take nothing out of the wheat when ground but the broad brann, but this doth not do for they millers &c mix so much bad wheat with it that it is not liked off.

As a human being Carrington was in tune with his local area and had some sympathy with the plight of the poor - he often gave money away out of his own purse. At Christmas he was increasingly generous:

> **[1804] Tusday 25** Being Christmas Day to church at Bramfield. Gave all the poor a dinner. Fetched in the cart except old Brux. Gave him &c 1s.

Collectively the parish vestry meeting also made special arrangements to ease the situation. In November 1799 'Vestrey at Bramfield, Mr Preston overseer, to settle somthing theese dear times on the large famileys. A man with 3 or 4 children to have ½ p[ec]k of flower (*flour*) per week &c &c'.

Carrington was an active member in several local benefit clubs, paying a subscription at their regular meetings held in the White Horse at Hertingfordbury, the Rose and Crown at Tewin and the Green Dragon at Hertford. Local funerals were often paid for out of the funds collected.

As a farmer, the high prices achieved for his produce gave him substantial financial reward, enabling him to purchase government stocks at the Bank of England and invest in property. He played the market and on several occasions reports re-selling for a significant profit within a relatively short time.

Local administrator

There is no doubt that Carrington was well respected as a farmer both for his financial dealings and business acumen; but in addition he served his local and county community in a variety of offices. In 1810 his son records in his own diary that his father had 'served the office of High Constable for the Hundred of Cashio and Assessor and Collector of Taxes for the Parish of Bramfield forty years'.[10] In addition, from time to time, he was appointed by the vestries of both Bramfield and Tewin as Surveyor of the Highways and Overseer of the Poor. All of these necessitated a great deal of travelling about the county, negotiation skills, honest dealing and financial expertise in the handling of often large sums of money.

As one of the Chief Constables for the Hundred of Cashio, in the Liberty of St Albans, to which he was appointed by the St Albans Justices in 1771, he was responsible for the supervision of the constables of the seven parishes in the Eastern Division (namely Bramfield, Codicote, Hexton, Newnham, Norton, St Pauls Walden and Shephall).[11] Historically the Hundred of Cashio in Hertfordshire was the area under the former jurisdiction of the Abbot of St Albans and included all the St Albans parishes and a compact block to the north, west and south-west of these,[12] together with the scattered parishes of Carrington's eastern division. This area became known as the Liberty of St Albans and after the dissolution of the abbey in 1539 held its own Quarter Sessions courts in St Albans. On the formation of the Borough of St Albans in 1553 the town also had the right to hold its own Sessions quite separately from the Liberty, but Carrington did not attend these. The position of Bramfield within this organisation is somewhat ambiguous. The parish is listed under the Hundred of Hertford in Domesday Book and the inhabitants continued to give suit to the Hundred court at Hertford until 1260, at which

[10] HALS: DE/X3/17.

[11] Michaelmas Sessions, 1771 [*HCR* vol IV p3].

[12] This block of parishes includes Barnet, Elstree, Abbots Langley, Redbourn, Rickmansworth, Ridge, Sandridge, Sarratt and Watford.

point the Abbot, as the owner of the manor of Bramfield, asserted his authority and 'annexed it to the Hundred of Cashio'.[13] However, even after 1539, Bramfield business was dealt with at the Quarter Sessions of both Liberty (at St Albans) and County (at Hertford). John Carrington certainly attended both sets of Quarter Sessions.[14]

Before each Quarter Session of the Liberty Carrington arranged to meet his parish constables to discuss what presentments should be made to the court. These could relate to criminal offences of all kinds, including prosecutions for selling goods at short weight. The appointment of parish overseers of the poor had to be ratified at Quarter Sessions and separate sessions were often held in other places to confirm victuallers' recognizances to enable landlords to sell alcohol. Much of this administration necessitated the making of lists: those liable to pay tax of all kinds, men liable for service in the militia and even in 1801 the taking of the first national census. All of these duties relied very heavily on Carrington's familiarity with the local area and the people who lived there. The mass of new legislation enacted because of the war led to a huge increase in his work load.[15] In July 1803 this caused him to remark 'nothing but soldiering. Three times a week to St Albans to draw and swear inn'.

Sometimes he travelled to St Albans only to find that the paperwork had not been completed, or a man drawn for the militia did not turn up. The short-lived Peace of Amiens, signed in March 1802, did not help matters as soldiers were stood down only to be redrafted a year later when war resumed.

Carrington also saw it as his duty as constable to attend the Quarter Sessions and Assizes in Hertford because sometimes Bramfield cases would be heard there. Notes that he made on the Assize calendars of prisoners amongst his surviving papers also show he had a lively interest in the civil cases which were decided before the Assize judges.[16] For example a case heard at the Lent Assizes, 4 March 1799, concerned the sale by Mr Camp of Three Houses, in

---

[13] *VCH Hertfordshire,* vol 2 pp319-322, quoting Assize Roll 325 m20d and 32d.
[14] S Lewis, *Topographical Dictionary* 4 vols (1831) describes Bramfield as 'in the Liberty of St Albans though locally in the Hundred of Hertford'.
[15] A comprehensive description of the legislation relating to the militia and volunteer forces can be found in Branch Johnson, '*Memorandoms For...',* pp16-18.
[16] HALS: DE/X3/14.

the parish of Knebworth, to Mr Bigg of the Hoo, St Pauls Walden, of a horse which subsequently proved unable to work:

> The state of the case is this Camp sold Bigg a horse for £30 for a sound horse. Bigg kept the horse 13 weeks and the horse not going on very well wanted to prove unsound and after calling a matter of 30 wittnesses on both sides their was nothing found a miss in the horse onley to have the meegrams at times and some times work kindly and feed and some times not. So Camp gained the cause.

His familiarity with local conditions and his attitude to aspects of the law are demonstrated most clearly in the extraordinary efforts he made to free Thomas Witty from a death sentence in March 1796. He called on the local gentry before travelling to London to see both the county and Hertford Borough MPs. His trouble was rewarded as

> a repreeve come down to the goaler at Hartford the night before the execution and to me the next morning of the execution about 10 clock at Bacons that our request was granted for his life and likewise his sentance was to Bottinebay (*Botany Bay*) for 7 years onley. The said Thos Witty was borne at the Horse & Groome, Stanborough near Hatfield, a young man about 32 having a wife & 4 children, his offence was for steeling 1 fat sheep out of a drove passing to London, value 1 guinea, in Nov[embe]r last in that distressed time when corne sold at £3 per load.[17]

Local character

Carrington's work as Chief Constable and local Tax Assessor, as well as his business as a farmer, meant that he was known personally to most of the landowners of the district, to parish officials, and to a wide range of farmers, craftsmen and labourers. He himself employed men and local families, and met and conversed with all ranks of society, gleaning local gossip from the upper servants of the landed gentry, their bailiffs, stewards and housekeepers.

He had obviously received some education, although spelling was not always his strong point, and he ensured his children were educated too. The 'Arithmetic Book',[18] as the family traditionally called the volume used by

[17] 'Arithmetic Book', page 77 [Appendix One].
[18] See Appendix One.

Carrington for some of his notes, contains mathematical calculations for such practical matters as the price of produce sold and how to calculate the area of a field and the size of trees. Some pages are signed by W Carrington, John's younger son William.

In John's later years William increasingly managed the farm, leaving his father free to take time off for trips to London and on one occasion in August 1804 to Brighton to see John Randall and his family, former tenants of Bramfield Place Farm. He visited a great number of hostelries throughout Hertfordshire and north London, but in his defence, this was where business deals were transacted, parish feasts were organised and benefit clubs met.[19] Carrington was also a member of the Society of Hertford College Youths from 1786, the Hertford change ringers, but a social member rather than a ringer.[20] As well as those from all parts of Hertfordshire, the membership list of this society surprisingly reveals a large number of members from London and as far afield as Leatherhead in Surrey and Lewisham in Kent. Carrington's circle of acquaintances reached far and wide.

John Carrington and his wife also regularly took in lodgers, some of whom stayed for decades, such as Lieutenant Timothy Hopkins, RN, who died in June 1800. The Lieutenant was almost totally blind and Carrington made frequent trips to London to look after his financial affairs. Another was Mr Cock (we are never told his Christian name) who came to Bacons in November 1802 and remained until his death in March 1812. The various lodgers were presumably a source of income, and some may have been hired help, but others were, or became, close friends.

Carrington's friendship with the London antiquarian and engraver Joseph Strutt is clearly declared in a poem penned in the Arithmetic Book after Strutt's death in 1802.[21] Joseph, his son William and the apprentice Townley came to live at Bacons in about 1790 and left for London again in March 1794.[22] Carrington visited the British Museum with Strutt in May 1790 and accompanied him in December of the same year on a business visit to

---

[19] W Branch Johnson counted more than 80 inns mentioned by Carrington in his diary [Branch Johnson, '*Memorandoms For…*', p1].
[20] HALS: DP48/29/14.
[21] 'Arithmetic Book', page 51 [Appendix One].
[22] 'Arithmetic Book', page 80.

Gorhambury, St Albans, to inspect some paintings.[23] Their friendship continued after the family had left Bacons and Carrington frequently met him in London at The Hole in the Wall and Strutt and his son returned to stay in Hertfordshire on several occasions.

From both the Lieutenant and Strutt came topics of conversation which interested Carrington and gave rise to entries in his diaries: naval battles and matters of antiquarian interest are often noted. But Carrington's information did not all come from conversation and gossip. In the course of research for this edition it has become clear that Carrington must have seen various newspapers and printed books in general circulation, possibly during his visits to London. The *Northampton Mercury* of 26 June 1790 reported on the ringing of the new peal of bells at Adderbury in Oxfordshire, giving the weight of the tenor bell as 26 hundredweight, which Carrington notes.[24] The loss of the Margate hoy in February 1802 was also reported in the press, and the duel between Montgomery and Macnamara in April 1803 was reported in *The Times*.

As a property owner, Carrington would have been allowed to vote at county elections.[25] A number of election squibs survive amongst his papers but his reports, although detailed, are usually simple statements of events that nevertheless do shine a light on the persuasive power of food and drink in the winning of votes. The 1802 county election was different – Carrington declares that it was very much a local issue which lost William Baker of Bayfordbury his seat in July of that year:

> **[July] Monday 12** Begun the pool (*poll*) againe & the pool closed about 6 clock and Baker near 300 behind Lamb. So he gave it upp, & Plumer of Gilston, & Lamb of Brocket Hall was cheared as members for this county. There was no open housen for treating this time, so every freeholder bore his own expences. Baker had served 2 sessions of Parliament for the county before, with Plumer, & a very good man, but he gave his vote in the house for a new tax on malt of 8s per q[ua]rt[e]r which gave a dislike to the mal[t]sters of Ware and other places & they all voted against him.

---

[23] 'Arithmetic Book', pages 41 and 59 [Appendix One].

[24] 'Arithmetic Book', page 1.

[25] Hertfordshire had three MPs – one for the county, and one each for the Boroughs of Hertford and St Albans.

Carrington also notes the contested St Albans Borough election in May 1796 between Samuel Ferrand Waddington, the Hon Richard Bingham and the Hon James Walter Grimston of Gorhambury, St Albans. Grimston was expected to take over the family interest in the town, but the election came sooner than expected when Grimston was still a minor and he had to withdraw. Bingham, sponsored by his brother-in-law Earl Spencer, served as the town's MP until June 1800.[26]

Until the last two years of his life Carrington remained very active, walking long distances, riding further, and participating fully in harvest and sheep-shearing.[27] He regularly attended local markets and fairs, in themselves potential sources of profit as well as local intelligence. The entries in his diary show his wide range of interests from the technical developments of the latest chaff cutting machine he saw in 1804, to ancient coffins dug up in Ware in February 1802.

The Diary

The Carrington papers were deposited in the Hertfordshire Record Office (now Hertfordshire Archives and Local Studies, HALS) in 1943 by Miss Hilda Wickham of Hertford, a descendent of John Carrington's granddaughter Ann.[28] The collection consists of 13 volumes of John Carrington senior's diaries dating from March 1798 to May 1810, together with a small bundle of his papers, the 'Arithmetic Book', and 7 volumes of a diary written by John Carrington junior from May 1810 to December 1812. Before being deposited the pages of the diaries had been folded and sorted loosely into date order then roughly stitched into small volumes, the largest of these measuring 33cm in height by 24cm wide, the smallest 19cm by 16cm. Each volume contains about 40 individual pages, but not all have hand-written text on them.

This is not a diary in any organised sense as Carrington had simply used whatever paper came to hand on which to write his thoughts and doings. He utilised the backs of various types of official forms sent to him in the course of his duties as Chief Constable and local Tax Assessor, including notices entitled 'Statutes and Regulations concerning Alehouses' (1799); instructions,

---

[26] 'Arithmetic Book' page 120 [Appendix One; and R Thorne (ed), *History of Parliament: House of Commons 1790-1820*].

[27] J Broad, 'Farmers and Improvement, 1780-1840' in R W Hoyle, ed, *The Farmer in England, 1650-1980* (Farnham, 2013).

[28] HALS: Accession 125.

tables and forms for tax assessment; sale posters; and militia service returns. Carrington wrote wherever there was space, both horizontally and vertically, in margins and between lines of type, sometimes leaving a confused chronological trail.

In his early researches Branch Johnson was greatly helped by an orderly transcript made of the diaries by Mrs Rosanna Ekins of Hertford, an aunt of Miss Hilda Wickham. However this transcript was not deposited at HALS and it is evident from Branch Johnson's work published in '*Memorandoms For…*' that papers he had originally seen with this transcript were lost sometime before 1943.[29] Branch Johnson began work again on the diaries in 1947 and his early work was serialised in the *Welwyn Times* newspaper from 19 September 1947 to March 1948. A new transcript of the diary was re-typed by Miss Eileen Lynch, a member of the archive staff, and this is available on the open shelves in the Reading Room at HALS.

'The Arithmetic Book', a name given to it by the Carrington family descendants, is a very different type of volume from the diaries themselves. It is of a standard size and form (25cm by 20cm and 3cm in thickness) with a board binding covered in parchment. The name 'John Carrington' is faintly written on both the front and back covers. Many of the pages have beautifully scripted mathematical rules and tables, ornamented with scrolls and spirals, which have been transferred from printing plates. Essays, such as 'Of Decimal Fractions', are in a consistently fluent and legible style by an unknown writer – not the handwriting of John Carrington senior. Spaces and blank pages are filled with notes of miscellaneous events, poems and diary-like entries which are undoubtedly the work of the elder John Carrington. The earliest reference in these is to the year 1725 when Carrington notes the date of execution of 'Johnathon Wild the noted theeftaker & the receaver of stolen goods'.[30] The majority of other entries refer to dates in the 1770s to 1790s: all of the notes and miscellaneous entries could have been written at any time during this period. The latest is 1802, when Carrington refers to his friend Joseph Strutt, demonstrating that he continued to use pages in the 'Arithmetic Book' even after beginning his diary. Other pages have schoolboy sums, and one or two are signed W Carrington, probably John's younger son.[31] Another

[29] See end of 'Arithmetic Book' [Appendix One].
[30] 'Arithmetic Book' page 24.
[31] 'Arithmetic Book' pages 28, 44, 91 and 92.

page is covered in doodles and signatures which could be the work of either John Carrington, father or son.[32] It is not clear who the other writers may be and the volume itself yields up no clues.

After publishing a general history of John Carrington's life and times in 1956 and a much shorter pamphlet in 1970 Branch Johnson produced an edition of the diary itself.[33] '*Memorandoms For...*' was published in 1973 but the length required by its publisher automatically precluded a full transcript of the diary and Branch Johnson lists, with some regret, the many items omitted from this work.[34] The present edition seeks to rectify these omissions and publish, for the first time, a full transcript of the diaries of both John Carrington senior and junior and the jottings from the 'Arithmetic Book' in two volumes. The first contains seven volumes of John Carrington senior's diaries covering March 1798 to the end of 1804 and the contents of the 'Arithmetic Book'.[35] The second will complete John Carrington senior's diaries, ending in May 1810, and will also include the diaries of John Carrington junior, covering May 1810 to December 1812, together with some related papers.[36]

Acknowledgements

I am grateful to the staff and visitors, both past and present, of Hertfordshire Archives and Local Studies for all their help and considered insight into the times of John Carrington. Ken Griffin's monumental work on Hertfordshire convicts and transportees has been invaluable. Especial thanks go to Dr John Broad for allowing me access to his unpublished papers. Also to the committee of the Hertfordshire Record Society for their patience and forbearance in the production of this volume, especially to Heather Falvey who read the final text and spotted typographical errors I had missed. Finally my thanks must go to my husband George, whose computer expertise I could not do without.

Susan Flood, May 2015

---

32 'Arithmetic Book' page 212.

33 W Branch Johnson, *The Carrington Diary, 1797-1810* (Letchworth, 1956) and W Branch Johnson, *The Hertfordshire Pepys, John Carrington of Bramfield and his Diary from 1797-1810* (Letchworth, 1970).

34 Branch Johnson, '*Memorandoms For...*', p19.

35 HALS: DE/X3/1-7 and 15.

36 HALS: DE/X3/8-13, 17-23 and 39.

INTRODUCTION

General editorial method

- The majority of Carrington's original spellings (including those of place names) have been retained. However where the meaning would have remained unclear the modern equivalent has been placed in italics within round brackets eg (*Michaelmas*) or (*Whitwell*). Carrington consistently uses the spelling 'there' in all cases. This has been silently altered to 'their' when the context requires it. Likewise ye (the) and yt (that) have been modernized throughout.
- Abbreviations for load (ld), per (pr), Quarter Sessions (Qr), which (wch), what (wht), have been silently extended. However 'Ld' meaning Lord and qr meaning quarter (in weight) remain as in the original text.
- All punctuation has been modernised to make the text flow more easily.
- The use of capitals has been modernised.
- Christian names and surnames have been left as they were written in the text.
- Words inserted above the line by the original writer are written thus <Tewin>.
- All diary entries have been placed in chronological order apart from summaries placed at the end of months or years by the author himself.
- Editorial notes are given in Italic text within round brackets.
- A question mark before a word signifies the most likely reading of a word eg (*?since*).
- (Round brackets) used in the original text have been reproduced.
- Square brackets are used when inserting letters into words abbreviated in the text eg s[ai]d.
- All numerals have been standardized into Arabic format and sums of money represented in the form: £6 13s 8d.
- Money: twelve old pennies (12d) = one shilling (1s); twenty shillings = one pound (£1); one guinea = £1 1s 0d. One shilling equates to five new pence (5p).
- Archaic words or expressions have been explained in the Glossary not in footnotes.
- All Bible references have been standardised to the text of the King James Bible first published in 1611.

- The spelling of place names are those used in J E B Gover, A Mawer and F M Stenton, *The Place Names of Hertfordshire* (CUP 1938).
- Throughout the diary Carrington refers to the majority of people, both friends and family, by their surname only. Where it has been possible to identify such individuals additional information has been placed in the Index of Names.

Abbreviations used in the footnotes

BL	British Library
CUP	Cambridge University Press
d	died
EHAS	East Herts Archaeological Society
HALS	Hertfordshire Archives and Local Studies
HCR	*Hertfordshire County Records vols II, IV, VIII and IX*
HRS	Hertfordshire Record Society
LMA	London Metropolitan Archives
ODNB	*New Dictionary of National Biography* (online edition)
OED	*Oxford English Dictionary* (online edition)
OUP	Oxford University Press
RCHM	Royal Commission on the Historical Monuments of England
TNA	The National Archives (formerly the Public Record Office)
VCH	*Victoria County History*, followed by county

THE DIARY OF

JOHN CARRINGTON, FARMER OF BRAMFIELD,

1798-1810

Volume 1, 1798-1804

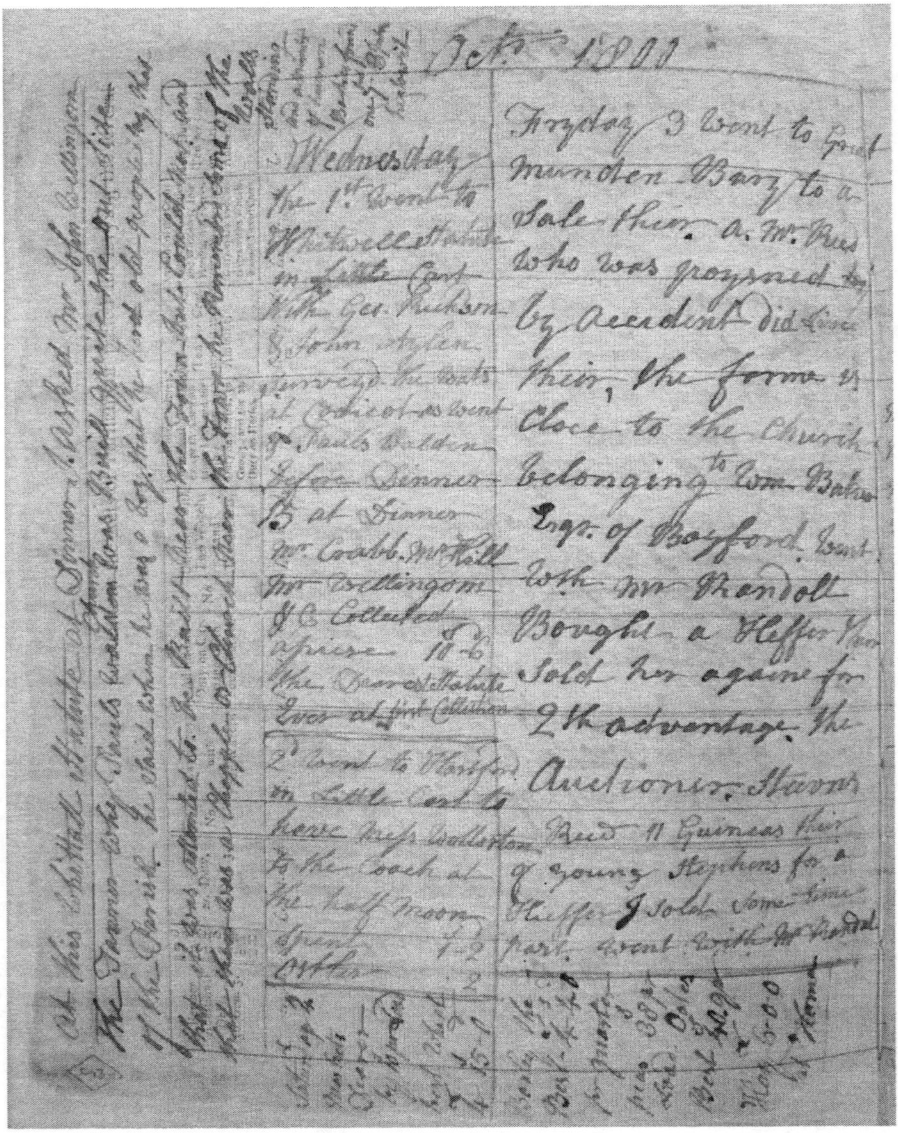

Oct. 1800

Wednesday the 1st Went to Whitwell Statute in Little Cart With Geo. Hickson & John Ayten surveyed the oats at Codicote & went to Pauls Walden before Dinner & at Dinner Mr. Crabb. Mr. Hall Mr Bellingam & C Collected

2d went to Hertford in Little Cart to Have Miss Wollaston to the Coach at the Half Moon Spent 1-2

Fryday 3 Went to Great Munden Bary to a Sale their. a Mr. Rees who was poysoned by Accident did Live their, the Farme is Close to the Church belonging to Wm. Baker Esqr. of Bayford. Went with Mr Randoll Bought a Heffer & then Sold her againe for 2/- advantage. the Auctioner Stevens Recd 11 Guineas their of young Stephens for a Heffer I sold some time past. went with Mr Randal

Page from John Carrington's diary for October 1800 (*HALS: DE/X3/3*)

1798 (*HALS: DE/X3/1*)

1798 MARCH 10 Went on jorney to the Angell Inn, St Albans. Met Marques of Salsbury and Deputy Lieutenants and Justices to drauft the Supplementry Millitia.[37] Such a number into the old militia. Paid from the Liberty one guinea for this. Staid all night. The Marquess gave us a good diner or raither supper. Very late.

APRIL Easter Monday 9th the terable fall I had about 9 clock at night, over some hurdles in Red Field coming home from my sons at Tewin, being turnops they had set the hurdles [across] the path.[38]

April 19 Went to Quarter Sessions St Albans - the great tryal about poor rates for the parish of St Peters. As one Britton, farmer of the s[ai]d parish and some others opposed the rest of the parish about the uneaquality of the rates. Sergant Sheephart & Counsler Asspens and 2 more Counselers names unknown was there.[39]

April 26 Jorney to St Albans to the Angell wth all my Constabls, to recive instructions from the Lieutenants and Justices for the defence of the country in case of invation from France. Ld Grimston, Esqr Osburn, Gape, Vandermuling there.[40]

The latter end of this month Mr Henery or Councler Cowper Esqr begun to pull down Tewin Water House, though the house had not been built much

[37] In 1797 by 38 Geo 3 c19 a Supplementary Militia was to be raised to augment the home defences against the very real threat of invasion from France. Hertfordshire's quota was to be an extra 500 men. Cheif constables like John Carrington were responsible for drawing up the list of men to be balloted [See J R Western, *The English Militia in the 18th century, The Story of a Political Issue, 1660-1805*, (1965), pp205-272 and 449].

[38] Turnips were grown mainly as a food crop for animals, so the hurdles may have been set up to keep stray animals out of the field.

[39] John Wane and others successfully appealed against the rating of St Peter's parish, St Albans reducing it from £431 10s 0d to £429 10s 6d [HALS: LSB2 p210-211].

[40] James Bucknell, 3rd Viscount Grimston of Gorhambury, St Albans; John Osborn, mayor of St Albans 1798; Joseph Gape (died Apr 1801) had been mayor in 1797; possibly Joseph Pomfret Vandermuelen who had served as mayor in 1793 [A E Gibbs, *The Corporation Records of St Albans* (St Albans, 1890), p294].

above 7 yrs.[41] But he not liking the plan of it and as his coz (*cousin*) Lord Cowper hath given him it to live in for life he now is puling down with intention to build a more nobler house on the same spott, and making great alterations in the gardens, and turning the course of the river to make a more famous water fronting the house and turning the road and footpaths which used to go by the house.[42] Upwards of one hundred men at work.

MAY 5th Saturday Jorney to the Angell, St Albans. All my constabls except Pauls Walden to carry in the returns from the instructions given us for the defence of the country. Bourcher,[43] Osborn, Gape &c there, Gent[le]m[en] Lieutenants.

May 11th Fryday went to Bull at Ware to meet Receiver Genarl of the Taxes, Mr Boyde of Ware Park.[44] Paid all windows, horses, coach &c taxes due 5 of April last and left due on land £32 16s 8d.[45]

---

[41] Henry Cowper (d 1841) was a descendent of Spencer Cowper the brother of William 1st Earl Cowper and was therefore a distant cousin of the 4th and 5th Earls. Together with his father Lt-General Spencer Cowper (1726-1797) he acted as guardian to the young sons of the 3rd Earl when they were sent to England in 1781 from their home in Florence [HALS: DE/P/F424]. The reversion of the Tewin estate had been purchased by the 3rd Earl Cowper in 1785 and it finally came into his possession in 1789 on the death of Lady Elizabeth Cathcart. The house was leased to Henry Cowper from 1791 [HALS: DE/P/T2401-3; DE/P/E281]. He was clerk to the House of Lords and chairman of the Hertfordshire Quarter Sessions, which he resigned in 1821 [HALS: DE/P/F424/22].

[42] Humphry Repton first visited Tewin Water on 16 May 1799 and had completed his Red Book by July in which he refers to the diversion of the footpaths and road. Carrington includes more information in the Arithmetic Book p83 (see Appendix One) and in diary entries dated 26 July and 4 Oct 1798 and 7 Nov 1800; the footpaths and roads were officially diverted by a Justice's order of 1797 [see HALS: Highway Diversions Nos 116-118 and the course of the new road on the southern bank of the river is clearly shown on HALS: DE/P/P14; the Red Book is HALS: D/Z42/Z1].

[43] Charles Bourchier, former Governor of Madras purchased Marshall's Wick near St Albans in 1788, and changed its name to Sandridge Lodge [Arthur Jones, ed, *Hertfordshire 1731-1800 as recorded in the Gentleman's Magazine,* Hertfordshire Publications 1993, p145].

[44] Thomas Hope Byde, whose family held the manor of Ware from 1668 to 1829 [*VCH Hertfordshire* vol 3 p388].

[45] Land Tax was first imposed in 1692 but not until 1798 (38 Geo 3 c60) was it made a permanent tax collected annually without the need for further acts of parliament.

May 12th Saturday Jorney to St Albans, the Angell, to make further returns from the instructions. All returns rec[eive]d but Pauls Walden as had not made aney they was complained of and given a further time till Tusday next. Charles Bouchier, & old Thos Gape,[46] Vandermuling &c there. Went to Town Hall. Recd order from Mr Donvell &c for 7 ginuas for examing w[eigh]ts & ballances.[47]

May 14th Sunday Set off wth cart & 2 horses & Wm Corral's servant to London to fetch one Gill's goods and wife to Tewin. Came to Wrestlers, Highgate 9 clock night. Set off 4 clock morning Monday, to London by 6. Set off about 10, stopt at Bull, Kentish Town. Came to Stagg, Finchley Common. Waited there, got home about 9 clock the same night (for 25 shillings). I nether eate nor drinkd in London.

May Saturday the 19 the raising fiest (*feast*) at Tewin Water. The surveyor gave the treat.

Went to the Angell, St Albans to appoint assessors for Land and other Taxes but the orders was not redy. So no appointm[en]t till the 2d June

Expence in all 8s Nothing got.

Hertfordshire lists survive amongst the Quarter Sessions records held at HALS and from 1780 were used as the qualification for the right to vote at county elections; window tax was collected from 1696 (7 & 8 Will 3 c18), a tax on carriages from 1776 (16 Geo 3 c34), pleasure horses from 1784 (24 Geo 3 c38) and horses used for industry from 1795 (36 Geo 3 c15 & 16) [W Kennedy, *English Taxation* (1964)].

[46] Thomas, died 19 Jun 1799 aged 83, and was the father of Revd James Carpenter Gape, vicar of St Michael, St Albans [Jones, *Hertfordshire, 1731-1800,* pp251-2].

[47] An Act of 1795 (35 Geo 3 c102) provided for the appointment of Inspectors or Examiners of weights and measures. As one of the four High Constables for the Liberty of St Albans Carrington was appointed an Inspector of Weights at the Easter Sessions 1796 for the parishes of Bramfield, Codicote, Hexton, Newnham, Norton, St Pauls Walden and Shephall [*HCR* vol IV p49]. Charles Domville, was a Justice of the Peace and later chairman of the Liberty Quarter Sessions.

Geo[rge] Ayscough Esqr was married at Hertford on Whisten Monday the 28th of this month to Mrs Neall of Herton Cottage near Windsor.[48] The next day to Bacons.

JUNE Sheep shore Saturday 9th of this month

Saturday 2d Went by Tewin Water, Digswell Hill & Water End. Jorney to St Albans to the Angell to appoint assessors for the Land and other Taxes. Gentlemen Commissioners there Esqrs Bourchier, Gape, Phillimore, V[ander]mulien, Simon Howerd &c. Cowper clerk of this meeting. Sedgwick of Rickmansworth surveyor of windows and other taxes.[49]

Mr Follett & wife from Sallopin Coffee House came to Bacons Fryday the 9th of this month and left Sunday the 24th.[50]

Marketts for the three month past much the same: wheat 31s per load; barley 28s per qr; oates 21s d[itt]o; peas, beens 20s; hopps 1s 6d per pound; hay 40s; straw 20s; malt 44s best pale per quarter wholesale.

Once upon a Certain Day,
Ears & mouth fell out they say,
Says Ears to Mouth w[ha]ts all this Ryott,
Pray Lets live in peace & quiott,
Yr so Noisey and quorelling,
And always on yr Neigbour Railing,
O says Eyes my hart it skipps,
To see how he Doth shake his Lipps,

---

[48] 'George Coles Ascough of the parish of St Giles Cripplegate, London bachelor' married Thomazin Neal, by licence, at All Saints Church, Hertford on 29 May 1798 [HALS: DP48/1/11].

[49] William Robert Phillimore held the manor of Elstree from 1789 until his death in 1846 [*VCH Hertfordshire* vol 2 p350]; Simeon Howard of Rickmansworth; John Cowper of St Albans, clerk to the Liberty Justices; John Sedgwick, member of a long established Rickmansworth family.

[50] Salopian Coffee House, Charing Cross, kept by Thomas Follett, a friend of Carringtons and a frequent visitor to Bacons. The house was well known in the late eighteenth century as the London headquarters of the engineer Thomas Telford (1757-1834), a sociable and entertaining companion with a wide circle of friends [see *ODNB* and Ben Weinreb, Christopher Hibbert, Julia and John Keay, *The London Encyclopaedia* (3rd ed, 2008)].

And if I could Hear as well as see,
Moast Shourly a fritned I should bee.

The Revd Mr Newton came to settle at Tewin Tusday the 19 of this Month 1798.[51]

Memarandom the Parish of Bramfield was Surveyd by 2 men: Mr Field of Hexters End (*Haxters End)* in the parish of Northchurch, Harts and Mr James Gutteridge of Eaton Green near Luton, Bedfordshire in the latter end of last month May 1798. They was 4 days in going over all the grounds at 2 guineas each a day £16 16s. It was done by agreement of ourselves upon account of not being eaquilly rated in the poor rates. So we agreed to be rated by their surveying. So som lands was sunk and some risen.

JULY Sunday 8 went to London wth Whitefoot in John's cart.[52] Carried Mrs Parker & Nanney Pierce up who had been to see us a week at Bacons & Ware. Took them up at Ware. Came home Tusday the 10. Brought down to Bacons Mrs Beck and her maid and young John Beck. Put up my mare at Bear and Raged Staff, Smithfield.[53]

12th Went to Quarter Sessions St Albans on Whitefoot mare. Mr [John] Randall overseer for Bramfield went with me to give notice to Mr Cowper, attorney St Albans to act for the parish of Bramfield against an appeal from Esqr Emmott of Goldings as being he thinks over rated for some of his land in Bramfield parish.[54] To come on next Sessions. For the parish was surveyd by

---

[51] Thomas Newton appointed to the rectory of Tewin on 25 Feb 1797 held the living until his death in 1843. He was later a JP for the North Riding of Yorkshire. Carrington refers to him again on 10 Apr 1803 [J A Venn, *Alumni Cantabrigiensis* part 2, 1752-1900 (CUP, 1940) and www.theclergydatabase.org.uk].
[52] Whitefoot is the name of Carrington's mare.
[53] The Pearce or Pierce family were relatives of Carrington's wife Elizabeth. The Beck family from London were the children and grandchildren of Carrington's eldest sister Mary, wife of Simon Beck of Hertford (see family tree).
[54] Richard Emmott, died 1820 aged 73. He appealed against the setting of the Bramfield poor rate. The hearing was held over until the next sessions where no further action was taken. The present house at Goldings dates from c1870 and has been recently converted into apartments [HALS: LSB2 p226-7].

2 survey[o]rs in May last & some of his land was set more value in the poor rates then before & likewise some othirs.

Saturday 14 Mr Wolloston, his child & nurse & her child came to Bacons by the evening coach from London.

Thursday morning the 26 about 8 clock one Rich[ar]d Tyler, laborough (*labourer*) of Bramfield dropt down dead in Hunsdons Walk Field as hoeing turnops wth John Leever & Burges of Tewin, never stird hand or foot. I hope (*helped*) carry him to Bramfield. He lived in the poor house. Left a wife & children, aged about sixty years.

26: Ringing Fiest at Hertford.[55] Dinner. Dresed at Falkon Mrs Romseys, dined at Town Hall, about 130 at dinner. Tickets 7s 6d. Mr W[illia]m Kinder master of St Albans. Mr Kirby of Hertford, Mr John Cass of Ware, Mr Stephen Worrell of Hertford, Mr Fordle, stewards.

Thursday 26 of this month my grandson christned George Carrington. Diner at 2 clock. Dined in the parler at Rose & Crown, Tewin. Mr Webb there & some relations from Suffolk. Mr Dolling, Mr Fokes, clerk of the works at the new house building at Tewin Water by one Mr Henery Cowper. This estate did belong to one Lady Cathcart but she dying in the year 1789 the estate came to Ld Cowper. He imeadeatly pulled down the old house she lived in and built another and one Ld Townsend lived in it till 1797. Ld Cowper coming of age he had warning to quitt which he did & Ld Cowper gave the place to his coz Henery Cowper to live in for life. And he is now pulling it down againe and building againe.

Monday 30th of this month begunn harvest though others on forward lands sooner. A great deel of wheat in shocks. Good cropp of wheat.

---

[55] Church bells were often rung on feast days and other special occasions. Carrington was a member of the Society of Hertford College Youths from 1786, a social member rather than a ringer [HALS: DP/48/29/14]. William Kinder, the master in 1797/8 may be the former mayor (in 1777 and 1788) of St Albans who died 12 Jan 1805 [Gibbs, *Corporation Records*, pp158 and 294].

AUGUST Wednesday 8th went to Pauls Walden Bury, Lord Burfords.[56] Rec[eive]d a drauft of £40 of him.

August 11th Saturday Jorney to St Albans to Angell wth 3 of my constables Pauls Walden Wrenn, Hexton John Day & Smith of Codicote, to recive instructions in making lists of the mens names for each of the parishes as one man is wanting in each parish for the Supplementry Millitia. Charles Bourchier, John Osborn, Thos Gape Esqrs there. To meet againe the 25 wth list at Angell. Went on Whitefoot, by Digswell and Waterend, came home the same way. Saw the great fieast at Tewin Water given by Henery Cowper Esqr to his workmen as building a new house there. Dined in the warren in the avenew about 130, good dinner & 3 barrels of bear (*beer*).

Fryday 17th Went to Wm Gear's funerall who lived at the Windmill, Waterford. Buried at Bengeo. Aged 52 yrs.

Sunday 19 Coz Thos Beck came to Bacons, walked down. Next morning returnd by coach. Coz Cooks & Davis & wife came to Bacons in post chaises. Went to dinner at brother Hastlers, from thence they went to London.[57]

25 Jorney to the Angell, St Albans to deliver in the lists from my 3 constables. Bourchier, Osborn, V Muling Esqrs there, to meet againe on Saturday 8 of Sept next for ballotting. Went by Digswell and Water End, came home the same way. Harvest home tonight.[58] High wind today.

---

[56] Aubrey Beauclerk (1765-1815) styled Earl of Burford until the death of his father, the Duke of St Albans in 1802. He was a tenant at St Pauls Walden Bury as this estate was already owned by the Earls of Strathmore [*VCH Hertfordshire* vol 2 pp405-6]. The £40 may well have been a payment towards his Land Tax as St Pauls Walden was one of the parishes in Cashio Hundred for which Carrington was responsible.

[57] The Cooks, fishmongers in Billingsgate were relatives of Elizabeth Carrington. The Heaslers (or Hasler) kept the Spread Eagle at Amwell End, of which Carrington owned the freehold, bequeathing it to his daughter Mary Ann.

[58] The gathering of the harvest was the climax of the rural year, an event which involved all local villagers. As a local farmer Carrington would have been responsible for his workforce, often supplying food and drink and a celebratory meal at the end [see D Hey, *The Oxford Companion to Local and Family History* (OUP 1996) and R Hutton *The Stations of the Sun, A History of the Ritual Year in Britain* (OUP 1996)].

Finished harvest 25, a fine harvest good wheat, barley midling, peas d[itt]o, oats good.

Sunday 26 Went to dinner at George, Codicote wth Mr Meriott from Gravesend & Mr Dolling & Mrs Howard from Tewin. Mr & Mrs Warren from Charlton near Hitchin came to Bacons Wednesday 29 and sleep 2 nights & left the 31.[59] Had been to Hertford to recive their rent from workhouse.

When ship wreck happns in Cornwell *(Cornwall)* on the coast, as it offen doth, if in church time if they hear of it, the congregation will leave the parson to pick up w[ha]t they can find, as it so happned on a time, and the parson spoke as follows:

> Oh Breathren wether are you rushing,
> Why all this elboing & pushing,
> If you wont suffer me to teach ye,
> Hear me one word I beseech ye,
> One moment onley pray forbear,
> Let us all at aney rate start fair.

SEPTEMBER The wather glass sunk from 3 degrees above fair to 2 degrees below. Changable the 3d of this month, and yet no raine, but windey & kind of storms & rises againe above changeable the 6th & 7th. The 10th thunder & now rain. Follett & wife came to Bacons. Went away Saturday 22. Pol went with them.[60]

Saturday the 8 Jorney to St Albans to the Angell to draw for my 3 parishes in Supplementry Millitia, (for Codicote No 60 Rich[ar]d Gray, labourer; Hexton No 18 James Russell, laborur; Pauls Walden No 20 Henery Moss, porter). Mr Bourchier, Osborn, Gape, Vander Muling, Esqrs there and Mr Grover from [Hemel] Hemsted, clerk there. Next meeting on 22 to swear in. Went by Diggswell and Water End. Came back the same. Went on Dimond.

Sunday the 9th Went to Bush Fair with Mr Randal [and] Richardson.[61] Bought 6 Welch Runts or yearlings for Mr Schribier of Tewin House at £4 2s

---

[59] Arthur Warren, son of Carrington's former master Richard Warren of Marden Hill, Tewin [W Branch Johnson, *'Memorandums For…'*, (1973), p36].

[60] Carrington's only daughter Mary Ann was affectionately known as Pol(l).

[61] Probably John Randall of Bramfield Place Farm. George Richardson, was church clerk of Bramfield, licensee of the Rose and Crown, Aston, then the Bulls Head, Hertford, then the Blackbirds in Parliament Square, Hertford.

each, £24 12s 0d. The great storm at the fair of thunder & raine at 1 clock. John Templeman brought the beast home for three shill[ing]s and beer &c. Hopps it is said very much mist in cropp & rissen to 2s per p[oun]d.

Monday 10 Great crickett match singell wicket. One Mr Fennix from London playd against three - Taylor from Ware, Field of Datchworth, & Wals of Stoney Hill (*parish of Bengeo*). Fennex beet them 3 noches in the 2 innings.[62]

Tusday 11 The same three playd again against one Mr Ray from London and Ray be[a]t the 3 again all the 3 innings against one, playd on Tewin Upper Green. Ray got 11 & they 3 got but 9. 2 innings.

Saturday the 15 Jorney to St Albans to Town Hall to renew licences. All my parishes met. I answerd for Mr Derds, Bramfield & paid for his licens £1 16s 6d.[63] Burges constable stood bound wth me. Dined at Piggotts Red House wth Codicot people & the 3 widows there, Mrs Raymond, Mrs Alvey, Mrs Farrow.[64] Went by Hatfield Road came home the same wth Burges. W[e]nt on Dimond. Hatfield bells ringing being the Marquiss Salsburys birth day.

Monday 17th Wotton Statute.[65] Dined at Crawleys, White Horse about 70 at diner. Hired S Freeman there for £6 10s. Gathering 5s per head.

---

[62] William Fennex, originally from Buckinghamshire, was an innovative batsman and an excellent bowler. He was the first to hit the ball by stretching forward without leaving the crease. He was paid to play and betting on the outcome was usually heavy. He died penniless in the workhouse c1835 [Derek Birley, *A Social History of Cricket*, 1999 pp51-79].

[63] William Deards had been licensee of the Grandison Arms, Bramfield. Until 1828 landlords had to furnish two recognizances (sureties) to the Justices of the Peace for the good conduct of their houses before a licence to sell ale could be issued.

[64] The Piggotts were relatives of Carrington's mother Mary. Thomas Piggott (died 1802) kept the Red House Inn, St Albans. The three widows all ran public houses in Codicote: Raymond at the George, Alvey at the Goat and Farrow at the Red Lion.

[65] Statute fairs were hiring fairs so called because an Act of Parliament of 1677 (29 Cha 2 c3) endorsed the yearly bonds made between farmers and their servants. Traditionally these would have expired on Old Martinmas Day (23 Nov) but certainly after the harvest was over at the end of the farming year [D Hey, *Oxford Companion*, p218].

Thursday 20 Gathering 5s. Codicot Stattute at George, Mrs Raymonds. I was there. 22 at dinner.

Saturday 22 Jorney to St Albans to Angell to sware in the Supplementry Millitia as drawn on the 8th above. Only Codicote man sworn in Rich[ard] Gray, labourer & he found a substitute,[66] Hexton man to[o] short, drawd again Thos Berry, labourer. Pauls Walden man not to be found. They give him a longer time to seek after him to 13 Oct[obe]r againe.

Tusday 25 Hartford Statute at White Hart, Camps. I dined, 21 at dinner. Gathering 8s.

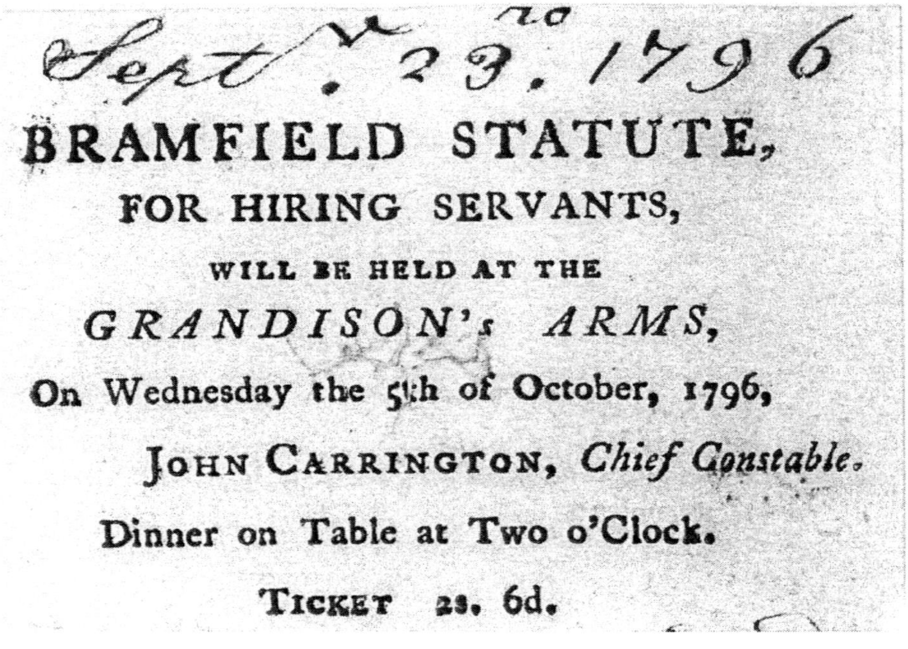
Sept. 23. 1796

BRAMFIELD STATUTE,

FOR HIRING SERVANTS,

WILL BE HELD AT THE

GRANDISON's ARMS,

On Wednesday the 5th of October, 1796,

JOHN CARRINGTON, *Chief Constable.*

Dinner on Table at Two o'Clock.

TICKET 2s. 6d.

Ticket for dinner at Bramfield Statute Fair, 5 October 1796
(*Hertford Museum*)

---

66 Any man drawn in the militia ballot had the right to find a substitute to serve in his place [HALS, *Tracing Your Family History in Hertfordshire* (Hatfield, 2003), p94]. On 5 July 1803 Carrington paid a man £20 to serve instead of his son William.

Wednesday 26th Bramfield Statute. 26 at dinner. Gathering 6s.

Kimpton Statute Wednesday 19. Was not there.
Wellwin Statute Monday the 24. I was not there.
Whitwell Statute Wednesday 26. Was not there.

OCTOBER Thursday the 4th went to Quarter Sessions St Albans. No great busness there only one fellon, a young woman for steeling 2 pair of stockings from a shop at High Barnat. Gilty. 3 months imprisonment.[67] Came home sooner & dined at Elsoms, Digswell wth Mr Pallet, Lord Cowper's stew[a]rd & Mr Dean, Mr Pennyfather & others when settled for the road to go across the field from Diggswell.[68] Spent 4s 6d.

Saturday 13 Jorney to St Albans to the Town Hall, to appoint surveyors. Went from thence to the Angell to swear Moor of the Supplementry Millitia in. Balloted againe for Pauls Walden & draud one John Reeves jnr, labourer. To meet againe at Angell Saturday 3d of Novr. Came home by Hatfield & drank tea at Palmers.

Sunday 14th Dined at Cole Green, Mr Palletts wth Best & Gilbirtson.

15th Dined at Feathers, Tewin Upper Green. Lord Cowper's wood fiest.[69]

Thursday 18 Dined at Cowpers Arms, Birch Green, S[a]m[ue]l James. Lord Cowper's wood fiest.

Fryday 19th went to Codicot and to Whittle (*Whitwell*), to see the 2 estates belonging to the 2 Miss Pilgrims.

Fryday 26 the great meeting at the Grandisons Arms, Bramfield as Esqr Emmott had given notice of his appeal against the poor rate last Quarter

---

[67] On 14 August 1798 Elizabeth Davis of Chipping Barnet stole two pair of worsted stockings, the property of John Bone [HALS: LSR/2 Michaelmas sessions 1798].
[68] Elsom was landlord of the Cowper Arms, Digswell. A map c1799 marks the 'Cowper Arms' at Digswell Water [HALS: DE/P/P14]. There was also a Cowper Arms, at Birch Green, Hertingfordbury, landlord Samuel Janes or James, which transferred to Cole Green about 1850 [W Branch Johnson, *Hertfordshire Inns part one, East Herts* (Letchworth 1962)].
[69] Virtually all estate owners periodically set aside an area of woodland for felling and sale. The sales would often take place in a public house usually accompanied by a meal or feast.

Sessions as been over rated. As our parish had been surveyd by 2 men Mr Field and Mr Guttredge he sent Mr Kitchener & Mr Lucass to survey over againe. And they all 4 men met as above and the parish wth 2 atturneys, and was settled very amicamly wth a good dinner.

Octob 26th paid Taxes 1st & 2nd quart[ers]s payment for 1798 at the Bull at Ware to Mr Boyde

Paid towards Land	£20 0s 0d
Paid towards New Assessed Taxes	£50 0s 0d
	£70 0s 0d
Paid the arrears of Land left May Last	£32 16s 0d
Totall paid	£102 16s

Mr White of Satridge (?*Sandridge*) was killed by a fall from his horse a coming from Eastwick Petit Sessions this month near Hunsdon Mill.

NOVEMBER Saturday the 3d Jurney to St Albans the Angell to swear in 1 man from Hexton & 1 man from Pauls Walden in the Supplementrey Millitia. Reeves from Pauls Walden was given 1 month longer to find substitute. Went wth Dimond in little cart with Sall Carrington to see her father Jonson & she found her brother Billey Jonson listed about 1 week past in the Essex Fenceables or Light Horse and gon to Ireland.[70] They was a recruting at St Albans.

Tho[ma]s Culver, shoomaker of Tewin many years, died the **5th** in the morning.

Bramfield tythe feast at Grandisons Arms the **5th**. Old Mr Lloyd and son Tho[ma]s was there.[71] Rained all day. I went from thence on Dimon to Tewin being clubb night.[72]

---

[70] Sall (Sarah) Johnson was the wife of Carrington's eldest son John (Jack).

[71] Revd William Lloyd, Rector of Bramfield (1786-1800). The Revd Thomas Lloyd, his son (1772-1851), was Rector of both Sacombe, Hertfordshire 1807-51 and Fordwich, Kent, 1802-1851 and domestic chaplain to Earl Cowper [Venn, *Alumni Cantabrigienses*].

[72] A Benefit Club to aid members and their families in times of sickness, unemployment or death. This club at the Rose and Crown was founded in the 1750s and was the second oldest known in Hertfordshire. It was wound up in 1809. A

Tusday 6th Dined at Panshanger wth Mr Russell, cook.

Thursday 8th the fair, dined at Cold Bath, Griffiths wth Randall.

Fryday 16 went wth Mr Pallet, Lord Cowper's stew[a]rd to vew the 2 estates belonging to the 2 Miss Pilgrams. Went to Whittle (*Whitwell*) to vew that first in the tener of Mrs West, a house & barn & 16 acres. Then came to Codicot to vew that of Cooks, a house, barn & 18 acres, and Cook which married one of them agreed to have the Codicote, and the other at Whittle for Miss Pilgrim of London.

Sunday the 18 went to London on foot from Cheshunt. Rode so farr & Curriell brought the horse back. Slep 1 night at Mrs Goodalls, 2 nights at Becks & 1 night at Cooks. Came home on Thursday wth brother Hasler in Flack's coach to Ware for 5s 6d inside. Saw the King go to the Parliament House on Tusday the 20th wth his great state coach and 8 horses, creame collerd and very finely dressed and the prosession very quiatt.[73] Stayd ½ [h]our and then returnd as quiatt home. Went to the Treasury to Mr Pollock and took for Mr Hopkins £30.[74] Went to the bank took £10 10s for 2½ qrs stock in 4 per & in 3 per cent.

Thursday 29 the collers (*colours*) given to the Hartford Association Gent[le]m[e]n by Alderman Gillman may[o]r, brewer & grocer. The collers was conveyd to the great church (*All Saints, Hertford*) and a sermon preached by the Revd Thos Lloyd to the mayr & aldermen & Association &c &c from the 8th chapter of the 1 Book of Kings and the 66 verse.[75] After Church the Association withdrew to Bayley Hall, and there formd in ranks with their muskets & fixt boinets (*bayonets*), and then the collers was brought from the

---

statute of 1793 (33 Geo 3 c54) gave tax relief to those whose rules were agreed and registered by the Justices [HALS: QS/MB14 Michaelmas 1794 and *HCR* vol VIII p444].

[73] The state opening of Parliament.

[74] Lieutenant Timothy Hopkins, a naval man and lodger at Bacons. He was almost totally blind and Carrington looked after his financial affairs. He records his death on 5 June 1800 below.

[75] One Kings, ch 8 verse 66: 'On the eighth day he sent the people away: and they blessed the king, and went unto their tents joyful and glad of heart for all the goodness that the Lord had done for David his servant and for Israel his people'.

church and presented to their Capt[ai]n, young Barran Dimsdall[76] by Mr Gillman mayr, & the Revd Thos Lloyd. Then the Captn presented them to the Association wth musick playing & 3 volleys fired. And then marched through the town some time, and to the Town Hall to dinner given by their Captn, the Association about 100, trades people &c. The collers cost abot £12.

Markets this month:

Wheat per load	£1 13s 0d
Barley per quarter	£1 12s 0d
Peas per load	£1 5s 0d
Oates per quorter	£1 4s 0d
Malt per quarter	£2 6s 0d
Hops per pound	£0 2s 3d

DECEMBER The 1st of this month Saturday sent John to the Angell, St Albans in my stead to attend the meeting for the constables in bringing in lists for the old Millitia.

Mr Reed of Great Munden Bury poysend by accident this month, as follows, he thought him silf not quite well and sent his man to the Doctrs for somthing to take and orderd him to bring a viall of vitterll (*vitriol*) for to dress his sheep on some complaint. But the nurs or housekeeper gave him the vitterll and he languishd 2 days in great misery and died.

Tusday 18 Ven[i]son fiest at my sons Rose & Crown, Tewin. The haunch & turkey was given by Mr Webb, Tewin. 14 at dinner at 5s 6d per head. Gave waiter 2s 6d.

Mr Webb	Mr Randall
Mr Whittenbury	Mr Richardson
Mr Bowley	Mr Dolling
Mr Tayler	Mr Brooks
Mr Hanken	Mr Fokes
Mr Preston	Mr Pridmore
Mr Pool	My Self

[76] Dr Thomas Dimsdale (1712-1800) and his second son, Nathaniel (1748-1811), also a doctor, had both been created Barons of the Russian Empire by the Empress Catherine the Great for inoculating her and her court against smallpox. Carrington presumably refers to Nathaniel.

Good compney, plenty of punch, stayd supper. Brok up ½ p[a]st 10.

Wednesday the 26 of this month the Earl of Essexes house in London burnt wth most of the valuable furniture. The house was eleunimated as being holiday and a going to have a card party at supper, and a candle fell out of the sconce upstairs into a sofa and all the house was in flames at top while they was at diner below. The Earl's country seat is at Cashiobury near Watford, Harts.[77]

The price of corn &c ending the year:

Wheat	32s per load
Barley	32s per qr
Oates	25s per qr
Peas	25s 6d or 26 per load
Malt	46s per qr
Hopps	2s per pound

Watton Woodhall by H G Oldfield, *c*1800 (see diary entry for 7 June 1799) (*HALS: DE/Of/7/160*)

[77] William Anne Capell, 4th Earl of Essex (1732-1799) [J Burke, *Genealogical and Heraldic Dictionary of the Peerage and Baronetage of the British Empire*, 6th ed (1839)].

1799 (*HALS: DE/X3/1*)

1799 JANUARY the beginning of this month lost a good fatting young heifer found dead in the morning. Supposed to be choked in the night as eating turnops. Mr Scales the athist (*?atheist*) supposed to be, died this month at Hertford wheare he had lived some years. He came from London, master butcher there.

Saturday the 12 of this month jorney to St Albans to the Angell to draw some parishes for the old Millitia what men was wanting - 2 for Pauls Walden, 1 for Codicote, 1 for Sheephall, to swear in the second of February next. Went in Dolling's cart with Sall my dughter in law & grandson Jack, my mear (*mare*) Dimond.

Thursday 17th went to Quarter Sesions St Albans on Dimond with Burges, Bramfield constable. Met my other constables at Red House, Coz Piggotts according to appointment to make out our bills for the defence of the contry & Supplementry Millitia, for each constable was allowed 5s for 10 mile, & 7s 6d if above, for as maney jorneys as they was ordered to meet at St Albans on they occations. No great buisiness at Sessions. Came home with Burges by Cole Green, as being frosty the beten road the best.

Saturday 19 had the flurey wth Billy Simpson when I throwd him down in little room for his imperdence.

Sunday 20 Went to Gilston Park Wm Plomers, Esqr MP for the County of Hartford with my son John & Mr Randall of Bramfield Place by order of Mr Jonson of St Albans to request a favour of Mr Plomer.[78] To request the same of Cololn (*Colonel*) Burgoyne who lived about 2 mile from Plumers, to reliece (*release*) Mr Jonson's son William who 2 months back listed into the Calolns Light Horse at St Albans and is gone to Iarland. We was kindly recved at Mr Plomers and he wrote to Col Burgoyne that night to London and John my son was to go to Plumers againe on Tusday morning to hear further, wich he did and then he must go to London on Wednesday the next day,

[78] William Plumer (1736-1822) MP for Hertfordshire, 1768-1807, had some years previously abandoned the ancestral mansion of Blakesware, near Widford, for New Place, Gilston. Blakesware was demolished in 1823, although rebuilt in 1852. New Place was rebuilt in 1878 and renamed Gilston Park [*VCH Hertfordshire* vol 3, p321].

which he did & rote a petition and sent to the Duke of York and returnd without answer as yet.[79]

Tusday the 30 [29] walked to Ware market, stayd, dined at Haslers and came home. Called at Mr Noah Young's brewhouse to inquire after Mrs Young, his wife, which was very ill. She died the next morning. Lord Cowper at Pansanger likewise very ill. Doct[o]r this day from London & likewise from Hertford.

Thursay 31 of this Month I was at Jacks, Tewin when a man came from St Albans in little cart to fetch my son's wife as her sister Suky Jonson was very bad. They sent for a post chaise from Wellwin to go in as the afternoon was the most turable driven snow from the east ever was known.

FEBRUARY: This month begins with deep snow and sharp frost.

Fryday the 1st of this Month the deepest snow for maney years. It begun about 3 clock the last day of last month and continead till this morning. It was a driven snow from the east and fild all places full through tyles of huses and lanes unpassable. The market on Saturday the next day very small, as people could not get there. Mr Raymond, farmer of Potters Heath in the parish of Wellwin walked to market, but was found dead the Sunday next day, within 80 poll (*pole*) of his house. Supposed to have perished through the snow as maney others likewise ded as we herd of. He was buried at Wellwin the Sunday the 18th following aged 62.[80] Mr Raymond left Hartford in good time, between 3 & 4 clock the afternoon. Very sober man.

Likewise Mrs Woodcock of Impington had been to Cambridge market & she fell into a pit of snow & was found alive after lyeng 8 days & nights 3 miles of Cambridge.

Saturday 2 Sent my son William to the meeting at Angell, St Albans, to swear in 2 men for Pauls Walden, 1 for Codicote & 1 for Sheephall which were drawn the 12 of last month for the old Millitia but all the men did not appear. So to meet againe at Angell the 23 of this month. He carried my bill in of 6 jorneys of the Supplementry Millitia wich is 1 guinea jorney, and the

---

[79] Frederick, Duke of York and Albany (1763-1827) was the second son of George III and commander in chief of HM forces [Burke, *Genealogical and Heraldic Dictionary*].

[80] William Rayment was buried at Welwyn on 18 Feb 1799 [HALS: DP119/1/3].

Gentmn signed it, and he brought home 6 guineas paid by Mr Boyes the Treasu[r]er for Cashio Hundrd.[81]

Suckey Jonson at St Albans died Monday the **4th of this Month**. Buried the Sunday following.

George Agustas Nasau Clavering, [4th] Earl Cowper died at Pansanger Tusday morning 5 clock the **12th of this month** aged 22 years 6 months.[82]

Fryday 15 Jorney to Town Hall St Albans to recive instructions from the Comm[is]s[ione]rs of Taxes for the new tax of all income, but no papers was brought by Sedgwick the surveyor, so obliged to return without doing buisiness, and they are to be sent to us.[83] The waters very much out on the road to St Albans from Hatfield. I ne[ve]r saw the like before on that road. Went on Dimon by Cole Green, back same way.

George Augustas Nasau Clevering Cowper buried on **Tusday the 19th of this month** at Hartingfordbury church in the family vault there. Taken from Pansanger about 8 in the morning with herce and six, 4 coaches in six and his own coach in six, over the water at Naves Acre up by his park pales to Cole Green. There all his capitall tenants met the herce & joyned the prosesion wth white hatbands, gloves and sashes, walked gently from thence to the Church. The pall bourn by his tenants. Mourners his brother Francus & Coz Henery Cowper Esqr. Buried about 11 clock in the day time by the Revd Thos Lloyd his chapplin. Aged 22 yrs 6 months. The herce and all the horses white feathers. Nothing of eating or drinking at Pansanger or else wear for aney, onley his tennants went back from church and dined at his steward's Mr Palletts, Cole Green.

Sunday 24 Went to Hardingfordbury church wth Mr Randall to hear the funeral sermon preached for the late Earle Cowper by the curate. The text

---

[81] John Boyce, St Albans Town Clerk, 1792-1817 [Gibbs, *Corporation Records*].

[82] George Augustus 4th Earl Cowper (1776-1799) died unmarried aged 22. He was succeeded by his brother Peter Leopold Louis Francis Nassau Clavering-Cowper 5th Earl Cowper (1778-1837).

[83] Income tax was introduced in 1799 (39 Geo 3 c13) as a way of making extra revenue to finance Britain's involvement in the Napoleonic Wars. It was set at a rate of 2s per pound on incomes over £200. Returns held at TNA Ref E182 give names of individual tax payers by parish [D Hey, *Oxford Companion* and A Hope-Jones, *Income Tax in the Napoleonic Wars* (1939)].

was the 4th & 5th verce of the 39th psalm in the Bible.[84] A full congregation all his tenants appearing with their wite sashes & hatbands & then they wear ordered dinner at Samual Janeses his L[or]d Ships Arms. I and Mr Randall dined at Mr Hankins, butchers and then went to the Wite Horse & staid late, Mr Sewillses.[85]

Wednesday 27 a fast throuout England, went to Bramfield church.[86] Sermon preached by Mr Vergen, curate of Hardingfordbury, text the 2d chap of Joel 15 verce Blow the Trumpet &c.[87]

MARCH 4th of this month the assizes at Hertford.

Sunday the 10 I went to Pauls Walden Bury, Lord Burfords. Was made welcom by Mr Peters, his buttler with companey there with Oldmeadows, D[octo]r at Wellwin.[88] We drinkd wine plenty and I thought best to sleep at Bull at Whitwell, one Dixons, as being dark and I came home next morning.

Mondy 11 Dined at my sons Rose & Crown, Tewin, with Mr Pallett, Lord Cowper's stew[ar]d, being Lord Cowper's wood sale there.

Fryday 15th went to the Bull at Ware to meet the Receiver General, Mr Thos Hope Byde of Ware Park. Paid him £50 on the additional taxes. £15 left behind.

Monday 18th Dined at Crawleys the White Horse, Wotton turnpike meeting wth Bush, Pearman, Clapham, Butterfield, Walls, Sarrege, Jaeremiah Crawley

---

[84] Psalm 39, verses 4 and 5: 'Lord, make me to know mine end, and the measure of my days, what it is; that I may know how frail I am! Behold, thou hast made my days as an handbreadth; and mine age is as nothing before thee: verily every man at his best state is altogether vanity.'

[85] Thomas Sewills was the licensee of the White Horse, Hertingfordbury at least until 1806 [HALS: QSVR1806].

[86] Ash Wednesday, the first day of Lent traditionally a period of fasting and penitence in commemoration of Christ's 40 days in the wilderness, culminating in the Christian festival of Easter four weeks later.

[87] Joel ch 2 verse 15: 'Blow the trumpet in Zion, sanctify a fast, call a solemn assembly'.

[88] Robert S Oldmeadow, surgeon of Welwyn. Carrington records his death in Mar 1803 below [Welwyn Archaeological Society, *List of burials in Welwyn churchyard*, (Welwyn 2004)].

& Hall &c. Paid 3 years duty for the parish of Bramfield £8 15s 6d for about 80 pole of the Turnpike road by Goldings.[89] The large bit of rost beef there for diner. Spent 3s. Comisioners there Dickerson, Prist, Blindall, Caters, Twinn, Kimpton &c, Alington clerk.[90]

19 Went to Ware with Mary Ann, slep there, came home the next day. Saw Joe the Hatter going to be hanged in the road from the gaol.[91] He stood up in the cart with wite hatband on, in mo[u]rning w[hi]te hankerchief, vas[t] number of people. He said he was inisent. See by callender.

Tusday 26 Dined Mrs Derdses, Grandison Arms, Bramfield as being our vestrey day, Mr Randall the overseer. Preston app[ointe]d for the year ensuing.[92] Rost beef, leg motton puddings. Mr Searanke there.[93] Good company, plenty of punch. Burges constable, Derds church warden, Geo Richardson church clerk. Mr Stephen Austorn of Hartford, vestry clerke.[94]

---

[89] This was the amount payable to Watton Turnpike Trust for the maintenance of a short stretch of road in Bramfield parish for which the trustees were responsible [HALS: TP8/2, minutes of the trustees, 1778-1819].

[90] John Baron Dickinson (d 1829), maltster and barge owner of Ware, who with John and Thomas Green, also of Ware, ran a private bank closed in 1816 [HALS: 79951X and Jack Parker, *'Nothing for Nothing for Nobody' A History of Hertfordshire Banks and Banking* pp18-19 (Hertfordshire Publications, 1986)]; the Revd Morgan Price, rector of Knebworth from 1788 to 1830; probably Thomas Blindle, farmer of Knebworth (d 1826); John Caters, surveyor of Watton; John Tween; Thomas Kimpton of Bardolph's Farm, Watton (d 1811); Henry Alington, attorney, mayor of Hertford 1813 and 1821 and clerk to the Watton Turnpike Trustees from 1796 to 1842 [HALS: TP8/2].

[91] Alexander Hobbs, 22 years old, alias Joe the Hatter, had been found guilty of Highway Robbery at Chipping Barnet, stealing a black silk cloak value 40s, the property of Ann Connor and 6 shillings the property of James Hill [Assize Calendar in Carrington's own papers, HALS: DE/X3/14].

[92] Bryan(t) Preston of Broadoak End Farm, Bramfield, overseer of the poor, 1799-1801. Vestry minutes for the parish of Bramfield survive only for the years 1750-1778 and 1803-1818, so for the intervening years this diary is the only source of information for the appointment of the parish officers [HALS: DP/22/12/1-2].

[93] Francis Carter Searancke (1754-1835), brewer of St Albans, was mayor in 1801 and 1808. He moved from the town in July 1817 [Gibbs, *Corporation Records,* pp167 and 294].

[94] Stephen Austin I set up as a printer in Hertford in 1768. He remained Bramfield vestry clerk until his death in 1818. His son, Stephen Austin II (d 1845) became official bookseller to the East India Company's college at Haileybury, Hertford

Easter Wednesday 27 Dined at George, Wotton (*Watton at Stone*) with the farmers as being their vestry day. Hall & Monk overseers. Came home by Goldings, refreshed there, good cheer.

Saturday the 30 Jorney to the Town Hall, St Albans to appoint overseers for the year ensuing. Went with Mr Randall the late overseer for Bramfield and appointed Mr Preston.

Sunday the 31 of this month the charity sermon at Tewin preached by the Revd Thos Lloyd. Lord Cowper & his brother Spencer, Mr Henery Cowper &c there. A good congregation. Collection £26 0s 0d.

APRIL This month still cloudy, wet & cold.
Thursday 4th Jorney and to deliver the papers on the Income Act to St Albans Quarter Sessions. Went by myself on Dimon by Money Hole. No great buisness there, most Codicote people there on Jury. Jeeves was sworn in constable for Pauls Walden but they would not take the papers as must come again to be sworne before the Commissioners.

Wednesday 10 Jorney to Codicot, Pauls Walden & Hexton. Sleept at Red Lyon, Widow Wilkens.[95] Came home next day by Norton & Sheephall. Surveyd those parishes of their w[eigh]ts & ballances and deliverd notices for their assessors of each parish to attend the meeting of the Commissioners at the Town Hall, St Albans on Saturday next the 13 to make their returns on the Income Act. Expences on this jorney 13s.

Saturday 13 Jorney to St Albans Town Hall. All the assessors in the Hund[red] to make their returns to the Commissioners of the Income Act and to be sworn that they have done their duty faithfully to the best of their knowledge. Went on Smiler, the colt, by Hatfield.

Sunday 28 Went to Ware, from thence to London inside of Ramsey's Coach. Slep at Mrs Goodalls first night. Monday went to the Treasury, took £40 of Mr Pollock for Lieutenance Hoppkins. Slep Monday night at Folletts the

---

Heath. His grandson, Stephen Austin III (1804-1892) developed the printing of Oriental texts. Messrs Stephen Austin also published the *Hertford Mercury* newspaper from 1772, which under various titles has continued to the present day [James Moran, *Stephen Austin of Hertford* (Hertford, 1968)].

[95] The Red Lion at Hexton, run at least from 1786-1790 by Sarah Wilkins [HALS: LSVR1786-1790].

Salopin Coffee House. Tusday went to the Bank took ½ yrs difedend of the 3 per cent, ½ years d[itt]o of the 4 [per cent]. Went to Mr Farmers & Adams paid £46 19s 6d. Came from thence to Long Lane, Cos Becks. Slept there. Came home the Wednesday by Carter's coach to Hertford. On the Tusday saw Follett exersize and went to the Feathers, St Albans Street and then came home to supper and then went to the Brewers Arms, Milbank Street, Mr Blackbirds. Stayd late.

Account of Markets this **April 1799:**

20th of this month market day at Hertford. Wheat per load £1 18s 6d, hay per load £3 10s 0d, barley per quarter £1 16s 8d, straw per load £1 10s 0d, oates d[itt]o £1 9s 0d, clover seed 6d pound, peas per load £1 7s 0d, hopps 2s 4d pound, malt per qr £2 12s 0d, tears per load £1 8s 6d.

No grass. No vigetables. No turnops. Occaisond by the long winter and the wather still continues wet and cold. The farmers in general, except some few on the light lands, has not sowd half their barley yet. I have not sowd half mine this 22 of April. Obliged to feed the sheep with hay and oates, maltdust, brann, chaff &c &c.

MAY Fryday 10 Went to the Bull at Ware to Reciver General Mr Boyde. Paid £76 5s all taxes for the year 1798, and £40 on the Land, and £20 paid before on the Land, so there is left due on the Land Tax for 1798 £32 16s

Sunday 12 Dined at Mr Randalls, Bramfield Place Farm with Mr Rook of Bengeo and Mr Pooll of Waterford Hall.[96] Stayd late.

Monday 13th Witten (*Whit*) Monday was Hartford May Fair. Sold Gilbirt horse there to Mr Archer, butcher of Hertford for 12 guineas. Great plenty of cattle of all sorts.

Sunday 19 Went to Aston with Geo Richardson, to see the Rose & Crown he is about taking there in possesion of Parker.

---

[96] Waterford Hall, Stapleford, built *c*1600 was inherited in 1778 by Richard Emmott of Goldings, who sold it in 1811 to Samuel Smith of Watton Woodhall [*VCH Hertfordshire* vol 3 pp477-8].

Saturday 25 Jorney to St Albans to the Angell to be appointed assessors for the taxes for the year ensuing, Osborn, old Gape, Vandermulin commissioners. Went on Dimon.

Wednesday 29 Went to the Feathers alehouse, Tewin, Jos Whittenburys, with Coz Thos Beck from London & my son John to meet Mr Benj[ami]n Whittenbury of Quino Hall (*Queenhoo*) to recive bill & tax as usuall.[97] Paid him likewise for 4 cows 6s. Gave him for his son Thos 2s.

<Tewin> **Thursday 30th** in the Morning died sudenly old Will[ia]m Watson, wheeler. He had been blind some years, aged 77 years.

Thursday 30th A court held at Tewin Bury by order of Francis Earl Cowper, Mr Neale steward there, & Nickelson his clerk. Onley Mr W[illia]m Gripper and myself there, as coppy holders.[98] The chieff buisness there was to admitt Mr Frances Dean to take up that little farme on Tewin Upper Green formerly called Piggotts Farme, only house, cottage, barne, stable &c and about 30 acres land. Likewise Mr Fordom of Hartford, brewer at the s[ai]d court took up some pieces of land belonging to the Feathers alehouse on Tewin Upper Green.

JUNE [7] Fryday afternoon went with Mr Randal & Richardson to Paul Benfields Esqr, Wood Hall, Wotton (*Watton at Stone*), to see the house & gardens.[99] Was used well by Mr Murrey, the gardener. Went from thence all of us to Wilshers the Bull at Wotton, supt there and stayd late. Had a cattelog or perticulers given me of Wood Hall Park and all the estate as it is to be sold by auction at London by Skinner & Co the 26, 27, 28, 29 of this month.

---

[97] Queenhoo Hall, Tewin was built c1550. It stands on high ground 1½ miles NE of Tewin church commanding extensive views over the valley to the south [*VCH Hertfordshire* vol 3 pp483-4].

[98] Carrington had inherited from his father a copyhold house on Tewin Upper Green, which he bequeathed to his son John [HALS: DE/P/T2027 and Acc 3772].

[99] Paul Benfield, an engineer in the East India Company's service left his employment after a chequered career with a fortune of half a million pounds. He purchased Watton Woodhall in 1793 after the death of Sir Thomas Rumbold, and becoming bankrupt sold the property to Samuel Smith in 1801 [Philip Woodruff, *The Men who Ruled India* 2 vols (1953-1954); see also diary entries for 3 Aug 1799 and 20 May 1801 below and *VCH Hertfordshire* vol 3 p162; sale particulars for the estate dated 1801 are held at HALS: DE/AS/4371-2].

Saturday 8 Jorney to the Town Hall, St Albans which all collectors met for the s[ai]d Hundr[e]d of Cashio to recive their assessment of the Income Act which was given in the 13 of April last for the Commissioners to examine and to sighn for the collectors to gather by. Went on a little poney that was sent to me to keep from John Aylon which is mad Briges of Amwell. Went by Turnpike, come home the same way.

Satturday 22 My sheep shore. Sheearers was Mardall, Sewill, James, Burton, and Sparks. Sheep 76. Dolling, Mr Randall, Richardson, Randall nephew &c there

Sunday 23 at George, Codicote with Mr Merriott from Graves End (*Albury*), went with Mr Dolling in his cart.

Thursday 27 Went to Clubb Fiest at [Green] Dragon, Cambels Hartford. Came home in time with Thorrowgood in cart with Burges from Bramfield as I being stew[a]rd went the next afternoon. Paid the bill £22 6s 8d.

Sunday 30 About 3 clock afternoon died John Whittenbury of Green Hill in the parish of Bramfield of a voialent fever which has raged in the parish of Bramfield these 2 months pased and 7 persons having died within theese 2 months in the s[ai]d parish, as Wm Hart, W Fife, & son, &c &c.[100]

> Account of persons quallified to serve on juryes at sessions and assizes in my Division in the Liberty of St Albans for 1798 for county Herts:

[100] There is no reference to 'fever' in the Bramfield burial register in 1799, but there were indeed seven burials recorded since the beginning of April when the more usual number was 3-4 per year. William Hart was buried on 8 April, John Whittenbury, aged 35, on 2 July but there is no mention of Fife [HALS: DP/22/1/3].

Bramfield	Sheephall	Norton
John Carrington Hen Hunsdon Richd Burges, constable	Samuall Crook Esq Ewd Andrew, constable	Ewd Payne Geo Freeman John Hayse Thos Street, constable

Hexton	Codicote	Pauls Walden
Willim Young Esq Ewd Holmes John Day, constable **Newnham** None James Gardner, constable	Ewd Pearce Richd Hale, Esqr Phillip Morgan Underwood Males Rich Pedder Geo Bayley Charles Lane Joseph Mathews Thos Cook John Harper Thos Clarke Wm Smith, constable	John Wellingham Thos Willingham Robt Fullwood John Hill James Dixson John Lines Geo Wyman Rich Jepp John Camp Wm Wren, constable

(*HALS: DE/X3/2*)

JULY 5th of this Month Carried my wooll to Hodsdon to one Skate, recived 30s as per todd at present and wat will alow further to be paid after mine 12 todd. Mr Webb carried his and Ben Whittingbury his in their wagon and Fields of Coltsford (*Coltsfoot*) his.

Sunday 7 The great meeting of the Quakers at Robley Heath as for 20 yrs past.[101]

Saturday 13th this Month Markets wheat per load at Hartford 51s, barley 45s qr, oates 38s d[itt]o, peas per load 29s, malt 25s qr, hopps 2s 8d p[oun]d.

[101] A small Quaker meeting and burial ground at Rabley Heath, on the boundary of Welwyn and Codicote, is known from 1655 and was held by Quakers until July 1800, when it was sold to Cornelius Cuyler for £350. These funds were to be held in trust for the benefit of poor Quakers [HALS: QSMisc 1471; NQ2/1A/21].

Sunday 14 Went to Codicote with Miss Wolston. Met Mrs Wolston & Mr & Mrs Watherall at Mrs Hunsdons at Hallords (*Hollards*).[102]

Thursday 18 Went to Quarter Sessions, St Albans. Went from thence to Hemell Hempstead to Mr Grover attorney, clerk to the meetings of the militia for the Hund[red] of Cashio. Took of him £7 10s 6d for my constabls for their meetings for the defence of the country & got my warrant of him for my 3 meetings for the same 3 guineas to be taken of Mr Byd, Reciver General. Went on little poney, got home by nine clock. Went by Money Hole, came back the same.

Saturday 20 Markets cheepr wheat 48[s] per load

Sunday 21 Cos Cooks came down in a little cart. Returnd back the same day & Stephen & Rebeccah returnd with them who had been at Bacons some time. They brought us a kitt of salmon.

Monday 22 Went to Earl Burfords at Pauls Walden Bury. Recived of his L[or]d Shipp £50. Was treated very kindly by his L[or]d Shipp with good rost beef & bear. Went from thence to Gusterd Wood to cricket match between Datchwarth lads and Kimpton. Datchwarth was winners by great odds. Came down to the 2 Brewers at Kimpton, Mr Hines and refreshed. Came home with Mr John Aylon and Ware people. Went on Dimon.

Wednesday 24 Dined at my sons Rose Crown, Tewin with all my constables. When parted money for defence of the relme. Spent bill £1 2s 0d.

Thursday 25 Dined at Town Hall, Hartford the ringing fiest. Large compiney diner. Dresed at Mrs Ramseys the Falken. Tickets 7s 6d. Cos John Beck went to London today as having been with us 5 days. Came home on Whitefoot. Currell fetched me 11 clok.

Fryday 26 Went to the Bull Inn at Ware to Receiver Gener[al]. Paid the remendr of all tax up to April 5th last except Land. Dined at sisters Eagle with Mr Munns, Mr Samms, Mr Baker from Wormley.

---

[102] William Hunsdon was at Hollards Farm, Codicote, from 1791 until his death in 1798, his widow until 1803. Their son Henry farmed at West End Farm, Bramfield.

Monday 29 Will went to Mr Grovers, aturney Hemill Hemstead. Bought 6 acres of barley of Mr Stephens, auctinear at the Grandisons Arms, Bramfield at £7 15s 0d per acre Mr Moodys, the Slipe Field near the church.

Wednesday 31 Dined at Earl Cowpers Cole Green House wen his Lordship gave all his tenants a diner and I was asked. We dined in the Great Marble Hall his L[or]dship at the head, and Henery Cowper Esqr and [Revd] Thos Lloyd. Great plenty, and Mr Mullett broke the glass door.

31 Mr Randall of Bramfield Place Farme lost 2 fine cows bursted or hoved in his clover.[103] Lord Cowper had the carcakeses for his hounds. The clover had been mooed (*mowed*) and groing fresh againe and there came a lettle wet soon after they was put in being the first time.

> Hartfordshire. Lord Lieutenants for this county for time back: Wm Earl Cowper of Cole Green House was for years, but he died Sepr 18 1764; after him the Earl of Esex of Cashio Bury was appointed Octr 19th 1764 and he resignd it to Lord Cranburn (*Cranborne*) now Marq[ues]s of Salisbury, March 1 1771.[104]

1799 AUGUST Thursday the 1st of this Month was the great feast given by Lord Rumney at Cox Heath, Lord Lieutenant for the County of Kent to all the Hors Yeomendry and Foot Associations in the said county.[105] 60 lambs, 700 fowls, 300 hams, 300 tongus (*tongues*), 300 buttocks of beef, 300 sr lynes (*sirloins*), 220 joints of veal, meat pies 220, fruit pies 220, &c &c. Seven pipes of port bottled off, 16 butts of ale, small beer &c and more wine was at hand and ale if required. The King, Queen and royal family was there, and dined there in a marquee near the Association's dinner tables.

---

[103] Known as Bloat: on eating clover cows' stomachs react badly and expand very quickly; If not treated immediately the cows literally burst.

[104] William 2nd Earl Cowper (1709-1764); William Anne Capel, 4th Earl of Essex (173201799); James Cecil, 7th Earl and 1st Marquess of Salisbury (1748-1823).

[105] Charles Marsham, 3rd Baron Romney of Romney, Kent (1744-1811), Lord Lieutenant of Kent and great grandson of Sir Robert Marsham of Bushey Hall, Hertfordshire. 'This Nobleman had the honour of entertaining his Majesty George III, 1 Aug 1799, at his seat in Kent, when the King reviewed all the Kentish Yeomanry, amounting to nearly 6,000 men in his Lordship's Park' [Burke, *Genealogical and Heraldic Dictionary*].

Saturday 3d Wotton Wood Hall, Paul Benfield's sale at the Falkern Inn, Hartford of the growing cropps, of Gubbens (*Gobions*), Perry Wood and Wotton Green Farmes. Also all the stock at Wood Hall as carts, waggons, horses, cows, plows, harrows, blacksmiths shopp, glaisers shopp and wheelers shopp, carpenters & joyners timber &c and all mooveables (except the goods in the Great House), a vass quantity of wine of all sorts, and beer likewise. Sold the beginning of this month 6 days sale on the preemeses at Wood Hall Park, Wotton. Sold by Mr Dyke.

Wednesday the 7 Meeting at Rose & Crown, Tewin to receive the Levy Money.[106]

Fryday 16 the Hitchin Assosiation received their collers (*colours*). Dinner in Wiltshirs garden.[107]

Tusday the 20th begun harvest.

Sunday Night 25 Ball, a fine mare, fell into the gravell pitt Blakemore Wide Way, my horses got out of Stable Field and she following them & being bling (*blind*) I lost her. Worth £[blank].

Monday 26 Gave dinner at Rose & Crown, Tewin to Mr King, lawyer of Ware. Brother Hasler, Mr John Aylen, Mr Dolling, Old Squier, in settling the house Tewin Upper Green, but Wm Clarke did not attend, so nothing done.

Wednesday 28 the Ware Volunteers or Assosiation received their collers (*colours*) in Ware Park given by their Captaine Barron or Barnat Dickenson of Ware Town, gent[le]m[a]n. They went to church, from thence to Ware Park to recive their collers & excersise, from thence marched to Ware & rcived a good dinner given by their Captaine allso.

Saturday 31 Carried 5 tod 26 pound more of my wooll to one Spencers at Hertford for Mr Larken. Recd of Mr Larken 35s todd.

Saturday 10th I sold som wheat at 47s 6d per load.

Saturday 17 Markets dearer being very wet 49s 6d per load.

---

[106] The money to fund the raising of the Supplementary Militia was to be levied from local landowners and collected by the constables [Western, *English Militia*].
[107] Hitchin Volunteers; William Wilshere, lawyer of Hitchin was the captain.

Saturday 24 Markets much the same 50s d[itt]o.

Saturday 31 Markets much the same 49s d[itt]o.

SEPTEMBER Sunday 1st Charles Moody Esqr left Bramfield after liveing at the Rector's house 4 years and went to live at Coopers Sale in Esex.[108]

Sunday 8th went to Tewin church. Herd a very good hestoricall sermon preachd by the Revd Mr Newton there from the Begining of the World to thiese Days Text 17 Chap Acts 11 Virce.[109]

Monday 9th Went to Bush Fair on Dimond. Bought of John Perry from Denbeth Shiere (*Denbighshire*) in Wales 6 heifers & 2 steers, the heifers at £4 10s, steers about £6 per head.[110] Old Mr Schribier of Tewin House had half of them, 3 hefers & 1 steer the next day.[111]

Saturday 14 Jorney to St Albans Town Hall to renew licenses. Mr Donvell & Vandermuling justices, Cowper and Boyse clerks, Went on Mr Randall's poney by Money Hole. Came home by Tewin Gate. We all dined at Cos Piggotts the Red House, except Pauls Walden people, they at the Blew Boor.

Sunday 15th Dined at my sons Tewin with Mr & Mrs Jonson from St Albans & his son Will[ia]m Jonson & his wife, & Mr Mullett come after dinner. Old Mr Jonsons treat. Gave £1 1s 0d.

---

[108] Moody died 29 Sep 1799 – see diary entry below. Coopers Sale is now Theydon Garnon, Essex, and takes its name from the family of Gernon which held the capital manor from the 13th century. From at least the late 16th century, and especially in the 18th and early 19th centuries, the parish was known also as Coopersale, but this name was subsequently restricted to that northern part of the ancient parish served by the district church of St Alban, Coopersale, consecrated in 1852 [*VCH Essex* vol 4: *Ongar Hundred* (1956), pp258-262].

[109] Acts ch 17 verse 11: 'These were more noble than those in Thessalonica, in that they received the word with all readiness of mind, and searched the scriptures daily, whether those things were so'.

[110] John Perry from Denbighshire was a drover [P G Hughes, *Wales and the Drovers* (1943, reprinted 1988)].

[111] Tewin House, on the east side of the approach to Tewin church, was built in 1716 and twice visited by George I for its magnificent decoration. In a diary entry made at the end of June 1807 Carrington records its demolition [HALS: DE/X3/10].

On Thursday 19 was buried at Bramfield about 10 clock for noon, John Bourchier Lloyd aged 17. Herce & 4, coach in 4. Brought from Esqr Emmotts, Goldings, he died there. Buried behind the church near Doctter Spillsbury preacher to the Charter House, D[octo]r of Divinety who was buried there some time back, as corner stone in the wall near that place will tell you.[112]

Bramfield parish church by J C Buckler, 1832 (*HALS: DE/Bg/3/11*)

[112] The Bramfield burial register records both John Bourchier Lloyd and, on 18 August 1787, 'Thomas Sainsbery DD Vicar of Ponteland, Bishopric of Durham, Rector of March Baldon in the County of Oxford & preacher to the Charterhouse, aged 50' [HALS: DP22/1/3]. Any inscriptions on the exterior walls of the church are no-longer visible after extensive Victorian alterations and the application of cement render. Charterhouse public school was founded in 1611 by Thomas Sutton on the site of the Carthusian monastery in Smithfield, London. It transferred to Godalming in Surrey in 1872 [Weinreb et al, *London Encyclopaedia*].

Thursday 26 Went to Codicote statute with Mr Dolling and son John in his cart and my horse Witefoot. Held at the George, Mrs Raymonds.

Sunday 29 of this Month Died in his chair at Cooper Sale in Esex, Charles Moody Esqr after being gon from Bramfield 1 month. Buried at the said parish church the Saturday following in the church.

Satturday 7 Markets much the same, wheat 48s per load.

Saturday 14 Markets much the same, old wheat 48s load, new 44 & 46 per load.

Saturday 21 Marketts, old wheat 48s per load, new 46 that's good, for wheat is corse, a great deal not in yet, the wather so wett.

Saturday 27 Markets dearer by 6s per load, old wheat 55s per load, new in propotion occaitoned by the harvest being not got in. Wather continus still wett. Barley 40s qr, oates 40 d[itt]o, peas 28s per load. Malt has risen greatly within this 2 weeks the wholesale 56s per quarter on acpt (*account*) of the wett. The barley mostly half not in & black.

OCTOBER Tusday 1 Died John Osborne Esqr, mayor of St Albans, aged 67, one of the D[eputy] Lieutenants & Justices of the Liberty.[113]

Thursday the 3d went to the Bull at Whittwell Dixsons to their Statute. Dined with Mr Crabb, Mr John Hill, Mr Evens & Mr Thos Hill from Hartford &c about 20ty good companey. Staid all night, and the next day came home by Wellwin, and being their Stattute staid and dined there at Mr Battens, White Hart. Mr Wm Pennyfather of Diggswell, chieff constable. About 30ty at dinner. Came home erley with Mr Hill from Hartford on Dimon.

Thursday 3d of this month finished harvest begun Augst the 20, but the wather being so long wett, and a great maney not done yet, and some has been done the 3 weeks. The cropps are slight, no reeks (*ricks*). And markets are rising on acpt (*account*) of the wett, and corne out much still.

---

[113] John Osborn had been mayor of St Albans in 1798. He died as an alderman on 1 Oct 1799 [Gibbs, *Corporation Records of St Albans*, pp151 and 294].

Fryday the 4th Welling (*Welwyn*) Statute. Dined there as I came from Whittwell.

Monday 7th Wotton Stattute. A wet day. Dined at Whittinburys, the Feathers, Tewin Upper Green. Esqr Mackys wood pay day.

Thursday 10 Mixs (*Michaelmas*) Day.[114] Went to the Quarter Sessions, St Albans. No great buisnes there. Onley more of Old Britton and his side and the parish of St Peters in law in settling the parish rates. Counseler Asspaness, & Willsher, the law[y]er for Bretton &c. Counseler Watson & Swannell, the law[y]er for the parish. Britton gainer but another hearing to be next Sessions. Went on Dimon with Burges, went by the (*Cromer*) Hide. Came back the same way. Saw a great deal of corne not in yet, barley, wheat, oates & peas. This being St Albans fair. Very wet againe as we came home.

Saturday 12 Jurney to Cowper Sale in Esex, a vilage about 3 mile from Epping, to one Mrs Moodys there at the Rector's house near the church. Settled with Mr Brindley, Mr Moody's executor. Paid him for all that hay, corne & grass I had of Mr Moody, & he paid me my bill and half a years taxes to this Mixs (*Michaelmas*). Slept there Saturday night. Came home on Sunday on Dimond. Came from Epping Church to Ware in one hour 10 minuits (*minutes*).

Monday 14th Dined at my sons Rose & Crown, Tewin with Mr Pallett, Lord Cowper's stew[a]rd. Lord Cowper's wood sale. Paid Mr Pallet for wood bought out of Bansleys Wood £6 5s 0d & he paid me for pigg 25s. Hartford Statute at White Hart.

Wednesday the 16 Bramfield Statute. 24 at dinner.

Saturday 19 Jorney to Town Hall, St Albans, appointing surveyors. Dined at Coz Piggotts, Red House. Paid the Levy Money to Mr Boyse, treasurer. Went on Dimond. Saw wheat & barley still out in the fields as I went. Very great raine. Corne still abroad and hay. Great floods so whet cannot sow the wheat.

Fryday 25 Went to Bull at Ware. Paid for Mr Byde, Recever Gen[eral] £32 16s 0d on Land for 1798 and £40 0s 0d on Land for this 1799, and £20 0s 0d

[114] Michaelmas day is actually 29th September but the Quarter Sessions held around this date is known as the Michaelmas Sessions.

on the Income [Tax] for 1799. Dined at Eagel with Mr Samms and Mr Munns, & the baker, and Mr Ben Whittenbury, a qr of rost pork.

26 Mr Twinns sale at Amwell End, Ware. Was there, bought 20 of his ½ qr sacks.

Wednesday 30th Dined at Jacks, Rose & Crown Tewin, with Mr King, Mr Dolling, Mr Farr, Mr Harrington, Coz Wm Clarke, & Coz Sarah Hudson wen settled that place Tewin Upper Green to me, I to give Wm Clarke £20 & Sarah Hudson £20.

> **Saturday the 5th** Markets dearer, wheat 60s per load, barley 40s per quarter, oates 45[s] that's good, peas 29[s] load.
>
> **Saturday 12** Markets much the same, good wheat 60[s] per load.
>
> **Satturday 19** Markets much the same, wheat good 60s.
>
> **Saturday 26** Markets rather dearer, good wheat at 62s, barley that's good 45s qr.

This Month ends with wet. Some people not done harvest yet and growing hay all spoyled. The Fenns all drouned and the corne spoyled. Oates are 45s quarter that's good, hopps 3s per pound to 4s per p[oun]d latter end.

Thus endeth Octr. A great deal of corne still out in different parts of the county, and the latter hay all spoyld by the wett. The Fenns are all a sea.

NOVEMBER Tusday 5 Tythe fiest at Bramfield. Dined at Wder (*Widow*) Derds, the Grandisons Arms. Old Mr Lloyd & young Mr Thos Lloyd, & Mr Byron there. Came in shayes (*chaise*) from Ramseys, a very wet day, a flood.

Wednesday the 6 Mr Newton, rector of Tewin, and Mr Pallet, Lord Cowper's steward, with Mr Dean of Tewin Burry, & Mr Webb &c &c went a possessioning of the bounderys of the parish of Tewin.[115] A good supper at

[115] A perambulation of the parish boundaries was traditionally undertaken at Rogationtide (near the 5th Sunday after Easter) and was meant to ensure the community knew where the boundaries were and maintained them. Carrington describes the Bramfield parish boundaries in detail in the entry for 30 May 1803 below. At Bramfield the children joined the walk and plenty of food was provided

the Rose & Crown Tewin, I was there as being the meeting of the Assosition for Prosicute Felons.[116] I came from Ware as had been to fetch a load of malt, 10 quarter at £3 3s per qr. Never known so dear.

Sunday 17 Set of for London. Slep at brother Haslers at Eagel. Went to London on the Monday morning by the Ware Coach, got to London by ½ p[a]st 9 morning. Breekfasted at Mrs Goodalls. From thence to the bank and then to Coz Cooks, Billingsgate. Slept there Monday night, from thence on Tusday to the Treasury. Took £40 of Hoppkins money from thence to Cos Beck, Long Lane. Spent the evening with Mr Strutt at Vauns, the Hole in the Wall.[117] Slept at Coz Becks Wednesday afternoon. Came home by Ware coach to Eagle. Slept there. Came hom Tursday to Bacons in Cockell's cart with sister.

The 24 of this Month the treble bell of Tewin Church, being crackt, was new cast by John Briant of Hartford, and the recasting and fixing cost £10.[118] Mr Fran[ci]s Dean, Tewin Bury churchwarden. The s[ai]d Briant had 5s per year to keep the church clock in good order, which gose well.

---

along the way [See Ronald Hutton, *The Stations of the Sun: A History of the Ritual Year in Britain* (Oxford, 1996), pp277-87; S Hindle, 'Beating the Bounds of the Parish: Order, Memory, and Identity in the English Local Community, c1500–1700', in M Halvorson and K E Spierling, eds, *Defining community in early modern Europe* (Aldershot, 2008), pp205-28; H Falvey & S Hindle, *'This little commonwealth': Layston parish memorandum book, 1607-c1650 & 1704-c1747,* HRS vol XIX, Appendices 2, 3 and 4, are transcripts of the perambulations of Layston and Wyddial, Hertfordshire].

[116] Local associations of property owners formed to supplement official rewards offered for information leading to criminal convictions. Most of them disappeared after the formation of permanent police forces. In Hertfordshire the boroughs of Hertford and St Albans set up forces in 1836 and the remainder of the county in 1841 [N Osborn, *The Story of Hertfordshire Police* (Letchworth, 1969)].

[117] Joseph Strutt (1749-1802), antiquary, painter and engraver who had lived with Carrington in Bramfield, 1790-94. The Hole in the Wall, Kirby Street, Hatton Garden, London, kept by Vaughan.

[118] John Briant of Hertford, bellfounder (1749-1829) cast several complete rings of bells in Hertfordshire and more in other counties, as well as adding to peals all over England. He set up a bell foundry on the west side of Parliament Square, Hertford c1779. In 1782 he was elected a member of the Society of Hertford College Youths [Joyce Dodds, *Hertfordshire Bellfounders* (Hatfield, 2003), pp165-291]; a printed list of the bells cast by Briant can be found in HALS: DP/48/29/14].

Wednesday 27th Dined at the Grandisons Armes, Bramfield, Widow Derds, with Mr Preston, Mr Randall, Mr Richardson, and Mr Samuall French from Hartford. Mr French gave legg motton and Mr Preston a small haunch of venson, & Mr Randall 2 bottles of wine. Had 3 bo[w]ls of punch & brandy and beer. They spent 2s 6d each and I 5s. Mr Nickolds and Mr Harress, Esqr Boyd's keeper and another gentleman from Ware joynd us after dinner, & dined likewise and spent there 2s 6d each.[119]

Fryday Evening 29 Vestrey at Bramfield, Mr Preston overseer, to settle somthing theese dear times on the large famileys. A man with 3 or 4 children to have ½ p[ec]k of flower (*flour*) per week &c &c. Onley Preston & I, & Derds & Burges there.

Mrs Cannon at Hatfield Hide died this week, the last week of this month.

Saturday 9th Markets dearer, wheat £3 5s 0d per load.

16th Markets dearer, wheat £3 9s per load, barley that's good 45s per qr, oates 40s qr, peas 30s per load, malt £3 6s per qr, hopps 3s 6d p[oun]d. Maney people not done harvest yet hear abouts, all sorts corne still out, the wather has been wet for 3 months past.

Saturday 23d Markets much the same, wheat at £3 8s per load, barley that is good 50s qr, oates that is good 50s qr, peas good 35s per load, good old malt £3 10s 0d per quarter, hopps 4s p[oun]d.

Satturday 30th Markets much the same, wheat 65s per lo[a]d.

DECEMBER Monday Morning the 2d was married at Tewin Church, the Revd Tho[mas] Lloyd of Hartford to Esqr Macky's daughter of Marden.[120] Maried by Revd Vergen of Hardfordingbery (*Hertingfordbury*).

---

[119] Under an act of parliament of 1710 (9 Anne c27) all gamekeepers had to be registered with the Clerk of the Peace and a certificate issued to the lord of the manor. George Harris had been registered as gamekeeper for Thomas Hope Byde of Ware Park from 1788 [*HCR* vol VIII, Appendix VII].

[120] Thomas Lloyd married Frances Mackey by licence on 2 Dec 1799 [HALS: DP106/1/6].

Monday 2d I was took in by a swindler who came into the house with a glass quort (*quart*) bottle saying it was for the collick, from the famous Dr Willess & the price 2s wich I gave him, which was all a lye.[121] Nothing but water.

Wednesday the 4 Venson fiest at the Rose & Crown, Tewin. I gave the haunch and the other found a turkey and ham. Companey at dinner was Mr Dean, Mr Webb, Mr Randal, Mr Mullet, Mr Dolling, Mr Preston, Mr Pooll, Mr Hanken, Mr Jonson, Mr Pridmore, Mr Harrington, Mr Whittenbury and myself. Good dinner, & tea, & supper. Wine & punch, plenty good company, money 7s 6d each.

Tusday the 10th walked on foot to Ware, to spend the evening at brother Haslers with friend, as his son William being out of his prenticeship having served 5 years to one Skegg, glaiser at Ware. Supper 1 filit of veal, 1 hamm, 2 leggs mutton, & apple pye &c &c. Plenty of punch & good companey. 29 at supper 3s per piece. Myself, Mr Golley, Mr Elless, Mr Baley, Mr Cockel, Mr Dunn, Mr Dennis, Mr Skegg, Mr Page, Mr Dawson, Mr John Aylon, Mr Woker jnr, Mr Ginn jnr, Mr Ekens, Mr Norton, Mr Cowper, Mr Treacher, Mr Hudson, Mr Cotton, Mr Shadbolt, Mr Hitch, Mr Taylor, Mr Hyde, Mr Freshwater, Mr Field, Mr Ginn, Mr Walker, Mr Hobbs, Mr Haradone.

Wednesday Morning 11th Joseph Andrews or Anderson of Ware drounded him self in the New River Head. Young man, a wife 3 chil[dren]. I saw him come in, the lime cart brought him to the George. Kimpton sent for the doctor but to no purpose.

Tusday 17th a privet court for the Manner of Tewin was held at the Rose & Crown, Tewin by Mr Neal atturney of Hartford, steward of the said maner, to admitt Wm Hunsdon tenant to the s[ai]d maner, late his father's Little Farme on Tewin Lower Green in the tenner of Lawrance Carpenter.[122] Mr Dean of the Bury and I was the coppy hoders there. Mr Cherry of Hartford, & Mr Ewderd (*?Edward*), & Mr Hall there. Mr Hall let Mr Hunsdon have £210 on

---

[121] Is this a reference to Francis Willis, one of the physicians who attended George III? [Roy Porter, 'Willis, Francis (1718–1807)', *ODNB*, Jan 2008].

[122] John Neild, attorney of Hertford was the steward of the Manor of Tewin from 1789 until his death in Aug 1803, recorded by Carrington below. He was buried at All Saints on 27 Aug [HALS: DP48/1/25]. Carrington and Francis Dean were sworn as the homage [HALS: DE/P/T2027].

morgage on the same place. Mr Hall is their landlord of Hollerd Farm wheare Mr Hunsdon and his mother lives, Codicote.

Thursday Night the 19th Camps House entred and robed by 2 ruffens which almost killed Camp & his wife and robd them of all. This is a small farme house between Stanstead and Hunsdon and the 2 men Criswell and Burges was hanged for it on the 14th of March 1800 in a field near his house.[123]

21 Flack's coach broke down about the Shipp, Tottenham a coming from London to Ware, and Mr Baker of Anstey killed on the spott, and several more hurt.

Thursday Night 26 Thos Kettle labourer of Bramfield and plowman to Mr Henery Hunsdon of Bramfield a going to London with waggon loaded with straw, stoped to bait at the Queens Head, Wormley and gitting up on the waggon after the bait for the horses, slipt off the waggon and killed him self on the spott instantly. Was brought home after the jury sat, and buried at Bramfield Tusday the last day or 31.

> **7th** Markets cheeper, best wheat £3 per load. I sold for 59s per load.
>
> **14th Saturday** markets dearer, best wheat £3 5s per load.
>
> **Saturday 21** Markets dearer by 8s per load, wheat at £3 12s per load, good barley £3 per qr, peas 36s per load, good oates at 45s per quarter, good old malt £4 10s per quarter, hopps 3s 6d per pound.
>
> **Saturday 28** Markets dearer. I sold for £3 15s per load to Mr Roberts of Bayford Bury, stewrd to Mr Baker, he bought it for the poor of Bayford. And I sold 5 quarter of barley to Mr Hudson of Ware at £3 per quarter.

Thus his ended this year 1799. The latest harvest ever known, corne out till the end of November, and the dearest ever known. Wheat £3 18s per load,

---

[123] William Cresswell (32) and James Burgess (37) had burgled the dwelling house of Nathaniel and Mary Camp, violently assaulting and maiming them and stealing three gold rings (worth 21s), a silver tablespoon (5s), a silver teaspoon (5s), a silver pap spoon (2s 6d) and a pair of silver buckles (5s). They were executed on 14 March near to where they had committed the crime [Information from Ken Griffin; see also diary entry for 3 Mar 1800 below].

barley £3 per quar[ter], oates 45s, peas 38s per load, malt £4 8s 0d per quarter, hops 3s 6d pound.

South west view of St Peters church, St Albans, by J C Buckler, 1831 (*HALS: DE/Bg/3/127*)

1800 (*HALS: DE/X3/2*)

1800 JANUARY Monday [6th] went to Quarter Sessions at Hartford. When Mrs Page, braiser (*brazier*) of Hartford wass called to the barr and tryed and found gilty for buying 2 iron wedges value six pence knowing them to be stolen and she lay in prison till the nixt Quarter Sessions Monday 21 April, and she got relieast and come hom in St Andrews Street, Hart[for]d.[124]

Tusday 7 Spent the evening at Mr Randals, Bramfield Place with Mr Rooke, Mr Pool, Mr Randal's brother William, Mr Kirby, when drawd King & Queene.

Wednesday the 8 Dined Wd Deards, Grandison Arms Bramfield a dinner given by Geo Richardson. Mr Preston, Mr Randal, Mr B Whittinbury, Mr Hunsdon, Mr Hanken, Mr Derds, Mr Burges, my self, & Richardson thar. Mutton &c. Money 3s 6d.

Thursday 16 Jorney to Quarter Sessions St Albans. No great buisness there though 4 counslers there about parish buisness on settlement of a man and family.[125] Went by Cole Green on Dimon. Came home by Grubbs Barne (*parish of Tewin*). Stopt at Jacks (*Rose and Crown, Tewin*), with Elsom &c.

Fry Evening the 17th Came from Ware by Bengeo. Stopt at the Globe & Compases there, one Robt Johns. Stayd till nine clock with Mr Gripper of Hartford, and Butterfield & Turner. Butterfd came to Waterford with me.

Saturday 18 Went to old Mr Fairman's buirall at Ware, a walking buriall from his house near Ware Mill to Ware church.[126] His old frinds paul bearers with sashes, hatbands, & gloves. I had a hatband & gloves. Buired about 5 clock, aged 94, on the east by south end of the churchyard. Went on Dimon. Came home by Waterford & Bramfield.

---

[124] Elizabeth Page was convicted at the Epiphany Sessions 1800 but the judgement was respited by the court, entertaining a doubt as to the legality of the conviction. She spent 99 days in gaol before being released [HALS: QSPB vol 2 and QSR vol 9 p11].
[125] The settlement case was in respect of Elizabeth, wife of James Sumner alias Smith and her four children, Sarah, Rebecca, James and Frances from the parish of Chipping Barnet to Northampton Town [HALS: LSR3 and LSB2].
[126] Joseph Fairman, maltster. Carrington attends a sale of his effects on 11 March below.

Saturday 25 Jorney to the Town Hall, St Albans as a meeting of the Justices and the bakers in the Hund[red] of Cashio being sumond to appear about baking but one sort of flower (*flour*), the wheat to be dresed so as to leave all in but the bran. Went on Dimon, and so it was done, but it was so corse & bad, & did not agree with the constitutions. Maney was hurt & some died & it was orderd to be made againe as usuall.

Sunday 26 Dined at Wd Deardses, Grandisons Armes Bramfield with Camp at the White Hart, Hartford & Geo Richardson, & Andrews, clarke. Spent 3s.

> **4th** Markets cheeper, best wheat £3 14s per load. I sold 4 load for £3 14s per load to Mr Roberts for the poor of Bayford.
>
> **Satturday the 11th** Markets rather dearer, best wheat £3 16s, barley best £3 3s qr.
>
> **Saturday 18** Markets much the same.
>
> **Saturday 25** Markets something dearer, wheat £3 16s per load &c.

FEBRUARY Sunday 2d My sister Martha Warby buried at Tewin church aged 86 years. A great number of people at the funeral. She died Monday morning the 27 January last month. She was a very charitable good woman, good to the poor and had been a good housekeeper at Tewin Lower Green upwards of 50 years at the butcher's shopp there, joyning the bakers there. And died as she lived, much respected and lemented by all. Had brought up a large family of her own, 5 sons, 2 daughters in great cretet (*credit*), and after that supported her grand children.

Fryday the 16 Jorney to London on Mr Wollaston's horse of the Charterhouse, London wich I had had a keeping at 3s 6d per week. Mr Randall of Bramfield Place Farme went with me on his poney. Dined at the Coach & Horses, Cheshunt 2s 6d. Slep at Coz Becks. Next day went to the Treasury. Recd of Mr Pollock £30 for Mr Hopk[in]s. Dined with Mr Wolleston, slept with Coz Beck. Sunday went to St Gilses church with Coz J Beck from thence to Ld Grandisons. Well entertained, from thence to Ld Cowpers. Slept at Becks. Monday with Coz Thos Beck to the hopp merchants, paid him £54. Had 2 bottls of his cyder. From thence to Coz Cooks No 1 Billingsgate, slept there. Next day went to the bank. Bought 2 hundrd in the 4 per cents for £156. Took ½ yrs of the 3 per cents. Slept at

Becks. Wednesday morning came home in the Hartford coach from Snow Hill. 6s coach. Mrs Ramsey's coach at the Falkon – Benjamin coachman.

Fryday the 16th of this month & Saturday 17th the great fire in Tems (*Thames*) Street, the stoore houses all burnt close to the Towr of London. I saw it a burning on the Tusday following the 20th and the great quantity of coffe[e] wich lay burnt on Towr Hill. Thousands of bushels. Supposed £500,000 damage.

Saturday the lst Markets much the same, wheat at £3 16s, barley £3 qr.

Saturday 8th Markets rather dearer, wheat the best £4 the load. I sold 4 load at £3 17s 6d per load to Mr Newman for the poor of Bayford by sample to be delivrd next Saturday.

Saturday 15 Markets much the same. I sold som wheat for £4 the load.

Saturday 22d Markets rather cheepr, about 2s per load.

MARCH This Month begins with sharp frosty wather, & clowdy, little son, wind NE.

Monday 3d the Assizes at Hert[for]d, Judge Heath, High Sheriff Justinen Cashmager from Pottrels (*Poterells*), North Mimms, foor man (*foreman*) of the Grand Jury Sr John Sanders Sebright.[127] Maney fellons, but the assizes over a bout 4 clock Tusday. Next day 8 condmed and on Fryday the 14 was 2 out of the 8 hanged. Criswell and Burges for robing Camp between Stanstead & Hunsdon, whome they broke into his house & robed & beat them much. The gallows was carried from Hartford and fixed in the field near Camp's house on the right hand as you go to Hunsdon. Supposed to be ten thousand

[127] Judge John Heath (1736-1816) was raised to the bench in 1780 and regularly rode out on the Home Circuit from his house, Hayes Park, Middlesex [Patrick Polden, 'Heath, John (1736–1816)', *ODNB*, Jan 2008]; Justinian Casamajor (d 1820) inherited the mansion and estate of Poterells, North Mimms in 1792 [*VCH Hertfordshire*, vol 2 p255]; Sir John Saunders Sebright, 7th Baronet (1767-1846) of Beechwood, Flamstead was sheriff 1797-8, Captain of the Herts Yeomanry Cavalry, 1798 and MP for Hertfordshire, 1807-1834 [R G Thorne, *The History of Parliament, The House of Commons, 1790-1820*, vol 5 (1986)].

persons there. I was charged to attend the execution from Mr Grover the Under Sheriff from [Hemel] Hemstead and as soon as turnd off, I and Mr Randall went to the Crown at Whitford (*Widford*) & dined, and stopt at brother Haslers and bought they howsen (*houses*) of Aylon at Whitford for £80. Paid Aylon £10 down & 3 ginuaes (*guineas*) gave him for the bargen.

Tusday 11 Went on foot to Ware to Mr Jos[eph] Fairman's sale. Bought a 6 inch cart £4 8s 0d, a hen coop 8s, and 40 sacks £3 14s 0d. Slept at Eagle and went to Ware church the next day, Wednesday being a generall fast. The text was in the Psalms 'O God our fathers have decleard to us the great works thou diddest in their days & in the time of old'.[128] Came on foot to Hartford in the afternoon, to the clubb at [Green] Dragon. Came home with Jack in Watson's cart.

Sunday 16 in the afternoon whent with John Day to Mr Rain at Newgate Street near [Little] Barkhamstead. The dark night, got lost coming home. Came by Rocksford (*Roxford, Hertingfordbury*), went by How Green with Aylon.

Monday the 17 Dined at Crawleys the White Horse, Wotton Turnpike meeting with Mr Mason, Hollingsworth, Thos Hinson, & Samms, Walls, Sarrage, Cloppham, Hall, Picketts from Sacomb, Ambrose of Grigerys, & Jerimah Crawley. Large piece of rost beefe but not well don, small fillitt of veal & hamm. Drank onley gin & water. Spent 2s, ostler 6d. Paid one qrs duty for Bramfield parish £2 18s 6d. Commssinors there Barron Dickenson esqr, Mr Green, Mr Blindall, Mr Kimpton, Mr Flack, Mr Twinn and the Revd Dr Carr, & Mr Kitchener.[129] Went on Dr Andrew's horse. Come home by Gubbens (*Gobions Farm, Stapleford*) ½ p[a]st 7 clock.

Tusday 18 Esqr Macky's wood sale at Rose & Crown. I drawed No 1 in Hooks Bushes.

Wednesday 19 Waters, otherways Munt, hanged at Gallows Hill, Hartford, for robing England, the Duke of Leeds' stew[ar]d in complace with one Hill,

[128] Psalm 44 verse 1: 'We have heard with our ears, O God, our fathers have told us, what work thou didst in their days, in the times of old'.

[129] John Carr LLD (1732-1807), Master of Richard Hale School, Hertford 1763-1788 and Mayor 1792, 1799 and 1800 [R Gander, *Richard Hale School*, Tewin (2008)]. Other commissioners were: John Baron Dickinson, Nathaniel Green, Thomas Blindle, Thomas Kimpton, William Flack, John Tween and Edward Kitchener [HALS: TP8/2].

but Hill was saved. Wen they come to the gallows there was no hangman & the man had som hopes, but the gaylor (*gaoler*) made his man do the job.[130]

Sunday afternoon 23 Went to Hardingfordbury (*Hertingfordbury*) to see Mr Jonson, from thence to the Park, Samuall Baker's Esqr.[131] Was made welcom by Mr Hoppwood buttler, Wrenn gardner, Porter groom. Called at Jonsons, saw Pallett and Grubb drinking wine there. Stopt a little & came home.

Monday 24 Went with Jack & Blindall to Woollmer Green to look at Blindall's estate there, 7 acers of land & 2 houses & barn about £19 per year. Dined at the W[i]d[ow] Crows, the Red Lyon. Blindall treated. Went on Andrews' mare.

Monday the 31 Spent the afternoon at Goldings, Esqr Emmotts with Samm Janes, Mr Phipp, & Mr Paine from an invitation of Mr Smith the buttler, plenty of wine &c &c.

> This month March 1800 marketts:
> The avridge price wheat £4 per load, barley the best £3 10s per quarter, oates the best £2 15s per quarter, hopps 4s pound, malt the best £4 10s per quarter, peas 40s per load, clover seed the best 15d per pound.

APRIL Tusday the 1st Dined at Samm Janeses, Earle Cowper's Arms, Birch Green, on 2 salt fish & h-bone of beef, with Phipp, Mullet, John Smith,

---

130 Francis Godolphin Osborne, Duke of Leeds, lord of the manor of North Mimms, d 1799. Richard Waters alias Munt robbed William England, the Duke's steward, of a purse valued 2d and £162 in bank notes on 3 Dec 1799. Thomas Hill who was similarly accused was acquitted. *The Cambridgeshire Reporter* relates that the Middlesex hangman engaged to execute the prisoner did not arrive, a local man took fright although offered one guinea, a convict from the gaol was persuaded to act, but before he did so 'an understrapper of the prison had relieved the unhappy man from his distressed situation, and the Sheriff of a disagreeable dilemma'. This was the last execution to take place at Gallows Hill, Hertford [TNA: Hertford Assize records, information Ken Griffin].

131 Samuel Baker lived at Hertingfordbury Park until his death in Dec 1804 and his brother William (who owned them both) at Bayford House, later known as Bayfordbury [Patience Bagenal, *Hertingfordbury Park and its links with the Bayfordbury Estate* (Hertfordshire Gardens Trust, 2000)].

Humfrey Field, Cheek, Hickman, & Pain from Chesham (*Buckinghamshire*), & Sewill. Spent 7s.

Wednesday 2d Spent the evening at Mr Randalls, with his brother Wm & a Mr Brown from London.

Saturday 12 Dined at the Turks Head, Hartford for dinner & punch 2s 6d. One Millard keeps this inn.

Saturday Night the 12th Died Charles Schribier Esq of Tewin House, aged about 80ty. Was buired the Monday following the 21st in a vault in Endfield Church. Was taken away about 7 clock in the morning from Tewin House in herce and six, 3 mourning coaches in four, and his own coach behind emty. He had not lived at Tewin above 12 years as about that time he pirchesed the estate of Esq Macky for £22,000. Then Macky bought Marden Estate for £7,000 and build a new house there finished in the year 1792. Old Esq Schribier was a Dutchman and he left the estate to his eldest son William Schribier, who came to Tewin to live there from Suffolk & made great alterations in the offices of the house, for the worse, & distroyd the fine engin which used to serve the house and offices with water and then sunk a well. A great simpleton.

Easter Monday the 14th Dined at Rose & Crown, Tewin, my sons. The parish vestrey. Buttok of beef, leg motton rosted, puddings &c. Mr Webb the late overseer, Mr Dean, church warden. Mr Hanken chosen for the year ensuing as overseer. After diner I spent the afternoon with Mr Blower, gent from Bulls Mill (*Stapleford*), & a French Count which dined there in the barr. Some good punch. The wet Easter Monday.

Easter Tusday 15 Dined at Grandisons Arms, W[i]d[ow] Deards Bramfield, Easter vestrey, Brynt Preston, overseer. Buttock beef, leg moton, ryse pudings &c. Esqr Searanke there. The expence for the poor this year &c was 7s in the pound.

Thursday 17th Went to Sheephall (*Shephall*) on Dimon. Waid the w[eigh]ts there. Came home by Wotton. Dined at the White Lyon with the farmers, being their Easter vestrey with Mr Kimpton, Mr Caters, Mr Hall & Monk overseers &c &c. Collection 2s 6d each.

Monday 21 Went to the Quarter Sessions Hartford. Went from thence to Goldings, Esqr Emmotts, to dinner as being his birthday. Comming home lost my way. Got down to Bulls Mill, young Cloppham came hom[e] with me, being a very dark night, was on the little poney, he led me out of the way.

Thursday 24 Jorney to St Albans Quarter Sessions on Dimon. Dined at Coz Piggotts with Lane, Pedder, Mathews, Cook, & Clarke all on the Jury from Codicote, & Smith constable. Spent with horse £0 3s 0d. No great businiss at Sessions. Went by Hatfield. Recd one yrs tax of Esqr Searanke £6 12s 0d. Came home by Grubbs Barne. Very wet. Stopt at Mr Patients.

Saturday 26 Dined at Bull with Mr Randall, Mr Elless from Ware. Spent 2s 6d. Went from thence to the Bell. Paid Mr Gripper a bill £35. Mr Hudson was with me from Ludlo[w] (*Shropshire*).

> **Saturday 5** Markets much the same, wheat at £4 per load, the best £4 2s 0d.
>
> **Saturday 12** Markets much the same, best wheat £4 4s 0d. I sold some for £4 2s 0d per load to Mr Robarts for the poor of Bayford.
>
> **19th** Markets much the same. The first Saturday the market bell rung againe, as hung in one corn[er].
>
> **Saturday 26** Markets rather dearer on acpt of the great wet wather, great flood today. Cannot sow our barley. Wheat at £4 6s per load, barley the best £3 12s qr, oates £2 10s qr, peas £2 per load.

(*HALS: DE/X3/3*)
MAY Fryday 9th Went to the Bull at Ware. Paid taxes to the Reciver General, Esqr Byde on the Income Tax for the year 1799. Money in full £107 17s 9d. Sallery £1 11s 0d. On the Windows and other Horses &c taxes on account for 1799 £50 0s 0d. Dined at brother Haslers with Samms, & Mrs Watson, & Mr Hunt's daughter. Spent the afternoon there with B Whittenbury, & his son in law Penefather in ginn & water. Went on Dimon, spent 2s 0d, ostler 3d. As went saw Mr Best the may[o]r of Hartford buired at St Andrews Church Hartford, a herss and pair, 3 mourning coaches in pair. He was a master carpenter at Hartford. He was about 40 years of age, a good kind of man, and died in the 8th month of his mayorlty all most suddingly.[132]

---

[132] John Best, mayor of Hertford, 1799/1800 [L Turnor, *History of the Ancient Town & Borough of Hertford*, (Hertford, 1830), p130].

Wednesday 21 Went on Witefoot to [W]idford to look at house which was [?to be] sold this day by auction by ... at the Griffin at Stanstead .... Bought none. ... to Ware in Mr Steven's chaise ... at sisters Haslers. Come home on foot next day, as young Wm [H]asler has my horse (*Remainder of page torn away*).

Fryday 23 Went to Lord Millborn's (*Melbourne's*) races Brockt Hall in the Park.[133] Saw the Prince of Wales there. Rode Lloyd's horse from Diggswell home. The races begun on yesterday the 22. A great maney people there ... 8d.

Saturday 24 Sent Will to St Albans the White Hart as being the day to appoint assessors. I went to Lord Millborn's races againe. Went to Red Lyon with Blindl & Dr Squier. Spent 1s. Spent at Diggswell 6d.

Sunday 25 in the Evening a Quarter Master of the Ryall Waggoners attillery quartering at Hartford hung himself with his [?sa]sh on a tree ... between Hartford .... (rest torn away).

JUNE the 3d Shore my sheep. Cold, showry wather. Shore them by the schoore (*score*).

Thursday 5th Died Lieutenant Timothy Hoppkins, at Bacons Farm, Bramfield. He had been at board with me at Bacons upwards of 20 years. He was a native of Wales, and was put prentice to a fisherman when young, but was pressed from thence into His Majesty's Navy in the war with Spane, 1739.[134] He was in the Duke, man of war of 90 gunns, in the command of Admirl Balshan of the Victory of 100 brass guns, in companey togather in that great storm when the Victory and all was lost in 1743 but the Duke was saved, though I have herd him say they all expected likewise to perish.[135] He had

---

[133] Sir Peniston Lamb, 1st Viscount Melbourne. Brocket Hall was designed by the architect James Paine and completed in 1760. The racecourse was behind the mansion and is clearly shown on a map of 1798 [HALS: DE/P/P15].
[134] Sometimes called the War of Jenkin's Ear, 1739-1742, which brought about the fall of Sir Robert Walpole's government in 1742.
[135] HMS Victory, commanded by Admiral of the White, Sir John Balchin (1670-1744) was lost in a violent storm off Alderney on 5 Oct 1744 after successfully liberating a Royal Navy convoy blockaded in the River Tagus, Lisbon, Portugal by a French fleet (*ODNB*; a detailed report of its history and the discovery of the shipwreck with her

been in maney engagements at sea, and in taking maney places & ships and was made Lieutenant of the Navy in the year 1760. He had the offer of Captaine of a 90 gun ship about the year '89, but his age & infirmitys obliged him to decline. His sight failed him, and he was almost totaley blind 9 years before his death. He was buried at Tewin Church on Tusday the 10. Aged about 82 yrs. He served their Majestys George 2d & 3d upwards of 60 years as a good & faithfull servant. His carrector such bold, corugs (*courageous*), genaros (*generous*), & an honest man.

Fryday 6 Jorney to London to acquaint Mr Pollock, Mr Hopkins' agent of his death, & his sister. Went with Mr Pallet in his 1 horse chair of Cole Green. Put up at the 4 Swans, Bishopgate. Done my buisness in the town. Came to 4 Swans to dinner with Mr Pallet & young John Beck. Came home the same day with Mr Pallet in chair to Cole Green, waked (*walked*) through the park home to Bacons. 11 clock night.

Fryday 13 Was the Grand Reveiw in Hatfield Park on a fine plane or riseing ground the east side of the Marques Salsburys house, of all the yeomendry, and all the Associations in the County of Hartford and the Hartfordshire Millitia. Reviewd by his Majesty and Duke of York, and the Prince of Wales, &c &c. The Queen and Princeses and most of the ryoll family there. The troops of horse & foot as follows:

Captn Lambs Troop Horse	60 men
Captn Calverts about	55
Captn Hales about	50
Captn Villers d[itt]o	55
Captn Sr John Sebrights d[itt]o	40
Captn Hankins d[itt]o abot	40
Hartford Association foot	90 men
St Albans d[itt]o about	80
Hitchin d[itt]o about	80
Hatfield d[itt]o about	70
Ware d[itt]o about	70
Hunsdon & Stanstead d[itt]o	60
Stortford about	80

bronze cannon by Odyssey Marine Exploration in 2009 can be found at: www.shipwreck.net).

Wormley & Cheshunt about	80
Royston & Barkway d[itt]o	80
Captn Sr George Prescotts	
Troop of Horse Yeomendry	55 men
And the Hartfordshire Millitia about	300

They was all entertaind with good diner under the east side of the house and cannon fir[e]d wen the King … about 9 clock & fierd again . ... Left about 4 clock. The Marques gave all the soldiers a good dinner in the park.[136]

Sunday 15 Charrity sermon preached at Tewin Church by the Revd James Riddell, Curat[e] of Hardingfordbury. I was there and dined at Mr Bruxes, Tewin & spent the afternoon with Brux & Richardson at Jack's. Spent 1s 6d. Gave at church 2s 6d. But a small congregation. None of the Cowpers. Collection on this sermon 17s 0d

Monday 16 A Coart held at Tewin Bury princpally to admitt young Schribier to the coppyhold belonging to Tewin House by the church, as accasined by the death of his father old Mr Schribier, which died on the 12th of April last, but he not attending so no buisness done, only good diner. Mr Neall, the stew[a]rd of the sd maner & Mr Nicholsson, his clerk there, I, and Mr Gripper, Mr Dean, & Mr Pallett, all as was there.

Wednesday 18 Went to Codicot with Mr Dolling. Deliverd the paper to Wm Warren, put up at George. Spent 2s.

Sunday 22 Jorney to London with sister Hassler and Mary Ann in little cart. Dimon, put up at White Lyon livery stables, White Lyon Street near Spittle [Square], Bishopgate Street. Went to Coz Becks slept there. Next day went to the Treasury with Mrs Edwrds, Mr Hopkins' sister to one Mr Pollock, Mr Hopkins' agent to settle. I rec[eive]d £68 for board & his funerll &c and she recd all other moneys that was in Mr Pollocksis hands. Came from thence to the Sallopin Coffee House, Mr Folletts to dinner, from thence to the Whole in the Wall and spent the evening with Mr Strutt. Slept at Coz Becks. Next day

[136] This was undoubtedly the most spectacular ceremonial event in Hertfordshire military history. *A Narrative of the Preparations made at Hatfield* written by Lord Salisbury gives the total of troops taking part as 1,594 [HALS: 70920]. It is described in great detail in *The Gentleman's Magazine,* June 1800, reproduced in Jones, *Hertfordshire, 1731-1800*, pp138-142.

Tusday went to Coz Cooks, and we all spent the evening at the Ryall Sirkett, St Georges Fields.[137] Went into the pitt 2s each. Mrs Cook had her pocket picket. Went home with Mrs Watson in coach to Bell, Holborn. Slept again at Long Lane, Coz Becks. Came home next day Wednesday, brought young Stephen Cook with me in the cart, & young John Beck came with us on Mr Follett's horse.

Thursday 26 Clubb fiest at the [Green] Dragon, Cambals Hartford. I was there, no fowls, but a plaine dinner. Came home with Thorowgood in his cart 9 clock.

Saturday 28 Jorney to St Albans to the White Hart to be appointed Collectors of his Majesty's Taxes &c &c. Went on Dimon by Stanboro. Came home againe by Stanboro. Spent at St Albans Coz Piggots diner 1s 6d, ginn and water 6d, osler 6d. Spent at Stanborough 6d.

> **Saturday 7** Markets dearer, best wheat £4 7s 0d per load.
>
> **Saturday 14** Markets dearer, best wheat £4 10s 0d per load on account of the cold, cloudy, dark backening wather. Wind NW, very cold & sharp.
>
> **Saturday 21** Markets dearer, best wheat £4 16s 0d per load and all other things in proportion. Oates 50s per quarter, good barley £3 d[itt]o, good peas 50s per load, beens 3s per quarter. Beef good 1s or 14d per p[ound], ordnery 10d, butter 15d d[itt]o, cheese 1s good, ordnery 9d.
>
> **28** Markets dearer, best wheat £5 0s 0d per load.

Thus ends the markets in June. The wheat on the ground but middling and late now but a shooting that which was sown first, and the late sown not near shooting as had not come up till after Christmas. Vass (*vast*) crops of grain which is much wanting, for price in London is £7 10s 0d per load.

JULY Tusday 1 Went to Gravley to Mr Warrens on Dimon. Came home by Knaboth (*Knebworth*) to look on my horse & steer in the park, a keeping

[137] The Royal Circus Theatre, opened in 1782. Burnt down in 1803, it was rebuilt and in 1809 renamed the Surrey Theatre, surviving until about 1920 as the Surrey Music Hall, Blackfriars Road [Weinreb et al, *London Encyclopaedia op cit*].

horse at 4s per week & steer at 3s 6d. Called at Pristes, & Jonses, & Blindalls, Derds End, all places made welcome. Spent at Woolmer Green & Burnham Green 1s. Gave Skeggs' famley Burn[h]am Green 6d. Gave the 4 boys at Burn[h]am Green 6d. Gave the Warren's maid at Gravley 6d.

Wednesday 2d Went to Ware in little cart, to carry Miss Wolleston away who took coach there for London. Saw the Harts Millitia come in with the Marquess Salsbry. The Ware Association met them between Ware & Hart[ford]. Spent 10d.

Sunday 6 Dined at Eagle, Ware with Coz Cooks from London. They came over night & slept at Bacons. Spent & gave 3s.

Wednesday 9th Tewin fair spent at Whittenburys with Ben Whittenbury 7d. Spent at Jacks with Dolling, Blindall, Harrington, Palmer, Richardson & Butterfield 2s.

Saturday 12 Jorney to St Albans, to the White Hart to receive instructions on the Income Act. Went on Dimon by Waterend. Dined at Coz Piggotts 1s 6d. Spent 6d, horse & hostler 10d. Came home to Hartford and spent there at Bull 6d.

Sunday 13 Dined at Mr Randalls. Walked down to Waterford in afternoon with Randall, Mrs Gears, spent 6d.

Tusday 15 To London with Mr Randall in his cart & my Dimond mare. Carried Step[he]n['s] shays (*chaise*) up with us. Went by Potters Barr, then the new road by Southgate. Dined at Southgate, got to London by 7 clock, put the horse up at the Bear & Staff, Smith[fiel]d. Slept at Coz Cooks first night, 2 night Coz Becks. Came home Thursday Hartford Road.

Spent at Esington (*Essendon*) as went		9d
At Southgate dinner	2s	
½ the horse keep at London	4s	6d
Spent at Coach Horses Cheshunt coming down, Taskers	1s	3d
Spent at Hartford Heath at Whittingsburys		11d

Brought Miss Wooleston down with us in cart. Set out from London five clock, home by 10 night. This Tusday night the great fire at Horrell Mr Youngs. Burnt 5 barns, 4 hovells. Supposed set on fire.[138]

Sunday 20 To church at Bramfield. After dinner went to Ware with Miss Wolleston in Randall's cart. Went by Hardingfordbury (*Hertingfordbury*), came home to Bantfield (*Bramfield*) and left the cart, walked home after. Spent 10d.

Sunday 27 Went to Ld Cowpers in the morning, from thence to Bramfield church, and the afternoon to Jacks at the Rose & Crown, Tewin to meet my constables for presentments for the Assizes. Spent there 4s.

Monday 28 Went to the Assizes Hartford to give in presentments. Judges were Lord Kinion and Grouse.[139] Dined at Ramses, the Falkon. Drank tea there with Mrs Watson. Saw her safe to the ball at the Town Hall. Came home by my self on foot, 11 clock. Spent 3s.

Tusday 29 Went to the Assizes againe. Herd Shock Oliver's tryall before Ld Kinion.[140] Was cast for death. Got £2 14s for Mrs Tatt. Came home in little cart with Sheath.

Wednesday 30th Went to my sons at Tewin, the christening of his child Susanah. Brother & sister Hasler, John Aylon, Mrs Watson, there from Ware, Billey Jonson & wife & old Mrs Jonson, Mr Pridm[o]r[e] & wife there, Mr Dolling &c there. Good dinner & plenty of wine & cyder. Gave 3s 6d. Came home 3 in the morning with young Clopham.

---

[138] The fire at Mr Young's 'an eminent farmer, near Essendon' was reported in great detail in *The Gentleman's Magazine*, July 1800, reproduced in Jones, *Hertfordshire 1731-1800*, p143. Another fire occurred on 11 Sep – see diary entry below.

[139] Sir Nash Grose (1740-1814) a fellow of Trinity Hall, Cambridge was called to the bar at Lincoln's Inn in 1766, a serjeant at law, 1774 and appointed a judge of the King's Bench and knighted in 1787. He died at his home on the Isle of Wight on 31 May 1814 [*ODNB*]. Judge Kinion was Lloyd Kenyon, one-time Lord Chief Justice [Douglas Hay, 'Kenyon, Lloyd, first Baron Kenyon (1732–1802)', *ODNB*, Oct 2009]. Carrington records his death at Bath in April 1802 below.

[140] James Oliver was hanged on 8 August 1800 [see diary entry of that date for more details].

Thursday 31 Was hanged at Hartford Ann Mead about 14 years of age, for poyseing one of Proctor's children about 1 yr ½ old of Royston.[141] She lived with them as servant girll & her mistress & she had words so she took revenge on the child, her body was given to Dr Bradley for descettion (*dissection*).[142]

Saturday 5 Markets rather lower, best wheat about £5 per load. This is midsumer fair day, I sold Prince horse for £15. Spent & gave 2s. Came home with Ewington.

Saturday 12 Markets cheeper by 10s per load or more according as they can sell. The wather fine. Full markets notwithstanding so dear.

Saturday 19 Markets cheeper by 5s per load. Fine, dry wather. Wheat begining to change coller (*colour*).

Saturday 26 Markets still cheeper. Wather very hot & dry still. Best wheat now about £3 18s per load, & oates 35s per qr.

AUGUST Sunday 3d Dined at the George, Codicote, Mrs Raymonds, with Mr Merrett from Graves End *(parish of Albury)* & Mr Dolling, & Mrs Howard. Gave hostler & horses 1s. Went on Dimon horsback. Gave Nathon Killby 6d. A very hot day.

Monday 4th Dined at the Grandisons Arms, Bramfield with Mr Stevens auctioner when sold Mr Moody's cropps of oates, barley & wheat. I bought some wheat at £10 10s per acre & oates at £8 2s 6d per acre & Mr Searanke bought the rest. Onley Sam Hide bought the 6 acres calld the Slirpe, being not good, for £6 6s per acre.

Tusday 5 Went to Ware on Witefoot. Spent with young Stephens &c 1s 3d.

---

[141] Ann Mead, aged 16 murdered Charles Proctor, aged 16 months, by feeding him with a spoonful of arsenic. After hanging, her body was dissected and anatomised [TNA: Hertford Assize Records: information from Ken Griffin]. The details of her trial on 20 June 1800 are recorded in *The Gentleman's Magazine*, June 1800, reproduced in Jones, *Hertfordshire, 1731-1800*, p143.

[142] Dr Henry Bradley, was 'surgeon and apothecary' to Hertford gaol at least from 1799 until his death in 1812 at a salary of £20 [*HCR* vol IX pxxiii].

Thursday 7th Dined at the Town Hall, Hartford, the Ringing Feast. Dined about 105 dinner. Dresed at Falken, Mrs Ramseys. Master John Calvert jnr. Tickets 8s 6d.

Fryday the 8 was hanged at Hartford gallows, James otherwise Shock Oliver <Oliver was a butcher> who in companey with 2 more did endever to stop and rob one Carter, & Mr Fossey, in the parish of Clothall a coming from Baldock fair. They bid them stop, but they did not, so they rode by their side and shot at them, & Carter swore to Oliver, but Fossey could not. A reward of £50 was offerd for Oliver & he was taken at Dudley in Staffordshire by one Warrick, and brought to Hertford, & Carter & Fossey appearing against him. Carter swore that he was the man that bid them stop & fired at them, so he was found gilty. Death. Oliver came from St Neots (*Cambridgeshire*), had wife 2 children.

Satturday 9 Jorney to St Albans the Town Hall to deliver in the inncome papers. Went by Hatfield. Came home by Water End. On Dimon. Stopt at the Widow Tatts, Diggswell Hill. All the 3 ponds dry at St Albans & cleand out.[143]

Sunday 10 afternoon went by Woolmers to Bayfordburry. Spent the evening with Mr Robarts.

Wednesday 13 Dined at Mr Randalls, and after dinner, he and his brother William & I went to Bulls Mill to Mr Blowers. From thence to Waterford, Mrs Gears <the Windmill>. Spent the evening there. Mr William treated. Mr Evens there.

Satturday 16 went to market with Dimock in cart in the afternoon. Met Ashley. Spent the evening with him & his friend Mr Flowers at the [Cold] Bath till 11 clock. Ashley he treated, I gave 6d.

23 [Saturday] Went to market in little cart with Miss Wooleston. Dined at Bull. Came home by 4 clock. Spent 2s.

---

[143] One pond at the lower end of St Peter's Street, a second at the junction of St Peter's Street and Hatfield Road, a third at the fork of the Harpenden and Sandridge Roads [Branch Johnson, '*Memorandoms For ...*', p55].

Sunday 24 Dined at brother Haslers at Ware, with Coz Cooks from London. Spent 1s. Gave Kit & Will Frances 1s. A very wet day. Now the raine is come as been dry for 65 days.

28 Thursday Sister and Mrs Watson from Eagle came over to Bacons in Cockel's cart with Jack and spent the afternoon.

Fryday 29 Spent the evening at Mr Hunsdon's harvest home with nephew John Beck, Miss Wolleston & Poll, Mr & Mrs Burges, Mr Bentley &c. Good companey. Staid till 12 clock. Made his harvest home but innd no barley & some wheat out yet.

Saturday 30th Made our harvest home as being a month. Though most of our barley out & some wheat, as being whet the week past and stoppt our inning. Never is the barley known to be grown so much in the swath in so little a time by the oldest man liven, for a great deal of the grone barley in the field was dried after thrashing without steeping & made good malt. Most farmers dried some, 10qr or 5 at a time at 1s per quarter, till Goverment stopt it and no more to be dried so without paying duty. I dried some quarters in the barn by the son (*sun*) in June till it would gring & made me good beer.

Sunday 31 afternoon went to Wotton Wood Hall with Miss Wolleston in little cart.

> **Saturday 2d** Markets cheeper by 10s per load or more as according as they could sell, for the wather continues still so dry and hot, brings the harvest on. We are now cutting wheat. All things lower except hopps. I sold my wooll to one J Cate of Hodsdon, & carried in today at 35s per todd.
>
> **Satturday 9** Markets cheeper very considrable on account of the hot dry wather. I begun harvest the 4th of this month, the best wheat now about £3 per load.
>
> **Satturday 16** Markets dearer by 15 per load. Every body buisey in harvest. Small market and the cropps are found to be small. The best wheat £4 per load. The wather still continuas hot & dry.
>
> **[Saturday] 23** Markets much the same or rather dearer, best wheat £4 6s per load. The wather now altered, now showery. Came by thunder on Tusday the 19 past. Had been dry for 65 days all burnt up.

Saturday 30th of this month went to market in Jack's cart with Dimon, Miss Wolleston & John Beck. Came home by 2 clock. Markets wheat £4 8s 0d per load or 5 bushell.

15th of this Month the great fire at North Mimms near the church begunn about 10 at night. After they left harvest cart the boys fell asleep in stable with lantron (*lantern*) and set fire. Burnt 12 large hay reeks, 1 large wheat stack, 1 peas d[itt]o, all the barns and outbuildings, 2 horses, hoggs &c, carts & waggons, fowls to a great amount.[144]

SEPTEMBER Wednesday 3 Jorney to St Albans to Cowpers the clerk to settle my Inncome Tax. Gave him for doing it 3s 6d. Spent 1s.

Thursday [4th] Went to Codicot to deliver warrant for Licensing. Spent 6d at the Goat with Hill & Bayley. Came home with Hunsdon's people in waggon as they had been to Hollards to help them in harvest and Mr Hen[ry] Hunsdon lost a good horse there by giving him well water to drink.[145]

Sunday 7th Jorney to Coopers Sale, Essex to see Mrs Moody, wet afternoon. Slept at [Stanstead] St Margets, young Mr Stephens. Next morning set of for Coopers Sale. Found them all well, Mrs Moody was out for a month. Spent the night till 4 clock Tusday morning, with som friends the servants had asked to sup with, one Mr Godfrey & Mr Gillderson & wife, & a Miss Green. Then set off for Bush fair about 9 clock Tusday with Godfrey & Gillderson, and Mr Nicholls. Spent at the fair in barber's booth 5s 6d. Came from the fair to Coopers Sale. Slept there again Tusday night, came home Wednesday. Stopt at Epping Place saw the giant 8 foot 4 ½ inches high. Stopt at [Green] Dragon Hertford at clubb. Got home 11 clock.

Thursday Night the 11th of this Month was another fire at Horrell, Mr Youngs a great oate reek set on fire but onley burnt that the wind was faverable, otherwise all his wheat stacks &c must have been burnt. I saw it.

---

[144] *The Gentleman's Magazine* gives the date for the fire as 18 Aug 1800. The Farm belonged to a Mr Brown and the incident is reported in great detail [See Jones, *Hertfordshire, 1731-1800*, pp143-4].

[145] Henry Hunsdon (buried 20 July 1803, see diary below) was the farmer at West End Farm, Bramfield (demolished 1969), his widow continuing there until her own death in 1805. He was appointed Overseer of the Poor for Bramfield 11 Apr 1801. His mother still lived at Hollards Farm, Codicote.

The 15th of July last was the other fire at Horrell, Mr Youngs. Burnt 5 barns, 4 hovells, some wheat, some oates was set on fire. I saw it.

Fryday 12 Went with old Mr Jonson from St Albans with son Jack to Mr Warrens at Graveley to treat with him about the Rose & Crown Tewin. Came from thence to Hartford. Dined at Cambells the [Green] Dragon with Mr Johnson. Spent there 3s. Spent at [Cold] Bath coming home 1s. Staid too late, got merry & foolishly said I would sell my wheat tomorrow for 10s per bushell, but Will would not, for he sold it for £4 6s 0d per load.[146]

Saturday 13 Jorney to the Town Hall, St Albans to renew Licenses. Went with Burges constable. Dined at Redhouse with Codicote people. Spent 3s. Came home, Burges and I spent at Jacks Tewin 1s.

Monday 15 Went to Stanstead [St Margarets] with Mr Randall & Mr Rooke. Dined at Crown Mrs Shippses. Spent 2s 6d. Came home by Ware, slept there at Eagle. Tusday went to the sale at Sarracons Head. Sacomb 2 estates sold by Mr More. Spent 2s. Came home in the evning.

Saturday 20 Went to market in little cart with Mary Ann and Miss Wooleston. Came home forward and went to Bramfield Mrs Deardses to spend larges (*largesse*) with my people. The great shew of wild beast, a large elefont & lyons etc etc today at Bull Plaine, Hartford.

Monday 22 Went to Wotton Statute on Dimon. Dined at Crawleys the White Horse with the High Constable, Mr Thos Kimpton. About 70 at dinner. No meet of aney sort, but fowls and geese & tongue & hamm, a flummery dinner. Spent 6s. Put Dimon upp at the Bull. Spent there 1s. Came home with Thos Sheith. I hired there a man & boy. The great shew of wild beast there, large elefont & lyons &c. Stopt at W[i]d[ow] Deardses, Brantfield (*Bramfield*) as came home, with Sheath, & Tom Corricott, & Stoton, Randall's lad, and Dimmock. Spent there 6d. Dimon brake her windows 5 panes, I paid her for it 1s 6d.

Sunday 28 Mr Bourchier took possession of the liven (*living*) of Bramfield and preachd there.[147] The text was 3d chap of Acts 6th verce.[148] A very good

[146] See market entry for Saturday 13 Sep below. Will was John's son.
[147] The third Edward Bourchier (died 1840) to hold the Bramfield living, although not in succession. His grandfather came there in 1740, his father in 1775.

preacher as being the first time and he red prayers in the afternoon. Church very fool both times. He took possession on the Fryday 26 before as going into church & tolling the bell &c. He gave the ringers for jangling the bells on Sunday after church 10s 6d.

Tusday 30th went to Ware with sister in little cart. Slept there. Spent the evening with Baker & Aylon. Spent 2s.

> **Saturday 6** Markets much the same or rather dearer as being a fine week, people buisey. Market small, best wheat £4 12s per load. Went to market in little cart late. Came home with Mr Brux & went to Tewin with my people, spend larges (*largesse*).
>
> **Saturday 13** Markets rather cheeper though I sold 3 load today to Mr Johnson for £4 6s per load. Will sold it, for I went to St Albans.
>
> **Saturday 20th** Markets cheeper by 8s per load or as people chuse to sell for there has been great rioting at London and maney other places on acpt of the dearness of provision these weeks past.[149] Best wheat about £4 4s 0d per load.
>
> **Saturday 27** Markets rather dearer, best wheat about £4 8s 0d. There was a great to do in the market today, for a fortnight back I sold a load to the Association of Poor Men held at Cambells the Green Dragon for 10s per bushell & promisd them some more. Therefore they got a great cheair into the market with a mobb to cheair me but I hid myself, but it had an affect on some of the great dealers, and they was forsd to fly.

OCTOBER Wednesday the 1st went to Whitwell Statute in little cart with Geo[rge] Rich[ar]dson & John Aylen. Surveyd the wats (*weights*) at Codicot as went & Pauls Walden before dinner. 15 at dinner Mr Crabb, Mr Hill, Mr Wellingom &c. Collected apiece 10s 6d at first collection. The dearest Statute ever. At this Whittall (*Whitwell*) Statute at dinner I asked Mr John Wellingom, the tanner, why Pauls Walden <church> was built quite the out

---

[148] Acts ch 3 verse 6: 'Then Peter said, "silver and gold have I none; but such as I have give I thee: in the name of Jesus Christ of Nazareth, rise up and walk"'.
[149] The riots in London were particularly fierce but Birmingham, Nottingham, Coventry, Norwich, Sheffield and Oxford were other centres of disturbance [Asa Briggs, *How They Lived*, vol III, *1700-1815*, (Oxford, 1969) p299].

side of the parish. He said when he was a boy that he herd old people say that it was attemted to be built near the town but could not and that there was a chapple or church near the Town.[150] He remembrd some of the walls standing and a numbr of human bodies found, one 7 foot 3 inchs. He saw it.

2nd Went to Hartford in little cart to have Miss Wollaston to the coach at the Half Moon. Spent 1s 2d. Ostler 2d.

Fryday 3 Went to Great Munden Bury to a sale there. A Mr Reed who was poysned by accident did live there. The farme is close to the church, belonging to Wm Baker Esqr of Bayford. Went with Mr Randoll. Bought a heffer, then sold her againe for 2s advantage. The auctioner (*auctioneer*), Steev[e]ns. Rec[eive]d 11 guineas there of young Stephens for a hieffer I sold some time past.

Tusday 7 Went to Ware on poney. Slept there at brother Haslers with Coz Thos Beck from London. Spent there 2s. Gave Wm Frances 6d.

Wednesday 8th Bramfield Statute 26 at dinner:

Mr Meers	myself
Mr Bowley	Mr Hunsdon
Mr Randall	Mr Hanken
B Whittenbry	Mr Ramsey
Mr George	Mr Cheek
Mr Thomas	Mr Preston
Mr Richardson	Mr Batten
Mr Bassett	Mr Hickman
Mr Crawley	Mr Wiltsher
Mr Grayham	Mr Walls
Old Bush	Mr Randall of Hartford
Mr Burr	Wm Adams for Searank
Mr Camp	Mr T[homas] Beck from London
John Day from Hexton.	

Expence apiese 9s.

[150] A chapel at the Manor of Bradway in Bendish had been built in the fourteenth century by Abbot Michael of St Albans. Known as the chapel of St Clement it existed well into the sixteenth century and remains may have been seen in the eighteenth [*VCH Hertfordshire*, vol 2 pp405-11].

Thursday 9 Went to Bramfield. Spent next day after Statute with Mr Aylon & Richardson in the afternoon 1s 9d.

Saturday 11 Went to market on poney. Dined at White Hart, Camps. Stopt at [Cold] Bath saw the battle between Mr Edmans & Parnwell. Spent 3d, spent at Camps &c 4s.

Sunday 12th went to Hartingfordbury church, a charity sermon preached by the Revd Gilbirt Beresford for the Sunday Schooll of that parish.[151] Gave 2s 6d. Dined at Billy Johnsons there, put Dimon up at White Horse. Spent, gave hostler 6d.

Monday 13 Dined at Feathers Tewin, Whittenburys, Lord Cowper's wood fiest, with Mr Pallett the stew[a]rd, & Mr Dean of Tewin Bury, and all the wood buyers of Tewin Woods. A buttock beef, leg motton boyled, a haunch of d[itt]o rosted. Mr Pallett paid all eating & drink.

Saturday 18 Jorney to Town Hall St Albans to appoint surveyors. Justices, Wm Donvell Esqr and Thos Baker Esqr that signd the warrants. Went on Dimon by the [Cromer] Hide. Came home the same. Dinner & spent 3s 6d, hostler 6d.

Tusday 21 Went to Ware to meet Mr Raine at the Soraisons (*Saracens*) Head. Slept at sister Haslers. Spent and gave 2s 4d.

Fryday 24 Went to the Bull at Ware to pay taxes to Mr Boyde, Rece[i]ver Gen[era]l. Paid £72 7s 0d for all taxes for 1799 and £50 towards the taxes for 1800. Went on poney & came home by one clock. Spent at Ware 3d. Treated the Revd Mr Nickolson at [Green] Dragon Hartford a pot 4d as come home.[152]

Saturday 25 Went to market on poney. Dined at the Ramm, widow Denshers on stakes with Mr Pall &c. Spent 1s 3d. Spent at Bull after with Mr Randall, Crow & Taylor 6d, ostler 4d. Spent at [Cold] Bath as come home with Smith, Wray & Draper 10d. Came home by 7 clock.

---

[151] Gilbert Beresford (1774-1843) was Rector of Fordwich, Kent from 1799-1802, a living also in the patronage of Earl Cowper [Venn, *Alumni Cantabrigiensis*].
[152] Revd Thomas Nicholson (c1750-1832), Curate of St.Andrew's Church, Hertford, 1791 until his death.

Tusday 28 Went to Ware. Dined at sisters. Came from thence to Hartford, and went with Thowdy to one Bolts at [Little] Barkhamsted. Bought a hieffer of him for £6. Spent at 3 Horsshoos there with Bolt &c 10d. Spent at Ware 9d. Gave 4d.

Fryday 31 Esqr Jinnings left Bramfield as having lived at the Rector's house about 9 months, as he took it when Mr Moody left.

> **Saturday 4th** Markets dearer by 10s per load, best wheat £4 15s 0d, barley the best £4 4s 0d per quarter, peas 38s per load, oates best 40s qr, hay £6 0s 0d at home.
>
> **Saturday 11th** Markets much the same. A full market.
>
> **[Saturday] 18** Markets dearer best wheat £4 16s 0d per load.
>
> **Saturday 25** Markets cheeper. Large market, wheat £4 10s 0d the best, barley the best £4 4s 0d the quarter, peas 36s, oates 40s.

The 24 of Last Month Mr Wm Limbury of Newgate Street near Little Barkhamsted about 2 clock in the morning had 14 geese stolen, but Limbery following them fought with the men most desprately & got the geese againe though all killed and the men got off.

NOVEMBER Saturday 1st Went to market on poney. Put him up at Mr Chapmans. Went to the Ramm, paid Bolt for the hefer, and from thence to the Vine. Took part of stakes with Mr Paull & Cannon 1s 3d, from thence to Bull 6d, from thence to the [Cold] Bath Griffithses. Spent there with Mr Randall 1s. Came home with Randall & Mrs & supt there. Gave to Stotan the boy 6d, gave Chapman's boy 3d.

Sunday 2d went to Bramfield church. Spent the evening at home with Mr & Mrs Randalls.

Monday 3d at home, onley went to Tewin clubb. Spent 6d.

Tewsday 4th went to Bramfield to meet the Revd Mr Bourchier. Took the Land [Tax] of him 33 acres for 50 per anam, tythe & rate free.

Wednesday 5th Went to the tythe fiest at Bramfield the last of the Revd Lloyds, for now Mr Ewd (*Edward*) Bourchier hes taken possesion of the living of Bramfield. Mr Thos Lloyd and Mr Ewd Bourchier there. Very few of the farmers there. A loyne of rost beef, 2 leggs of motton & pudings &c. I went at 4 clock from thence to the Association meeting at Tewin with John Aylon. Mr Pallett & Dan Webb, Patient, Brux, Dolling, Simon, Field, Johnson, Randall there. Spent a pies (*apiece*) for their dinners and all 4s. A loyn of beef, calves head, pidgins, pies etc.

Thursday 6 went to Hartford with Mr Randall. Dined at Cambells, [Green] Dragon. Spent 2s 4d. Came hom to Bramfield with Randall. Supt there, home at ten.

Fryday [7] went to Bakers for Whittenburys pittion (*petition*). Came to Pansanger, rode with the gentlemen when went to survey the new rodes which are to be made by Lord Cowper from Poplar Green to Hartford, & Hatfield. Came home & went to Jacks and spent with Mr Dolling 2s 3d when he paid me for six load of wheat £25 10s 0d.

Saturday 8 Went to market on poney. Dined at the Shipp, Cooks, on red huring with Pinock and bargeman when took my malt from Grippers in 2 carts, being the fair, spent in all 1s 9d.

Monday the 10th Jorney to London on poney, to Ware from thence to Sr George Prescots, Cheshunt with Mr Aylon to interseed for Whittenbury of Hartford Heath for Licenses.[153] From thence to Waltham X (*Cross*) 4 Swans. Was well entertained at Sir Georges by his orders and his buttler Mr Charmberlin a harty good fellow. From the X to London the same afternoon in post chaises cost, 2s 6d. Expence at X &c 1s 4d. Whittenbury rode poney back. Slept at Coz Becks. Next day to St Jameses and saw the King go to the parliament, & come back. Very quiet. Dined at the Salopin Mr Folletts with young John Beck & Nancy Hunsdon. Gave 1s. From thence to the Whole in the Wall, Kirby Street. Spent the evening with Mr Strut &c. Spent 1s 6d. Slept Coz Becks. Next day went to the Bank. Took dividend and from thence to Farmers in the Borough, hop merchant with Coz Thos Beck. Paid him for hopps. Well entertaind, went to Coz Cooks from thence the Whole in the Wall. Spent the evening with frends again. Spent 1s. Slept at Beck againe. Next day to St Jameses End of the town Mr Jinningeses. Spent the evening

[153] George Prescot of Theobalds Park, Cheshunt, died 20 July 1801 aged 54 (see diary entry below). Whittenbury became licensee of the Jolly Pindar, later known as the East India College Arms and now the College Arms, Hertford Heath. See also diary entry for 29 Mar 1801 below.

with Strutt the Whole [in the] Wall. Spent 1s. Slept at Becks againe and Fryday morning set out for home on Mr Brindley's horse as bringing down to Preston Yard for the winter. Set off from Bedford Road. Spent there 6d. Will Worby came with me, the new road allmost to Higate.[154] Came home in 3 hours.

Tusday 18 Went to Ware market with Mr Randall. Dined at sister Haslers. He was offerd 4 guineas per quarter for his barley, but Mr Randall would not let it go for that sum. Spent there 1s 9d. Came home with him and drank tea at his house, gave his boy 3d.

Wednesday [19] went to Goldings on poney, was made welcome. Came home by Waterford. Spent & gave 1s 2d.

Thursday [20] went to Ware on poney, brought malt home from Cadmore. Spent on putting up 1s 6d.

Saturday 22 Went to market on poney, put him up at [Cold] Bath. Dined with Chapman at Vine on saregs (*sausages*) <gave & spent 3s 4d>. Came home with Mr Randall & 2 brothers.

Sunday 23 Went to Goldings, from thence to Bramfield church. From thence in the afternoon to Jacks, Rose & Crown, Tewin with Mr Randall & his 2 brothers. Spent & gave 1s 8d.

Tusday 25 Went to Ware on poney. Slept at Eagle. Great flood there. Came home on Wednesday morning. Spent & gave to maid and Will Frances, 3s 6d.

Sunday 30 went to Cowpers Sale, Essex on Dimon, Mrs Moodys. Slept there. Came home on the Monday. Gave there 1s 2d for my horse to the man & cleand boots. One Mr Saveall, the church clerk told me the church steeple which is all brick was built by an alderman and his 2 wifes. The church clerk's house is part in the church yard very close to the steeple. I saw the inscription on the tower of the building, the aforesaid in old Roman letters, and the date was 161 and the other figar was broke off. So it was built in the

[154] Probably a reference to the major improvements being made at this time to the Great North Road from Islington to Highgate by the Turnpike Trustees.

years from sixteen hundred & ten to nineteen.[155] I was at home by 5 clock and went to Tewin clubb on poney.

Saturday the 1st Markets rather cheeper, best wheat £4 10s 0d per load.

Saturday the 8 Market much the same.

Saturday 15 Markets dearer, best wheat £3 17s, barley good £4 8s per qurter, oates 45s qr, peas 36s load, hopps 4s p[oun]d, malt £5 qr the best.

Saturday 22 Markets dearer, best wheat £5 per load, barley £4 4s per quarter, peas 40s load, oates 40s qr or more.

Saturday 29 Markets much the same. I sold wheat for £4 16s 6d per load or 5 bushills.

DECEMBER Tusday 2 Went to Hitchen market with Mr Randall in his cart. Went by Codicot, came hom by Stevnege. Dined at the Angell. Dinner 1s 6d. Spent further 10d. Stopt at Woolmer Green at Red Lyon, Mrs Crows. Spent 1s. Stopt at Mr Randalls supper. He went to take for 10 qr of barley sold to a person there, at £4 10s per quarter.

Thursday 4th Sent for to Mr Randalls. Spent the evening there with Mr Odle from 3 clock till 9. Gave 1s.

Sunday 7 Went to Bramfield church. After diner went to Eagle at Ware with Mr Sadler & Mr Randall. Stayd till moon up 10 clock. Spent my part 2s. Home ½ p[a]st 11 clock.

Thursday 11 went to Hertford to Cheeks taylors. Spent at [Cold] Bath with Chapman 6d. After came home went to Bramfield to see Land Nickolds from Cowpers Sale. Spent there 2s.

---

[155] The church of All Saints, Coopersale: 'About 1520 the west tower was added. It is of red brick, with some blue brick, of three stages with an embattled parapet. The date is recorded on a stone panel on the outside of the south wall, where it is stated that Sir John Crosbe, late alderman and grocer of London, and his wives Anne and Annes gave £50 towards the building of the tower.' So Carrington's comment about the date being 161- is incorrect [*VCH Essex* vol 4: *Ongar Hundred* (1956), pp269-271].

Fryday 12 Spent the evening at Tewin Jacks with Thos Sheath & Pridmore.[156] Spent 1s 2d.

Sunday 14 Went to church. After dinner, went to Mr Palletts Cole Green. Gave his maids 2s.

Tusday 16 Went to Hitchin market with Mr Randall in his little cart. Dined at the Angell, dinner 2s. Came home erley. Gave Stotan 3d.

Wednesday 17 Dined at the Grandisons Arms, Bramfield wood fiest. Bassett took the money. Onley Mr Higgs, Mr Chapman, Allen, Basset, Day, blacksmith and I dined. 2 leggs motton. Expence 2s. I spent more and Gardner came home with me 1s. Gave him 6d.

Tusday 23 Went to Ware with Mr Randall in his cart, with his son John. Dined brother Haslers. Came home by Bramfield with him in cart. Spent & gave 2s.

Saturday 27 Went to market on poney. Went by Emmotts. Deliverd bill to Mr Smith. Came home with Mr Randall and 2 brothers from Bull. Stopt at Bramfi[e]ld, got fuddled. Spent and gave 2s 6d.

Sunday 28 Spent the evening at Jacks Tewin with Mr Randall, his 2 brothers, Simon and William. Spent 1s 6d.

Tusday 30 Went to Ware on poney. Spent with Mr Hitch & Whittenbury of Hertford Heath 1s 6d.

Markets this Month:

> **Saturday 6th** Markets dearer, best wheat £5 3s 0d per load, best barley £4 10s 0d per qr, best oates £2 13s 0d qr, peas £2 8s 0d per load. Went to market on poney, went to Ware. Dined there spent 4d. Came home from Hartford with Mr & Mrs Randall to Bramfield. Gave & spent 1s.
>
> **Saturday 13** Markets much the same, best wheat £5 5s 0d per load. I sold four load today for £20 to Mr Whittingstall. Went late on poney.

---

[156] John Pridmore, schoolmaster of Tewin had been appointed between 1794 and 1798 and leaving in 1839 [*The History of Tewin* (Tewin, 2009), pp83-5].

Stopt at Bull with Randall & Richardson. Came home to gather with Will. Spent & gave for Will & I, 3s 4d.

Saturday 20 Markets much the same, best wheat £5 5s 0d. Spent today 2s. Came hom by self in little cart from [Cold] Bath.

Saturday 27 Markets much the same. Thus ends the year wheat at £5 3s 0d per load, barley per qr £4 10s 0d, oates per qr £2 10s 0d, peas per load £2 8s 0d, hopp per pound 4s 0d, malt per qr £5 5s 0d.

Thus endes the most extrordaney (*extraordinary*) year 1800. When things of all kinds was never known so dear, wheat £5 per load, or 5 bushell, barley £4 10s per quarter, oats 55s d[itt]o, peas 50s per load, butter 18d p[oun]d, cheese 1s d[itt]o, beef 7d. All these are on avradge. Good malt £5 per quarter, hopps 4 shillings per pound, hay that's good £7 per load. I sold some for £5 10s to a hay carter to sell again. Turnopps sell from £3 to £12 per acre, straw 40s per load, apples 40s per bushel. This year a very wet barley seed time and so was the wheat se[e]dtime before, which occasions the yeald very bad, which is one reason for its being so dear. There was 65 days of dry wather this year from the 14th of June till the 19th of August. There was one very great high wind this year Sunday the 9th of November from 12 clock in the day till ½ past one, when William Turner from Hartford with hirce and coach was buired at Tewin church the same time one clock. Iarland was united with England this year.[157] New halpence this year and last year. New penny piesses quoined in the year 1797. St Peters church steeple of St Albans or the tower all taken down this year even with the roof of the church and then tyled inn. 10 bells in the steeple, it was supposed it was so old & decayd would fall. Though 7 years back £2000 was laid out in repairing of it which I saw dayley as I went to St Albans. It was a very large abby tower, large & high, & build up againe with brick and finished in the year 1806.[158]

---

[157] The Act of Union which joined the English and Irish Parliaments, 1 Jan 1801 (39 & 40 Geo 3 c67).

[158] 'In 1756 the tower arches were taken out and loftier ones inserted, and the tower heightened, and in consequence it soon fell into a dangerous state. In 1785 it was underpinned with upright baulks of timber, nine in the lower part of each pier, a makeshift arrangement which began to fail almost at once. The vestry showed the greatest reluctance to amend this piece of jerry building, which had cost no less than £2,790, and could only agree to patch the failing beams with plaster. By 1799 the tower had become so dangerous that it was at last taken down to the top of the

This year Lord Cowper begun altring the roads to Hartford. 1st Tewin Road by Hooksbushes Wood, gose straight, before went round by Pansanger. 2d road from Wellwin, gose straight upp from Popler Green, before round by Naveacre. 3d road from Bramfield to Hatfield or Essington (*Essendon*) streight from Popler Green, threw his old park close by his mansion house called Colegreen House, now pulled down.

June 14th 1800 Died Lord Grandison at his house in Park Lane, Carringtons Place, aged about 50ty, buried in Iarland.[159] This Lord was the owner of Bramfield Estate and now it is Lady Cartwright (*Gertrude*) Villers, his onley daughter as heair to all his estates, now about 23 years of age and she maried the Marques of Bute's son Lord Henery of Luton Hooe (*Bedfordshire*).

This year Mr Thos Rook of Bengeo Great Farme near the church sold 100 fatt sheep for £7 per head, and 100 load of hay at £7 per load, and most of his wheat £5 10s per load or 5 bushells, but his last 3 or 4 parsells at £5 16s 6d. This he possitive declared to be true, as he told me so his self. This year I sold som wheat at £5 5s per load, and barley was 5 guineas per quarter, the dearest year ever rememberd or recorded, for every thing dearer than the year 1794.

(*Remainder of page for this year torn away and decayed*)

---

crossing arches, and in 1801 the belfry floor fell, a final disaster which brought about the desired rebuilding. The transepts were then taken down and the chancel shortened' [*VCH Hertfordshire* vol 2, pp412-424].

[159] George Mason Villiers, 1st Earl Grandison (1751-1800), whose family had held the manor of Bramfield since 1732 [*VCH Hertfordshire* vol 2 pp343-5].

1801 (*HALS: DE/X3/4*)

JANUARY 1801 Saturday the 3d Markets much the same. I sold 3 load to Mr Mullett at £4 18s. Went on poney. Dined at Bull, came home with Mr & Mrs Randall. Drank tea there. Spent & gave 2s 10d. Got drunk this time.

Sunday the 4th Went to church at Bramfield 2 clock, Mr Newton preached. Mr Randall & I went to Windmill Waterford, Mrs Gears, in the afternoon. Spent & gave old Mr Gear 3s 9d.

Tusday [6th] Dined at Mr Randalls Bramfield Place, with Mr Webb of Tewin Hill Farme, Miss Betsey Webb, and Mr Pridmore, schoolmaster at Tewin, and his wife Mrs Pridmore. Good dinner, tea & supper. Left about ½ past 12. Gave 1s 6d.

Saturday 10 Markets rather dearer, best wheat £5 3s per load. I went on foot. Dined at 2d (*second*) table Bull with James Kent & Chamberlen &c &c. Spent 2s 6d. Came home by self erley.

Monday 12 Went to the [County] Quarter Sessions at Hartford. Served on the Jury till 8 clock the evening. Found gilty Jinnings, Warren, one for steeling flower (*flour*) & one for steeling barley& the 2 women from Baldock.[160] Went from thence to Ware. Slept there 2 nights. Came home on Wednesday. Spent & gave 5s 6d.

Thursday 15 Went to Quarter Sessions St Albans on poney with Mr Preston. Dined at Redhouse with Pauls Walden people, Reed, Smith, Brown & Mr Preston & the young man & woman as they brought. Dinner 1s 6d. Spent 1s. Qrn of corne 6d. Gave hostler 3d.

Saturday 17 Markets, best wheat £5 5s 0d per load. Went to market in little cart. Dined at Archers, paid him, & sold him steer & one l[oa]d hay for £22.

---

[160] Isaac Jennings had stolen 5 bushels of threshed wheat from Jacob Bosanquet of Broxbournebury (9 months in Bridewell); William Warner was found guilty of uttering a counterfeit seven shilling piece to William Sams, victualler of Cheshunt (6 months gaol); the two women from Baldock were Hannah, wife of Richard Lee, and Sarah, wife of John Gobby who had stolen 6 wooden stakes used for fastening hurdles, the property of John Kingsley at Willian (Lee acquitted, Gobby three months in Bridewell) [HALS: *HCR* vol II, pp193-4; *HCR* vol IX pp23-25, QSB vol 17 and QSPB vol 3].

Came home with Bobb on Dimon. Spent 1s 2d. After came home, went to Tewin & spent the evening there with Townley as he came this day from Aldnam (*Aldenham*) to see us.[161] Spent at Jacks 2s 6d.

Sunday 18 Walked about with Townley and after diner went part of the way home with him as far as Cole Green. Stopt at Mr Palletts, from thence to Tewin. Spent & gave 2s.

Fryday [23] Spent the evening at Sewills, White Horse Haddingfordbury (*Hertingfordbury*) with Mr Randall. Spent 1s, gave 2d. Home 7 clock. Very bad this time.

Saturday 24 Markets rather dearer, best wheat at £5 6s 0d per load. Went in little cart with grist to mill. Dined on stakes at the Ramm with Thodey. Spent there & Bull 2s 4d, ostler 4d. Geo Richardson came home with me in cart 9 clock. Paid Gripper today for making malt.

Sunday 25 Went to Mr Cloppom's buring of Bulls Mill.[162] Buried the south side of Staplef[or]d church, aged 87. Mr Walls, Mr Preston, Mr Hankin, Mr Mitchell, Mr Emmott, and myself paull bearers. Staid tea & supper. Gave boy 6d. Came home 11 clock. Green, Bengeo undertaker stole my old hatband.

Tusday 27th dined at Hunsdons when the wedings was kept there, George Richardson, & Thomas Whittenbury.[163] Gave 4s. Great plenty & Mr Hoare the fiddler.

28 Went to privet court to Tewing Burry, onley Mr Gripper & I coppy holdrs, Neal, clerk & Mr Pallet all that was there. I rec[eive]d & Mr Gripper 2s 6d each.

Thursday 29 Dined at Colegreen Mr Palletts, Lord Cowper's rent fiest. Buttock of beef, a lyne (*loin*) of veal & mutton, pudings &c. Plenty of good

---

[161] Townley, now living in Aldenham, was apprentice engraver to Joseph Strutt while he was at Bacons Farm, 1790-1794.
[162] This is James Clapham aged 87, the father of James who married Mary Ann (Poll) Carrington (see family tree) [HALS: DP/104/1/3].
[163] George Richardson married Rebecca Hornet and Thomas Whittenbury married Maria Redman at Bramfield on 27 Jan 1801 [HALS: DP/22/1/4].

beer & punch. Jack Frances came for me on poney. Home about 10 clock. Gave 2s 9d. Got drunk this time.

Saturday 31 Markets much the same, best wheat £5 8s, barley best £4 10s, oates £2 15s, peas £2 11s. Came home with Randall on poney. Spent & gave 2s 6d. Sold broadhorns cow & calf today at Bull to one Mr Tinmoth at the Kings Arms, Endfield Highway for £10.

FEBRUARY Sunday the 1st went to Bramfield church. Afternoon went to Jacks Tewin. The man paid me for 1 week carts & horses in making the new road from Hooks Bushes to Hartford £3 12s.[164] I spent on him & his men & with Thos Sheath all togather 6s.

Monday 2d Spent at clubb when John Cock came with me to Mackey's gate 4d.

Tusday 3d went on foot to Ware, with Mary Ann. Slept there, came home the Wednesday, by Goldings. Dined there, from thence to Waterford the shooting match at pidgons. From thence to Bramfield the vestrey. Home by 9 c[l]ock. Spent in the whole & gave 3s. Gave to the workhouse 1s. Mary Ann went back having lost her money.

Saturday 7 Jorney to St Albans to Town Hall as a meeting of the Justices and all overseers to consider what substitute instead of wheaten bread for the poor, or to save the wheat as much as possable as it bears the price of £5 10s per load, and barley £4 10s per quarter.[165] Mr Donvell the Chieff Justice, Boyse clerke. Went in little cart, with daughter [in law] Sarah, Jack & Suckey from Tewin. Spent dinner & gave 3s 6d.

Saturday 7th Marketts much the same, best wheat about £5 11s 0d per load or 5 bushell. There is an order by Act to take nothing out of the wheat when

---

[164] This is one of the new roads the course of which was altered by Lord Cowper to skirt around his park at Panshanger, now part of the B1000 (see diary entry at end of 1800).

[165] This meeting was called in response to a letter from the Duke of Portland, Home Secretary, sent to the Lord Lieutenant 'recommending the adoption of certain measures to obviate the distress which the industrious poor are likely to suffer from the unfavourable season, which will probably lead to a rise in the price of wheat and other grain' [*HCR* vol IV p93].

ground but the broad brann, but this doth not do for they millers &c mix so much bad wheat with it that it is not liked off.

Tusday 10 Went to Ware on poney. Stayed but little while. Stopt at goal as came back. Gave Joseph Sellitt as is in there 1s. Home 4 clock. Spent & gave 6d.

Wednesday 11 Went to Mrs Haynses buring from Cole Green to Hardingfordbury church.[166] Stopt at White Horse, Sewills with Mr Jonson & Mullett &c. Spent & gave 2s.

Thursday 12 Went to Bramfield to see Mrs Cathrine Bourchier buired in the family vault in the church. She was brought from Reding in Barkshire. A herse and four & coach in four. Buired about 2 clock aged 62.[167] Spent at Mrs Derdses with Richardson 1s.

Fryday 13 a general fast. Went to Tewin church. After dined at Jacks my sons with Geo Richardson, the church clerk of Bramfield, as no churching there. Spent 1s 3d.

Saturday 14 Markets much the same, wheat the best £5 10s per load. I sold some today for £5 3s load. Went on foot. Dined at Bull. Came home with Mr Randall, drank tea there. Stotan came home with me with lanthron (*lantern*) as very dark 10 clock. Spent at Hartford 2s. Gave Stotan 6d. Got verry drunk this time.

Sunday 15 Went to Tewin afternoon. Spent with Blott & Thos Sheath at Jacks 1s 9d.

Monday [16] went to Tewin Rose & Crown in afternoon. It was Ld Cowper's wood sale. I bought 2½ roods of wood of one Hale the woodman out of Bealls Wood for £1 1s 0d. I paid him 3s 6d stubb money, that was all, for I did not go to dinner. Spent 3d.

---

[166] Mrs Dianah Haynes was buried at Hertingfordbury on 12 Feb 1801 [HALS: DP50/1/7].

[167] Catharine was the widow of the Revd Edward Bourchier of Bramfield, who had died on 14 Dec 1785, aged 47. Her monumental inscription on the south side of the chancel in Bramfield church states: 'Catharine his widow, 2nd daughter of William Wollaston Esq of Finborough, co Suffolk, grand-daughter of the author of *Religion of Nature Delineated* d. 4 February 1801 aged 62'.

Tusday [17] went to Ware on poney. Took 13 ginues (*guineas*) for a young cow & calf sold to Mr Hooper at the Great House, Amwell End.[168] Gave & spent on Cockell who fetched her, and to Wm Frances 5s 6d.

Sunday [22] went to Bramfield church. In afternon went to Tewin. Spent there with Mr Otway & another gentm from Wellwin.[169] Rec[eive]d £5 of one Smith for carting in Lord Cowper's new road. Gave him to dring (*drink*) 2s 6d. Gave his man 6d.

Saturday 21 Markets dearer by 3s per load, best wheat £5 15s per load. I went to markett on foot, Jack Frances with little cart with 20 bush[ell] oates and he brought home 3 load peas. Came home with Allen. Spent and gave to Crawley & Butterfield 4s.

Tusday [24] went to Ware. Spent there and at Ramseys as came home on poney 2s. Gave Hall 6d.

Wednesday Evening [25] Went to White Horse, Hardingfordbury drinking clubb. Spent 6d. Great storme as went.

Saturday 28 Markets dearer, wheat best £5 18s 0d per load & some say £6. Went on poney. Sold some black oates for 49s qr. Went to the [Green] Dragon the sale of Lord John Townsend's land.[170] Came home with Mr Randall as far as Lye Lane. Spent at Bull, dinner 1s 6d, at Cambels the auction 6d, at Griffithses 6d, osler 4d.

---

[168] Amwell House, Amwell End, Ware, is now part of Hertford Regional College. During the 1770s parts of the house were rebuilt and extended by John Scott, the Quaker poet (1730-1783) – see Carrington's reference to the building at the end of 1803. From 1906 to 1964 it accommodated Ware Grammar School for Girls [*VCH Hertfordshire* vol 3, p383; J T Smith, *Hertfordshire Houses Selective Inventory*, (RCHM 1993) pp193-4; D Perman, *Scott of Amwell, Dr Johnson's Quaker Critic*, (Ware 2001), pp113-14].

[169] Canadian born William Otway (died 1828 aged 65) kept a private school in the Old Rectory, at Welwyn from c1799, carried on by his son William and daughter Elizabeth until c1840 [W Branch Johnson, *Welwyn, By & Large, Historical Gossip from a Hertfordshire Village* (Welwyn, 1967) p43].

[170] Lord John Townshend (1757-1832). The Townshend family acquired Balls Park, Hertford, through the marriage in 1723 of Etheldreda or Audrey Harrison, daughter of Edward Harrison of Balls Park, with Charles Townshend of Kings Lynn (1700-1764). For further references to the sale see diary entries for 1, 4, 9 and 24 Aug 1801.

Hear Lies our Sovringn Lord and King,
Whose word no man relied on,
He offen said a foolish thing,
But never did a wise one.

Rochester said this on King Charles the 2d in his presence.[171]

MARCH Sunday 1st Went to Tewin church. Stay diner at Jacks at Tewin to meet my constables to receve presentments for the assises. Spent 1s 6d.

Monday 2 Went to Jos Whittenburys, Tewin Upper Green, Mackys wood sale. Bought one rood. Spent onley 9d. From thence to the Clubb.

Tusday 3 Went to Ware on poney with Mr Archer when went to look of the land bought by Mr Fletcher, & I was to have it if I liked it. Stopt at [Green] Dragon, saw Fletcher, told him I did not lik[e] it at the prise £436. Treated him & Bolt. Spent there 2s 10d.

Thursday 5 Went to the Assizes. Dined at [Green] Dragon with Mr Randall, Billey Johnson & Field &c, &c. Spent in all 3s. Judge Heath gave Hall 6d.

Fryday [6th] went to Ware by Bengeo with cart. Carried Purlivent wood,[172] & brought home from Ware 5 qr malt had of Stoton at £4 10s 0d qr. Spent 2s.

Saturday 7 Markets something cheeper. Very dull market. I went on poney Dimmock with cart. Brought home 5 qr malt bought of Gripper at £4 12s 0d qr re[a]dy money. Came home with Mr Randall to his house, drank tea there. Spent & gave in all 3s. The man whippt at cart tail 50 yards by Jo Sell. Got fuddled.

Sunday 8 Went to Bramfield church, afternoon to Tewin. Stay but little, spent 3½d. Gave Crawley 2d

Monday 9 to Schribiers twise and spent at Jacks 6d.

---

[171] This is a very famous quotation from John Wilmot, 2nd Earl of Rochester, entitled 'The King's Epitaph' [*Oxford Dictionary of Quotations*, (Oxford, 1941), p309; Frank H Ellis, 'Wilmot, John, second Earl of Rochester (1647–1680)', *ODNB,* Jan 2008].
[172] The Revd Henry Purlewent of Bengeo (1747-1807) died as rector of Brampton St Botolph, Northamptonshire in July 1807 [J Foster, *Alumni Oxonienses* 4 vols (Oxford, 1891)].

Tusday 10 Went to Ware. Slept there, to London next day on the Ware Coach. Slept at Coz Becks. Next day to the Bank. Recd ½ qrs divedend of 3 per cent due Xms (*Christmas*) last, & bought 2 hund[red] in 3 per cents consolls, for Poll, & one hund[red] for myself. From thence to hopp merchant, paid him £61 odd. Slept at Becks againe but spent this evening at the Whole [in the] Wall with Strutt. Next day went to Jinnings & called on Mr Sadler. Spent the evening with Strutt the Whole [in the] Wall. Next day dined at Mr Lloyd & spent the evening at Coz Becks. Sat upp drinking with Jack & Tom till 3 clock morn[in]g. Came home Satturday afternoon on the Ware coach. Slept at Ware. Came to Bacons next day. Spent & gave in all 13s.

Satturday 14 Markets cheeper of all sorts but wheat about 8 shillings per load.

Monday 16 Went to Crawleys White Horse, Wotton Turnpike Meeting. Paid there one qrs duty £2 18s 6d for Bramfield Road. Commissioners there Dickenson Esqr, Byde Esqr, Hanken Esqr, Twinn, Cater, Kitchener, Kimpton. Surveyors there, Butterfield, Mardall, for Bengeo, Saredge, and for Sacomb the church clerk there & others was Walls, Bush, & Crawley. Dinner plumb puding, leg mutton, rost beef. Dinner each 1s 6d. Spent in punch & ginn & water 1s each. At Bull 3d.

Satturday 21 Markets much the same. Best wheat £5 8s 0d per load. Went to market in cart with Dimmock. Brought home a pockett of hopps. Cost £16 per hundred. Came home on foot with Richardson & Will, this being Lent fair. Never was known cattle so dear especley (*especially*) cows. I was asked 14 ginues (*guineas*) for a small heiffer near calveing. Sheep £3 10s per couple. Dined at Bull. Spent in all 2s 10d.

Sunday 22 To Bramfield church. Dined at Randalls, from thence to Tewin Jacks with Mr Randall. Spent with him, & Richardson and Billey Johnson 2s.

Monday 23 afternoon went to Ld Cowper's, Pansanger to frank 3 letters. Got merry.

Tusday 24 went to Ware on poney. Spent there 1s. Came home erley, and went to a committee of Tewin Clubb wen Wm Currell a member was excluded as dissembld on the society. Spent 4d.

Wednesday 25 Went to the White Horse Hardingfordbury Sewills, to a spending club in the evening. Stayd till 11 clock, with Mullett and Johnson, Phipp, Smith, Hanken, Hickman, Chesher &c. Spent & gave foolishly 2s 6d.

Thursday 26 Went round Bramfield parish with Mr Preston of Broadoak Farme & Mr Randall of Place Farme, in taking account of the number of inhabitants:[173]

Males	91	Houses 28
Feamales	101	Famileys 42
All	192	

Dined at Grandisons Arms, Widow Deardses on fresh codd & salt fish. Mr Vaux of Green Hall dined with us & he sent home for 2 bottles of port wine and brandy and water &c.[174] We drinked till 10 clock at night. Old Mr Benj[ami]n Whittenbury was with us sometime.

The number of males & feamales in the parish of Tewin taken the 8 of this month:

Males	248	
Feamales	225	
All the inhabitance Totall	473	No of howses in the s[ai]d parish is 73.

Saturday 28 Jorney to St Albans, Town Hall to recive instructions and papers on the Income Tax. Dined at Redhouse Coz Piggotts with other assessors as Woodfield, Simpkins, Young, Kirkby, & Parker, Coz Pierce &c.

Dinner	2s
Spent in punch	1s
Horse & hostler	9d

Went on poney by Cole Green. Came home the same by 6 clock.

Saturday 28 Markets rather dearer, wheat £5 12s 0d, best barley qr £4 12s 0d, best oates qr £2 14s 0d.

---

[173] This was the first decennial census of population taken in 1801 when only total figures are recorded without any details of individuals. Carrington was paid 10s 6d for the work [*HCR* vol IV p99].

[174] John Vaux of Green Hall Farm, Bramfield, later of Bramfield Place Farm, gentleman farmer and overseer, 1802-3.

Sunday 29 Went to Darmers (*Dalmonds*) to Ricketts, near Brickendon.[175] Very dirty countrey. Dined there, then he & I went to Hartford Heath to one Whittenburys who keeps a publick house new built up neare the pond, by the road side the 2d year of opening it. Spent there with Reckett, John Aylon, & Brother Hasler which happend to meet us there from Ware 9d. Gave Recket's boy 6d. Gave Whittenbury's d[itt]o 3d.

Tusday [31] Went to Ware with Mary Ann in little cart in afternoon. Came home by 7 clock. Spent there & gave Wm Frances 1s. Gave a solder 3d. Gave Hall 6d.

> This month meat was never known so dear. Pork per stone the whole hogg 7s 6d & 8s, motton 14d per pound, beef the same, g[oo]d joynts. The very best wheat was sold today as this being the dearest market at Hartford at £5 18s 0d per load or 5 bushells, barley at £4 12 s per quarter, peas & oates in proportion.

APRIL Saturday 4 Went to market on poney, and Jack Frances took 8 cuppels [sheep] which I sold to one Kingsley at 49s per cuppel. Money £19 12s. Markets much the same in corne &c. Wheat about £5 10s per load. Spent & gave hosler and came home with Randall 2s 3d. Gave Stoten at Randals 6d for coming part the way with me.

Sunday [5] Went to brother Haslers with Coz Cook from London in my little cart to dinner there. When Jack from London & George from Cheshunt & all his chilldren there. Mr Randall came in afternoon. I slept there and walked home in the morning by Bengeo, & Goldings. Spent 2s. Gave maid 6d, Will Frances 6d.

Monday 6th W[en]t to Tewin with Mr Aylott.[176] Spent at Jacks 10d.

Tusday 7th Dined at Bramfield the Grandisons Armes the Wd Derdses, as being our Easter Vistry (*Vestry*). Good dinner round beef, leg mutton, pudings &c. Mr Vaux of Green Hall treated us with 4 bottls of wine & some of his beer. Our poor rates are 7s in the pound this last year. Staid and spent

---

[175] James Rickett (d 1833) of Dalmond Farm [Branch Johnson, *'Memorandoms For…'*, p68].

[176] Aylott, Eylott, or Ilott boarded at Bacons, 1801-2, a 'timber hewer' (see diary entries for 23 Jul 1801 and 21 Jun 1802 below).

after bill paid by Mr Preston overseer 1s. Mr Hunsdon overseer for the year ensuing, Mr Randall & Jos Derds continue church wardens, and Burges constable.

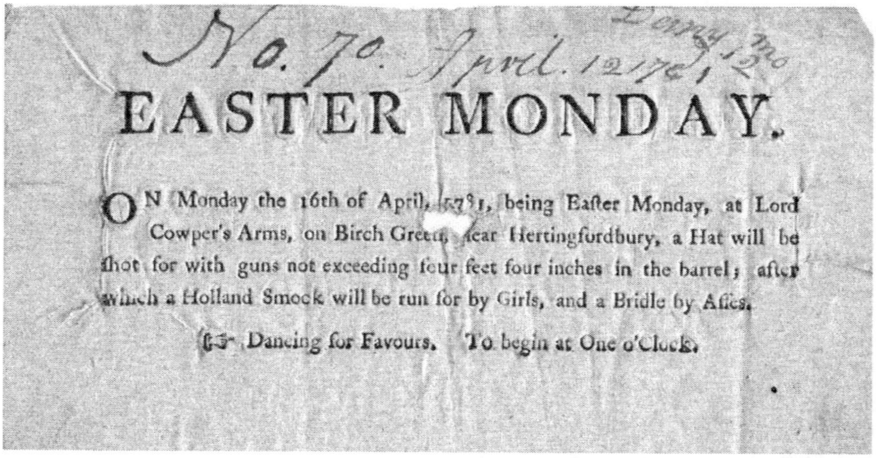

Advertisement for Easter Monday festivities at the Cowper Arms, Birch Green, 16 April 1781 (*Hertford Museum*)

Wednesday the 8 Went to Wotton (*Watton at Stone*) Easter Vestrey held at Crawleys the White Horse. Dined with them, good dinner & wine & punch. Spent 1s. Went on poney round by Goldings. Came home forw[ar]d & stopt at Mr Randalls & supt there with Mr Wilson from Balls [Park] & his wife & sister. Gave the maid & boy 1s 2d.

Saturday 11 Went to St Albans on poney to the Town Hall to recive overseers returns of the popilation, & likewise to appoint overseers for the year ensuing. Went with Burges constable, Mr Preston overseer, & Mr Henry Hunsdon for the year ensuing. Spent & for horse & hostler 3s 3d. Spent at Birch Green coming home Sam Janeses, Cowpers Arms 1s 6d.

[Saturday] 11 Markets much the same. Best wheat, £5 7s 0d.

Sunday 12 Went to Ware on poney. Dined at Haslers. Came home by Wades Mill. Saw Mr Mears at Trotters, Hartford & at Blackbirds. Spent 1s 6d.

Monday 13 Went to Bramfield wood sale. Had 4 roods wood but Stratton came too late so I let him have 2 roods of it. Spent dinner and all 3s.

Fryday 17 Went to Tewin with Mr Eylott. Spent at Tewin Upper Green Whittenburys with Harrington in beer at 7d per pott 1s 6d. Spent at Jacks as came home 1s.

Saturday 18th Markets cheeper, went on poney. Spent & gave 2s 6d.

Sunday 19 Went to Hatfield in the morning on poney with Mr Randall to Lawyer Palmer, then to church at Bramfield, then to Tewin Hill Mr Webbs, then to Tewin Lower Green Jacks.[177] Met old Mr & Mrs Johnson, Mr Aylon, & Billy Johnson & wife & Scott, gardener at Tewin Water & Mr Dean there and brother Hasler in the parler. Spent 1s 6d.

Tusday 21 Went to Esqr Emmotts, Goldings being his birthday. Got fuddled, fell of my poney. O for Shame.

Wednesday 22 Went to [Cold] Bath Mr Griffithses with Mr & Mrs Randall on horseback. Spent there in beer 1s. Then I went to the White Horse, Hartingfordbury to the clubb there. Spent my quota 6d. And it being their finishing vestry.

Fryday 24 Went to Tewin Jacks with Mr Eylott. Spent 9d there. Got fuddled.

Saturday 25 Jorney to St Albans in cart with Mr Aylon to meet Commissioners at the Town Hall to swear to the returns of the Income Tax. Dined Redhouse, I paid for Aylon's diner both 4s. Came home to [Se]wellses Hardingfordbury then Aylon went home. I spent there in ginn & water 1s 3d.

Saturday 25 Markets cheeper, 6s per load.

---

[177] This and several later journeys, one in Sep 1801, to Bradfield, near Reading, Berkshire, were on behalf of Randall, who was leaving Bramfield Place Farm. Carrington attends the sale on 27 July.

Sunday 26 afternoon went to Codicote on poney to carry warrant for Levy Money & a summons for Smith of Bendage (*Bendish, St Pauls Walden*).[178] Put up at Gate. Spent 1s 3d.

Monday 27 Went to Whittenburys Tewin Upper Green with Mr Eylott. Met B[enjamin] Wittenbury & Mr Harrington. Spent there 6d. Came home by Jacks. Spent there with Scott & footman 2s 6d. Gave Ann Kimpton when slept at Bacons 6d.

> Thus ends this month. Marketing all thing seemingly to be gitting lower. The wather very dry & has been all this month. Now the end very hot & dry. Easter Tusday the 7 som driving showers & on Sunday the 12 some snow but all gon directly and cold dry NE winds all the month.

MAY Saturday 2d Jorney to St Albans, in little cart with Mr Aylon to the Town Hall to appear against Smith of Bendage (*Bendish*), and Wright of Sheephall for short weight. Smith find 14s 6d & Wright 14s 6d. Spent there 4s 6d. Came home forward to Hartford with the constable of Redburn with a foot pad, who attemted to robb a poor man there, and was taken and had before Mr Byde & sent to goal this night.[179] Spent at Hartford with Aylon 2s. Mary Ann came home from Hartford with me.

Markets Saturday 2d Cheeper by 10s per load or as they could sell, for the best wheat is not above £4 4s 0d per load.

Sunday 3d Went to Bramfield church, Mr Newton preached as Tewin church being repairing. Afternoon to Tewin, spent 1s.

Wednesday [6] Went to the clubb Hardingfordbury. Supt there. Dr Field gave it, as leiveing it. Bobb & Jack Frances came for me.

Fryday 8th Went to the Bull at Ware to meet Esqr Byde, Reciver Generall of the Taxes. I paid all the Income Tax & others as Windows &c for 1800 and £40 on Land for 1800. Dined at Brother Haslers with Samms from Hodesdon

---

[178] The summons was for selling goods at short weight. See diary entry for 2 May below.

[179] William Pearson was charged with hitting John Durrant with a stick at Redbourn with the intent to rob. He was acquitted at the Hertford Assizes on 20 Jul 1801 [TNA: Hertford Assize records. Information from Ken Griffin].

& spent the afternoon with him & Iredale, baker at Wormley & Mr Aylon. Spent 2s 6d. Gave Will, hostler 3d. Went on poney home by 9 clock.

Saturday 9 Markets cheeper, the best wheat not above £4 per load. I went to Hartford on poney in the afternoon. Spent at Bull with Cadmore, & Draper from London, Mr Randal &c 1s, at Bull Head Richardsons 8d, at [Cold] Bath Griffiths 4d, gave hostler 4d. Came home with Schriber's butler as was rather late 10 clock. Very drunk this time.

Sunday 10 To Bramfield church. Mr Pridmore & the Tewin Singing Girls there, tayler Amherst with base viol. From thence to Ware with Mr & Mrs Randall, I on poney & they single horse. Went by Bengeo. Spent at Eagle 2s. Came home by Hertford by 8 clock.

Wednesday 12 Went to Hartford Fair on poney. Dined at Richardsons the Bulls Head, with Coz Thos Beck & Grayham. Spent there 1s 6d. At Bull 1s, hostler 4d.

Thursday 13 Went to Brocket Hall on poney Ld Milburns races. 3 days the Prince of Wales & Duke of Bedford there & a vast number of gentry &c.[180] One of the gent[leme]n that rode fell from his horse & was much hurt, his name was Buttler Danvers. Spent there & at Tewin 18d.

Saturday 16 Markets much the same or if aneything dearer. Went in afternoon on poney. Spent 1s, hostler 3d. Came home by Mr Randals. Gave Stotan his boy 3d.

Sunday 17 Not to church but went to Sheephall on poney. Spent there with Parker and Bygrave 1s 6d. Poney fell down with me in Horeses Lane. Hom ½ p[a]st 8.

Wednesday 20th Went to London on poney by Potters Barr, and then by Southgate. Put poney up at the Angell Inn, Islington. Went directly this day to Garraways coffeehouse to see Pauls Benfield of Wotton Wood Hall sale.[181]

---

[180] Francis Russell, 5th Duke of Bedford. Carrington records his death at Woburn Abbey on 2 Mar 1802 below.

[181] Garraway's Coffee House was in Exchange Alley, Cornhill, London. Famed as one of the chief auction houses of the City, it was begun in 1669 and was well known to Charles Dickens. It closed in 1872 and was later demolished [Weinreb et al, *London Encyclopaedia*].

3 days sale of the house & park, and farmes &c. The house & park, the first lott, sold for £25,500, Bardalls Farme for £16,500, Wotton Green d[itt]o £6,450, Patchenton d[itt]o £9,850, Gubbens (*Gobions*) d[itt]o £8,900, Little Gubbens d[itt]o £3,200, &c &c all the rest of the farmes. I came away the first day before the sale over. Slept at Coz Becks. Came home the next day Thursday the Hartford Road. Horse & spent about 6s.

Saturday 23 Jorney to St Albans to White Hart to Commissioners to appoint assessors of Land & other Taxes. Went on poney with Mr Eylott by Stanborough. Spent at St Albans dinners &c, at Piggotts 2s 3d. Corne & hostler 1s 6d. Spent as came bak at Stanbrough 6d.

Saturday 23 Markets dearer by 10s per load, the stock of wheat in hand is thin, & the country factors come to London market to supply them & that rises the markets. Wheat is the best £4 12s 0d per load.

Sunday 24 Went on poney to Bramfield church, Mr Newton preached from Tewin. From thence to Ware to dinner at Hastlers, with Mr Johnson & wife from St Albans, & Mr Johnson and wife from Hardingfordbury & my son John & wife from Tewin. Gave & spent 2s 6d.

Wednesday 27 Dined at Tewin. Went to recd Levy Money, onley Norton, Pauls Walden & Codicote there. Spent 2s.

29 Fryday Rode over to Pauls Walden Burry, Ld Burfords to see for money, but he was not there. Got som refreshment from James Flack the buttler. Gave boy 6d.

Satturday 30 Markets rather dearer, best wheat £4 16s. Went to market on poney, dined at Bulls Head with Clapham with mutten stakes. Spent there 1s. From thence to the Bull, spent there with Mr West from London & Chapman & paid Mr Gripper for 3 qr malt £13 10s 0d. Spent 1s. Gave old Hall 1s. Gave hostler 4d.

Sunday 31 Not to church but dined at Mr Randalls, Bramfield Place [Farm]. Stayd evening to tea with Mr Odall. Gave maid 6d. I set out to go to Lord Burfords on poney, and to ask Randall [to go] with me, but very wet afternoon.

JUNE Monday 1 Road over to L[or]d Burfords, Pauls Walden Bury. His Ld Ship is going to leeve there today, & so buisey that he could not see me, so must call again, got nothing. Came home by the 3 Howsen (*Three Houses, Knebworth*) & The Noad (*The Node, Codicote*). Cald on Coz Pierce but he wass very ill, just had a great fall from an old building. From thence to Tewin clubb, hom ½ p[as]t 9 clock. Went on poney spent nothing.

Tusday the 2d Went to Ware on poney. Spent with Aylon & Chamberlin at Weat Sheaf 6d. Spent at Eagle with Wand &c and sold him ½ load hay & 2 ton of straw for £7 15s. Spent 6d. Gave 2½d.

Wednesday 3 Went White Horse Hardingfordbury the clubb, paid for 3 nights 1s 6d. Mr Eylott came home with me on poney 10 clock.

Thursday 4 Went to Mr Prestons with Mr Aylott but he not at home. I came back by Randalls on poney.

Fryday 5th The evening to Mr Hunsdons sheepshearing with Mr Aylott. Stayd 12 clock. Bassett, Bowley, Sheath, Peck, & Burges, &c &c there.

Saturday 6 Markets rather dearer wheat at £4 16s 0d per load. I went in little cart by self, gray poney. Dined at the Plow, Onwins. Spent 3s. 250 French prisenors came into Hartford today from Eping going to Stilton Barrecks.[182] Spent at Bull with Aylon & Randall when Jack was foolish 1s. Spent at [Cold] Bath & Jack silley there 9d.

Sunday 7 Not to church for Coz Cook from London & took me in postchises to dinner at Ware. I stayed all night & came hom Monday and Sall with me. Spent 2s 6d.

Wednesday 10 Went to Hartford to the clubb at [Green] Dragon on poney in the evening. Gave hostler 2d. Came hom in Thorrowgood's coch and Simon rode the poney to Pietle Gate.

Thursday 11 Dined at Ld Cowper's rent fiest in the garden under a booth. About 60 at dinner at Mr Pallett's, the stew[a]rds, Cole Green.

Fryday 12 Afternoon went to see Preston with Mr Aylott. Drank the fine Burton Ale there.[183] Gave his boy 6d.

---

[182] Prisoner of war camp at Norman Cross, near Stilton, Lincolnshire.

[183] As early as 1623 Burton ale was being sold in London. Priced by the bottle it was therefore expensive and designed for the fashionable market. It maintained a strong

Saturday 13 Markets cheepr, best wheat about £4 18s 0d. Went on poney. Dined at Bull second dinner 1s 4d, spent in parley with Aylon &c 6d, gave Hall 2d, gave the lame man 2d, gave hostler, 4d. Came home forward. My sheep sheering 64 sheep - sheerars T[h]o[ma]s Sewill, Mardal, Wiggs, & Sparks. Shoore by the schoore (*score*) but I gave the men refreshment. Very cold day, wind north and high, I howsed the sheep.

Sunday 14 To Bramfield church. Mr Thos Lloyd preached his last sermon there as Mr Ewd Bourchier is to come to live at Bramfield and takes the living. He came from Reding in Berkshire. The afternoon drink tea at Mr Randalls.

Tusday 16 Afternoon went to Knaboth (*Knebworth*) Park with Mr Randall, & Mr Probet, to see Mr Randalls 2 colts in Knaboth Park. Stopt at Woollmer Green Red Lyon wd (*widow*) Crows, had 7 tankets (*tankards*) of 6pney (*6 penny*) & bread & ches (*cheese*) &c. Spent my post 1s 4d. Gave hostler 2d.

Wednesday 17 Went to the evening clubb at White Horse, Hardingfordbury. Home at 10. Spent 6d.

Saturday 20 Markets cheeper, best wheat £4 10s 0d, other wheat a great deal cheeper. Went on poney. Went to Mr Neals with Aylon, son John, brother Hastler & Lawyer King. Spent at Bull with them 1s 10d. Spent at Ramseys Falkon 1s. Spent at Richardsons the Bulls Head on sammon with Schribier's footman as was, & Randall the constable of Hertford 1s 4d. Gave hostler and spent at the Bull when took my poney 10d. Came home 12 clock with Schribier's footman. Too late.

Sunday 21 To Bramfield church. Dined at Mr Randalls with his brother Simon & Mr Probet. Gave maid 6d. Afternoon to Tewin. Spent with the sheepshearers 1s.

Thursday 25 Went to clubb fiest, Green Dragon on poney. I came home in Simons cart. Jack rode poney home 11 clock. Al good companey, plenty goos & ducks.

---

reputation for quality [Peter Mathias, *The Brewing Industry in England, 1700-1830,* (Cambridge, 1959) pp174-5].

Fryday 26 Went to Hatfield with Mr Randall & Mr Probet. Dined at One Bell,[184] went up to Marqueses House. Spent 3s. Gave h[o]stler & others 9d. Home by 9 clock. I fell of my poney in Sandy Lane, hurt my shoulder.

Saturday 27 Markets much the same, the best wheat £4 10s 0d. Fine dry hot wather & good hay tim[e] & though want rane but all things somthing cheeper. Went to St Albans today for signing Land Tax & other papers at the White Hart. Dined at Redhouse with Coz Pierce &c Woodfield from Hexton. Diner 2s. Spent aftr 1s. Gave hostler 3d. Corne 6d. Stopt at Smiths the 3 Horse Shoos, one glass ginn 2d. Came home by the [Cromer] Hide by 6 clock.

Sunday 28 Went out noware as hurt my shoulder as a fall from poney in Sandy Lane, a coming from Hatfield.

Monday 29 Went to Hartford on poney. Stopt at Goldings as came home to deliver Mr Eylotts bill. Called at Randalls as came home by 11 clock.

> Our God & soldier we adoar,
> At the brink of ruin, not before,
> When dangers past how are they requited,
> God is forgotten & the soldier slighted[185]

Tewin church thorowly repaird & the pews altred &c this June & May past. Frances Dean of Tewin Bury, churchwalden *(churchwarden)*.

JULY Wednesday 1st Went to the clubb at Sewills Hardingfordbury White Horse in the evening on poney. Clubb & spent 9d, hostler 1d.

Saturday the 4th Markets dearer, best wheat £5 per load. Went to Hartford on poney & to Ware to see brother Hasler who had a hurt by a horse. Spent 6d at Hartford at Richd Gears at the Runing Deer 1s. Gave hostler 2d.

---

[184] One Bell: now known as the Eight Bells, in Park Street, Old Hatfield.

[185] These lines originally written by Francis Quarles (1592-1644) in 1632 (*Divine Fancies*): Our God and soldiers we alike adore, Ev'n at the brink of danger; not before: After deliverance, both alike requited, Our God's forgotten, and our soldiers slighted [A Partington ed, *Oxford Dictionary of Quotations*, rev 4th edn (OUP, 1996) p533].

Sunday 5 To Bramfield church, afternoon to Quino Hall to Mr Ben Whittenburys. Cald at Webbs at Tewin Hill, from thence to the Feather, Upper Green. Spent with Mr Whittenbury & Aldredge there 7d. Spent at Jacks Lower Green 3d.

Monday 6 Carried my wooll to Hoddesdon to one Skeats there & 7½ tod at 34s down if afford more to be payd afterwards. Gave 1s. Spent at Cooms, Queens Head there 8d. Spent at Hartford as came home as being the Midsummer Fair 1s 6d. Went after in evening to Tewin clubb. Spent there 3d.

Wednesday 8 Spent at Tewin fair with Geo Richardson, the two Hickmans, old Sewell, & Wm Johnson from Hardingfordbury at the Rose & Crown Jacks 2s 6d. Gave away in halfpence 10d.

Thursday 9 Dined at Mr Randalls, & went to Hatfield to Mr Searanks with Mr Randall. Stoppt at the One Bell, some brandy, water & beer but he paid all, home by 7 clock.

Fryday 10 Dined at Mr Randalls with Mr Gutteredge from Eaton Green, and Mr T[h]o[ma]s Smith near Lutton (*Luton, Bedfordshire*). Went to Hartford after dinner with Mrs Randall.

Saturday the 11 <Went to Bank this day took ½ yrs 3 per cent>. Went to London with Mr & Mrs Randall in their cart, by Hatfield. Called on Mr Searanks. Stopt at Gally Corner and breakfasted.[186] I slept at Coz Cooks. Spent at Holland Coffe[e] House Myers from Hartford 1s.[187] Next night slept at Coz Becks, next night at d[itt]o. Spent there 3s. Next night at d[itt]o. Spent 1s, gave maid 1s. Spent & gave more 1s 6d. Came home on Wednesday. Dined at Ware brother Haslers, Mr Randall treated with dinner. Saw Lady Grandison 80 steps high before I came to her, in her house.

Saturday 11 Markets dearer, best wheat £5 10s. Some said more as £5 16s. This was the dearest market of all this year.

---

[186] On the Great North Road south of Potters Bar.

[187] Holland Coffee House is in Lower Thames Street, London. Burnt down in 1814, rebuilt and burnt down again a few years later [Branch Johnson, *'Memorandoms For...'*, p 68].

Thursday 16 To the Quarter Sessions St Albans, on poney by Money Hole. Came home by Grubbs Barn, no great busness onley a tryall of Watford and a parish in London as appeall against an order, and a man for steeling som linnen from Barnat and a woman for recveing the things, the man to be impresend 2 months & the woman transported.[188] Spent 2s 6d. Went and drank tea with Isacc Piggott. Great thunder today.

Fryday afternoon 17th Spent at Jacks at Tewin with Simon Worby 7d.

Saturday 18 Markets cheeper, or as they could sell, for a fine day and the harvest at hand. The mealmen will buy no more but from day to day as the price so great. I dined at Richardson's Bulls Head 1s 8d. Spent at Bull, home with Aylon 6d.

Sunday 19 Went to Bramfield church. In the afternoon to Tewin Jacks to meet constables for presentments for the Assizes, Crowtt [of] Paulswalden, Smith of Codicote, Burges of Bramfield all that was there. Spent 1s. Spent the other 4 sixpences, 2s. Old Mr Aylon with us there, as dined at Bacons before I went.

Monday 20 Went to the Assize Hartford, Lord Kinion & Judge Groose. Little busness for Ld Kinion but 2 tryalls & both over in 1 hour. Stratton's gardner was one, he lost it with Rook. The Assizes ovr by 2 clock. Tusday 3 condemd. Spent at Bulls Head with sister Hasler & Mr Parker & children in sammon 2s 6d. Foreman of Grand Jury S[i]r John Seebright.

Tusday 21 Evening spent at Jacks at Tewin with John Beck & Simon 1s.

Thursday 23 Spent at Jacks at Tewin with Mr Eylott that boarded at Bacons with us, and Coz John Beck from London, and Simon Warby in bear (*beer*) and gin & water 2s 6d.

Fryday 24 Afternoon went Pansanger Lord Cowpers. Drank som good ale with Jack Togood, from thence to Randalls. Drank tea there.

---

[188] The Watford woman being removed to the parish of St James [Piccadilly], Middlesex was Ann Phillips. The man charged with stealing 3 shifts, a shirt and a waistcoat, value 3s, at Barnet was Thomas Goodman who was imprisoned for 2 months. Mary Lee was charged for receiving these goods, the property of Elizabeth Bagnall, for which she was sentenced to 7 years transportation. She was afterwards pardoned [*HCR* vol IV, p98].

Saturday 25th Markets cheeper by 15s per load. Fine dry hot days & some places a reapen wheat which maks the markets lower. Went to market on poney, from thence to Ware. Dined there, came back to the Bull. Spent there with Aylon &c 1s 3d. Gave hostler 3d. Spent at Ware 6d.

Sunday 26 Dined at Jacks Tewin with old nephew John Beck. From thence Bramfield church, in evening to Pansanger to Lord Cowpers. Drank in the hall some good ale with Joseph Toogood, & young Campen & Ewd Harress. Spent at Tewin 6d.

Monday 27 Mr Randall's sale of all his standing cropp of corne, at Bramfield Place. Mr Young of Horwell (*Horrell*), and Mr Dean of Tewin Bury was the greatest purchaseers 61 acres of wheat at about £14 per acre to gether, one field was sold at £16 per acre, barley £11, togather oates & peas £10 acre. The sale at Tattle Hill Barne.[189] Spent at Mrs Derdses 1s.

Tusday 28 Went in cart in afternoon to Rich Gears the Running Deer Porthill with Mr Eylott, & my old nephew John Beck. Went by Bengeo. Bro[ugh]t home 1 qr pollard. Spent there 9d. Spent at [Cold] Bath 6d.

Wednesday Evening [29] To the club Hardingfordbury on poney, 6d. Ostler 1d.

Thursday 30 afternoon went to Datchworth, with Mr Eylott to look at Thos Fletcher's house which is to be sold by auction. Stopt at Horns. Spent 1s 6d.

> This month, Tewin church thorow repaird inside & out. Great alteration in the pews.

AUGUST Saturday 1st Markets cheeper. Went to market on poney. Afternoon went to the sale Green Dragon by Wilson. Bought Cherretree Farme & Steels Wood, Datchworth.[190] Came home with young Mr Blendall to Bacons with me. Spent 2s. Gave Fletcher 2s, ostler 6d.

---

[189] Tattle Hill lies in Bramfield parish between Waterford Lane and Broadoak End.
[190] Cherry Tree Farm was part of the Manor of Datchworthbury owned by Lord John Townshend of Balls Park, Hertford. It was situated on the east side of Datchworth Green. The farmhouse was demolished in the mid 19th century but the farm cottages, much modernised, are now known as Cherry Tree Hall - see also diary entries 9 and 24 Aug below [W Prowle and J Walker, *A History of Datchworth* (Datchworth, 2014) pp116-17].

Sunday 2d Went to Tewin church the first opening after a thorow repair, and the charrity sermon preachd by Revd Ewd Bourchier from Bramfield. Gave 2s 6d. The afternoon went to Ware with Mr Randall in his cart with one Rickett. Spent 1s.

Monday 3 Went to the Robbin Hood & Little John at Robley Heath to meet my constables. Rost beef & pudings for dinner. We spent 2s 6d each. Newnham constable not there, Old Oney from Codicote dined with us. I came from thence to Tewin clubb.

Tusday 4 Went to Ware, dined at Eagle with Mr Randall and Mr Ricket & Aylon. I went to meet Wilson auctionear to pay deposit money, but he not come. I came home by Ware Park. Stopt there, drank some ale. I spent 7s.

Thursday Evening 6 To Grandisons Arms, Wd Derds being Lady Grandison's rent fiest taken by one Peacock, stewerd from London. Spent with Hunsdon, Bassett, Allen & Jack 6d.

Sunday 9 To Bramfield church. The afternoon to Balls [Park], Lord John Townsend, to pay his steward Wilson the deposit money for Cherretree Farm at Datchworth £100.

Saturday 8 Markets much the same, very small market. Some new wheat at £4, Mr Thos Rooks of Bengeo. Fine wather, all busey in the harvest, ½ the wheat inn.

Wednesday 12 Went in the afternoon to Redlyon, Digeswell Hill Mrs Tatts with Mr Randall as by appointment to runn his poney with Harringtons, but they did not runn. Spent nothing.

Thursday, Fryday, Saturday Went not from home, busey in harvest, fine wather.

Saturday 15 Markets cheeper as they could sell the bes[t] wheat £3 or under per load, as the wather fine and most the wheat inn.

Sunday 16 To Ware in foor noon, home to dinner. Afternoon to Hartford by Bayford Burry by [?Harts] Horns to Archers to pay draft. Spent at Blackbirds with Thody 6d. Home by Randals. Gave Stotan 6d.

Monday 17 Went with Mr Randall to Whitwell to see Mr John Hill in his cart after Codicot Bury Farm whear one Mr Bayley lives as he is going out. Dined at Dixons the Bull. Spent the afternoon with Mr Hill there. Home by 10 clock.

Tusday 18 Went to Ware on poney with Mr Randall. Dined at brother Haslers. I treated 3s. Came home by Horrell Mr Youngs. Cald on Mr Pallets Colegreen, home 9 clock.

Saturday [22] Jurney to St Albans the White Hart, to recive papers for the Hair Pouder (*Powder*) and Court (*Coat*) of Arms Tax.[191] Dined at Redhouse with Mr Randall which went with me. Dinner 2s. Spent horse, corne & hostler 3s. Home by ½ p[a]st 7, our Harvest Home Supper, as done in three weeks the wather so fine. All the harvest as ever known except 2 acres, of barley, 4 acres of peas at Bramfield still out.

Saturday 22 Markets cheeper, the best wheat about £3. All wheat inn & mostley all other corne.

Sunday 23 Not to church, the poney fell down with me a going, so I came back, and afternoon to Tewin with Mr Eylott to Jacks. Spent there for I treated 2s.

Monday 24th To dinner at Tewin when I sold Mr Edmans of Wotton the estates I bought of Ld John Townsend at Datchworth. Spent 8s. Mr Harrington, Edmans, and Mr Aylon, and Lewis from London at dinner. Mr Randall came after. Gave old Gass 1s.

---

[191] The Hair Powder tax was first levied in 1795 (35 Geo 3 c49) to be paid by employers of servants required to wear hair powder (see also p11 of the Arithmetic Book, Appendix 1). The Coat of Arms tax levied from 1793 to 1882 was payable by anyone carrying armorial bearings, whether or not they were valid. Anyone keeping a coach or other carriage, and using or wearing any armorial bearing, paid annually £2 8s; anyone not keeping a coach, &c but liable to the house and window duty, paid annually £1 4s and every other person 12s annually [E Baines, *A History, Directory & Gazetteer, of the County of York* (1823); http://familysearch.org/learn/wiki/en/England_Taxation_1700s_to_1900s_(National_Institute)#Hair_Powder_Tax_.28or_Duty.29_1795-1861]. See also entry dated 4 Sep below.

Wednesday 26 Went to North Mimm Place with Mr Randall, formerly the Duke of Leeds, to enquire after Waterend Farme.[192] Was made welcome by Timothy Iarland the bayley (*bailiff*). Came home throu Essington (*Essendon*) & so to Hardingfordbury clubb. Spent & gave 1s 6d. A little fresh this time.

Satturday 29 Markets the same, best wheat £3. Went to market in cart with Little & 2 load wheat sold for 50s. Dined at Bull. Spent & dinner 2s 6d. Gave Hall 6d. Spent at [Cold] Bath 1s 6d. Came home on foot with Mr Eylott.

Sunday 30th Not to church but went to Ware in little cart. Took Mr Ilott up at the goal, carried him to Ware. Dined at sisters Haslers with Emmott & Claphams daughters. Mr Eylott, I and John Aylon spent the afternoon there. I spent 3s. Gave hosler Wm Frances 6d. Home by 8 clock.

Monday 31 Went to Tewin with Coz John Beck who came from London this morning to acquaint us of the death of his brother's wife, and to be buried at Tewin on Wednesday nex[t].[193] So we acquainted Mr Newton the parson, & Sheath the clerk, and fixt on a place for the grave & he returned againe the same day by the coach.

> **Wednesday 12 and Thursday 13** the two very remarkable hot days this month.

SEPTEMBER Wednesday 2 Attended the funerall of my Coz Thos Beck's wife from Long Lane, London at Tewin church. We met them at the entrance of Tewin Lower Green, a herce & 4, coach in 4, all drest in black feathers & a board of fathers on the mans head & mutes & bearers from London. The prosesion very slow to church. Buried about ½ past 3 in the afternoon. The herce returnd to Hartford to the ½ Moon for the night. The coach stopt at Tewin at Jacks the Rose & Crown, ware we all dined and slept, the undertaker Mr Howdon, John & T[h]o[ma]s Beck & his son, & Mrs Beck's brother. Next day Thursday the 3 then returnd to London in the coach. They set off from Tewin at ½ pst 2 clock. I rode in the coach with them to Ware, & young

---

[192] George William Frederick Osborne, Duke of Leeds, and his wife Charlotte sold the Manor of North Mimms in 1800 to Henry Browne [*VCH Hertfordshire* vol 2 (1908) pp251-261].

[193] See diary entry for 2 Sep below when 'Priscilla Beck from London' was buried at Tewin [HALS: DP106/1/2].

J Beck rode my poney there. They set off from there about 4. I spent there 1s 6d. Spent at Ramseys with Hickley & George Kent as I came home 1s.

Fryday 4 Afternoon rode round the parish to recive papers from those that had armorial bearings or used hear (*hair*) powder, the coat of arms was 2 ginues (*guineas*) per year, hear powder 1 ginuea (*guinea*) per year. Stopt & drank tea at Mr Randalls. Gave Stoton 6d.

Saturday 5 Jorney to St Albans Town Hall Licensing Day. Dined at Piggotts, Red House. Spent the afternoon with Codicote people upstars with the 3 widows, Mrs Rayment at the George, Mrs Alvey at the Goat, and Mrs Farrow at the Red Lyon. Spent with them & diner 3s 6d, ostler 4d. Came hom with Burges. Stopt at 3 Horseshews, Smiths, spent 7d. After went to Tewin drinking larges, when Aylott jumt out of window. Markets much the same.

Sunday 6 To Bramfield church. After dinner to Tewin to Jacks. Spent with Old Dr Squire and Sewill from Hardingfordbury 8d. Gave Old Luck 3d.

Tusday Evening [8] To Tewin with Mr Ilott. Spent 2s.

Wednesday 9th Went to Bush Fair with Mr Randall & Mrs Randall, they in their cart, I on their poney. I bought 2 two year old steers at £9 pease (*apiece*). Brought home by Deavonshire the next day. Spent at the fair 3s. Stopt at [Green] Dragon clubb as came home. Yearlings or calves £5 5s per head.

Thursday 10 Foornoon to Hartford for a few things. Treated Hall 6d.

Fryday Morning 11 Set off from Bacons 8 clock to go below Reading with Mr Randall on horsback, I on his poney throw St Albans, to Whatford, to Rickmanswith. Refreshed there at the George, one Mr Browns, from thence to Ammersom (*Amersham*), then threw part of Esqr Garratts Park to Wickome Heath or Mopp End, from thence to High Wickome (*High Wycombe*). Dined there at the 3 Tunns, from thence to Great Marlow over the Theams (*Thames*) to Besom (*Bisham*) which is the first village in Barkshire, from thence to the Bath Road. Near Hear Hatch to Twiford (*Twyford*). Stopt at the Kings Arms there & slept there at one Nathaniell Sandys about 55 mile or 60 the first day from Bacons. Next morning by 7 clock from Sandys to Theale 5 mile from Reding. Turnd of[f] there throw Inglefield to the Starr at Bradfield. Refreshed there at Simmonds who keeps the Starr. Went from thence to the farm at Bradfield, held by one Cox. Did not like it, I called it Mop Hole. Returnd directly to Reding to dinner at the Feathers kept by one Mr Jones on the Market Hill. Set of from thence about 5 clock and came to Mr Sandys at Twiford. Slept there againe the 2d night. Set off next morning Sunday at ½ past six. Came by Maidenhead Thicket through Maidenhead to Slow (*Slough*), put up at the White Hart there one Godards about ½ past 9. Breakfasted there, then walked up to Windsor to see the Castle. Saw it all round & went up the Round Tower, & Eaton Colledge. Then returnd and saw Dr Herscels, as we came by his house instrements between Windsor & Slow (*Slough*) to vew the sun, moon & starrs with.[194] They are much like shipp masts 60 foot high with ropes & pulleys to raise his great tillyscopes with wich are 40 or 50 foot long and as bigg as a large timber tree of 2 or 3 load of timber. Then we refresh againe a little at Slow (*Slough*), and took our horses againe ½ past one clock to Uxbridge 9 mile. Did not stop there, frome thence to Rickmansworth the George againe. Dined there ½ pst 4 clock. Converst with Norress, shoomaker there. Set off for home ½ pst 5. Met Mr Rook by Lord Esexes park. Home by 10 clock. Stopt at the 3 Horseshews & at Red Lyon, Hatfield just to refresh our horses. Mr Randall went after a farme at Bradfield and I went with him, but it did not answer the advertisement. So in the 3 days we rode 160 mile or upwards. Reding is a large town, 3 large churches with peals of 10 and 8 bells each, a good market, but no market house. Harefield is betwixt Uxbrige & Rickmansworth a pleasant village, the church close to the great house or in the park ware at preasant lives Esqr Beans, in Middlesex.[195] We stopt there as came from Slow.

---

[194] Sir William Herschel (1738-1822), originally a musician from Hanover, came to England in 1757. He discovered the planet Uranus in 1781whilst living in Bath. King George III appointed him Royal Astronomer and gave him a house in Slough, later known as Observatory House, to which he moved in 1786. The house was demolished in 1963. It is here that he built his largest telescope which had a 48 inch mirror and a focal legth of 40 feet. A telescope made by him for his sister Caroline, an astronomer in her own right, is at the Science Museum, London [M Fraser, *History of Slough* (Slough, 1973, 2nd ed 1980) pp129-133; http://iya2009/william-herschel, International Year of Astronomy web site accessed 14 Aug 2010].

[195] The great house immediately south of the church was seen by Lysons, and in a print of 1800 appears to have been of two stories built on an H or half-H plan. The two wings which projected at the front may have represented the lodges to an earlier house. Between these the building is of five bays; these and the wings themselves are surmounted by small Dutch gables with finials. The central pedimented doorway with a Venetian window above it dates from the 18th century as do the sash windows

Satturday 12 Markets dearer, best wheat £3 or upwards.

Monday 14 To Tewin afternoon. Spent the evening with Mr Strutt at Jacks who came from London 3 days past & lodged there. Spent 1s 6d.

Tusday 15th To Ware in cart with Mr Strutt. Dined at brother Hasler. Spent the afternoon with Aylon & Chamberlin there. Spent my part 1s 6d. Gave 6d.

Wednesday 16 To Tewin Jacks. Spent the evening with Mr Strutt it being Kimpton stute (*statute*). Maney came from the statute, Cambell, Fletcher &c. Spent 1s.

Thursday 17 To Tewin. Spent the evening with Mr Strutt & brother Hasler, & old Mr Gass came up there. Brother Hasler went home. Spent 1s. Mr Dean & Billy Johnson with us.

Fryday afternoon 18 To Tewin Mr Eylott to Jacks. Spent the evening there with Mr Strutt, Ashley & Flowers, just as a coming away. They was at Bacons for a day or 2 shooting. Home 12 clock late. Spent 2s.

Saturday 19 Markets much the same, very large market supposed to be 1500 load wt *(weight)* barley at about 45s per quarter, peas 30s per load, oates now about 28s per qr, or 30s. Now a great dropp in hopps, buy the best for £5 per hundred [weight], and ½ year past was sold for £20 per cwt. Went to market on poney, spent 2s 6d. Come home by Randalls.

Sunday 20 The Duke Cumberland or Prince Ernest dined at Tewin Water, his men quarterd at Hartford & Ware &c the 15 Reg[i]m[en]t of Lite Horse & he took lodgings at the Lumber House for 1 month and was at Hartford a month or more.[196] He is Coll[o]n[el] of the s[ai]d Regment.

---

on the main front. By 1813 it had almost all been demolished [D Lysons, *An Historical Account of those parishes in the County of Middlesex which are not described in the Environs of London* (1800), p109 and *VCH Middlesex* vol 3 (1962), pp 240-246].

[196] Ernest Augustus, Duke of Cumberland, and from 1837 King of Hanover, brother of George IV (1771-1851). On 3 Sep he was presented with the freedom of the Borough of Hertford [Turnor, *History of Hertford*, p437-8]. Lumber or Lombard House, in Bull Plain, Hertford once the home of Henry Chauncy (died 1719), Hertfordshire's first historian. Now the Hertford Club.

Sunday 20 To Bramfield church, afternoon to Tewin. Spent the evening at Jacks with Mr Strutt, Simon & James Walby. Spent 1s 2d.

Monday 21 Went to Esqr Vincents near the Crown at South Mimms Wash, with Mr Randall in his cart about a farm. Came home thorow South Mimms, to North Mimms, and so to the Greyhound, Hatfield Wood Side, one Georges. Dined there. Spent there with Mr Smith, & Waller, church clerk Hatfield 2s. Stopt at Esington (*Essendon*), Clerks. Spent 1s.

Wednesday Evening [23] To clubb at Hardingfordbury Sewills White Horse onley Jos Hickman, Sewill, & I there. Spent my 6 pence & left. Some to come in.

Thursday 24 Went to Lord Cowpers Cole Green, to see the great house as the workmen are now puling of that great house down. They begun it the beginning of this month, it hath been built 95 years. Gave Mrs South there 1s. Spent at Tewin afterwards with Mr Strutt at Jacks 1s 6d.

Fryday 25 Went againe to Ld Cowpers to see the great house a pulling down. Returnd with Mr Ilott & Mr Strutt to Jacks and spent the evening there at Tewin till 11 clock. Spent 2s.

Saturday 26 Went to market on poney. Dined at Bulls Head Richardsons on stake & onions. Spent there 1s 4d. At Bull 6d, ostler 4d. Came home to Ld Cowpers at Pansanger. Gave there for poney 6d. Markets much the same, best wheat about 58s per load 45 quarter &c.

Sunday 27 To Bramfield church Mr Bourchier preached. Afternoon to Rose Crown Jacks Tewin. Spent there with Mr Strutt 6d.

Monday Evening [28] To Jacks Tewin. Spent the s[ai]d with Strutt, it was the Tewin Surveyors Vestrey, Benj[ami]n Whittenbury & Mr Dean. Spent there 1s 6d.

Tusday To Ware being the **29** Mxs (*Michaelmas*) Day. Dined on stakes with Mr Aylon. Came home forward & went to Tewin the crickett, first when Jack playd against the taylor & beat him. Spent with Strutt & Mr Ilott 2s. Spent at Ware in collecting money for wood 3s. Gave Frances for poney 3d.

> **24 of this month** Mr William Limbery at Newgate Street near [Little] Berkhamstead, had his gees stolen about 2 clock in the morning, a

man and coming by saw them under a hedge ly all kiled. Went & told Limbriy & Limbrey went & found them but he was attacted in bringing them off but he got the better of the rogues & had them againe.

OCTOBER Thursday 1st Spent the evening at Mr Randalls Bramfield Place Farm as somthing like a harvest home supper given to his men, though he had no harvest for he sold his cropp on the ground. Stopt till 12 clock. Good supper, gave maid 6d. Gave Stoten for poney 6d.

Fryday 2d Spent the evening at Jacks with Mr Strutt as he a going to London in the morning. Mr Ilott with me. I paid 10s 6d as there was an old reckning left some nights before, & we staid late.

Saturday 3d Markets cheeper, best wheat 52s per load. Went on poney. Spent at Denshers with George when paid him for bringing bullocks home from Bush Fair 1s. Spent at Bull with Aylon & hostler 8d. Spent at Red Cow Wallers the second day opening house 6d. Gave hostler 4d.

Sunday 4 To church. Dined at Mr Randalls. Evening to Pansanger Lord Cowpers to enquire after the pease (*peace*), from thence to Tewin.[197] Did not stop. Gave Dame Culver 2s 6d.

Monday 5 To Wellwin and bought a hieffer of Parker for £8 13s 0d. From thence to Whittenburys, Mackey's wood fiest. Spent my part 1s 6d. From thence to Tewin clubb & home.

Tusday 6 Afternoon to Hartford. Caried 10 qr barley to mak malt at Grippers. Brought 2 pocket of hops home, & 2 load of wheat, & 1 load tears. Came home to Tewin with 2 gent[leme]n from London to see old Gass. They slept at Jacks, and I spent with them, & Mr Ilott 1s 6d.

Wednesday 7 To Hardingfordbury clubb in the evening on poney. Spent 8d. Home 9 clock, onley 7 there.

Thursday 8 Jorney to St Albans Quarter Sessions. No great business there onley one felon for steeling a pair of boots, in the parish of Watford.[198] Dined

[197] Preliminaries to the Peace of Amiens between England and France were signed in London on 1 Oct 1801.

at Red House with Coz Pierce, & Morgan, & Alvey from Codicote. Spent for diner & dring 2s 6d, corne & hostler, 9d. Went on poney by Colegreen, home by the [Cromer] Hide. Searank sat chairman as being chosen may[o]r, but Donvell did the buisness, home 6 clock.

Friday 9 The evening to W[i]d[ow] Derdses Bramfield to give her licence. Spent there with Burges 1s.

Saturday 10 Markets cheeper the runing price about 48s per load. I dined today at the [Green] Dragon at Cambels the bottom Maidenhead Street. Mr Randall gave the dinner, 2 geese, legg of lamb & pudings, it being the day appointed to recive the money for his cropp of corne sold before harvest. 12 at dinner, Mr Randall paid all wine & punch. Mr Deane, Mr Field, Pool, 2 Youngs, Hanken, Mr Pallet, Mr Wilson auctinear &c &c. Came home to Mr Randalls drank tea, Mr Ilott with me. Stopt there till 2 clock in morning Sunday on account of the thunder and lightning which begun about 7 in the evening. The lightning as much I think as ever I remember, but the thunder very favourable. Peace now thorowbley (*thoroughly*) settled & tonight London illuminated. Peace, Peace, Peace, now rattefied and settled all of a suding, quite unexpected, though not before it was wanted. Hartford & London againe illuminated on the Monday night the 12th, great rejoyceing.

Sunday 11 Not to church, dined at Mr Randalls. In evening to Jacks with Richard, Mr Dollesses man, home 8 clock. Spent 8d.

Monday 12 Dined at Tewin the Rose & Crown, Lord Cowper's wood fiest. Spent my part 1s 6d, the maid 1d. 2 buttocks of beef, 2 leggs moton (*mutton*). Went from thence to Hartford on poney being the town lited up for peace. Rode through the town, & come home immeadiatly. The town much illuminated.

Tusday 13 To Tewin in evening with Mr Ilott. Spent at Jacks 2s. Home 10 clock. Sister Nancy [Pierce] came with us home, as had been at St Albans with Sall being the 2d fair day. They had Dimon.

Wednesday 14 Afternoon to old Phipps sale at Hardingfordbury Street, farmer as retiring from buisness and resining the farme to his son at

---

[198] John Coil stole a pair of boots the property of Davis Darvill of Rickmansworth, victualler. He was found guilty and sentenced to one month in gaol and to be whipped on market day at St Albans [*HCR* vol IV p100].

Pansanger, as Lord Cowper his inclosed the Pansangr farme in his new park, and is now pulling Colegreen House down, and is said to build a new one at Pansanger. Spent at Sewills, the Wite Horse, 4d. Went from thence to the clubb at Hartford. Came home with Simon. Went on poney by 10 clock, hostler 2d. John Ramsey auctinear at Phippses & at Hartford, Maidenhead Street another sale by Manser Judds, the hatter. I bought 6 hats the same evening for 4s 6d. A little fresh this time.

Thursday 15 To Mr Derdses Bramfield the Surveyors' Vestrey. Onley I, and Burges and Derds, & Preston there. Spent 5s and home by 9 clock.

Saturday 17 Jorney to St Albans, Town Hall to appoint surveyors, Mr Cowper, Mr Boyse clerks, Justices Esqr Donvell & 2 more. Dined at Redhouse, dinner 2s. Spent after with Stratton 6d, horse & hostler 10d. Went by the [Cromer] Hide and came home the same on poney by 5 clock. Markets much the same, best wheat about 50s.

Sunday 18 To Hardingfordbury church, a charity sermon preachd by Mr Newton of Tewin for the Sunday Schools there. Gave 2s 6d. Went from thence to Ware. Dined and spent the evening there with John Aylon, & one Tubbman, and one Pamplon schoolmaster, with cockt up hat, at the Swan Denneses till 11 clock. Spent there 1s. Slept at Eagle & spent there 2s. Gave Will and maid 1d. Home in morning Monday 9 clock. Got fuddled.

Monday 19th To Esqr Emmotts to carry in my bill. Refreshed very comfortly. Shook hands with the Esqr & Pedder, & Ladys.

Wednesday 21 Went to London with Richards. Counsels (*Counsellor*) Dallesses man rode his horse, & he had my Dimon in Randalls cart. Stopt at Whittenburys Hartford Heath. Stopt at 4 Swans Waltham X. Was not in London till 12 clock at night. I came home next day in cart, Barnat (*Barnet*) Road. Home 8 clock evening. Richards paid all expences but it cost me over and above 5s. Went to see Mary Scott who lives at the Black Bear, Pickadilley (*Piccadilly*). Went no wear else. I slept at Delleses.

Fryday 23 Went to the Bull at Ware to pay taxes. Paid Esqr Byde £71 13s 0d. Cleard the Land [Tax] for 1800 and £20 towards taxes for 1801. Onley Mr Pierson & he there. Dined at Eagle with Mr Rogers, Mr Munns, Mr Samms, Mr Iardale, baker from Wormley, & John Aylon & self. Spent 3s. Spent afterwards with Mr Ilott and Chambrlin & Aylon 1s. Gave Will

Frances 4d. Home by 9 clock. I rode Dimon, Mr Ilott had been to Wades Mill on poney.

Saturday 24 Markets much the same, the average in market 46s load, barley 45 per qr, peas 28s per load, oates best 30s qr. Went on poney. Dined at Bull, Mr Ilott dined there. Dinner 1s 4d. Spent there after dinner 1s. Spent at Richardsons Bulls Head when Chapman paid me for 3 load of wheat. Gave hostler 5d. Came home with Sheath.

25 Sunday To Bramfield church, the rest at home.

26 Monday Went to Ware in poney. Settled with brother Hastler. Spent 1s 9d with Chamberlen & Aylon & paid Tho[ma]s Constable for well rope, & putting on some boards.

Thursday 29 Spent at Tewin in the evening Jacks with Mr Ilott. Staid late 3s 6d.

Fryday 30 Afternoon to vestrey at Mrs Derdses Bramfield to grant rate to Mr Hunsdon, overseer. Bourchier, Vaux, Preston, Hunsdon, & I there & Mr Auston, the vestrey clerk.

Saturday 31 Markets cheeper, best wheat 45s per load, barley 45 per quarter. Went on poney. Spent at Richardsons 6d. At Bull 6d. Hostler 4d. Came home by Mr Randalls and home at Bacons by 9 clock.

> This month Lord Cowper's House, called Cole Green House, begun to be taken down after standing 95 years, a very large strong brickt house, & fine paintings and all. Totally taken down & carried away, distroyd. It was built by his present Lordship's great grandfather, Chanceler Cowper.[199]

NOVEMBER Monday 2d Spent at clubb Tewin 4d. This day was the sale at Mr Randalls, Bramfield Place of all the farming stock, a vast wet high windy day. I bought a colt there for £8 13s 0d.

Tusday 3 Spent at Rose & Crown Jacks Tewin in taking my rents & Mr Meears my part 6s & he 6s.

---

[199] William Cowper (1665-1723), Lord Chancellor, 1707, and created 1st Earl Cowper, 1718.

Wednesday the 4th Dined at the Rose & Crown Tewin, being the annuall dinner of the Association for Apprehending Fellons & Robers. Dinner calves head, a hamm & turkey, pudings & pyes &c, wine & punch. Mr Pallett, Mr Webb, Mr Patient, Mr Preston, Ben Whittenbury, Dolling, Simon Walby, Brux, Mr Hanken, Richd Dean, Ben Squier, S James, & myself, and John. Spent each 5s. A very wet day & dark rainey windy night. Home with Mr Ilott by 12 clock.

Thursday 5th Tythe fiest at Mr Ewd Bourchiers, Bramfield. Dined in the landry (*?laundry*). Buttock of beef, lyne (*loin*) of veal, & pudings, good ale & punch. The first feast of Mr Bourchiers. Mr Hunsdon, Preston, Allen, Thos Whittenbury, Derds, Burges and self & Will there and some women there likewise.

Saturday 7 Markets much the same. Went on poney, dined before I went. Spent at Bull & gave hostler 1s 6d. Came home by Randalls forward.

Monday 9 To Watchshod (*?Hertford*) fair.[200] Carried a load of wheat to mill. Little went with me in Cook's cart. Bought 1 bush[el] of inons *(onions)* 3s. Came home by Richd Gears at the Running Dear, had 6 bush[el] of Pollard. Spent 1s.

Tusday 10 Afternoon to look [for] my hoggs. Refreshd at Esqr Emmotts, by the woods to Hardingfordbury. Spent at Sweills (*Sewells*), White Horse 6d, at old Wellses 6d. Did not find them, but herd of them there in the woods.

Wednesday 11 To Bramfield wood fiest. Rost ribbs, & byled (*boiled*) beef, pudings &c. Gatherd for dinner 1s. Spent in punch Wm Ramsey made it, 2s 6d. Lost my way in 6 acres coming home it was so dark & foggy, home 7 clok.

Saturday 14 Markets dearer by 3s per load, best wheat at 50s per load. Went on poney. Dined at Bull, home 8 clock. Dinner at Bull 1s 4d. Spent at Richardsons 1s, hostler 4d. Home by Randalls 8 clock.

---

[200] 'Watchshod' is an unusual spelling for Carrington and it is not clear where exactly he means; he uses the form Watchard on 8 Nov 1804 below. Branch Johnson suggests Hertford [Branch Johnson, *'Memorandoms For ...'*, p106].

Tusday 17th Mr Randall's sale of Bramfield Place of his household goods. Spent with Smith in liquers from Wd Derds 7d. Gave Preston's boy 2d as went from sale with Hanken to Mr Prestons and I sold him Backelhill turnops at 40s per acre.

Wednesday Night about 9 clock the 18th Mr Randall & wife and his brother Simon left Bramfield Place Farme.

Thursday 19 Afternoon spent at Mr Gears at the Windmill at Waterford with Mr Randall the day after he left Bramfield, another man from Grantom (*?Grantham, Lincolnshire*) 1s 6d.

Fryday 20th Dined Whittenburys Tewin Upper Green, Tewin tythe fiest. Buttock beef, leg moton, fillett of veal, pudings, plenty of punch.

Saturday 21 Markets dearer, best wheat at 55s per load. I went on poney at ½ past 12 clock. Spent at [Green] Dragon with Wm Johnson 6d, at Bull 4d. Gave hostler 4d. Home at 6 clock.

Sunday 22 Not to church but went to Esqr Bakers. Dined there with Mr Bigg, his buttler, and the housekeeper & Mr Kinsey, the gardner. Came away with Byott the blacksmith, to Hadingfordbury (*Hertingfordbury*). Was well entertained. I spent at Hadingfordbury foolishly 2s.

Monday 23 Spent the afternoon Colegreen Mr Palletts. Gave to Mrs South & the maid 2s.

Tusday 24 To Ware. Went to the auction at Ellises the Punch House. 2 freehold houses sold by Dunn belonging to Mr Allen of High X *(Cross)* near the church yard, first for £140, second for £128. Stopt & spent there with Mr Scott, Mr Mickley & Cass &c &c 1s 6d. Slept at brothers, home morning 6d.

Wednesday 25 Went to Mrs Derds. Spent there with Bassett at 1 clock 8d.

Thursday 26 Afternoon to Jack. Spent 2½d.

Fryday 27 The great snow, it lookd thik in the morning. About 8 it began and snowd very fast all day, the wind NE frose very sharp at night and Saturday night likewise but on Monday a thaw.

Saturday 28 Markets cheepr. I sold some for 50s per load. Dined at Bull at the first table 2s 6d. Spent at Richardsons 7d. Gave Hall 6d. Gave hostler 4d.

> Memorandom sold Mr Preston **Monday 30** Bramfield Place field turnops & the Hopp Ground turnops & 2 steers at Bacons for £51. Buckell Hill turnips 10 acres for £20.

DECEMBER Wednesday 2d In evening to Tewin Jacks with Mr Ilott. Spent 2s.

Thursday 3 Paid Baldock, bricklayer for 9 days work at 18d & board for new laying some part of the kitchen &c 13s 6d.

Saturday 5th Markets cheeper, best wheat at 50s. Went on poney. Dined at Richardsons with Dolling & Pridmore. Dinner 1s. Spent after there 6d. Spent at Bull 6d. Gave Hall 6d, ostler 4d.

Sunday 6 Not to church, but went to Wotton to see those places near the Waggon & Horses that Aylon bought for £56 at the auction at Ware on Tusday last. Spent at the Bull at Wilshiers with Edmonds 2s 6d. Drank coffee at Edmonds. Gave 6d. Came home with Johnson 8 clock.

Monday 7 To Tewin clubb, spent after clubb 3d.

Tusday 8th To Ware on foot. Dined and spent after with Thorpe & Caswell's gardner 8d. Home 10 minuets before 6, in one hour & ½ to Bacons. Dirty walken (*walking*).

Wednesday Evening [9th] To the clubb at [Green] Dragon Hertford. Gave hostler 3d. Home with Simon by High Field.

Thursday 10 To Tewin Jacks to dinner of haunch of venson. I gave onley Mr Dolling, Sheath, Mr Ilott & Simon. Spent our parts 3s 6d. Home 11 clock. Gave the maid 1s.

Fryday 11 In the evening to Jacks Tewin to sup on hasht venson. Spent with Mr Ilott 2s.

Saturday 12 Jorney to Angell St Albans to carry in list for drawing millitia. Ld Grimston, Esqr Gape, Esqr Bourchier & Grover, the clerk. Went in cart to Sandredge (*Sandridge*) Lodge. Dined there. Gave the man there 1s. Spent at

Piggotts 2. Markets dearer, best wheat 56[s] per load. Sharp frost, very cold day.

Sunday 13 Not to church but was sent for to meet Mr Randall at The Bull Hartford, but he was not there, so I went on to Ware. Dined there, & then met Randall at Onwinns the Wor[l]ds End, Hartford. Spent with him there 4s 6d. Came home with Mr Ilott.

Tusday 15 to Ware on foot as sharp frost. Dined there with Coz Thos Beck as came down on Sunday last, so he went with me as going back & took coach at Haslers. Went to Driver's sale at Sarrasons Head & I staid all night. Spent 2s.

Saturday 19 Markets much the same, as being a fool market as the wather continues frosty & some snow. Went on foot today. Came home with Allen, when I and Mitchel stopt at the [Cold] Bath, & Mitchell & Harrod talked the scripter (*scripture*). Spent there with Mitchell 2s 6d.

Sunday 20 To church & walked in evening to Jacks at Tewin. Spent 3d.

Monday 21 Went on poney to Woollmer Green, with butcher Bowley, to the Redlyon the Wid Crows, to recive one yrs rent due Mixs (*Michaelmas*) last. Spent & gave 6s. Bowley came back with me to the Moatehouse, Bulls Green,[201] after that I fell off poney. Staid late.

Tusday 22 To Hartford to git some pease for the parson. Got none.

23 Wednesday To dinner at Jacks the Rose & Crown Tewin, a dinner on acpt (*account*) of Mosey Gillman to serve the house with beer.[202] Mosey Gillman spent £2 2s 0d, Mr Pallett £1 1s 0d, the rest all 8s a peece. 16 at dinner: Alderman Archer, Kimpton, Evens, Mr Mullet, Grubb, Johnson, and Field, Cambell, & Tice, Crawley of Wellwin, I and Ilott.

Fryday 25 Christmas Day to church at Bramfield. Spent the evening at Mr Hunsdons with Bowley, Bassett, Peck, Richardson &c &c. Gave maid 1s 6d. Gave Hoar the fiddler 1s.

---

[201] Probably Moat Farm [see, Prowle and Walker, *A History of Datchworth*, p122].

[202] Moses Gillman, brewer of Hertford, beer supplier. The Gillman family owned the Cross Keys brewery in Fore Street, Hertford [A Whitaker, *Brewers in Hertfordshire A Historical Gazetteer* (Hatfield, 2006), p122].

Saturday 26 Markets cheeper, best wheat 51s. I sent Will today so did not go.

Sunday 27 To Bramfield church. The afternoon to Ware on pony to take Witbury Hill rent of King. Stayd all night. Went to the meeting at Ware at 7 clock with brother Hasler, Aylon, & Chamberlen, the text was, there is but a step between us and death.[203] Came home with Mary Ann the next day. Called at Goldings & refreshed. Spent & gave 5s.

Wednesday 30 Attended the funerall of Mr B Whittenbury of Quino (*Queenhoo*) Hall to Tewin church. Spent at Tewin as came from church with Burges, Derds, Squier, and Bowley, Crowt, Hasden, &c 1s. Gave Whittenbury's boy 6d.

> Thus ends this year. Nothing very remarkable, onley the inhabitants the numbr of in every parish was taken by order of Act of Parliament this year in March last all over the kingdom. And Cole Green House was taken down in Sep[tembe]r last this year.

Deaths & Marriages this year 1801

Tusday the 27 January was married at Bramfield church, two couple, Thos Whittenbury of Quino (*Queenhoo*) Hall to Maria Redman, and Geo Richardson of Bramfield, to one Hornat, the wedings cept (*kept*) at Mr Hunsdons. Everything plenty, I gave 4s.
January 25 old Mr Clapham buired aged 87.
[January] 31 young Hubard of Sacomb buired aged about 26. Gladman of Wheathamstead died aged 50.
Febry Twinn of Ware Westmill died **7th** aged 55.[204]
Arkley, formerly lived at Nup End, buried at Wheathamstead this **8th** aged 50.[205]
Febry 11 Mrs Haynes died, buried at Hardingfordbury. She was neice to S[i]r Henery Vincent, Surr[e]y and neice to Richd Warren Esq of Marden.[206] Her miaden name was Vincent. Aged 75.

---

[203] Text is I Samuel ch 20 verse 3: [David said] '… but truly as the Lord liveth, and as thy soul liveth, there is but a step between me and death'.
[204] John Tween was buried at Ware on 14 Feb 1801 [HALS: DP116/1/5].
[205] 'James Arkley of Caddington in the county of Hertford' was buried at Wheathampstead on 8 Feb 1801 [HALS: DP122/1/3].

Mrs Cath[a]rine Bourchier buired at Bramfield this **Thursday 12**. Brought from Reding, Barkshire a herce in 4, coach in 4 all plaine. Aged 62.
Mr Thomas at the Bull Inn Hartford buired at Hitchen **Fryday 13th**.[207] He had lived at the Bull about 6 yrs. A young man, a wife & small children.
S[i]r Ralf Abercromey, generall was killed at the battle before Alexandray in Egypt on the **21 March** last.[208]
Mr John Proctor, mal[t]ster of Ware died and buired at Ware church, Fryday evening **May the 8th**.
John Andrew buired at Bramfield church **May 10**. Young man married Kittle's daughter.
Sall Munns wife to John Munns at Tewin died **Fryday morning May 29**. Aged 45 years. She used to make numbers of cakes to sell, & wiggs.[209]
Mr Ambrose of Grigorys Farme, Watton [at Stone] died this **June 1801**.[210] A good man aged about 71.
Mr George Prescott of Theobals Park, Cheshunt died suddingly of an apperpleet (*apoplectic*) fitt on **Monday night July 20th**.
Sepr 2nd Coz Thos Beck's wife bro[u]ght from London in herce and 4, coach in 4 to be buried at Tewin church aged 60 years.
About **Sepr 14** died at his seat at Hilsborough in Iarland, the Marques of Downshire, who about 12 years back lived at the Castle at Hartford and then

---

206 Sir Henry Vincent of Stoke d'Abernon, Surrey [Burke, J, *Genealogical and Heraldic Dictionary* (1839)].
207 A man with the surname Thomas does not appear in the Hitchin burial register for 1801, or the Quaker digest [HALS: DP53/1/5; NQ1/5D/1]. Carrington lists a second Thomas buried at Hitchin on 10 Jan 1802, who also does not appear in the above registers.
208 Sir Ralph Abercromby (1734-1801) was 'struck by a musket ball in the thigh and was evacuated to the fleet's flagship, HMS *Foudroyant*. … After rallying a little he faltered, and finally succumbed to septicaemia at 11 pm on 28 March 1801. He was buried on Malta, where a simple monument was erected to his memory' [David Gates, 'Abercromby, Sir Ralph, of Tullibody (1734–1801)', *ODNB*, Oct 2007].
209 Baroness Dimsdale has a recipe for 'Wiggs': 'Take 3 pound of Flour, one of butter; melt it in as much Milk as you think it will make it very light, and full half a pint of ale Yeast; Put the Ale and Yeast into the flour, and stir it as you do for a Cake, then set it by the fire to rise for half an hour, then work in one pound of Sugar and one Ounce and a half of Carraway Seeds; then let it rise by the fire a little longer' [H Falvey, *The Receipt Book of Baroness Dimsdale* c1800, HRS vol XXVIII, 2013].
210 'John Ambrose, farmer' was buried at Watton at Stone on 5 July 1801 [HALS: DP/118/1/2].

was Lord Fearford (*Fairford*), and was chosen Alderman of the s[ai]d Borrough, but since left and lived in Iarland.[211]
Sepr 20th was buried at Hartford All Saints church Mr Benj[ami]n Gillman, grocer & brewer, and Alderman of the Burrow (*Borough*) of Hartford. Died of the putred feever which is very much now at Hartford. Aged 31 yrs.
Tusday Octobr the 20 about 9 clock in the morning was buried at Tewin church at the chancell end Miss Litticia Mackey, daughter of Rob[er]t Mackey, Esqr of Marden. A herce in 4, a coach in pair white hat bands silk. Aged 21 yrs.
October 23 was buried at Hartford, All Saints church old James Kent aged 76. He lived up Castle Street, Hartford. He was a flower (*flour)* dreser and worked at the Town Mill and formerly a servant to me at the Seall Mill, a good man.
John Peek at the White Hart, Stapleford buired on **Thursday 29 Octr 1801** aged about 65. Was lame some years.
Sunday November 1st was buried at All Saints church, Hartford Mr John Beecroft who kept the Bell Inn, Hartford, aged about 60.
Sunday Novr 15 was buried at All Saints church Hartford Mr Wm Randall, staymaker at Hartford. Lived above the Blackbirds, Castle Street next the gate going into Bayley Hall. He was Sergant at Mace & used to take the toll of the market, and constable money (*many*) years. He belonged to the Association at Hartford. They marched the Dead March & fired over him. He was a ringer & they muffeld the bells. I was at the buring about 4 clock, a great number of people. Aged 63.
Wednesday 16 of this month Decbr Old John Wicks of Bramfield Bury buried at Wotton (*Watton at Stone*), aged 86. He had lived in that farme some years and a hard working man, and a great wood carter, perticler (*particularly*) of Bramfield Wood.
Monday Decber 28 Mrs South from Cole Green, aunt to Mr Pallett there, buried at Wotton. Formerly wife to baker South there, aged 62.[212]

---

[211] Arthur Hill, Marquess of Downshire (1753–1801). In 1786, he married Mary Bertie, nee Sandys. At the time of his marriage he was styled Lord Kilwarlin but from 1789 Earl of Hillsborough and from 1793 second Marquess of Downshire. [*ODNB*, Jan 2008].
[212] Sarah South of Hertingfordbury 'aged 78' was buried at Watton at Stone on 28 Dec 1801 [HALS: DP/118/1/2].

Queen Hoo Hall, Tewin, from the south by J C Buckler, 1833
(*HALS: DE/Bg/4/183*)

Wednesday 30th of December was buried at Tewin church old Mr Benj[ami]n Whittenbury of Quino (*Queenhoo*) Hall, aged 71 years. Carried in a herce and 2 horses, the paul bearers was I and Squier, Brux & Thorrowgood, Burges & Derds. This was he, that one Walter Clibbon & his two sons 3 foot pads, atacted at Oakenvelly Bottom on Saturday evening the 28th of December 1782 and Mr B Whittenbury got the better of them and shott dead the old man, & one of his sones he took, the other run away. And the Marques of Salsbury made him a present of a silver cupp for his valuer (*valor*). This sone so taken was hanged the March assizes following. Old Clibbon lived at Babbs Green either in the parish of Ware, or Thundredge, and used to go a robing with his sones every winter and done very great roberys, & murder, but now the rogue was stopt and the countrey sattesfied of their suspicions.[213]

[213] More detail concerning this event can be found in the Arithmetic Book pp166-7, Appendix One.

At Kirklees in Yorkshire near Hutherfield (*Huddersfield*) is a funeral monument of the famous outlaw Robin Hood with a inscription on it who died the 24th of December in the reign of Richard the first, 1247:

O vain man as thou art,
When will you then be wise,
To curs and dam thy hart,
And sware and blast thine eyes.

Remember yr but dust,
And sertainly soon must die,
And account then give you must,
For all you sware and lye.

O what terable dread,
Must seaze you with supprise,
When after such a life you have led,
To judgment you must rise.

On account of Battle of Ware who was took speechless by swareing at the Eagle and died in 5 days after 1798.

----

54 good guinuas *(guineas)* is exactly one pound averdupois w[eigh]t.

(*Last pages of diary written on pages of printed Income Tax Tables and the following note is made by Carrington*:-This was a Table of Income for every person to pay Tax according to their estates for the year 1800).

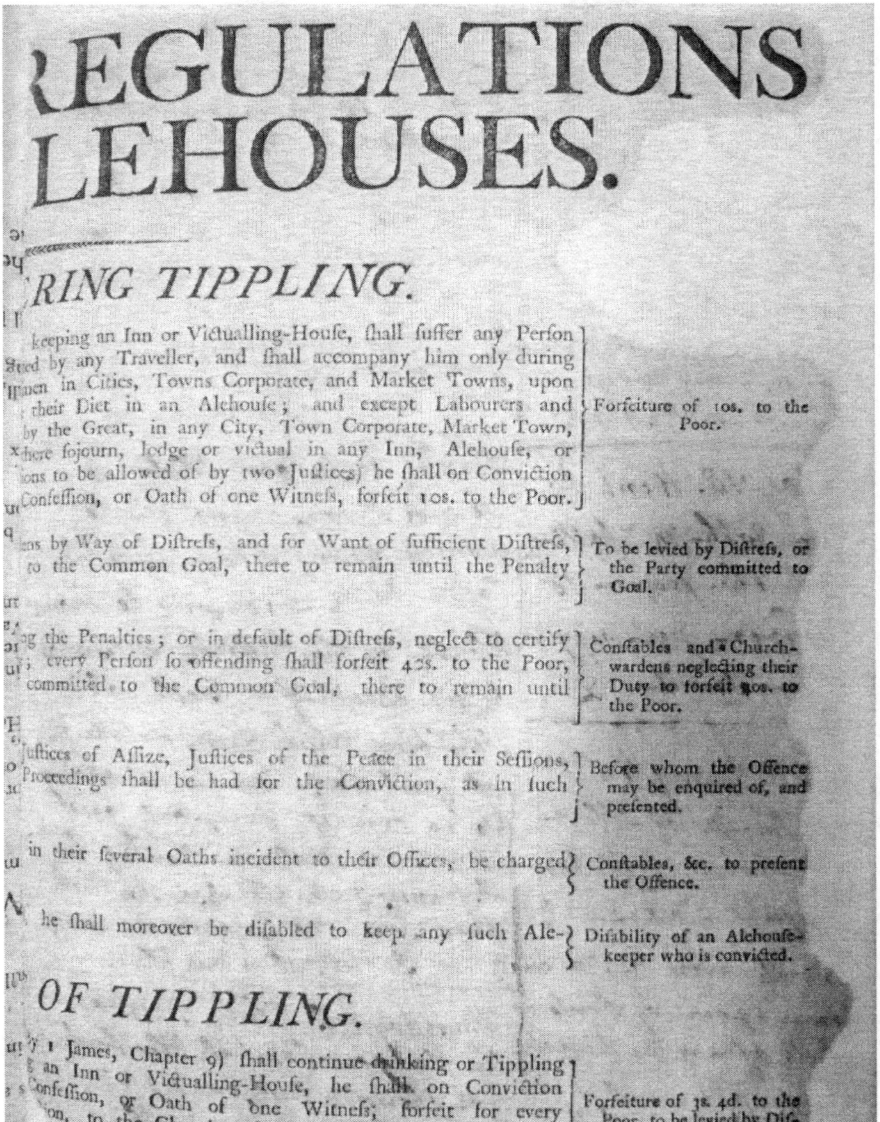

REGULATIONS
LEHOUSES.

RING TIPPLING.

keeping an Inn or Victualling-House, shall suffer any Person
ted by any Traveller, and shall accompany him only during
men in Cities, Towns Corporate, and Market Towns, upon
their Diet in an Alehouse; and except Labourers and
by the Great, in any City, Town Corporate, Market Town,
here sojourn, lodge or victual in any Inn, Alehouse, or
ons to be allowed of by two *Justices) he shall on Conviction
Confession, or Oath of one Witness, forfeit 10s. to the Poor.

Forfeiture of 10s. to the Poor.

ns by Way of Distress, and for Want of sufficient Distress,
to the Common Goal, there to remain until the Penalty

To be levied by Distress, or the Party committed to Goal.

g the Penalties; or in default of Distress, neglect to certify
every Person so offending shall forfeit 40s. to the Poor,
committed to the Common Goal, there to remain until

Constables and Church-wardens neglecting their Duty to forfeit 40s. to the Poor.

Justices of Assize, Justices of the Peace in their Sessions,
Proceedings shall be had for the Conviction, as in such

Before whom the Offence may be enquired of, and presented.

in their several Oaths incident to their Offices, be charged

Constables, &c. to present the Offence.

he shall moreover be disabled to keep any such Ale-

Disability of an Alehouse-keeper who is convicted.

OF TIPPLING.

1 James, Chapter 9) shall continue drinking or Tippling
an Inn or Victualling-House, he shall on Conviction
Confession, or Oath of one Witness, forfeit for every
on, to the Churchwardens, who shall be accountable

Forfeiture of 3s. 4d. to the Poor, to be levied by Distress, or the Party set in

Printed notice: 'Statutes and Regulations concerning Alehouses' used by Carrington for his diary, 1799 (*HALS: DE/X3/2*)

1802 (*HALS: DE/X3/5*)

JANUARY Saturday 9 Markets much the same, wheat per load 53s, barley per quarter 48s, oates 27s, peas 28[s] per load. Went to market on poney, put him up at Cold Bath. Dined at Bull 1s 4d. Spent at Bath with Knapp of Roblyheath (*Rabley Heath, Codicot*) who came with me to the hand post by Hooks Bushes 6d. Gave hostler 3d.

Sunday the 10th To church. Afternoon to Tewin. Spent there 1s.

Monday 11 Dined at W[i]d[ow] Derds, Bramfield, with Mr Peacock, Lady Grandison's rent fiest. Spent after 1s.

Tusday 12 To Ware on foot. Stopt all night. Spent there 2s.

Wednesday 13th To the clubb dinner at Sewils, Hardingfordbury. Spent 5s. Nedd Spencer came for me, my servant.

Fryday Evening 15th Spent at Esqr Mackeys at Marden when carried a fatt pigg and a loaf of bread for the way thorough his fields.

Saturday 16 Markets much the same. I sold good wheat today for 52s per load. Went to market on foot as being very frosty. Dined at Richardsons, Bulls Head 1s 2d. Spent there after with Odal &c 4d. Spent after at the Bull … Hollingsworth, & Young …, & Smith 10d. … at Cold Bath, Griffithes. … home with Pridmore.

Sunday 17th To Tewin church afternoon, from thence to Jacks. Spent there with Billey Johnson & John Hickman from Hardfordingbury 8d. Afterwards with brother Hasler & George & my son Willm 1s 6d.

Tusday 19 Evening spent at Tewin with Thos Sheath & Wm Sheath his brother, and John Sheath their uncle, church clerk of Tewin, & Thos Blindell, Simon Warby. … Hot pot … 1s 6d …. (*Corner torn off*)

Wednesday 20 Dined at the Bulls Head, Hartford at one Geo Richardsons, a Scotchman which keeps the house as a house warming. Companey was Mr Hasler, Pallett, Thorp from Great Amwell, myself, & Mr Hunsdon, Mr Burges from Bramfield, Mr Chapman, Simpson, Kent, and the watchmaker &c from Hartford. Din[n]er calves head, a hear (*hare*), pork & sasseges, pudings &

applpy *(apple pie).* Spent each 3s 6d. Gave James Warby's wife 6d. Pl[e]nty of punch, home 10 clock.

Fryday 22 Evening went to Tewin to see old Gass which lives in a room at Grimes, the blacksmith now 85 years of age. Gave him 1 pot of beer 4d. Spent at Jacks 3.

Satturday 23 Markets dearer, 2s per load, small market. Dined on stakes at Bulls Head with Hanken, butcher & Mr Chapman. Spent 1s 6d. Spent at Bull 6d. Came home by old Wellses with Mullet & Insom, sackcarer &c. Saw old Wells a bed very bad not like to live. Spent there with them 2s 6d.

Sunday 24 Not to church. Afternoon to Colegreen, Mr Palletts. Spent some time there with him & Woodhouse.

Tusday 26 To Ware on poney, went with Mr Aylon in evening to White Swan. Saw the fight with Hobbs, the glover, & Nutting the braiser, in the parler. Hobbs beat & served Nutting right for he was the offender. Spent there 6d. Slept at Ware the Eagle. Spent night & morning & gave 2s.

Saturday the 30 To St Albans to draw Millitia, & when came there the day was put off. Dined at Coz Piggotts the Red House with my constables, found Coz Piggott very ill thought a dying.[214] Came home with Burges, constable of Bramfield. Spent diner 2s after & corne & hostler 1s 9d

Sunday 31 To London on poney as far as Cheshunt, & Jack Frances brought him back, then found at Waltham X a reternd chaise for 1s 6d to London. Slep at Coz Becks, Long Lane, and came home on the Wednesday morning on foot to Ware. Slep there & home on the Thursday morning. Went to see Nancy Pierce at Mrs Goodalls, and found Mrs Goodall dead, but found Nancy Pierce with her other 2 fellow servants & refreshed there. Spent in all in London, & going and coming home 9s 6d.

> In this month was found a human skilliting (*skeleton*) between Tewin Lower Green & the Upper Green in an elbow in the rode opposite som[e] railing where the foot path is narrow. Found by one Thorrowgood, blacksmith, at Tewin Upper Green in digging for gravel.

---

[214] Thomas Piggott died the next day, leaving a son Isaac – see Carrington's list at the end of 1802 below.

Prat came into the Bell, St Andrews Street this month, after Brown leeving it.

FEBRUARY Thursday 4th Lord Cowper's rent fiest. Went there, paid £50 towards rent.[215] Jack Frances came for me.

Satturday 6 Markets cheeper, best wheat 52s. Went on foot, dined at Richardsons with Clapham & his son & wife & Newnham of Bayford on sassages &c. Spent my part 9d. Spent after in paying Haggers bill at Maidenhead 6d. Spent at [Cold] Bath in the parler with Pridmor & Thos Sheath 2½ d, which came home togather.

Sunday 7th To Bramfield church in morning, [Little] Barkhamstead parson preached.[216] In afternoon to Jacks, Tewin. Spent 4d.

Wednesday 10th In the evening to Mrs Gears at Windmill, Waterford with Mr Randall who came from London in a wiskey and cal[l]ed on me to spend the evening with him at Waterford. Staid till ½ past 10. Spent 3s. Jack Frances came for me on poney.

Fryday 12 Evening to Tewin Jacks. Spent there with Thos Sheath 8d.

Saturday 13th Markets cheeper something. Went on foot. Dined at the Bull 2d (*second*) table 1s 4d. Spent there afterwards 6d. Spent after at Bulls Head, George Richardsons with Miller the chimney sweeper from London, & Reckett, Gear, Pridmore & Mr Ilott 1s 9d. Pridmor & I and Ilott came home togath[e]r one clock.

Sunday 14 Not to church but staid at home all day.

Tusday 16 To Ware on foot. Caried 10 qr barley to malting on 2 carts and Ned went with me to Ware with on[e] cart, brought back 5qr oates of Chamberling at 10s per quarter. Staid there all night. Spent there 1s.

---

[215] This is the first mention in the diary of Carrington paying rent to Lord Cowper. William Warren had sold Bacons Farm to Cowper in 1801 [HALS: DE/P/T24-25; DE/P/T2027].

[216] Robert Orme vicar of Little Berkhamsted from 1790 was also vicar of All Saints, Hertford, from 1786 until his death in 1843 [J E Cussans, *History of Hertfordshire*, vol 2 p165].

Wednesday afternoon [17] To Tewin. Spent at Jacks with Mr Scott, gardner at Henery Cowpers Esqr, Tewin Water new house finished in the year 1800. Spent 1s.

Saturday 20th Markets somthing dearer, best wheat 52s load. Went on foot. Dined at the Bulls Head with Hunsdon, Burges & Clapham &c 1s 4d. Spent after there 10d. Home with Pridmore & I rode Molding's horse.

Sunday 21 To Bramfield church, Bowger (*Bourchier*) preached. From thence to Goldings and dined there, from thence to Windmill, Waterford Mrs Gears. Spent there 7d.

Monday 22nd In afternoon went to Waterford Hall, Mr Poolls to settle with him, Mr Ilott went with me. Staid supper till 11 clock. Dark & dirty home. Gave the boy for my poney 3d.

Tusday 23 Went to Bramfield Place Farm to meet Mr Peacock but he not came. However I spent the day with Bassett & Smith & Jack & his son there.

Wednesday 24 In evening to the clubb at Hardingfordy (*Hertingfordbury*). Staid late and spent with young Hickman after 1s. Jack Frances came for me.

Fryday 2[6] In the evening to Tewin. Spent 3d.

Saturday 27 Markets something cheeper. To market on poney. Dined with Mr Archer, butcher, and Robrts of Bayfordbury, & Archer's brother at the Half Moon, Medcalfs on stakes, when I paid Archer's bill. Spent at Bull after with Cadmore 1s, at Richardsons d[itt]o 7d, ostler 4d.

Sunday 28 To Bramfield church. Afternoon to Tewin Jacks. Spent 3d.

MARCH Monday 1st To Tewin to the clubb. Gave the maid 3d. Gave Deaf Jammey 2d.

Tewsday 2d To Ware on poney. Saw the 4 stone coffens with bones in them found on Satturday the 27 of last month. Spent 6d.

Wednesday 3d To Ware on poney by Ware Park Mill. Saw the 4 stone coffens agane. Saw one of them opned & saw the forme of a skelliting (*skeleton*) in it. The large bones and skull all perished dust. Maney people there. They was found on Satturday last by diging a ditch across the field, the field is called Bury Field, about 60 pole from Magpy Corner & 70 steps up the field to the Ware Park Road.

Fryday 5th To Vestrey at Bramfield, Mr Hunsdon, Preston, Derds, Burges, & Thos Whittenbury, & Auston & Richardson there. Spent after vestrey 9d.

Saturday 6 To market on poney in afternoon, to the White Hart, Camps, to pay Knight for 3 load peas & I bought 4 load more. Spent there with Guttredge of Artick (*Haultwick, parish of Little Munden*), & Chapman and Mr Strutt came to me as had been to Ware to see the stone coffins 2s. Hostler 3d. Markets dearer on account of said going to warr againe and fitting our shipps out.[217]

Sunday 7th To Tewin church, & dined at Jacks, Tewin, with Mr Strutt, & met my constables there for presentments. Onley 3 there, Sheephall, Pauls Waldon & Bramfield, the other fined. Spent besides the fines 1s each.[218] Moulding came with me to White Gate.

Monday 8th To the Assizes on poney. Left him at Chapmans. Gave old Hall 6d. Gave young Chappman 6d. Spent at Richardsons 6d. Went to church, did my buisness & home erley. Judge Heath.

Tusday 9 To the Assizes. Sargant Best, a trying in one court, & Judge Heath in the other. Herd in Sargant Best court S[i]r Abrahams Hooms for housebraking, Lord Clarendon of Grove Park Watford, for steeling images, & the man for steeling the gray mare, and the man for steeling the barley, & selling it to Susanah Howard at the Checquers at Barley, she knowing it to be stolen.[219] Refir to the callender. Home erley went to Tewin. Spent the evening with Mr Strutt, at my sons & Thos Sheath. Spent [blank].

---

[217] A false alarm about war being renewed with France.

[218] Absent constables appear to have been fined, the fines being spent in beer for the rest [Branch Johnson, *'Memorandoms For...'*, p80].

[219] Hooms: Sir Abraham Hume, 2nd baronet (1749-1838), lord of the Manor of Wormley. Thomas Villiers (1753-1824), Earl of Clarendon. Thomas Barnes, Richard Dukes, John Nolan and Susannah Davis were involved in the theft of many items from Sir Abraham Hume's house at Wormley. Susannah admitted evidence against the three other defendants and was acquitted while the three men were sentenced to death. They were all repealed to life transportation. It is not known what happened to Barnes and Nolan but Dukes was sent to Australia in 1803 aboard the *Calcutta.* Thomas Lowe and Joseph Richards were accused of stealing 600lbs of lead from Lord

Wednesday 10 To clubb at [Green] Dragon on poney. Spent after clubb 5d. Gave hostler 2d.

Thursday 11 Evening to Tewin. Spent at Jacks with Mr Strutt, Mr Ilott, Mr Brooks & Squier, Simon & Watson. Staid late 2s 6d.

Fryday 12 Paid Joseph Barns for 44 pole of ditchen at 9d.	£1 13s 0d
And for 3,500 of quick at 8s 6d per thousand	£1 9s 6d
And for bushing some few poles	1s 6d
	£3 4s 0d

This new fence is between Bansleys & Grissells.

Saturday 13 Markets much the same. I sold some wheat today for 52s per load. Went on poney. Dined at Bull 1s 4d. Spent there after 3d. Spent at Richardsons 6d. Gave ostler 3d. Spent at Cooks Maiden Head after 6d. Home erley.

Sunday 14th Not to church. To Tewin afternoon. Spent 3d.

Monday 15th To Wotton turnpike meeting at Crawleys, White Horse. Paid £2 18s 6d for Bramfield parish. Commissioners there Dickinson, Byde, Dimsdall Esqrs, Kimpton, Blindall, Green, Caborn, Twinn, Brown, gen[tle]m[e]n &c, surveyors, Hall snr, Hall jnr, Butterfield, Bush, Vyguss, and &c. &c. Dinner sr lyon (*sirloin*) rost beef, fillett of veal, green ham, puding. Spent each man 3s. Came home with Butterfield to Stapleford. Spent there 6d. Home 11 clock, sharp frost night.

Tusday 16th To Ware on foot. Went to the Bull to the sale there, some pieces of land & cow leaces sold by Mr Dunn, auctioner. Spent with Thorp, near Amwell church and Cadmore, meeler (*meal man*) & Aylon at Eagle. Slept there. Spent 1s 3d. Home next day on foot.

Clarendon's property, the case being respited to the next Assizes where they were both acquitted. John Manning was charged with stealing a grey mare worth £14 at Chipping Barnet and was acquitted, while Susannah Howard had her case thrown out for receiving 56 pecks of barley stolen by Thomas Layton. Layton received 6 months gaol for the offence and was fined a shilling [Information from Ken Griffin; TNA: Hertford Assize records].

Wednesday Evening 17th Went with Mr Ilott to Sewills, White Horse Hardingfordbury. Staid there till 10 clock. Spent my part 2s. I went on poney, a clubb met there.

Thursday 18th To Tewin Water to see Mr Scott, gardner to Henery Cowper Esqr there, but found him not at home, but met him with Sheath, church clerk of Tewin as I was coming home. Went back with them to Jacks and spent with them & Simon, Pridmore, & Molding, 10d. Peggy Clarke very ill at Bacons. Very doubtfull of her life.[220]

Saturday 20 Markets cheeper something, all sorts dull in trade. Went on foot. Spent at Richardsons 3½d. Spent at Bull in little room by myself, onley Bush at last 6d. Came home with Little, who came with little cart for peas & flowr (*flour*).

Sunday 21 To Bramfield church in morning, Bourchier preached. Afternoon to Jacks at Tewin. Spent there with Mr Robbarts, Mr Baker's bayliff 6d.

Monday 22 Went to Tewin in the evening to Jacks, Mr Ilott being gon before. Spent there with him till 11 clock 2s 6d.

Tusday 23 Afternoon went on foot to Ware. Staid all night. Spent there & gave 1s 9d. Came home Wednesday 24 in the morning. Stopt at the gaol & went into the chappell & herd the sermon preached by Mr Moor to the 5 persons goaing to be hanged, viz John Nowland, Thos Barnes, Thos Wite, William Izzard, & Alexander Horress.[221] As see the callender. Went in the evening to the clubb Hardingfordbury with Mr Ilott. Spent there over the clubb … (*torn off*). Home 10 clock. Went on poney.

Saturday 27 Markets cheeper, best wheat 48s per load. Very remarkable fine hot wather, went on poney. Spent at the Falken with sister & Nancy Pierce from Ware 1s. Spent at Bull 6d. Spent at the [Cold] Bath as came home at Winters, with Pallet 1s. Smith the hun[t]sman came with me.

Sunday 28 To Tewin church, Mr Bourchier preached. Dined at Jacks. After dinner went to Burnamgreen to look at Pallet's place. Spent at the alehouse there kept by Burges 8d. Came back to Jacks and spent there with Pallet from

---

[220] Peggy Clarke, a visitor from London, is to remain ill at Bacons for another year.
[221] See also diary entry above dated 9 Mar 1802. Revd James Moore was chaplain at Hertford Gaol for 41 years, resigning in 1815 [*HCR* vol IX pxxiii].

Eason Green (*East End Green, Hertingfordbury*) & Pallet from Easenton (*Essendon*), Clapham & Smith 2s.

Tusday 30 To Bramfield wood sale. Mr Peacock from London sold the wood & Bassett. I bought 2 acres in Park Wood. Sold ½ acre againe to Uncle of Chopmerend *(Chapmore End)* and I bought 1 acre ½ againe the next day of Bassett in Park Wood. Spent at the wood sale first gathering 2s 6d. D[itt]o more 1s.

> And the peace being finely settled now and great rejoyceings at Lond[on] and Hartford &c this night, so I gave 3 pound of candles to Mrs Derds to illuminate her house 2s.[222] Spent more & gave 1s.

APRIL Saturday 3d Markets still cheapr, the best wheat at 46 shillings per load. Went to market on poney being Lent fair. Dined no ware. Stopt at Richardsons, Bulls Head, from thence to the Bull, from thence to the Cold Bath kep by one Winter. Spent in all & gave away and my own men came home with me, Smith & Spencer. Spent at Richardsons 1s. Spent at Bull 6d. Spent at [Cold] Bath with Pallett of Eason Green (*East End Green, Hertingfordbury*), & Robertson from Enfield, Pallett's uncle, at the Bath when the woman was there 1s. Smith & E[d]w[ar]d Spencer, my cowman came home with me.

Sunday 4 Went to church at Bramfield, Mr Bowcher (*Bourchier*) preached. After to Bedwell Park to see the fire that happned there on Fryday night the 2d about 9 clock supposed to be set on fire. The fire was burning, not still out. 6 reeks (*ricks*), 5 barns & all the stables & other offices totalley burnt down. Went on poney with Pallet from Eason Green. Spent at Esonton (*Essendon*) the Kings Head, Clerks 6d. Great number of people there indeed.

Tusday 6 To Ware on poney. Stopt at Bull there, one Browns, to see the auction of house to be sold on Hartford Heath by one Dunn. Spent there with Aylon, Page, & Hobbs, & wooden legg man, in punch & wine 2s. Spent at Hastlers & gave 1s.

Wednesday 7th In evening to the clubb Hardingfordbury on poney. Robarts went with me from Bacons, Mr Baker's bayley 6d.

---

[222] The Peace of Amiens was signed on 28 Mar 1802 and the candles were by way of a celebration.

Saturday 10 Markets dearer, small market. Best wheat about 48s per load. Went on poney, dined at Rose & Crown on stakes from Halen 10d. Spent at Ramseys 1s 6d at Bull & came home with Lord Cowper's groom at Panshanger 6d.

Sunday 11th Not to church but went to Goldings about Mr Ilott who left Bacons yesterday, from thence to Mrs Gears at Waterford, the Windmill. Spent & gave 1s 4d.

Tusday 13 To Ware on poney. Spent brother Haslers 1s. Stopt at Hartford coming home. Paid Veanus (?*Vigus*) for 80 bush[el] of ashes at 3 [per] bush[el]. Spent 3d.

Wednesday [14] To Ware on poney by Pirlivents at Beng[e]o for malt. Spent & gave the men 1s 8d. Herd at Ware of the fire at Bramfield, the workhouse. Came home imeadiatly. Met the engen and people from Hartford. All burnt down in a few [h]ours. I saw it but the engen kept it of the parson's barne so it spread no further.

Thursday 15 To Bramfield to see about the fire yesterday which burnt the workhouse. It was insured for £150. It had been built about 20 years, thatchd. Spent at Mrs Deardses with Hand, the glayser from Hartford 1s.

Saturday 17 Markets much the same. Went on poney. Staid late at Bull with Pridmore & Pallet of Easongreen (*East End Green*). Spent in all 3s.

Easter Sunday 18th To Tewin church. In the afternoon went to Tewin Water, Henery Cowper Esqrs to see Mr Lee the buttler, & Scott the gardner. Stayd supper. Gave for poney 6d.

Easter Monday 19th To Tewin in evening Jacks. Spent there with Hanken butcher and in the Vestrey Room the parler with Dean, Webb, Patient, Dolling &c &c 1s 4d.

Easter Tusday 20th To our Vestrey at Bramfield, Mr Hunsdon overseer, Mr Vaux chosen for the year ensuing, Jos Derds, church walden, Burges constable. Dinner rost ribbs beef, large legg of mutton &c. Staid there till 3 clock in the morning with Hunsdon & Allen. Spent & gave 9d.

Wednesday Evening the 21 To the clubb at Hardingfordbury, the White Horse. My clubb 6d.

Thursday 22 To Wotton on poney to their Easter vestrey to settle about the workhouse. Dined at the Bull, Wilshers, with Mr Kimpton & Cater, Crawley, Burr, Parish, Edmunds, Stockbridge, Pendred, Hall, Wheeler, &c. Spent nothing. Chipperfield took the workhouse.[223] Gave for poney 3d. Spent at Tewin Jacks as came home 6d.

Saturday [24] To market on poney. Markets cheapr, best wheat 44s per load. Spent at Bull 1s. D[itt]o at Vine, Mumfords 1d. Richardsons with Clopham 6d. Gave hostler 4d.

Sunday 25 Not to church but went to Braffen (*Braughing*) to see the 2 plous (*ploughs*) I bought by auction. Spent on the tenants at Widow Lawrences at the Ax & Compases 10d. Spent at Ware coming home 9d.

Tusday 27 To Harford to carry barley 5 qr from Bramfield. Met Claphams 5 qr there at 34[s]. Gave the men some beer at the Green Dragon, Baxters who entred the 5 of this month there. Cambell being gon to the Angell. 3 potts of beer 1s. It rained all the afternoon therefore I stayd longer & spent 1s 6d.

Thursday 29 Spent at Bramfield Wd Derdses 6d.

Fryday the 30 Went to Codicote & Whitwell with Geo Richardson in little cart to inspect the w[eigh]ts & ballances. Dined at Dicksons, the Bull at Whitwell. Stopt at the Goat, Codicote. Expences 8s. Took 1 w[eigh]t from Camp, baker d[itt]o 2 from Smith, Bendage (*Bendish*).

MAY Saturday May 1st Jorney to the Town Hall St Albans with Mr Hunsdon, & Burges the constable of Bramfield to appo[in]t overseers for the year ensuing, John Vaux for Bramfield. Justices there, Searanke, may[o]r, Vander Muling, Kinder, Clarke, &c, Cowper & Boyce, clerks. Dined at Redhouse, dinner 2s. Horse & hostler 8d. Spent at Jonas Langtons at Stanborough as came home 2s. We went that way, so came back d[itt]o.

Saturday the 1st Markets still cheeper, good wheat at 40s per load, barley 34s quarter, peas 24s per load, oates 23[s] per qr.

---

[223] The Bramfield poor were temporarily lodged at Watton, where the workhouse was farmed by Chipperfield [Branch Johnson, *'Memorandoms For…'*, p80].

Sunday the 2d Not to church but went a walking with Mr Buttrey & Miss Scott as was.[224] They came from London to see us. In the afternoon I went part of the way to Hatfield with them, as they went that way for London. Came back to Jacks Tewin and spent there with Thorowgood, butcher from Ware & Geo[rge] Aylon till 9 clock 2s. Thorowgood came to Bacons with me & slept there, Aylon went home to Ware.

Monday 3 To Tewin clubb. Spent in ginn & water 1s.

Tusday 4 To Goldings in afternoon for the Land Tax. John Smith treated me with 1 bottle of old Mountane wine 33 years old.

Wednesday 5 Evening to White Horse, Hardingfordbury to clubb. 2 Hickmans & Moumford there 6d.

Fryday 7 To Ware on poney to the Bull, to pay taxes. Paid Mr Byde of Ware Park the recever £130 towards the Land, & Income Tax & all others for 1801. Onley Esqr Byde [&] Pierson there. Dined at Eagle with Mr Munns, Mr Iardale baker, Mr Samms & Geo Richardson. Spent each 3s. Gave ostler 3d.

Saturday 8 Small market rather dearer, best wheat about £2 2s per load. Went to market on poney. Dined at Richardsons Bull Head diner & spent there 1s 6d. Went from thence to the Bull, paid Clopham for 5 qr of barley at 34s qr & spent there with Mr Ilott, Tice, Clopham, Cadmore & Moton in gin & water 3s.

Sunday 9 To Bramfield church, Mr Newton of Tewin preached there. Afternoon to Jaks Tewin, spent there with Chapman & son & Forster from Hartford 6d.

Monday 10th Afternoon to Bramfield, Preston, Derds, Burges, & Hunsdon a vestrey. I staid all night with Hunsdon & Burges. Spent over the vestrey in gin & water 1s.

Tusday 11 Afternoon went to Tewin, to see after, Lowin, Lilley, & 2 Leevers, & Aylott & Chalkley, for their assalt to the W[i]d[ow] Derds, & breaking her windows, on Saturday night last, whome they met at her house this evening &

---

[224] Buttrey was the landlord of the Black Bear, Piccadilly. Mary Scott had become Mrs Buttrey – see diary entry dated 13 July 1802 below.

paid her 10s 6d, for damage.[225] It was done as they came from Waterford, a hunting a badger there, as they came by to Tewin. Spent 6d. Coz Thos Beck, & John as was at Mrs Goodalls came the 11th.

Wednesday 12 Clubb fiest, at Tewin. Spent there with Coz Thos Beck & John as was at Mrs Goodalls after I left the clubb 1s.

Thursday 13th To Tewin in afternoon with Coz Beck & John d[itt]o d[itt]o. Spent at the Fathers Upper Green 6d. D[itt]o at Jacks 1s.

Fryday 14 Gave Peacock for W[i]d[ow] Smi[th] which lost her horse 2s. Coz Beck & John left Bacons for London.

Saturday 15th Markets much the same, best wheat about £2 2s. Went to market on poney, went to the sale at the White Hart, of that 2 tenements near the Feather, Tew[i]n Upper Green late carpenter Oakleys. Sold by John Jaques of North Hall (*Northaw*). I bought it for £73. Spent there & at Ramses, & Bull &c 3s. Came home with Deaff Jimmey.

Sunday 16 Not to church, but w[e]nt to Ware on foot to dinner at Haslers with Mr Sussum & his wife, & his foreman, Jacks marster from London, taylers. They went after dinner to Esqr Bakers to see the hott house.[226] I met them in Hartford as I came home by 8 clock. Spent 2s.

Tusday 18 To Ware on poney. Saw the woman stand in the pillery at Magpye Corner at Ware, for allmost starving a girll about 7 years old to death. It was her husband's child.[227] She was mother in law. Dined at brother Haslers & spent 1s 1d.

---

[225] Carrington has arranged for this dispute to be settled by mutual agreement without going to court.

[226] A sale catalogue dated 1773 for Hertingfordbury Park, the home in 1802 of Samuel Baker, states that 'there are two hot walls, 2 pineries … a green house' etc [HALS: DE/Bk/C11/1]; at Bayfordbury or Bayford Park on the south side of the River Lea, the home in 1802 of Samuel's brother William Baker MP also had a fine kitchen garden with 'numerous forcing houses, pits and frames' [Bagenal, *Hertingfordbury Park*].

[227] Elizabeth wife of William Horton of Ware, labourer, for assaulting and starving her infant daughter in law (ie step daughter) Alice Horton. She was to stand in the pillory for an hour opposite her dwelling house on market day, and was also imprisoned in a solitary cell in Hertford Bridewell for 6 months [*HCR* vol IX p35].

Wednesday evening [19] To the clubb at Hardingfordbury, Phipps, Chesher, Gardner & other Phipp, & Hanken there. Home erley, onley the clubb money 6d.

Fryday 21 Spent at Tewin Jacks when attended old Thos Sewills funerall to the church from the Upper Green, over & above the clubb allowance 4d.

Saturday 22 Jorney to St Albans to the White Hart to appoint assessors of Land & other Taxes. Whent on poney by Stanborough, came home the same. Dined at Red House, dinner & spent 3s. Spent at White Hart 1s. Commissioners there, Howerd, Kentish, Kinder, & Cowper, clerk. Corne & hostler 8d.

Saturday 22d Markets dearer, bes[t] wheat 47s per load.

Sunday 23 To dinner at Mrs Raymonds at the George, Codicote with Mr Merriott from Graves End, & another gent[lema]n & Capt[ain] Luse, Mr Dolling, Mrs Luse, & Mrs Howard. A fillett of veal & nuckell d[itt]o, bacon & puding. Mr Merriott's treat. Hostler 6d.

Tusday 25 Evening to Jacks Tewin. Spent with John Tingy, which sailed round the world with Capt[ain] Walless in the year [17]61 & 62.[228] Spent 3d. Gave Bluitt at workhouse 6d.

Wednesday 26 Spent the night at Windmill, Warterford with Mr Randall, & his brother Simon, & Mr Pool. Mr Randall treated.

Thursday 27 Spent at Mrs Derdses, Bramfield at vestrey about rebuilding the poor house. Vaux, overseer, Hunsdon &c there 1s 6d. Staid all night.

Saturday 29 Markets dearer, small market. Went on poney. Spent at White Hart 6d, at Richardsons Bulls Head 3d. Spent at Bull when Preston paid me for turnops and the steers & all he owd me, in companey with Dunn of Ware, Hudson, Pamfling, linnen draper, & Hide 7s in wine. I treated Preston & gave him back 7s.

Sunday 30 To Bramfield church. Afternoon to Tewin. Spent by myself 3d.

---

[228] Captain Samual Wallis (1728-1795) sailed around the world in the *Dolphin* between 1766 and 1768, discovering Tahiti and the Society Islands [Glyndwr Williams, 'Wallis, Samuel (1728-1795)' *ODNB*, Jan 2008].

JUNE Tusday 1 A thanksgiven & churching for the peace throuout England. To Ware on poney by Bengeo. Carried Purlivent some wood there. Spent at the Bulls Head at Ware, Lewings with Butterfield 6d. Spent at Eagle & slept there 2s. Gave Will Frances & maid 1s.

Wednesday 2d To the clubb at Sewills, Hardingfordbury my clubb money & gave 8d.

Thursday 3 To Lord Cowper's rent fiest at Mr Palletts, his steward at Colegreen a good dinner & plenty of good liquer & tea. Gave John the wa[i]ter 6d. Gave 2 maids 1s. Gave Crawley for great coat for a great thunder shower 6d. Frances came for me on (*page torn*).

Fryday 4th In evening to Jacks at Tewin. Spent by self 3d.

Saturday 5 To market on the poney. Dined at the Bull, Mrs Thomases, dinner 1s 4d. Spent in little room after with Osburn, & Parker, Hagger & Charmberlin from Ware 1s. Spent at Angell with Chors 3d. Spent at Bulls Head, Richardsons with Charles Cate 7d. Gave hostler 4d. Stopt at Chapmans & paid him for 2 sacks of flowr (*flour*) & pollard and gave his son Joseph 6d. Markets much the same as last. I sold som at 45s load. Home by self 11 clock.

Sunday 6 To Tewin church, Mr Newton preached the text Mathew 12 chap 31 & 32 verses.[229] The afternoon to Ware, to see Cozs Cooks as came by Ware coach over night, & went home in a chaise this afternoon. Spent 1s.

Witten Monday 7 To Tewin in the afternoon Jacks & being clubb night spent & gave 1s 6d.

Tusday 8 To Tewin Jacks. Spent in companey with a Mr Jakes, who came from London, to agree with Mr Pridmore school marster at Tewin, for a child of his to come to schoole with him at Tewin as he took boarders 3d.

---

[229] Matthew ch 12 verses 31-2: 'Wherefore I say unto you, all manner of sin and blasphemy shall be forgiven unto men: but the blasphemy against the Holy Ghost shall not be forgiven unto men. And whosoever speaketh a word against the Son of man, it shall be forgiven him: but whosoever speaketh against the Holy Ghost, it shall not be forgiven him, neither in this world, neither in the world to come'.

Wednesday 9 To Tewin to the Rose & Crown Jacks, to recive the levy money. Mr Wellingham for Pauls Walden, Mr Salt for Norton, Mr Clerke for Codicot was all that met me. Dinner eggs & bacon. Spent my part 4s. Went from thence to the clubb at Green Dragon Hartford as being q[ua]r[ter]ly night on poney. Spent nothing. Gave hostler 3d. Came home with Simon Worby.

Thursday 10th To Tewin to smoke a pipe in evening with Capt[ai]n Loose, & Mr Dolling at Jacks. I treated them in ginn & water & 2 tankets (*tankards*) beer 3s, till ½ p[a]st 9.

Saturday 12th Market on poney, from thence to Ware to see John Aylon as being very ill. Dined at brother Haslers. Spent at Richardsons & at Bull as came back & hostler at Hartford 1s 6d, and at Green Dragon with Mr Chapman 1s. Markets much the same, the best wheat 47s per load.

Sunday 13th To Bramfield church. After dinner to Tewin. Spent at Whittenburys the Feathers at the Upper Green 6d. Spent at Jacks at the Lower Green with John Molden, Brux and Chamberlin from Hartford 1s.

Monday 14th Spent at Jacks at the Rose & Crown, Tewin with brother Hasler, & Mr Sissum from London who came over night to Bacons and went home this evening 1s 6d. We dined at Jacks. Swopt my poney for one other poney of butcher Smith of Codicote at the Rose & Crown, Tewin. Gave him 3 guineas ½ to boot.

Tusday 15th Went to Hartford in afternoon, was pres[s]ed to go to the Angell Mr Cambells as they was a canvessing the town for the Hon[oura]ble Spencer Cowper.[230] I had severall glasses of wine to drink success. Spent 1s. Spent at Gears as went for Pollard 5d. Home by 10 but left the town crasey.

Wednesday 16 To the clubb at Hardingfordbury. Spent over & above as recivd Mullett in againe & Smith paid me for straw £3 12s 0d, & Hanken the butcher paid me for 2 calves £7 10s 0d, & he told me that he sent 6 joynts of one of them & the head to the Duke of Bridgewater's at Woollmers for he bought that, & this day he came there and the bells was a ringing for him. I herd them. Woollmers was late Whitbreads.[231] Clubb & spent 1s 1d. Gave

[230] Parliamentary election for the Borough of Hertford. See diary entry for 6 July below.

[231] Woolmers Park, Essendon, was purchased by Francis Egerton, Baron Ellesmere, Marquis of Brackley, 8th Earl and 3rd and last Duke of Bridgewater from the brewer

Hanken's girl 1s. Shore my sheep 83. Shearers Thos Sewill, Geo[rge] Grant, Sparks & Wiggs. A very fine hot day.

Thursday 17 Afternoon to vestrey at Bramfield to settle to build the workhouse which was burnt 3 months back. Vaux overseer there & Mr Preston, Mr Hunsdon, & Joseph Derds, churchwalden & myself. Staid very late.

Fryday 18 To Esqr Mackeys at Marden to pay Malden his baylef (*bailiff*) for 2 load of peas money £2 16s 0d. Staid till 8 clock, had plenty of good sider (*cider*). He had company Revd Bourchier, Revd Thos Loyd, Cap[tai]n Jud.

Saturday 19 To market on my new poney. Dined at Bull, diner 1s 4d. Spent after there in barr 6d. Spent at Bulls Head when I paid Chapman for 1 sack flowr (*flour*) £2 11s and he paid me for 4 load wheat at 45s per load, 1s. Spent at Cold Bath as came home with Chapman 1s, hostler & gave away 10d. Markets rather cheeper, best wheat about 46s per load.

Sunday 20th To church at Bramf[iel]d. In evening to Pansanger Lord Cowpers, was entertained by the groom Mr Robarts & smoked severall pipes with him in the servants' hall till 9 at night. Good beer stale. Fuddled this time. Drank 20 hornes.

Monday 21 Afternoon to Cole Green Mr Palletts. Settled with him for the wood I bought at Pansanger & Bushes all £22. From thence to Jacks Rose & Crown, Tewin. Spent with Geo[rge] Passell & Aylott, the timber hewer from Hartford 1s 6d.

Thursday 24 To clubb fiest at Green Dragon, Hartford. John & I came home on foot togather. Spent after fiest 6d.

Fryday 25 Went on poney to Bayford Bury. Dined with Mr Robarts, from thence to Brickendon Ricketts, from thence Hartford Heath, from thence to

---

Samuel Whitbread in 1801 for £16,502.10s. He then commissioned the architect James Lewis to alter the house [H Malet, *Bridgewater, The Canal Duke, 1736-1803* (Manchester, 1977) pp159-160]. James Lewis (1751-1820) was surveyor to Christ's Hospital and was responsible for the dining hall and infirmary at the Hertford Girls' School in 1800 [H Colvin, *A Biographical Dictionary of British Architects, 1600-1840* (1978)].

Green Dragon at Hartford. Spent there 6d. Gave Robartses boy 2d. Home by 8 clock. Little fuddled last night.

Saturday 26 Journey to St Albans to meet Comm[i]s[sio]n[e]rs of Land & other Taxes to the assessments to sighn. Commisioners there at the White Hart, Charl[e]s Bourchier, Kentock, & Emmott, Cowper & Piggott, clerks. Dined at Redhouse with Parker from Sheephall & Woodfield from Hexton. Diner 2s, ½ p[ec]k corne 10d, hostler 4d. Went in little cart with Sall & little Jack. Spent & gave more 6d.

Sunday 27 To church. Afternoon to Tewin round by Okenvaley Bottom to see the road. Spent 3d.

Tusday 29 To Ware on poney in the afternoon. Spent at brother Haslers with one John Coe from Dunmore (*Dunmow, Essex*) who had been to Codicote and with Mr John Aylon 9d. Gave Will Frances 2d. Home by 7 clock.

Wednesday 30th To the clubb at Hardingfordbury in evening, a full company. Spent over and above the clubb 6d, [h]ostler 1d. Home by 10 clock. Got drunk last night.

> Electtinearing (*electioneering*) now all over the kingdom, the King and familey are gon down to Waymouth (*Weymouth, Dorset*) the mean time.

JULY Saturday the 3d To market in little cart & carried my wooll to Scates at Hodesdon 8 todd 5 p[oun]d. Recd £13 on acpt (*account*). Spent at the Maidenhead there, one Coomses, with Hale, blacksmith there 8d. Gave Scate's man 6d. Brought Samms from Hodsdon in my cart to Hartford. Spent at the Bull with Mr Wm Blindall from Wellwin & Mr Squier &c 1s 6d. Spent at [Green] Dragon with Ben Sq[uie]r 6d. Ben Squier came home with me. Gave hostler 6d. Markets rather dearer.

Sunday 4 to Tewin church on poney. With Steven in the afternoon to Tewin Jacks. Spent with Thos Sheath and Grimes the blacksmith in gin & water & beer 1s 6d.

Monday 5 To the clubb Tewin. Spent over the clubb with Auston, stonemason [of] Hartford & John Sheath church clerk who had being to Tewin church to put a stone down for Miss Liticia Mackey 3d.

Tusday 6 To Hartford on foot to the Borough Election when Spenser Cowper & Calver[t] of Hunsdon House, were chosen without aney opisition. The late members were Nathaniell Barron Dimsdale, & John Calvert of Albery (*Albury*) Hall Esqr which both resigned as soon as they was cheaird. I left the town about 1 clock.

Wednesday 7th Went to the town of Hartford, the nomination for members for the county on poney. Met Plomer & his companey at the goal. Rode into the field with them up Castle Street a medow belonging to Mr Neall at the Great Brick House. No oppisition so Plumer & Baker which served before was putt up again. No housen in town open for entertainment so we returnd soon. I came round with Mr Ba[ker] to his house & dined there, with Mr Bigg his buttler, & howsekeepr Mrs Ward, & Mr Kinsey garde[ner].[232]

Thursday 8 In afternoon to Ware in cart with poney. John Beck jnr went with me. Carried a sack of flowr (*flour*) to sister Haslers. Bro[ught] my grist and bran from mill. Spent with John Aylon (*manuscript torn*).

Saturday 10 No market as being the electtion day for the county. Rode with Mr Mackey & his son Thos & Burges to Mr Bakers to breakfast, from thence into the field. When Plumer, Baker & Peneston Lamb stood the pool (*poll*) but not over today.

Sunday 11 Went to Luton Hooe the Marques of Boots (*Bute*), with sun John to see Lord Henery Boote (*Bute*) which, about a month past, was maried to Lady Gartwood (*Gertrude*) Villers. Was admited to see them in the librey (*library*), the finest room I ever saw. From thence to Stockwood, Esqr Crawleys.[233] Dined there. Came home by Harden (*Harpenden*), went by

---

[232] William Baker (1743-1824) of Bayfordbury served as MP for the Borough of Hertford 1780-1784 and for the county 1790-1802, and 1805-1807. He had been critical of the introduction of the Income Tax and opposed the Treaty of Amiens as being too lenient to France. However Carrington declares that it was very much a local issue which lost him his seat – see diary entry for 12 July below. He was an officer of the Herts yeomanry until 1810 [R G Thorne, *The House of Commons, 1790-1820 Vol III Members A-F* (History of Parliament Trust, 1986) and HALS: DE/Bk/C38/2-11].

[233] Luton Hoo was purchased in 1763 by John Stuart, Earl of Bute (1713-1792) who enlarged the park and rebuilt the mansion to designs by Robert Adam; 'The house [at Stockwood, Luton, Bedfordshire] built by John Crawley about 1740 is a rectangular brick building with stone dressings, of two stories and an attic, with a balustraded

Kimpton on poney. Spent 2s. Mr Scott farmer, & his wife houskeepr to the Marquess of Boot, Mr Yardley farms the park, Mr Heath bayleff, Clopham butler to Crawley.

Lady Gertrude Villiers, after a miniature by Richard Cosway, 1810
(*Private collection*)

---

parapet and hipped roof. The principal entrance is on the north-east, under a pillared portico, and the central bays of the east and south fronts are set forward slightly from the general wall-face. The house has a central hall with a stair on the west side, and to the west, or more accurately, north-west, lie the offices and stables. The garden is on the south and west, and running due northwards from a point in front of the house is a fine avenue.' [*VCH Bedfordshire* vol 2 (1908), pp348-375].

Monday 12 Begun the pool (*poll*) againe & the pool closed about 6 clock and Baker near 300 behind Lamb. So he gave it upp, & Plumer of Gilston, & Lamb of Brocket Hall was cheared as members for this county.[234] There was no open housen for treating this time, so every freeholder bore his own expences. Baker had served 2 sessions of Parliament for the county before, with Plumer, & a very good man, but he gave his vote in the house for a new tax on malt of 8s per q[ua]rt[e]r which gave a dislike to the mal[t]sters of Ware and other places & they all voted against him. Baker gave no entertainement ... house at Bayford Hall (*Bayfordbury*) the nominat[ion] morning but thought himself sa[fe] & the election morning in the field they brought Lamb which .... "Lamb for Ever No Baker Out" (*manuscript is torn at edge).*

[Tues]day 13th To London on poney. Got there ½ p[a]st 10, went to the Bank with Cos Beck. Took dividends & sold out 200 in the 3 per cent consoladated at £73 5s 8d. From thence to Cooks, from thence home to Becks. Slept there. Next day to see Follett, & Land[lord] Nickolds & Dr Nevertons which married Mrs Moody.[235] Dined there, from thence to Mary Scotts as is Mrs Buttrey, from thence to the Hole in the Wall with Land[lord] Nickolds & Coz Thos Beck. Staid there with Mr Strutt till 12. Supt on sammon. Slept at Becks. Next morning set off for home to St Albans Quarter Sessions. From St Albans home by 10 at night. My horses expences in London at the Bear & Staff, Smithfield 4s 2d. Gave ostler 6d. Horses expence at St Albans 6d. Gave ostler there 6d. Spent & gave in London 4s 6d. Spent at St Albans & diner 2s 6d. Paid the levy money this [d]ay at St Albans to Boyse £120. Receved my fee, & afterwards ... to the gentlemen at the White Hart, Esqr Searanke may[o]r. ... Donvell, &c &c and receved order for 7 ginueas for [examin]ing w[eigh]ts & ballances paid (*manuscript torn*).

---

234 William Plumer (1736-1822), MP for Hertfordshire 1768-1807; Peniston Lamb (1770-1805), MP for Hertfordshire 1802-1805; eldest son of Sir Peniston Lamb, 1st Viscount Melbourne and brother of William Lamb later Queen Victoria's Prime Minister; captain Herts yeomanry cavalry from 1794.

235 Landlord Nicholls of the Pewter Platter, St John's Street, London EC1, then of the Bunch of Grapes, Smithfield, later of the Bell, Tottenham. St John's Street was the starting point of the main road north out of London from Smithfield via the Angel [Weinreb et al, *London Encyclopaedia*]. Charles Moody had left Bramfield Rectory (which he rented) in 1799, dying very soon afterwards in Essex – see diary entries for Sep 1799 above. His widow has now remarried.

Fryday [16th] Evening to Tewin Jaks. Spent there when Ben Squier & Willm Watson playd at the 4 corners for legg of motten.[236] Squier beat 5d.

Sunday 18th Dined at Ware at sister Haslers with Cozs Cooks & the new maried daughters & sons in law from London. Dinner & gave 3s 3d. Spent after with Mr Aylon & Clapham, 1s 6d. They set off for London in a coach & post chaises, & chier (*?chair*) about ½ p[a]st 5 clock. I home by 9 clock.

Saturday 24 Markets much the same, best wheat 46s per load. To market on foot. Spent at Falkon with Mr Gripp[er], Aylon and Ilott, in the auction room when the grass & corne was selling by Ramsey 1s. Spent at Spratts Little Bell as came home with Fletcher 1s. As I came home found Stoten by the Seal Farme, brought him home with me.

AUGUST Sunday 22d To Bramfield church in foor noon, from thence to Esqr Emmetts at Goldings to see Mr Smith, the buttler. Dined there, the cook's father there from London. In the evening to Tewin. Spent there at Jack[s], with Moulding, Pridmore, & Grimes &c 2s 6d.

Wednesday 25 To clubb at Hardingfordbury. Spent there over & above 6d.

Saturday 28 To market in little cart to carry a grist to mill. Staid while ground. Came home early to barley cart. Spent at Richardsons & gave hostler 1s 4d. Markets cheeper. Very small market, & very fine wather. Mostley done wheat harvest, few buyers.

Sunday 29 To Tewin church in the morning. After diner to Bramfield church. From thence to Tewin Rose & Crown. Spent with Mr French & French the blacksmith, & Balls [Park] gardner 1s. Gave Webb of Burnam Green 2 pints, 6d. Spent in beer with young Patientt and Ambrose Tayler &c 6d.

SEPTEMBER Fryday the 3d Finished harvest. Good cropp. Afternoon spent at Mrs Derdses with son John & Wilkins from London 6d and gave my men beer, 1s 3d.

---

[236] A form of bowling, four ninepins being placed in a square. See Glossary for more detailed information [Joseph Strutt, *Sports and Pastimes of the People of England; including the rural and domestic recreations, May-games, mummeries, pageants, processions, and pompous spectacles, from the earliest period to the present time* (1845 edition), p273].

Saturday the 4th To market in little cart, carried a grist to mill. From thence to Ware, Mary Ann with me. Braught Nancy Pierce back with us to our harvest home to night, home forward with the grist. Markets much the same, best wheat about 44s per load. Spent at Ware 6d. Spent at Hartford, Richardsons 6d. Jack & Mr Dolling, brother Hasler, George & Pridmore at the harvest home. Buttock, & 5 ribbs of beef, a hamm, pudings & pye &c &c.

Sunday 5 Not to church, but in afternoon to Tewin Jacks. Spent there with coz Pierce & his wife 1s.

Wednesday 8 Went to Sheephall (*Shephall*). Gave old Grimes 6d. Gave Parker's maid 6d. Came home by Tewin. Saw Ashley & Miles at my sons. Rode in Miles shay (*chaise*) to the clubb Hartf[o]rd. Came home in Thowrowgood's cart. Spend over clubb 3d.

Saturday 11 Markets rather dearer. I sold 3 load to day new wheat for 45s 6d per load. Jorney to St Albans on poney with Burges, the Licensing Day at the Town Hall. Esqr Searank may[o]r, Justices Donvell, Emmott &c &c there, Cowper & Boys the clerks. Dinner 2s. Spent after 1s. Spent at Stanmore (*Stanborough*) at the Horse & Groom Jonas Langtons as came home 7d.

Sunday 12th Not to church, but went to Ware in little cart with Mary Ann & Nany Pierce. Slept there. Next day went in little cart to Wantham X (*Waltham Cross*) with brother Hasler to renew his licens.[237] Came back to Ware to dinner with Cockell, Aylon, Walker his bondmen (*ie apprentices*). This was the time when Haress thretned to take away his lic'ns. Came home on the evening. Spent 1s 6d. Justices there S[i]r Geo Prescote, & Esqr ?Newjek, & Jessep, the clerk. We met Plumer agoing to dinner with them at the X.

Wednesday 15 Afternoon to Tewin. Spent at Jacks with Deaff Jimmey 6d. Gave W[i]d[ow] Culver 1s. It was the evening the women met in the orchard to play for a goose.

Thursday 16 To Tewin afternoon Upper Green a crickett match between the maried & single men. The mar[ied] beat 14 notches. Spent on the Green with

[237] Carrington is supporting his brother in law at the Licensing Sessions in the renewal of his licence to sell beer at his Public House the Eagle in Ware.

old Squier & Dolling 3d. 11 of a side the loosers 3s. The winners 1s to be spent.

Fryday 17 To dinner at Tewin Upper Green at the F[e]athers, Jos Whittenburys, with Mr Dean of Tewin Bury, Mr Webb of Tewin Hill, Mr Dolling baker, Mr Brooks, Mr Thorowgood blacksmith Tewin Upper Green, Mr Pridmore schoolmaster, Mr Thos Whittenbury Quino (*Queenhoo*) Hall, son John [and] Mr Bowley butcher. Large leg mutton & beef stakes, the Dean brought 2 bottles of ginn. Spent each 4s.

Saturday 18 To market on poney. Markets cheeper ½ crown. I sold 5 load at 43s per load. Dined no ware, went Neals the law[y]ers about Jack's buisness. Spent at Bull after with Ilott 1s 3d. Gave hostler 4d. Came home by Bramfield but did not stopp.

Sunday 19 To Tewin church. A charity sermon preached for the Sunday School by the Revd John Hey DD Rector of Passenham, Northamtonshire. Gave 2s 6d. Afternoon to Datchworth to see Titmus bricklayer. Spent at Tilbrey with Bennet 6d.[238] After to son John Tewin 6d.

Monday 20th To Wotton Statute. Dined at Wiltshers the Bull. Dinner 2s. Spent after with Waller from Ware & Tayler &c in the great room 1s. Spent after at Parkers White Lyon with Mr Stevens from Ware & Davis from the George, Hodsdon (*Hoddesdon*) 1s. Spent after at Widow Derds at the Grandisons Arms Bramfield as I came home as beer for my men 1s 3d. Gave away 6d.

On Tusday the 21 assended in a b[a]loon at London, Garneron about 5000 feet high and then cut with his knife the strings that fastned his carr that he sat in from the balloon and came down to the earth with a parachute over his head un hurt to save his fall.[239]

---

[238] In Carrington's time the Tilbury public house at Datchworth was a sixteenth century building situated near the church, not the present building on Datchworth Green. It was owned by the parish, the landlord regularly paying rent to the overseers of the poor. It was purchased in 1837 by William and Joseph Lucas, brewers of Hitchin [Prowle and Walker, *A History of Datchworth*, p83].

[239] Frenchman Andre-Jacques Garnerin (1769-1823) was probably the first man to descend from a balloon by parachute and gave many demonstrations in France and Europe. As Carrington records here, in 1802 Garnerin made a spectacular jump in England; in fact it was from 8,000 feet (2,440 m) [*Encyclopedia Britannica*, online

Wednesday 22 To the clubb in evening Hardingfordbury. Home by 9 clock. Clubb 1s. 2 nights.

Thursday 23d To Codicot Statute at Mrs Alveys at the Goat. 20 dined dinner each person 2s 6d. Spent after 3s. Good companey. I came away about 8 clock. Dined in a booth by the side of the barne by the road. A clarenet & french horne. I went round by Kneboth (*Knebworth*) and called on Mr Jones & Revd Prist Jones dined with me, ribbs of rost beef, fillett of veal, ham & fowls, pudings & pies &c.

Saturday the 25 To Waltham Abby (*Essex*) fair with John Moulding, Mr Makey's bayleff of Mardon to buy some bullocks but b[ou]ght none so dear. Spent there, and dinner at the ... Hound 3s 6d. Spent coming a long with John Devenshir home at the Crown & Thistle his house & at the [Green] Dragon 1s 6d. The wheat markets cheeper.

Sunday 26 To Bramfield church afternoon, Mr Bourchier preached.

Monday 27 To Giningsbury (*Jenningsbury*) sale. Lord John Townsend purchased the farm so Cherry the tennant left.[240] Bought 1 cow for £11 10s, heffer for £9.

On Wednesday 29 Was plaid a match at crickett, on Tewin Uper Green, between Benj[ami]n Squier & Bayley of Codicot on one side, (and Joseph Hickman & Woodhouse of Hartford braiser on the other side) for 2 ginues (*guineas*). Squier & Bayley beete them & memerandom I plid after they had done after dinner on the Lower Green, with Chesher, church clark at Hardingfordbury for 2s 6d.[241] And I beete Chesher 6 noctches single wicket, & won of Hardingfordbury men 15s. Spent at dinner whome 12 dined at Jacks 5s. Leg moton boyled, sholder rost, pudings &c &c. Memorandom this

---

verions: http://www.britannica.com/EBchecked/topic/226079/Andre-Jacques-Garnerin]. In 1785 another Frenchman, Blanchard, had dropped a dog by parachute.

[240] The estate of Little Amwell with Jenningsbury was held by Henry Dunster, who died on 23 Aug 1791. In accordance with Henry Dunster's will the manor was sold to George Townshend, Earl of Leicester, from whom it was purchased by Lord John Townshend of Balls Park, Hertford [*VCH Hertfordshire* vol 3, pp409-414]. Jenningsbury was subsequently pulled down by Townsend - see Carrington's note at the end of 1803. The present house at Jenningsbury is surrounded by the remains of a moat, possibly medieval in origin.

[241] John Chesher was the church clerk at Hertingfordbury [HALS: DP50/8/2].

29 of Sepr 1802 sold Mr Hanken the field of turnops by Mr Bourcher's garden, at 2 ginuas per acre, & some in Buckell Hill at 2 d[itt]o per acre by measure ment.

Thursday 30 Spent at the F[e]athers Tewin on Tayler bricklayr & laborer when came this day to mend the tyling at the house I bought, late Oakleys, 1s 6d. And memarandom this day the water was let out of May Pond as going to be cleaned by Mr Dean, Tewin Burry.

> In the year 1715 on the 22 day of April was the greatest eclipps of the sun ever known. It begun at 8 clock in the morning and lasted till past 10. The sun totally dark & the starrs appeared.[242]

OCTOBER Saturday 2d To market on poney, Jack Frances with cart with 4 load of wheat. Sold the wheat at 40s per load. Went to Ware to dinner, came back to the Bulls Head to take the money for the wheat. Came home with Mr Pridmore & Thos Sheath. Spent in all 2s. Markets cheeper, barley about 30s, peas 25s, oates 22s q[ua]rter.

Sunday 3d To Bramfield church, the service preformd by Vauxes brothr in law. The text Micah 6 chap 8 verce.[243] Afternoon to Tewin. Spent with Odall from Wotton & Mr Dean & son & Simon, Brux, Pridmore, & Scott, who left Tewin Water as gardner 1s 4d.

Monday 4th To the clubb at Tewin. Spent over 3d.

Wednesday Evening 6th To the clubb Hardingfordbury with Richard & Roberts from Pansanger. Clubb money & gave 7d.

Thursday the 7 The great crickett match on Tewin Upper Green, Ware against the County for 11 guines. But the County beat Ware people allmost

---

[242] Halley wrote about this eclipse in Edmund Halley, 'Observations of the Late Total Eclipse of the Sun on the 22d of April Last Past, Made before the Royal Society at Their House in Crane-Court in Fleet-Street, London', *Philosophical Transactions*, 29, (1714-1716), pp245-262.

[243] Micah ch 6 verse 8: 'He hath shewed thee, O man, what is good; and what doth the Lord require of thee, but to do justly, and to love mercy, and to walk humbly with thy God?'.

the first innings. A fine day, & suposed to be 1500 people there. Panshanger farme house & barnes &c puld down this mo[n]th, late Phipps.

Fryday 8 To Ware on poney. Spent at brothr Haslers 1s. Gave 3.

Saturday 9th To market on poney. Had 10 she[e]p there. Sold them to Mr Paresses, steward on the Chace (*Enfield*) near the Bald Fase Stagg for 20 ginues (*guineas*). Sold 4 load of wheat at 39s per load. Went to the Falken, saw Archers Green sold by Ramsey to Elless for £297.[244] Spent with Baker & others at Bull &c 4s.

Sunday 10 To Bramfield church. Afternoon to Tewin Bury, from thence to Tewin with Mr Dean. Spent there at Jacks with Dean, Sheath & Pridmore 1s 6d.

Monday 11th Mr Bourcher set of for France.[245]

Saturday 16 Markets much the same, wheat best 44s, barley 30s, oates 24s qr, peas 31s per load. Jorney to St Albans to the Town Hall to appoint surveyors, Esqr Do[m]vell, & Clerk justices, Boyce, clerk & Cowper. Dined at Red House. Dinner 2s. Spent after 1s. ½ p[ec]k corne & hostler 1s 2d. Went on Dimon by turnpike. Came home same by Tewin.

Sunday 17th Not to church, but went on poney afternoon to Woollmer Green Mrs Crows at Red Lyon to recive a years rent, which she paid. Staid late with Butcher, Bolley & the 2 Wheelers, Bassetts & the 2 Smiths. Spent & gave 5s.

Wednesday 20 Afternoon to Hardingfordbury clubb. Clubb money & gave 7d.

Fryday 22 To Ware on poney to pay taxes. Paid Mr Byde reci[e]ver at the Bull, all taxes for 1801 and £15 acpt (*account*) on the taxes for 1802. Onley Byde and Pierson there. Dined at the Eagle with Munns & Sams from Hoddesdon, & Jardall baker from Wormley, & Smith at Roxford. Diner each 1s 6d. Spent 1s 6d. Gave 4d. For dinner leg of mutton & rist (*rice*) puding.

---

[244] Archers Green Farm: on 5 Nov Carrington reports that the same property was sold to Lord Cowper for £397.

[245] Bourchier, like many others with family connections in France, took advantage of the peace to travel.

Saturday 23 To market on poney. Sold 4 load of wheat to Chapman at 41s per load. Spent at Bull with Insom & Hoton 1s, at Bulls Head with d[itt]o 6d. Came home by Thos Wellses, Hardingfordbury with Harrington and Pallett, Eason Green (*East End Green, Hertingfordbury*). Spent 1s.

Sunday 24 To Bramfield church. Thos Lloyd preached. After noon to Tewin with Pallett of Eason Green (*East End Green*), and Harrington. Spent at Jacks the Rose & Crown with them 1s.

Tusday 26 Afternoon to the Vestrey at Bramfield, grant a rate &c. Deards, Burges, and I and Vaux the overseer that was all as was there.

Wednesday 27 Evening to Jacks Tewin. Spent with Dolling 3d.

Fryday 29 To Tewin with Passell, the chalk drawer. Spent with him & his children at Jacks 1s 6d as having finished chalking Crabtree Field, Stable Field and half Cheretree Field.

Saturday 30 To market on foot. Sold 4 load of wheat at 40s per load. Dined at Bulls Head, dinner & spent 1s 8d. Spent after at Angell 6d. Gave Hall, barber 3d.

Sunday 31 Went to Ware on poney to meet King for Whitbury Hill rent but he not came, but I recivd £5 for wood, 2 load Denness at the George, ½ load Field, ½ load Aylon. Slept there & spent 2s.

NOVEMBER Monday 1st Evening to the clubb at Tewin.

Wednesday 3 To dinner at Rose & Crown, Tewin as being the yearly dinner of the Association for Prosicuteing of Fellons, mockturtle, sr lyne (*sirloin*) of beef &c &c.[246] Mr Dean, Mr Webb, Mr Patient, Brux, Simon Walby, T[homas] Whittenbury, Edmons, Mullett, Johnson, Sq[ui]r[e] Hanken, Elsom, Mr Johnson of Colegreen, Preston, myself. Each person spent 8s. Plenty of wine & punch.

Fryday afternoon the 5 To Tewin to take rent of my tenants and Mr Meers. Onley Sheath, & Harrowd. Paid of Meers as being the last of Archers Green for he has sold that to Lord Cowper by auction at the Falkorn Hartford for

---

[246] Baroness Dimsdale had several recipes for Mock Turtle made from the head of a calf [Falvey, *Dimsdale Receipt Book*, pp25-26].

£397, of my tenants, North, & Day & Squier, & Ward. Spent in bread & cheese and beer & gin & water 10s. The Noisey Lowin there.

Saturday 6 To market on poney. Dined at Bull & spent after 2s 6d, ostler 4d. Markets much the same. The mal[t]sters & factors of Ware have entred into an agreement to buy no barley at Hartford under £50 penalty & is the last day for this season.

Sunday 7th Went to the 3 Horshoos [Little] Barkhamstead to meet Cock to settle about boarding with me.[247] Spent there at one Boltons at the Horshoos in beer 6d, in gin & water with Cheek the carpenter there, Cock & Bolton's brother farmer 2s.

Monday the 8th Went to Hartford fair on poney to try to sell a cow, but did not siller (*sell her*). I should a took the first biding, 13 guines but I could reach but 12 after, so not sold. Ostler 4d. Refreshd at Lloyds. Spent 0.

Tusday 9 To Tewin in evening. Spent 3d.

Wednesday 10 Went to James Days Stocking Elms, at [Little] Barkhamstead to fetch Mr Cock to board at Bacons with cart 2 horses. Mr Day there had just lost his wife, buried at Hardingfordbury Tusday the 4th this month.

Saturday 13 To market on poney. Dined at Bull 1s 4d. Spent there after dinner 6d. Spent at Richardsons with John Aylon 8d, ostler 4d. Came home by Pansanger. Smoakt a pipe there with Robarts the groom. Gave to the boy there 6d. Markets much the same.

Sunday 14 To Tewin church with Mr Cock. Mr Johnson of Datchworth preached.[248] Spencer Cowper & Henery [Cowper] from Tewin Water there &c. In afternoon to Tewin. Spent there with Mr Dean of Tewin Bury and Pallett of Eason Green (*East End Green*) 2s.

---

[247] On 26 Mar 1812 Carington's son Jack records in his diary: 'This morning about 6 o clock old Mr Cock died at Bacons Farm where he has boarded for some years' [HALS: DE/X3/22].

[248] Charles Woolsey Johnson was rector of Datchworth for 43 years from 1785 until his death on 30 Nov 1828. He was one of the subscribers who contributed to the building of Datchworth School in 1820 [Prowle and Walker, *A History of Datchworth*, p152].

Tusday 16 Went to Ware on poney cart. Went with faggots, brought home 6 qr pale malt of Cadmore. Spent & gave 1s.

Wednesday 17 to the wood fieast at Bramfield. Paid Mr Peacock from London & Bassett £19 10s, for 3 acres of wood, in Park Wood. A round of beef, pudings, a great companey not dinner enough, the gathering was 2s each. Spent after 1s. Not stout dinner.

Fryday Evening 19 To Tewin with Mr Farmer from London, hopp merchant & Cock our border to Jacks Rose & Crown. Spent 1s 6d.

Saturday 20 To market on poney with Mr Farmer whch slept at Bacons. I went as farr as Ware with him as he went that way for London. Spent with him at Eagle 1s. Gave ostler 3d. Came home and stopt at the Ramm as had 13 sheep but did not sell them. Came home erley. Spent nothing at Hartford. Markets much the same.

Sunday 21 To Bramfield church, Lloyd preached. Afternoon to Tewin. Spent 3½d.

Tusday 23 To Ware. Slept at the Eagel. Spent at Swann & at the Wheat Sheeff [in] the Market Place, one Burr keeps it, with Aylon & Cadmore 10d. Spent at Eagle 2s. Gave Will & the maid (*manuscript incomplete*).

Satturday 27 To market on poney. Dined at Bull Head on sasages with 2 Claphams & Cock. Spent 1s. Spent after 6d, ostler 4. Markets cheeper, the best wheat near 40s per load, barley about 30s per qr.

Sunday 28 To Tewin church on poney. Afternoon to Wellwin, saw Mr E[d]w[ar]d Pennyfather's funerl as a walking funerl from Har[m]ergreen threw Lockley Warren. Buried in a vault in the ch[urch], aged 37. Spent at the Rose & Crown Nickoldses 6d.

Tusday 30 Spent at Tewin in the evening 3d.

> This month was buried Thos Tanson of Weston at Walkorn. He was drawn from Weston to Walkern in his waggon and two griseled horses. He was supposed to be the fatest and bigest man in this county, about 35 years of age.

> This month Pansanger Farme House, barnes, stables &c pulled down as the land being taken into the New Park & the roads turned 2 years back or the year 1800. The last tennant in Pansanger Farme, was Joseph Phipp, which went to Hardingfordbury Street Farme in occipation by his father which resigned it to his son as obliged to leeve Pansanger.

DECEMBER Wednesday the 1 Went to Hartford. Carried Wm Hasler some wood at a house by the Runing Deer, Poort Hill. Went from thence to the clubb at Hardingfordbury. Spent 6d.

Memorandom this 2 Day of Decbr sold Mr Hanken 8 acres of turnops more or less in Bansleys, from the gate way in the Hartford Road to Hooks Bushes Wood for 45s per acre & my whole flock of sheep are to go in his grass at Esington (*Essendon*) at 12 per wek. Hanken dined with us to day & I sold him the turnops above, & Robarts and wife spent the evening from Pansanger with us.

[Satur]day 4 Jorney to [A]ngell St Albans to [take] in lists for Millitia. Marquess of Salsbury, Lord Grimston, Vandermulin &c there. Dined at Redhouse, new people there. Spent 2s. Carried daughter Sall in cart & gran[d]son Jack had Dimon. Hom[e] ½ p[a]st 6. Ostler & corne 1s 2d.

Sunday 5 To Bramfield church, Mr Bourchier preached the first Sunday after his arivell from a broad as France &c. The aft[ernoon] to Tewin. Spent at Jacks 3½d.

Monday 6 To clubb at Tewin. Spent there over clubb 6d.

Wednesday Evening the 8 To Greendragon Clubb. Spent over & gave ostler 9d. Gave old Mr Hunt 6d. Gave Foster 5d.

Saturday 11 To market on foot. Came home with T Sheath in my cart which brought a grist to mill. Spent at Bulls Head with Mr Spittle & Sheath 1s. Spent at Bull with T Sheath & Green of Bengeo 6d. Markets much same.

Sunday 12 To Esington (*Essendon*) to see my sheep, 95 in Cloteros (*?Clitherow's*) Park.[249] Went to Essington (*Essendon*) church. Spent at the Kings Head the Widow Clerks, with Mr Simpson carpenter, Grubb church clerk, & Cowper at the mill 2s. Gave hostler 6d.

Tusday 14th To Ware on poney. Spent at Eagle with King when paid rent for Widbury Hill there 3s.

Wednesday 15th To the clubb Hardingfordbury. Coz Thos Beck met me there, as went before me to Eason Green (*East End Green*) to see John Day a farmer there, who formerly lived at Roxford together. Clubb 7d.

Thursday 16 to vensen fiest at Tewin Jacks, onley a side. Coz Thos Beck, Mr Dolling, Thos Shieath there. Spent 4s each.

Fryday 17 Dined at Tewin againe on a large codd from coz Cooks London with Dolling & coz Beck & Sheath when I let the house. Spent each 2s. I was fuddled.

Saturday 18th To market in little blew cart. Dined at Bulls Head, Richardsons on sasseg's & mutton chopps with Mr Cock, Butterfield, Aylon & Pallett. Spent 1s. Spent at Bull after 6d. Gave ostler 6d. Carried wheat to mill and brough[t] grist home & barly meall.

Sunday 19 To church, the afternoon at home.

Monday 20th To tythe fiest at Mr Bourchiers, Bramf[iel]d. Dined in the landrey (*?laundry*). Mr Bourchier dined with us. Dinner rost fowls, hamm, rost beef &c, plenty of punch &c. Home erley. Gave Webster his man 1s. Spent at W[i]d[ow] Derds after 1s.

Tusday 21st To Hartford on poney. Paid Webster for toll 5s. Spent at Bell, Beacrofts with Webster 1s 6d. Gave to the man that showed the sellar 6.[250] Gave John the wa[i]ter 3d, ostler 2d.

---

[249] Bird's Place, Essendon, owned by Captain Robert Clitherow is shown on the Ordnance Survey two-inch drawings of Hertfordshire, 1799-1812 [H Prince, *Parks in Hertfordshire since 1500* (Hatfield 2008) p135].

[250] The Bell, now the Salisbury Arms, Fore Street, Hertford, was first mentioned in 1431. The building has medieval stone work in the cellar [Department of

Fry Day 24 Being market day as Christmas Day on the Saturday. Did not go to market, but went to Wollmers, now the Duke of Bridgwaters as just bought it of Esqr Whitbread, and building a new part to the house & other out buildings greatley.

Saturday 25 Went to Bramfield church. After newn (*noon*) at home, in the evening to Mr Henery Hunsdons. Drank tea and spent the evening there with Mr Peck & wife, Mr Burges & wife, Mr Bowley & Joseph Bassett & Geo Richardson our church clerk at Bramfield, though he liveth at the Bulls Head at Hartford.

Sunday 26 To Tewin church after noon to Jacks Tewin with Mr Cock. Spent 3 pints of beer. Home earley to tea 7½d

Monday 27th The afternoon to Jos Whittenburys the F[e]athers Tewin Upper Green. Met a few friends there according to custom time past. Mr Dolling, Simon Warby, Thos Sheath, sun (*son*) John, Bassett, Waller, old Squier, Thos Whittenbury. Spent as treated 5s 3d. The rest 1s each. Wet evening.

Wednesday 29 In the evening to Hardfordingbury clubb. Robarts, Moor, Cheshers, & Mr Mullett all that was there besides my self, & Beck. Sewill the landlord treatted us with elder wine. Clubb 7d. Home with Robarts by ½ past 10 clock.

Thusday Evening 30 Spent at Jacks at Tewin 3d. Rumney & his son dined wth us at home to day.

Fryday 31 To Tewin Jacks with John Molden, Esqr Mackey's bayliff. Spent there with him and Thos Sheith as being the last evening of the years 2s.

> O Lord unto me, how great are thy merseis I declare,
> Poor mortall as I be, that thou should take such care,
> From perils & dangers & with long life, and blessd me then with helth,
> And half my days with a virtues wife, and gave me a sheare of welth,
> O what return can I then make, for such great blessings given,
> My unfeigned thanks for Christs is sake, and hope theyl be rec[eive]d in heaven,

---

Environment, *East Herts List of Buildings of Special Architectural or Historic Interest* (1988)].

O Lord grant to me thy heavenly grace, that I may obey thy will,
That when I leave this earthly place, I may find then favour still.

Other remarks this year 1802:

In the Month of **January 1802** was found a humane skilliting (*skeleton*) of a man or woman, between Tewin Lower Green & the Upper Green oppisite a narrow place of the foot path whear it is railed. Found by one Thorrowgood a blacksmith of Tewin Upper Green, but late of the Lower Green as moved at Midsumer last, by his dig[g]ing gravel about 15 inches under the surfice of the earth, on a little elboe place next the East Field hedge.

A very great high sowth west wind on **Thursday January 21** from 9 in the morning till evening. Great damage.

On Sunday morning **February 7th** about 3 clock a Margat[e] hoye, with 35 pasangers on board and the other loading was chieffly corne had not set sail much above ½ an hour was lost at or near Margate as saileing for London and 25 of the passangers with the master &c drownd.[251]

Saturday 27 of February this year was discovred in a f[ie]ld near Ware Mill, called Burry Field, by one … which was diggen a didtch across the s[ai]d field … stone coffins (*manuscript incomplete*). I saw one of them opened by 6 or 7 men lifting upp the lid it being so waitey, there was the form of a scull & the large bones of either man or woman but if you touched them cromling (*crumbling*) to dust. It is about 70 poles to the end of Ware called Magpy Corner or ware the Wotton Road enters Ware and 70 steps up the field to the road from Ware Park Mill, in Burry Field ware they was found. They was taken upp & remooved to a barne at the upper end of the field, and there they are at preasant for inspection & no account at preasant can be given of them, but the generall opp'nion they have being buried a thousand years or more or before Ware Church was built.[252]

---

[251] 7 Feb 1802: loss of a Margate hoy is reported in several newspapers. There was a very detailed report, for example, in *The Bury and Norwich Post: Or, Suffolk, Norfolk, Essex, and Cambridge Advertiser* (Bury St Edmunds), Wednesday, Feb 17, 1802, issue 1025. It reported what happened to the boat and listed the names, occupations and addresses of the survivors and of those who died.

[252] One of the coffins was kept by Carrington at Bacons Farm and referred to in his diary on 18 Dec 1807 and 7 Jan 1808. It survived the fire at Bacons in the early 1850s and was seen by William Strutt, grandson of Joseph Strutt, in 1885. But a few

Deaths & Marriages this year 1802

Mr Joseph Thomas, wheeler in Sow Lane, Hartford buried at Hitchen **Sunday 10th January.**

Mrs Blindall buried at Wotton on Fryday evening the **15th of this January**. Aged about 82. She was wife to Richd Blindall formerly of Watkins, her maiden name was Adams, formerly of Welches Farme, but since the loss of her husband, she lived at Wollmer Green with her son William, & was carried from there.

Sunday 31st Was buried at Whitford (*Widford*) one Barnat carpenter of Amwell End, Ware.[253] He was poiner to the association there at Ware.

Febry 2nd Millses wife, the letter carrier of Hartford, found dead in the bed in the night by him leeving a husband & 6 children.

Sunday 7 Mr Ruth farmer at the end of Ware Town towards Wades Mill buried, formerly Ware coachman.[254]

Coz Thos Piggott at the Red House St Albans died **31 of January** or last month.

Mrs Goodall of London died the **31 of January** last.

Sarah Burton widow buried at Tewin this **18th of this month** aged 96 years. She lived at a little house belonging to the Rectory of Tewin, at the upper end of Tewin Upper Green.

On **Monday the 8th of this February** was married at Tewin Church by bands (*banns*), one tayler (*tailor*) Piddey of Tewin to one Mary Ann Munns of Tewin Lower Green.[255] The taylor was a lodger at one Grimeses, blacksmith at Tewin Lower Green, late Thorrowgoods.

---

years later it 'had to my intense mortification just been smashed up by the orders of Lord Cowper's steward to mend the road' [William Strutt, *A Memoir of the Life of Joseph Strutt* (1896)].

[253] Thomas Barnard was buried at Widford on 31 Jan 1802 [HALS: DP123/1/3].

[254] John Ruth was buried at Ware on 7 Feb 1802 [HALS: DP116/1/5].

[255] Joseph Pitty married Mary Ann Munns at Tewin on 15 Feb 1802 [HALS: DP106/1/6].

The Duke of St Albans, Lord Burford's father buried, at Hanworth Midlesex on **Fryday the 12th** of this month. A herse in six, & 3 morning coaches in six, & his Grace's carrige.

Tusday 2 March Died the Duke of Bedford at his seat at Woburn Abby, Bedfordshire aged 35. This was son to him that was kild a hunting and died at Porters End, in the parish of Kimpton. He was buried at Chines (*Chenies*) Bucking[ham]shire, near Chesham.

Sunday 28 of ditto Was drowned by accident John Osburn, malt maker at the Pryory kill (*kiln*) Hartford to Mr Young, formerly to Mr Fairman, at the same kill. He was a native of Ware, and that day had been over there to see his wife, and came back to his kill, but the next morning his body was flooting at Dicke[r] Mill. Supposed he went to dip som[e] water in his pale as being dark and fell inn. He was a very stidey (*steady*) sober man, & had work[ed] for me in making malt as I had a great deal of Mr Fair[man].

Thursday 25 of March Fealex (*Felix*) Calvert of Hunsdon House & brewer in London shott him self. He was High Sheriff for this county in the year 1798.

April Fryday 2d about 9 clock at night the fire broke out Bedwell Park Farm near Esington (*Essendon*), in the tener of Esqr Corroe. Burnt all down in a few [h]ours, 6 reeks, 5 barns & all other buildings but the house, and that very much damaged.

In the **beginning of this month April** died Lord Kinyon at Bath aged 69 years. He succeeded Lord Mansfield and was Lord Chieff Justice of the Kings Bench in 1788.[256]

Bramfield workhouse burnt down Wednesday afternoon **14th this April 1802**. Was set on fire by the children for, as the chimney sweeper took the coles from the herth in a pan, and set them under the house it was thatched while he swept the chimneys they blowed them up & set fire to the house. The house was built in 1782. Lord Grandison gave timber, Esqr Emmott of Goldings gave 5 ginues, & the Miss Searanks of Hatfield 5 guineas, the rest by the parrish.

---

[256] William Murray, 3rd Earl of Mansfield (1777-1840) [Burke, *Genealogical and Heraldic Dictionary* (1839)].

May 21 Fryday afternoon was buried at Tewin church old Thos Sewill, laborer, of Tewin Upper Green aged 84. He was a member to the old clubb, held at the Rose & Crown Tewin, & the sociaty attended with their wands.

Butcher Warby of Whitwell buried this **Fryday 16 July** at Pauls Walden church.[257]

Monday the 9th of August John Tyler buried at Tewin. He worked at Mr Deans, Tewin Burry & had been to London with straw, and coming home at Bellbarr he got up to ride on the coppses of the cart & slipt through and the wheele went over his body and being heavy loaded with compast crust him allmost to death, but he lived from the Sunday morning erley the first as it was done, till the Thursday following. He was a stout young man aged 36 with wife & 4 children of Tewin.

Monday 2d of August Ettredge comonley called Toper, which used to work in the road from Stapleford to Hartford, killed at Waterford by Hookers cart of Hartford, as he was driving it. Stout man aged about 40ty, a native of Waterford.

Joseph Sewill died this **August.** He was a very stout, strong man and a very obstinate, abusive man 6 foot or upwards about 55 years old. Lived at Ware.

Timothy Casuall (*Caswall*) Esqr of Sacomb died this **Aug[u]st** the laterend at London, formerley a Member for the Borrough of Hartford.[258]

Thursday Bush Fair the 9 of Sepr Mr Perkns, carpenter of Stanstead, dropt down dead at the fair.

Fryday night the 10 of September, the male (*mail*) coachman killed at Ware. A little above the church his horses run up the high side & over turnd the coach on him, dead instantly.

---

[257] George Warbey was buried at St Pauls Walden on 16 July 1802 [HALS: DP113/1/4].

[258] Timothy Caswall (1733-1802), MP for Hertford, 1761-1768, and a Commissioner of Excise, 1789-180, was buried at Sacombe on 31 Aug 1802. He was a personal friend of William Pitt who visited him at Sacombe Park. Timothy acquired the Sacombe estate on his marriage to Mary Constantia Rolt. It was sold to the Smith family of Watton Woodhall on the death of Timothy's son George in 1825 [HALS: DP89/1/6; *VCH Hertfordshire,* vol 3 p137].

Saturday evening the 18th of Sepr William Day at the Water House Roxford, found dead on Cheshunt Common. He set out on the day before to go to Layton in Es[s]ex, and coming home againe supposed to drop down dead of his horse. Aged 55.

Monday 27 Sepr died Crout … maker in Hartford Market Place, and … to the Union Society Green Dragon …. (*manuscript incomplete*).

Tusday the 4 of Octr was buried at Hardingfordbury church Mrs Day of [Little] Barkhamsted wife to Mr Day of Stocking Elms in that parish.[259]

Sunday 17th October was buried at Diggswell church Farmer Pinack of Diggswell Lodge.[260]

Tusday Morning 16 Novr died Mrs Robartson at Amwell End.

Sunday night Novr 21 died Mr Ewdard Pennyfather of Harmer Green, buried the Sunday following 29th at Wellwin church in a vault on the right hand, at the entrance of the church, aged 36. An antham was sung taken out of the 7th chap of Job.[261] I was there a waking (*walking*) funerall through Lockly Warren.

Britton, gardner at Hardingfordbury, formerly under gardner to old Lord Cowper of Colegreen died this **Decbr 2d 1802**.

Mr Hide of Ware killed this month **Decembr 1802** by the sails of the windmill Wadesmill.

This year 1802 and 1801 I chalked some part of Bansleys the short work, and Crabtree Field, & Cheretreefield, & Six Acres, and Stable Field, 1 pitt sunk in Bansleys, 1 d[itt]o in Cheretreefield, 1 d[itt]o at the corner of 6 Acres by the X road, and 1 d[itt]o at the upperend of Crabtreefield, under the wood near the old pitts and this last pitt we carted the chalk to Stablefield, and part of Cheretreefield. Done by one George Passell of Burnham Green, and his wife

---

[259] Ann Day was buried at Hertingfordbury on 4 Oct 1802 [HALS: DP50/1/7].
[260] 'Henry Pinnock of Digswell Lodge, farmer, aged 52 years' was buried at Digswell on 17 Oct 1802 [HALS: DP34/1/3].
[261] Job ch 7 begins: 'Is there not an appointed time to man upon earth? Are not his days also like the days of an hireling?'.

and his three daughters and one son, they did their work alternatly. Cost me about £100.

The 9 Worthies, Joshua, David, & Judas Maccabuas, Jews

Hector of Troy, Alexander the Great, & Julas Caesar, Heathens

Arther of Britan, Charl[emagne] the Great of France, and Godfrey of Bouillion, Christians.[262]

[262] The Nine Worthies are a set of champions, first devised in the 13th century, who became a subject for poetry and art. They were meant to represent the greatest military leaders of all times: three pagans - Hector, Alexander the Great, and Julius Caesar; three Jews - Joshua, David, and Judas Maccabeus; and three Christians - Arthur, Charlemagne, and Godfrey of Bouillon (a leader of the First Crusade, which conquered Jerusalem). The Worthies constituted a kind of chivalric Hall of Fame to inspire nationalism. That is how they are presented by William Caxton in his Preface to his edition of Sir Thomas Malory's *Morte D'Arthur*. However, they were also used to deplore the absence of chivalry among the contemporary aristocracy [The Norton Anthology of English Literature, accessed 22 September 2010): http://www.wwnorton.com/college/english/nael/middleages/topic_2/deschamps.htm].

1803 (*HALS: DE/X3/6*)
JANUARY Saturday 1st To market on poney. Did not stop at Hartford onley to send some things by my cart home, but went to Esqr Emmotts to deliver my bills. Dined & greatly refreshed there. Gave to the groom 1s. Gave John Draper 1s.

Sunday 2d To Bramfield church, afternoon at home.

Monday 3d To Tewin clubb, & Xm[a]s (*Christmas*) supper. Spent nothing but gave old Field 3d.

Tusday 4th To Ware. Staid all night and had words with Harrington. Spent and gave in all at Dennesses at George & Eagle in taking money for wood &c 5s. Came home next day through Ware Park. Was kindly asked in by Esqr Byde, and well entertained.

Wednesday 5th Spent at Johns at the Globe at Bengeo, with Samms when left Esqr Bydes 1s. Richd Stalley buttler, James Knight footman, James Webb coachman, servants to Esqr Byde.

Saturday 8th To market on foot in afternoon. Spent at Richardsons Bulls Head with Clapham & Aylon 6d. Markets much the same, good wheat 36s per load, good barley 27s qr, oates 25s qr, peas 30s load. Home by self on foot erley.

Sunday 9th To Tewin church the Revd E[d]w[ar]d Bourchier preached, the afternoon to Tewin. Spent with Jos Draper & Simon 6d.

Wednesday 12th To the clubb Hardingfordbury with Roberts, the groom Pansanger. Spent the clubb 6d. Gave for Welch Rabet (*?Welsh Rarebit*) 6d. Gave the boy for poney 6d.

Saturday 15th To market on foot. Spent at Bull with Hanken & Mr Cock as I treated 2s. Spent at old Wellses as came home 1s. Gave Hanken's boy to light me home 6d. Godfrey of Tewin came home with me by chance for the boy's light we[nt] ou[t].

Tusday 18th To Tewin in the evening. Spent at Jacks with Grimes the blacksmith & young Patient 9d.

Young John Beck came on foot to Bacons the 17, and left to London 21 & Will went with him on foot.

Thursday 20th To Tewin. Spent with Pridmore the schoole master 6d.

Saturday 22d Jorney to St Albans to the Angell to draw for Millittia. Lord Grimston, Wm Grimston and Vandermuling there. For Bramfield drawd J[ame]s Allen. Dined at Redhouse. Went on Dimon.

Sunday 23d To Bramfield church, the man's child christned whos wife lay in at W[i]d[ow] Derdses. The afternoon to Tewin. Spent at Jacks with Robarts, Ld Cowper's groom & Kimpton, Spencer's coachman, & Thos Sheath 8d.

Wednesday 26 To the clubb fiest Hardingfordbury. Dinner leg moton, rost lyne (*loin*) of beef, pudings &c. Mullett, Phipps, Johnson, Hancock, Hanken, the 2 Hickmans, Moor &c there, 15 at dinner. Spent in punch all together 4s. I went with Robarts the groom from Pansangar.

29th To market on foot. Spent at Vine with Mr Cock & Day 1s. Mr Cock & I came home togather. Markets rather dearer.

Sunday 30th Set off to London on poney as far as the Woollpack, Cheshunt. Chapman my boy rode him back by returnd chays (*chaise*) to London from Endfield Highway. Staid till Wednesday wa[l]ked on foot Endfield Highway, then rode in Baker's carrivann to Hartford. Gave Riddle the man 1s. Spent on him 1s. Slepp (*slept*) in Long Lane Sunday night at Land[lord] Nickolds, Puter (*Pewter*) Dish, St John Street Monday night d[itt]o 3s. Set off on foot on Wednesday morning the 2d of February home.

Sunday night or Monday morning the 31 Hatfield church robbed.

FEBRUARY Thursday 3 Lord Cowper's rent fiest. 32 at dinner at Mr Palletts, the stew[a]rds. A buttock beef, lyone (*loin*) & fillett of veal, hamm and legges moton. My man & little boy came for me. Grant gave the cook maid 1s.

Fryday the 4 To Tewin with brother Hassler. Spent at Jacks 1s. Gave old Bluitt in the workhouse 1s.

Saturday the 5th To market on foot. Dined at Richardsons on fresh herrens (*herrings*), with Harrington & Bush from Wotton. Spent my part 1s. I found

6 good herrens 4d. Home with Chapman in little cart from the mill. Best wheat 38s per load, best barley 28s per qr. Markets much the same.

Sunday 6 To Bramfield church, after to Tewin. Spent by self 3d.

Monday 7th To Tewin clubb. Spent nothing. Deaf Jamey came to Makeys Gate with me.

Tewsday 8 To Ware on foot. Staid all night. Spent at the Swan Dennesses 6d, at Dennesses the George 6d, at brother Hasslers the Eagle with Cadmore & Aylon 1s 6d. Came [home] Wednesday the 9. Stopt at Hartford the Falkorn, had sassages, with Hassler &c as swareing in the Millitia. Spent nothing. From thence to the clubb Hardingfordbury & so home.

Thursday 10th Afternoon to Jacks, Tewin. Spent 2d.

Fryday 11 Evening to Tewin. Spent at sons with Mr Pridmore, the schoolmast[e]r & young Flindall 6d.

Saturday 12th To market on foot. Dined at the Redcow Wallers with Mr Cock & Thos Sheath on sasages. I gave the sasages. Spent 1s 6d. Markets much the same, best wheat 37s per load. Sharp, frosty wather. Sent John my son to the Angell Inn, St Albans to swear in the Millitia in my stead. Marques Sal[i]sb[u]ry, Ld Grimston, Wm Grimston, B Lewis there. John staid all night.

Sunday 13 Not to church. Afternoon to Tewin spent with Baker collermaker from Wellwin & James Wiggs from the Swan Wellwin keeps the Tap 1s 6d. Gave deaf Jimmey 2d.

Monday 14 To Wellwin in afternoon to post office. Spent at James Wiggs who keeps the Swan Tap 1s.

Saturday 19 To market round by Woolmers the Duke of Bridgwaters on poney. Dined at the Vine, Hartford, E[d]w[ar]d Moundford on stakes with Hanken butcher. Spent 1s 6d. Spent at Cold Bath as came home with Simpson 6d. Markets rather dearer.

Sunday [20] To Tewin church. Afternoon to Jacks the Rose and Crown. Spent there with Pridmore & Sheath 4½d.

Monday [21] To Tewin with Mr John Garner late ser[van]t to Mrs Goodall deceased. Spent 2s. He staid all night with us & went for London the next day by Ware.

Wednesday [23] To Esqr Godfry at Hardingfordbury Parsnage to see Mr Moore, gardner. From thence to the clubb at White Horse Sewills. Spent & gave Blind Bettey 2s.

Saturday 26th To market on poney. Dined at the Bull. Dinner 1s 4d. Spent after when paid Mr Chapman for 3 sacks of corse flowr £5 11s 0d with him and brother Hassler & Sanders, church clerk of Amwell & young Parker 8d. Spent more at Bulls Head with Guttredge of Artick (*Haultwick*) 6d. Spent more at Bull with Pridmore & taylor Pattey 1s. Gave hostler 6d & to the man that plaid the bells 2d.[263] Came home with Pridmore & Pattey, taylor. Markets much the same.

Sunday 27th To Bramf[ie]d church. Mr Newton preachd. Afternoon to Tewin Hill Mr Webbs, after to Jacks. Spent & gave 4d. Gave Widow Culver 1s.

Monday 28 To Hartford on poney for peas of Simpson. Spent at the Black Swan Taylors with Dr Rumney 3d.[264]

Only 9 days frost this month and little snow, other fine mild wather but a terable high wind on the 27.

MARCH Wednesday 2d To Vestry at Bramfield. Vaux overseer for a rate of 2s 6d in the pound for & toward paing the building a new workhouse or poor

---

[263] These are probably hand bells laid on a table, often played by a company of ringers. Here there appears to be only one man playing so they could have been suspended on a stand and struck by hammers [Strutt, *Sports and Pastimes of the people of England* (1845 edition) pp292-3].

[264] Dr Thomas Romney was contracted to St Andrews parish, Hertford, for medical services at least from 1787-8 at a yearly salary of 12 guineas [HALS: DP49/21/1]. See also R Dimsdale, 'The Old Poor Law and medicine in and around Hertford, 1700-1834 in (eds S King and G Gear) *Social welfare in Hertfordshire from 1600. A Caring County?* (Hatfield 2013) pp14-44.

house which is now just finished. Bassett carpenter, & Mumford bricklayer.[265] Cost neer £300. Spent & gave 1s 6d.

Thursday 3d To Tewin afternoon to Rose & Crown. Spent with Pridmore schoolmaster & tayler Paddy & Blindall 6d.

Saturday 5th To market on poney. Dined at the White Swan Pinaks. Spent there with Campen of Burchall (*?Birchall, Hertingfordbury*) &c 1s 9d. Spent at Richardsons 6d. Gave the blind higler from Walkon (*Walkern*) 1s.

Sunday 6 To Tewin church. Afternoon to Tewin the Rose & Crown to meet my constables to recive presents (*presentments*) for the Assizes. Smith and Camp & Parker & Burges. Spent each 1s 6d.

Monday 7th To the Assizes on poney. Judge Heath & Sergant Shephard, the Hon[oura]ble Spencer Cowper, fore man of Grand Jury. Little buisness.[266] Over on Tusday by 1 clock. Spent 2s. Went to church the text 5 chap Livitecus 17 verce.[267] High Sheriff, Brown Esqr of North Mimms Place.[268]

Wednesday 9th To the clubb Green Dragon. John Molding was ballotted in and Warby taylor was ballotted out. Gave ostler 4d. Spent & gave 6d.

Thursday 10th To Tewin Jacks. Spent with Pridmore, Paddy & Sheath 8d.

Saturday 12th To market on poney. Dined at Bull 2d (*second*) table. Dinner 1s 4d. Spent after with Parrott & Williams blacksmith 9d. Gave Ann Kimpton 6d. Gave ostler 3d. Markets dearer 2s per load.

---

[265] Joseph Bassett of Datchworth and Edward Mumford, bricklayer [HALS: DP22/12/2].

[266] There were just seven cases heard involving 14 accused, five of whom were given transportation sentences, two were sent to Hertford gaol, one was publicly whipped, two were at large and four acquitted [TNA: Hertford Assize records, information from Ken Griffin].

[267] Leviticus ch 5, verse 17: ‘And if a soul sin, and commit any of these things which are forbidden to be done by the commandments of the Lord; though he wist it not, yet is he guilty, and shall bear his iniquity’.

[268] Henry Browne was sheriff in 1803 [S Austin, *List of Sheriffs of the County of Hertford from the Accession of William the Conqueror to the present time* (Hertford, 1947)].

Monday 14th To Watton Turnpike meeting at the White Horse Crawleys. Dinner 1s 6d. Spent after 1s 9d. Gave ostler 3d. Commissoners Byde, Twin, Kimpton, dined with us. Sarige [&] Camken from Aston, Guant (*Gaunt*) from Bennington, Green & Butterfield of Beng[e]o, Jery Crowley & Mr Byde's two servants Knight & Webb. Diner rost beef, leg motton, & pudings.

Thursday 17th To Tewin to Johns Rose & Crown. Spent with Pridmore & Grimes blacksmith and young Patient 1s. Home with Chapman my boy.

Saturday 19th To market on foot. Dined at Bulls Head Richardsons on stakes. Spent 6d. Spent after at Bull with Gaunt from Bennington 6d. Markets much the same.

Sunday 20th To church. After to Esqr Emmotts. Gave young Derds 6d. After to Tewin. Spent there with Molding &c 1s.

Monday 21 To Hartford on poney to know about malt & barley. Dined at Mr Rutters. Gave 1s. Gave for Mrs Walker 2s 6d.

Tusday 22 To Ware. Dined brother Haslers. Spent after with Gripper, Aylon & Thorp 10d. Gave Will 2d.

Wednesday 23 To Clubb Hardingfordby. Spent clubb and gave 11d. Came home with Robarts.

Thursday 24 To Esqr Emmotts to take bill. From thence to Esqr Mackeys wood sale at the Feathers at Tewin Upper Green. Drawd No 1, a rood. Spending money 1s.

Fryday 25 Went to Tewin. Spent at Jacks by self 2d.

Saturday 26 To market on poney. Being Lent fair had my large cow there but did not sell. Dined at Bulls Head with stakes and sassages, with Oadall (*?Odell*) & Clapham, & Oakley of Kings Walden. Spent 1s 6d. Markets dull of all trade. Gave little boy at Chapmans for my poney 3d. Spent at Spratts with Cock 6d. Gave to old Hall & others 9d.

Sunday 27 To Bramfield church. After dinner to Tewin church. After spent at Jack when Thos Whittenbury paid me & with Simon & Cock 1s 8d.

Monday 28 To a committee at Green Dragon, Hartford of our clubb, when wanted to exclude Sajant and Robert Whittinbury as thinking took to[o] much money, but a further enquirey to be. Spent & gave 11d.

Tusday 29 Afternoon to Tewin church to meet Sheath the church clark, to choose a buriall place for Coz Ann Pierce who died on Sunday last. Spread Eagle, brother Hasslers Ware.

Thursday 31 Attended the funeral of Coz Ann Pierce from sister and brother Hasslers at the Eagle, Ware. Herce and coach & pair from Flacks, Hartford. Buried at Tewin about 2 clock.[269] Dined at son Johns Tewin. Aged 54. Coach came home by Bacons & drank tea.

Bramfield Poor House finished this month. The Assezes at Hartford the 7th. Brown Esqr of North Mimms Place, High Sheriff, Cherry Under Sheriff of Hartford.

Memorandom. Paid Thos Wildes 14s 3d towards the hedggreen in Cherry Tree Field this 16th. Paid him moor 12s. 52 pole long at 6d per pole.

The 26 of this month the Millitia of this county met at St Albans to be embodied.

Tyler's wife at Waterford hanged her self this month.

This month Mrs Derds at the Grandisons Arms Bramfield was rob[b]ed of £13 by a woman that lodged in her house, but she got £10 againe.

APRIL Fryday 1st Spent in evening at Mrs Derdses Bramfield with Burges 9d.

Saturday 2 To market on poney. Dined at Mr Archers as paid him a bill, afterwards to the Bulls Head. Spent there with Cock & Clapham 1s. Spent at Bull 6d. Gave hostler 4d.

Monday 4 To Wotton meeting againe, paid one yrs duty £2 18s 6d. Dined there with Serage, Vigus, Hall, Butterfield, Pool, Crawley. Dinner 1s 6d.

---

[269] Further details of the funeral can be found in Carrington's notes at the end of 1803.

Spent after in punch 1s. Gave hostler 6d. Commisioners there Byde, Dickenson, Cobham, Twinn, Revd Mr Prist, Dimsdale, Lloyd, Blindall, Kimpton.

Wednesday 6 afternoon to clubb Hartingfordbury. Spent over & above the clubb 6d. Clubb 7d. Came home with the groom at Pansanger, Roberts.

Thursday 7 To Ware on poney for the affidave (*affidavit*) of Nancy Pierce.[270] Spent at sister Hasslers, with Mr Potts. 20 years back he was gardner to Esqr Seamer (*Seymour*) of Pansanger, & Mr Hide, baker 1s.

Fryday 8 Afternoon to Wellwin to put letter in. Stopt at the Earl Cowpers Arms, Elsoms, Digswell Water. Spent there and treated Robarts a master miller formerly, but now works at Digswell Mill for Blindall master, 1s.

Saturday 9 To market on poney. Dined at Bull. Dinner 1s 4d. Spent after there 1s 3d. Spent at Richardsons 6d, ostler 4d. Markets much the same, best wheat 37s load, barley 26s qr, oates 23s qr, peas 24s per load. Herd to day that Edmonds Edmans (*sic*) is dead, at Margate.

Easter Sunday 10th To Tewin church. Mr Bowger (*Bourchier*) preached, for Mr Newton being gon into Yorkshire as his wife being out of her mind, and has been in some mad house some time. Went to Tewin after dinner. Spent at Johns with Crook from London, & Taylor, Gillman's clerk, Clapham, Brooks etc, gave 2s.

Easter Monday 11th Afternoon went to Hatfield on poney to Dr Penroses for stuff for Miss Clark at Bacons, & Sheath's daughter wich are both very ill.[271] Was well treated at Mr Cannons as went. Gave his boy 2d. Spent at Hatfield 4d.

---

[270] An Act of Parliament of 1679 (30 Cha 11 c3) designed to lessen imports of linen and encourage the woollen and paper industries declared that an affidavit was to be brought within eight days of a burial, under a penalty of £5, that the deceased was not buried in linen [J Southerden Burn, *The History of Parish Registers in England* (first pub 1829, reprint 1976)].

[271] James Penrose (1750-1818), was appointed surgeon-extraordinary to George III in November 1793, in succession to John Hunter (1728-1793). Both James and his father Francis (1718-1798) were buried in the churchyard at Hatfield, but no trace of their tombstone remains [D'A Power, 'Penrose, Francis (1718-1798)', revised by Jean Loudon, *ODNB*, 2004].

Easter Tusday 12 Spent at Bramfield W[i]d[ow] Derds our Easter Vestrey, as Mr Vaux our overseer had not provided aney dinner 1s 8d. Mr Vaux continues overseer, Jos Derds church w[ar]d[e]n, Richd Burges constable. We had some pork and eggs etc 7s ginn & water besides beer.

Easter Wednesday 13th To Tewin

Saturday 16th To St Albans on Dimon to Town Hall to appoint overseers. Dined at the Redhouse, newcomers one Grubb from Wemstead (*Whempstead*) by Wotton (*Watton at Stone*). Dinner 2s. Spent after 9d, ½ p[ec]k corne 8d, ostler 3d. The great ox at St Albans to day to be seen alive weigas (*weighs*) upwards of 500 stone. It was bread (*bred*) by John Spotteswoode Esqr of Spotteswoode in the county of Berwick upon Tweed, Scotland. It was sold from him to three persons in Sep[tembe]r last for 360 guineas and now drawn about the kingdom to be shown. Supposed to be the largest ever shewn.

Sunday 17 To Bramfield morning & Tewin afternoon church. Mr Bourchier preached. Evening to son Johns. Spent 6d.

Monday 18th To Quarter Sessions at Hartford. The long tryall of one Daws, sawer of Blakfann, for steeling of faggotts from the widow Pinock of Diggswell Lodge.[272] She set her sheepard & boy to watch and on the evening of the 4th of March last they saw a man binding 5 up in a string, but their dogg gave him a signall and he left them, but they followd him and asked if he was not Daws. He said supposed it was, and they both swore to him, but upon his good evidence and most excelent good carrecttor, he was acquitted. Aspness was his councell and it was not Daws but another man Will[ia]m Smith which lived at Grubbs Barn. But he took towards the house of Daws, as he confesed after the tryall over and as being dark they supposed to be Daws & swore to him and he was sent to joall (*gaol*) and under went his tryall. They had lost faggotts severall times which made them more strict as Wm Smith confest as took them after tryall.

---

272 William Dawes, sawyer of Digswell, had been accused for stealing five faggots, value 5d, from Sarah Pinnock. He was acquitted at the Easter Session 1803 [*HCR* vol IX p48 & 50].

Sunday 24th To Hartford church St Andrews. Saw Capt[ai]n Jackson buried there.[273] A herce & pair, 2 coaches & pair. Dined at Mr Chapmans. Spent after at Spratts at Little Bell, with Mr Chapman and Mr Fletcher the bricklair (*bricklayer*) that made the vault 1s 6d.

Wednesday 27th To Ware on poney. Dined at brother Hasslers. Spent 7d, gave ostler Frances 3d. Came home by Esqr Emotts for Land Tax, was well treated there. Gave boy 3d. From thence to Bramfield. Spent at Wd Derdses 6d. Wednesday evening to clubb at Hardingfordbury. Clubb 7d.

Thursday [28] Afternoon Widow Derds Bramfield. Spent 6d.

Fryday 29 To Hartford to send 4 spearibbs to London. Spent at Richardsons 3d.

Saturday 30 Went to market on foot by Broadoakend for taxes of Preston & Miss Hattons. Dined at Bull 1s 4d. Spent after 1s. Spent at Richardsons 6d. Markets rather dearer, good wheat 38s load, good barley 26s qr, good oates 23s qr, good peas 24s load.

The latterend of this month and the beginning of the next was the great fall of timber at Sacomb belonging to Esqr Cashwell (*Caswall*).[274] 1732 trees, 140 men to fall them. Timber, bark, & topps bought of Caushwell for £8,016 13s 5d. Surveiad by John Baker of Hatfield Hide. That is, it was sold for £8,016 by Baker for Casuall.

Gave to the old men in Tewin workhouse in beer at Rose & Crown Tewin 3s, Webster, Burton, Leever, Luck, Ward.

MAY Sunday the 1st To church at Bramfi[e]ld. Afternoon to Tewin. Spent there at Rose & Crown 3½d.

---

[273] Captain William Jackson was buried on 24 Apr 1803 at Hertford St Andrews [HALS: DP49/1/4].

[274] George Caswall (1762-1825) inherited the Manor of Sacombe from his father, who had died in Aug 1802 (see diary entry for this date above). He served as a Justice of the Peace from 1806-12 and 1819-20 [*HCR* vol IX p538]. Sacombe House, surrounded by a park of 150 acres, lies south-east from the parish church – see Carrington's note about the previous house and the rebuilding at the end of 1803. It was the scene of a destructive fire in 1911-12 [*VCH Hertfordshire* vol 3 pp136-139].

Monday 2d To Tewin clubb. Spent 1d.

Tusday 3d To Bramfield Vestrey when I, and Allen excepted (*accepted*) the office of overseers, for the Justices appointed us, as would not appoint Mr Vaux. Spent over the vistrey 1s.

Wednesday 4th To the clubb at Hardby (*Hertingfordbury*). Clubb there 6d. Spent after at the Crown old Wellses, with Auston the printer of Hartford 1s, which was wrong. Staid late.

Fryday 6 To Bull at Ware to pay taxes. Paid Mr Byde £130 on account of the land and other assessed taxes for 1802 and £15 in October last on account of this years, all other being cle[a]r[e]d. Dined at Eagle with Samms, Iardale, Clerk, Elsom, and Aylon. Diner & spent 3s. Diner sho[ulder] veal, bacon & pudings. Lent Clerk my poney from Eagle to Hartford & Elsom & I walked to the [Green] Dragon. Spent 8d.

Saturday 7th To market on poney. Dined at Bull. Dinner 1s 4d. Spent after with treating & gave Cannon 1s 3d. Markets rather dearer, best wheat about 40s. Staid late, was detained with Mr Preston on Jos Basset's account.

Sunday 8 To Tewin church. Spent in evening at Tewin Johns, with Schribiers and his brother coachman from Forty Hill, Enfield 9d.

Monday 9 Afternoon to Wellwin with letters. Spent at Tewin as came back 2d.

Wednesday 11 To Tewin clubb fiest. Spent nothing.

Thursday 12 Hartford May fare on poney. Sold my young mair Snipp to one Sanders of Corner Hall by [Hemel] Hemstead for £28. Dined at Richardsons Bulls Head on sassages with Mr Land[lord] Nickolds, nephew Thos Beck, & Mr Cock. Spent in all 2s 6d. After the fair evening to Tewin second fiest. Spent 1s.

Fryday 13 Spent at Tewin when supt on a large codd with Coz Thos Beck & Mr Nickolds from London, and Mr Dean, Whittenbury, Haydon, Cock, Simon, Beck & Nickolds. Slept at Simons, and erley in morning of[f] for London 2s.

14th To market on poney. Not dined but spent at Richardsons Bulls Head 1s. Went to Mr Allingtons the law[y]er with Mr Preston to settle Basset's account. Settled it at the Angell. Spent on the parish acount 4s 6d. Spent at the Bull when took poney 6d. Gave ostler 6d. Markets much the same. Staid late this 2 Saturdays nights in settling Basset's account or he must went to goal. I paid £56 and Preston £30 for him.

Sunday 15 Spent at Tewin afternoon at son Johns with Dolling's man 8d. Gave to the old men in Tewin workhouse, old Burton, Leever, old Webster, Joseph Lowin, William Ward & John Luck in beer 3s 4d. To church in morning at Bramfield.

Wednesday 18 To Ware on poney. Spent at Eagle 6d. Gave Will 2d. From thence to the clubb at Hardingfordbury. Clubb 6d. Home erley, ostler 1d.

Saturday 21 To St Albans on poney, to the White Hart to appoint assessors of Taxes. Commissioners, Howerd, Kentish & Day, not stopt dinner but refreshed, & came home by the races at Brocket Hall. Spent at St Albans 1s 2d, ostler & corne 7d. Spent at [Red] Lyon, Digswell Hill 6d. Spent at Tewin with Coz Tho Beck 2s & the baker &c.

Sunday 22 Not to church but went to Brickwall, the Angell one Barkers, to enquire after a great coat which nephew T[homas] Beck left at Ld Millburns (*Melbourne's*) races yesterday.[275] Spent there 6d. From thence to Battens the White Hart, Wellwin, no news of it. Spent there 1s. Nevy (*nephew*) Beck, Thos Sheeth, and son John & my self.

Wednesday 25 To dinner at the Crown old Wellses with Hanken, Preston, Hickman & Mr Sewill. I gave mutton to the amount of 4s & spent & gave 1s.

Thursday [26] To Hardingfordbury to settle with Mr Hankin butcher for turnops he had of me & meat I had. Settled on both sides and dined with him upstairs, as he been overturnd by the coach, of a calfs fry 1s. Gave his girl or daughter [blank].

Fryday 27 Spent at Wd Derdses over the Vestry 6d.

---

[275] Quarter Sessions records show that The Angel, close to Ayot Green, near Welwyn, now demolished, was run by John Barker at least from 1806-22 [HALS: QSVR1806-22]. Carrington's diary entry suggests that Barker was there earlier.

Saturday 28 Jorney to St Albans to sighn a rate. Refreshed at the Red House 1s, ostler 2d. Spent & gave the old turnpike man at 3 Horshews 7d.[276] Home erley on poney.

Sunday 29 To Bram[fiel]d church in morning. To Tewin in the afternoon Mr Bowcher (*Bourchier*) preached. Spent at Tewin 3d.

Whitson Monday May 30 Went the boundarys of Bramfield parish on poney with Mr E[d]w[ar]d Bouchier rector on foot, Jos Derds, John Squier of Tewin, Joseph Bassett of Datchworth, Joseph Mowbry, John Templeman, Thos Hornatt, Burges, Webster Mr Bourchier's serv[an]t of Bramfield, &c and children. Set of[f] in the Back Lane behind Green Hall at the corner of the wood down by the side of it, then turnd to the right by side of other woods along Hopground Fields X (*cross*) Waterford Lane by the fields hedges side strait to Esqr Emmotts little gate of the Wilderness, through the same le[a]ving house on the left down the medow X Wotton Road to the Serpendine River, along by the same allmost to the top of the meadow, then over the hedge into the road to the post Maple X Hill, then to the right up the fields by side of wood on the left, strait on through the fields leving Goldings Woods on the r[igh]t to the entrance of the lane from Bacons to Hartford, along the same by the wood on the left, then along Grinels, leve Bonsleys Wood on l[e]ft, X road along Cherretree Field leeving Hooks Bushes Wood on left to Gilberts Pikle (*Pightle*), then to ri[gh]t by Bacons Orchard down to Howses Lane, up the same along Howses, X Lane at the top down by Pikle Hedge, up the first park leving Tewin Wood on left, round the pond on the r[igh]t to corner of the wood over a gap into Midle Park up by side of the wood leeving a little piece at the top, then through the wood to the corner of Upper Park, then ½ round the same leeving the wood on left into Park Lane at the upper corner, X lane to a Huntingate through the wood into the field, round the same leving the wood on r[igh]t, along the bottom of Whittenburys fields leving the woods on r[igh]t to Okenvaley Bottom, X the rode up a blind lane to the Back Lane, X the same into Gubbens Field along the same leveing Alexanders Wood on r[igh]t to such a place to mark, then through the wood into Back Lane againe, then down the same to the place you begun.

The dinner when went the boundrys at Wd Deardses was 2 leggs moton, shoulder veal, pudings &c. Mr Vaux, & Mr Bourchier dined with us. Mr

[276] The turnpike gate was situated near the Three Horseshoes at Smallford on the Hatfield-Reading turnpike road [Branch Johnson, *'Memorandoms For ... '*, p93].

Bourchier gave 3 guineas as rector & Mr Vaux for the Lord of the Maner £1 11s 6d, the rest by the parish. We took 2 glass bottles of gin, lofe & chees with us, and beverd (*beveraged*) at Maple X Hill & had 13 quarts and lofe & chees from Tewin & drank it in Park Lane.

Tusday 31 Spent at Tewin Jacks with Pridmore 3d. Gave old Luck 3d.

> The Begining of this month the Hertfordshir Millitia marched from St Albans through Hartford for Chelm[s]ford Bariks & the Northamton d[itt]o & the Buckingham d[itt]o. I was pre[s]sed for 4 horses to draw 2 amonition (*amunition*) cart[s] from Ware to Hockerill by Stortford, on Tusday the 24 of the Buckingham, rec[eive]d 14s. Now nothing but sharp presing and raiseing forses, for war afresh. Now to warr againe with France, though not proclamd.[277]

> Bayford church taken down this spring and a new one building with brick, and the church servis is performd in a stable, fitted up for that purpose, near Bayford Place.[278]

JUNE Wednesday 1st To Clubb at Sewils Hardingfordbury, 6d.

Thursday 2 Spent at Mrs Derdses when paid her £2 which was left at the raising fiest of the new workhouse 6d.

Fryday 3 Went to Esqr Emmotts to rec[e]ive rate, was entertained. From thence to Mr Gears, Waterford. Gave Taylor & other man 5d. Spent with Walls, Dines & Clapham 6d.

Saturday 4 To market in afternoon on poney. Rec[eive]d £61 of Vaux at the Angell for rates, paid Mumford the same as by drauft 6 weeks after date. Spent at Mumfords 8d. Spent at Bull with Cheek 8d. Spent at Bulls Head with Cheek, 3d, at [Green] Dragon with Cheek 6d. Gave away 5d, gave ostler 3d. Markets rather cheeper, the best wheat about 40s per load.

Sunday 5 To Tewin church. Afternoon to Jacks at Tewin. Spent with Mr Dolling's man, the baker, & Thos Sheath 10d.

---

[277] War was not declared until the end of May.
[278] Carrington gives a fuller description of the work at Bayford church in his entry at the end of 1804.

South east view of Bayford church by J C Buckler, 1832 (*HALS: DE/Bg/3/1*)

Monday 6 Spent at Tewin clubb after with Thos Sheath when paid me for malt & hopps 5d.

Tusday 7 Sister Hasler and taylor Jack from London over at Bacons. Gave Jack 1s.

Wednesday 8th To Tewin dinner at sons the Rose & Crown to recive the levy money. Street from Norton, Rowe from Sheephall, Camp from Pauls Walden, no more there. Dinner rost shoulder moton, ghoosbry (*gooseberry*) pye. Diner each 1s 6d. Spent after 1s. Afterwards to Hartford clubb at [Green] Dragon on pony. Gave away 5d.

Thursday 9 Lord Cowper's rent fiest at Colegreen, Mr Palletts the stewrd. Dinner buttock, & sr lyne of beef, rost veal, ham & pudings. Good beer & plenty of good punch. Thunder & wet evening. Went on poney & Burton came for me with great coat. Gave Grant, the maid 1s, ostler 6d.

Fryday 10 Spent at Mrs Derdses, Bramfield when settled for the boundries of the parish & highway bill 1s. Gave away 1s.

Saturday 11th Jorney to St Albans to the Angell to draw againe the Supplementrey Millitia, onley Vandermuling, Gape, & Grover the clerk there. Drawd Ballard, Bowger's (*Bourchier's*) groom for Bramfield. Had stakes at Red House 1s. Spent after 1s, corne & ostler 8d. Spent at 3 Horseshoes came home, 1s 2d.

Sunday 12 To St Andrews church Hartford, young Mr Bush preachd the sermon before the Mayor & Aldermen who came there that day. From thence to Ware to dinner. Settled a mistake with Cadmore, & paid him a pound note, wittniss Wm Frances. Spent with Cadmore & Aylon &c 2s. Gave away 3d.

Monday 13th Foornoon to Bramfield. Herd the disturbance between Guttredge & J[a]ms Allen as Guttredge left his work and abused Allen, his master. Spent 6d at W[i]d[ow] Derdses with Whittenbury. Afternoon to Wellwin to put letters in post office for swaring in the Supplementrey Millitia. Spent at Tewin son Johns as came home when Thos Whittenbury paid me his rate at 4s in the pound, 3d.

Tusday 14th Afternoon to Bramf[iel]d. Spent at Mrs Derdes with George Richardson who came to marry Wm Derds & Wallses daughter. But all things not right, not married this day.[279] Vaux turnd his ser[van]ts away 3d.

Wednesday afternoon [15] To Woolmers on poney to see after my bill as Mr Garton, the surveyor, for they still go on with the build[in]g tho the Duke is dead.[280] From thence to the clubb Hardingfordbury. Clubb 6d. Gave 2d.

Fryday 17 Afternoon to Mr Webbs, Tewin Hill. Stopt some time. Gave boy 3d. After to Rose & Crown. Spent with Thos Sheath 5d.

---

[279] William Henry Deards married Rose Walls of Bengeo on 4 July at Bramfield, Richardson being one of the witnesses. Banns had been called on 22 May and 5 and 12 Jun and again on 19 and 26 Jun and 3 Jul [HALS: DP22/1/4].

[280] Carrington reports that the Duke of Bridgewater died on the 8 March (see his list at the end of 1803). He died at his London house and was buried at Little Gaddesden, Hertfordshire [Malet, *Bridgewater The Canal Duke*].

Saturday 18 To Hartford on poney. Dined at Bulls Head with Mr Cock and others, 2 dinners 3s. Spent after with Harrington, Bygrave & Cock 6d. Gave Hall 2d. Gave Jos Chapman 3d. Markets much the same. Home erley.

Sunday 19 To Tewin church. Afternoon to Tewin. Spent with Mr Crook from London & Brooks, Thos Sheath & Pridmore 7d.

Tusday 21 To Ware on poney. Staid all night. Spent at all places 2s. Gave 6d. Home next day with the 2 carts 10 qr malt of Stoten & Hudson.

Thursday 23 Afternoon to Tewin with Simkins from Newnham, when paid levy money. Spent 7d.

Saturday 25 Jorney to St Albans the Angell to swear in the Supplementry Millitia. Lord Grimston, Vandermuling the chieff there. Dined on stakes at Red House. Dinner & drink 1s 6d, ostler and corne 8d. Went on poney by Stanborough. Came home that way & spent there with Mr Stevenson Lord Salsbury's steward &c, 6d.

Sunday 26 To Bramf[iel]d church. Afternoon to Tewin with Mrs Buttrey, Mary Scott as was, & spent there with Mr Cock & Cheek from Barkhamsted, carpenter 1s.

Tusday 28 To Codicote & Pauls Walden on poney to examon w[eigh]ts & to carry 2 warrants one Smith constable of Codicote, & one for Chalkley of Pauls Walden for men drawn to serve in Millitia. Dined at Dixsons the Bull at Whitwell. Dinner &c 4s. Spent at Codicote as came back at Gote (*Goat*) with Smith 6d. D[itt]o at Bull with old Oney & Inglish 6d. And our three ages amounted Oneys 87, Inglishes 73, mine 77, in all 237 years. Spent after at Tewin Jaks 6d.

Wednesday Evening [29] To the clubb Hardingfordbury. Spent over the clubb 2d. Clubb 6d, ostler 1d. Mr Cock was with me. Went to see [William] Phipp buried of Eason Green, herse & coach.[281]

Thursday 30 To the clubb fiest at the Green Dragon, Hartford, one Baxtaws. Next ev[e]ning the first of July went down to pay the bill as being steward with John Brett & Smith of Amwell, presedent (*president*). The bill £23 1s 0d. Spent 6d each. Baxtaw gave as some cold beef & 5s punch.

---

[281] William Phipps was buried at Hertingfordbury on 29 Jun 1803 [HALS: DP50/1/7].

The armey of reserve raised this month besides the old Millitia & Supplementrey d[itt]o.[282] The devell to pay.

This month Bulls Mill House or Benwick Hall (*Stapleford parish*) puled down by order of Rich[ar]d Emmott Esqr of Goldings the owner, and to erect a dogg kinell in its stead. Their doing of buisness. It was a compleat hansom strong brick house and maney a good familey hath lived in it to my knowledge, as Willson Esqr, Emmit Esqr, a taylor.[283]

JULY Saturday 2d To market in little [cart] with Mr Cock. Put up at Rich[ar]d Gears, at the Dear, Port Hill. Dined there with Cock & Buterfild on bacon. I found 1s 3d. Spent 1s each. Very hot day. Thunder, I was forsed to stop at Cold Bath, but no raine. Spent there 6d. Markets much the same, best wheat about 39s.

Sunday 3d to Tewin church. Afternoon to Tewin. Spent 2d.

Monday 4 To Tewin clubb. Spent before the clubb with Mr Dean of Tewin Bury 4d.

Tusday 5 To St Albans to swear in Millitia at the Angell. Swore in John Walker for my son Will & gave him £20. Spent in all with Burges, constable, & Ballard who was drawn for Bramfield likewise at Redhouse & the 3 Horseshoose as we came home 4s. Gave 1s.

Wesnesday 6 To Hoddesdon with my wooll with Mary Ann in little cart, 6 todd all but 8 pound. Mr Scate was not at home. Gave his man 6d and did not stop but went to Ware to dinner. Spent there 1s. Gave Will Frances for

---

[282] When war was resumed in May 1803 the government requested that all the former voluntary troops be re-formed and in Hertfordshire six new associations were raised [J Sainsbury, 'Local Volunteers during the Napoleonic Wars' in D Short (ed), *An Historical Atlas of Hertfordshire*, pp176-7].

[283] Bulls Mill House: its exact site is difficult to determine, but it probably stood near Bull's Mill. Some old apple trees here suggest the site of the orchard of the hall. Between 1795 and 1803 Thomas Blore, the well-known topographer, resided at Benwick Hall for several years. He collected a vast mass of material referring to the topography and antiquities of Hertfordshire, which was afterwards used by Robert Clutterbuck in his history [R T Andrews, *Benwick Hall, Stapleford* in EHAS Transactions vol iv, p100; *VCH Hertfordshire*, vol 3 pp476-480].

my horse Smiller 6d. On Saturday followin Mr Scate paid me £10 as 35s per todd for my wooll & 25s as left due last year, at White Hart, Hartford. Spent 1s.

Thursday 7th To Bramfield in evening. Spent at Mrs Derdses 3d.

Saturday 9 To market on poney. Dined at Bulls Head with Mr Hanken & Mr Cock on veal stakes. I spent 1s 8d. Bought a horse sold by auction by Driver for £13. 29 sold belonging to the horse sold[i]ers at Hartford. Spent at Bull and gave the soldiers 1s 2d, ostler 4d.

Monday 11 To the Quarter Sessions at Hartford. Jack Templeman, young Derds & E[d]w[ar]d Lowin was to appear for assolt on Vaux, shepherd. It was made upp on their good behaver for the futer. They paid the constable's bill.

Tusday 12 To Hartford for a rate to be made by Auston. I staid till it was done at the Cold Bath. Spent & gave there 1s 4d. There was a great meeting at the Town Hall to day for the defence of the countrey as thretned by Bonepart to invade us.

Wednesday 13th To Tewin fair. Spent there 1s. Receved the notices by one Merriott from Grover, the clerk from [Hemel] Hemsted for raiseing an armey of reserve for the defence of the countrey.

Thursday 14 Jorney round to all my parishs to deliver notices to all my constables for to make new lists for to draw for men for the defence of the countrey. Slept at Hexton. Came home by Norton & Sheephall. Spent in all & stopt at Wotton (*at Stone*) when Lady Rumbold was rec[ei]ving rents 5s.[284]

Saturday 16 Jorney to the Town Hall St Albans to receive instructions for the defence of the countrey. Went on poney. Spent at Redhouse 1s, corne & hostler 9d. Spent at Stanborough 6d.

---

[284] After the death of Sir Thomas Rumbold in 1791 his house at Watton Woodhall was sold but he bequeathed the remainder of his estate to the children of his second wife Joanna. It is Joanna who probably visited Hertfordshire in 1803. Sir George Berriman Rumbold, second baronet (1764–1807) was the son of Sir Thomas and his first wife, a Miss Berryman. George married, in Nov 1783, Caroline, only child of James Hearne of Shanakill, County Waterford, Ireland [G Le G Norgate, 'Rumbold, Sir George Berriman, second baronet (1764–1807)', rev H C G Matthew, *ODNB*].

Sunday 17 Not to church but to Codicote in the afternoon to deliver warrants for the Hund[red] of Cashio to meet at Town Hall St Albans on next Thursday for defence of the countrey. Spent 1s. Spent at Jacks as came home with Thos Welch from near London, which came to day to see his friends & brought Sal Warby with him 8d.

Tusday 19 To Ware on the poney. Dined at Eagle & slept there. Spent the afternoon there with young Hudson when paid him for malt & Mr Stephenson and others. Sat in the back y[a]rd. Sultrey hott. Spent in all 3s.

Wednesday 20th Will went to St Albans Town Hall to carry in the list for the armey of reserve instead of Burges, constable & my self as being at Mr Hunsdon's buring at Great Amwell.[285]

Thursday 21 Jorney to the Town Hall on poney to settle inspectors in every parish of the Hundard of Cashio for the defence of the countrey. The Minister, church wardens & other princip[a]l inhabitants of every parish went. Lord Grimston the Head for Cashio, and some princip[a]l person for each parish as the Revd Mr Bourchier for Bramfield &c. Spent at the Redhouse with Derds, Parker, Bygrave, Chalkley for diner 1s, after 9d, corne & hostler 8d. Spent at Jonas Langtons at Stanborough with Chipperfield & others at the Horse [&] Groom as came home there, 1s.

Fryday 22 Spent at Tewin with brother Hasler & young Stephens from Ware 1s 6d.

Saturday 23 Jorney to Town Hall St Albans with Burges, Bramfield constable, on horsback to draw for the armey of reserve. Joseph Moobray was drawd for Bramfield. Dinner at the Redhouse 2s. Spent after & corne & ostler 1s. Went by Stanborough & came home that way & spent at the Horse & Groom there one Jonas Langtons 1s. At Tewin after 6d.

Sunday 24 To Bramfield church. Afternoon to Tewin. Spent with Mr Cock & Simon 7d.

Monday 25 To the Assizes on poney, left him at Chapm[an]s. Judges Heath, & Elingborough. Went to church the text 'shall we receive good at the hand

---

[285] Henry Hunsdon of West End Farm, Bramfield had died on 13 July and was buried on 20 July at Great Amwell [HALS: DP4/1/11].

of God, & shall we not receive evil'.[286] Esqr Brown of North Mimms sheriff, the Hon Spencer Cowper foor man (*foreman*) of Grand Jury. The fellons all tried the first day. Severall law tryalls and one between Bayley of Codicote, and Hill about rotten sheep. Bayley lost the cause.

[Tuesday] 26 Spent at Mr Derds 3d.

Wednesday 27 In the evening to clubb at White Horse, Hardingfordbury. Clubb 2 nights 1s, ostler 1d.

Thursday 28 To Hartford in little cart. Caried 7s worth of wood to the woman [in] Hartford workhouse. Went to Geers Port Hill for pollard. Spent there with Mr Rutter & Mrs Hasler, little boy w[i]th me 1s.

Fryday 29 Morning to Bramfield. Spent 2½d. Evening to Tewin to meet Waller, bricklayer on his bill for Thos Sheath's shop. Spent 9d.

Saturday 30 To St Albans the Town Hall to swear in the armey of reserve when Joseph Mowbery was drawn for Bramfield but he appeald off, so drawd again Esqr Vaux. Dined at Redhouse. Diner 2s. Spent after & horse 1s 6d. Spent at Smiths the Horshoos as came home with Burges 1s 6d & gave [blank].

Sunday 31 To Tewin church. Afternoon to Tewin. Spent there & gave 7½d.

> This month we are thretned to be invaded by one Boneparte, by the French, and England is to be divided amongst the French, and every man to be killed and the women to be saved. So we are raiseing of men from [age] 17 to 55 one class, and 15 to 60 the other class. So nothing but soldiering. Three times a week to St Albans to draw and swear inn, Burges the constable of Bramfield & my self, fine work.

AUGUST 1 Spent at Tewin clubb. Gave old Webster 4d. Spent 2d.

Tusday 2d to Ware on the poney [and] little boy with the cart to carry post to Witbury Hill. Spent 6d. Gave Will Frances 6d. Spent at Half Moon at

[286] Text is from Job ch 2, verse 10: 'But he said unto her, thou speakest as one of the foolish women speaketh. What? shall we receive good at the hand of God, and shall we not receive evil? In all this did not Job sin with his lips'.

Hartford as being called after to take papers from Mr Grover 6d as being a meeting this day at Town Hall for the defence of the countrey.

Thursday 4 Went to the ringing fiest at the Town Hall Hartford. Diner. Dressed at the Angell Cambells, 206 at dinner, ticketts 9s each. Home at ½ pst 10. Fell of[f] the poney at the turn out of the road into field. Walked home after.

Fryday 5 To the 3 Hors Shoos, one Pedders by Nup End (*Codicote parish*) to meet my constables. All there. Good dinner, rost ribbs beef & pudings. Spent each 4s. I gave Waters 2d, boy for horse 3d. Spent at Burnahm Gren (*Burnham Green*) 6d. Mr Guttredge with us & Bottom.

Saturday 6 To market on poney. Dined at Bulls Head with Hanken butcher on lamb stakes. Spent 9d. Markets dearer. Home forwd by Lord Cowper Pansanger. Gave hostler at Bull 4d.

Sunday 7th To Bramfield church. Afternoon rode round by old Clibborns[287] & so to Tewin with Mrs Buttrey so home to tea.

Monday 8 Begun harvest, in generall the cropps very great. Wheat laid & mildued (*mildewed*). Mrs Buttrey & Miss Web come down this Saturday 6th, went away on the Monday 8th. Miss Peggy Clark went with them.

Wednesday 10th In the evening to Hardingfordby clubb & spent after 1s. Staid late & lost my poney.

Satturday 13th Not to market as being buisey at Oates' cart. Markets much the same.

Sunday 14 To Tewin church. Afternoon to Bayford with Mr Cock, to enquire after a lad, one Slack, that I hired till Mixs (*Michaelmas*). Spent there at the alehouse one Sagents 1s.[288] Saw the new church a building with brick there about 3 foot high.

---

[287] Clibbons Post, the stake marking the burial place of the footpad, Walter Clibbon stands by the roadside at Oakenvalley Bottom in the parish of Tewin, on the road between Bramfield and Datchworth. Carrington's visitors often went to see it. It has been renewed as recently as 2009.

[288] John Sergeant was licensed at the Griffin, Bayford, at least from 1806 [HALS: QSVR1806].

Fryday 19 Jorney to St Albans with Burges constable to Town Hall to carry in the lists of all persons from 17 to 55 the first class & from 15 to 60 the 2d class & of carts & waggons to assist if invaded. Dinner at Redhouse and spent after & horse &c 3s 8d. Spent at Stanborough as came home 9d. L[or]d Grimston & full meeting there.

Saturday 20th To market on the Soger in the afternoon.[289] Spent at Bull with Mr Nickold, the parson & Aylon and ostler 1s 6d. Markets much the same. Small as being buisey in the harvest. I sold 5 load of wheat to day to Mr Farr of Burleys Mill for 40s per load.

Sunday 21 To Bramfield church. Afternoon to [Little] Barkhamstead with Mr Cock on horseback. Spent at the Horshoos there one Boltons 1s 6d. Gave Ballard 6d. Spent at Hardingfordbury 6d.

Wednesday 24 To Hartingbry (*Hertingfordbury*) Clubb 6d.

Saturday 27 To market in afternoon on the Soger. Put up at [Gren] Dragon to £12 for wheat of Ensom sold to Farr at Burleys Mill at 40s per load, 6 load sold.[290] Last day by sample. Markets much the same. Spent 1s 6d, ostler 3d. Gave old Dickinson 6d. Sold 5 load more to Farr to the same mill at 41s.

Sunday 28 Not to church but to Ware on poney to dinner as expected Coz Cooks down, but they did not come. So came home soon. Spent & gave there 1s 3d. Went to Tewin after to find some men to mowe. Spent there with Forster 8½d.

> The fineist harvest ever known & the most greatest, perticular barley. Never known so much and there's great plenty. A vas[t] numb[e]r of reeks, but we greatly want water.

SEPTEMBER Fryday 2d Went to Codicote on poney to deliver war[ra]nts for licensing. Spent and gave at the Goat 1s. Finished harvest.

Saturday 3 To market on poney in afternoon. Spent at Cooks Maidenhead 6d. Spent at Bull with Frank Stevens &c 1s. Gave ostler 4d. Markets much the same. I sold 5 load of wheat at 41s. Harvest home on Saturday Night and

---

[289] Soger (*Soldier*) is the name of one of Carrington's horses.

[290] Ensom was what Carrington calls elsewhere a 'sack carrier'. In 1804 and 1806 Carrington was to employ him in catching moles.

this night 3 howsen at Tewin was entred into and robed John Munnses, Robt Grimeses, & John Cutts, Tewin Lower Green.[291] The people was all from home as at harves[t] homes or drinking larges, but the man was taken that night and kept in hold till Monday & then comm[it]ted to goall by Hen[ry] Cowper, Tewin Water Esqr.

Sunday 4th To Bramfield church. Afternoon to Ware to dinner on poney as Coz Cooks down. Spent 1s. Gave 4d.

Monday 5 Afternoon to Mrs Derdses to carry her certivicate (*certificate*) for licensing. Spent there 3d. After to Tewin clubb, forfitt (*forfeit*) 2d. The man sent to goall for pilfering 3 houses at Tewin.

Wednesday 7 To Clubb Hartinbry (*Hertingfordbury*). Clubb 6d. Gave 1d.

Thursday 8 To Hartford for peas of[f] Brown. Gave his man 6d. Afterwards to the sale at Bulls Mill of the mater[i]als of the great house Esqr Emmet pul[l]d down, & are now a building a dog kinell, thats doing of buisness in deed. Fished Husmer Pond which never known so low as the springs being so & the dry whather. Catched plenty of fish. Sent some to Tewin by G[eorge] Burton, & some I carried to Esqr Macky.

Saturday 10th To St Albans on poney with Burges constable, as licensing day at the Town Hall, and balloting for some for Millitia, & armey of reserve. Gentlemen Mr Donvell & Cowper, & Boys &c for licensing, and Lord Grimston & Vandermuling &c for balloting. Dinner at the Redhouse with my constabls 2s. Spent after & horse &c 2s 6d. Spent at Tewin as came home 1s.

Sunday 11 Not to church but the afternoon to Wellwin on the Soger, to see Waller, brickman. Gave him £10 at the Checkers one Wallers.[292] Waller treated. Gave the lad 2d.

---

[291] William Jackson of Tewin, labourer, was tried on 4 Oct 1803 for stealing a linen shirt (6d) and a linen pocket handkerchief (4d) the property of William Ward. He also stole three pairs of thread stockings (3d), a muslin neck handkerchief (1d), a lawn neck handkerchief (1d), a silk handkerchief (2d) and a linen shirt (3d) the property of George Hall, and a calico handkerchief (5d) and a child's calico shirt (5d) the property of John Cutts. He was found guilty and sentenced to three months in Hertford gaol [TNA: Hertford Assize records, information from Ken Griffin].

[292] James Waller kept the Chequers, Welwyn at least until 1828 [HALS: QSVR1828].

Wednesday 14 To Hartingfordb[ur]y statut[e]. Spent there 1s. From thence to the clubb Hartford. Gave to ostler &c 5d.

Saturday 17 To market on poney. Sold 5 load of wheat at 37s per load. Dined on stakes at the Bulls Head. Spent there with Mr Cock 2s. Spent after at Bull 1s, ostler 4d. Went with my men after to Bramfield to spend their larges. Gave them 3s. Mr Burges with us.

Monday 19 To Wotton stattute. Dined at the Bull Wilshires. Diner 2s. Spent after 1s. Gave away 9d. Hir[e]d one Parker for horskeep[e]r from Benington for 2 guines ½.

Wednesday 21 To Hartford. Bought 2 wa[i]stco[a]ts 14s 6d. Spent at Rich Gears at the Runing Dear Port Hill 1s 3d. Came home by Pansanger, was made welcome by Mr House, Ld Cowper's hous stew[a]rd.

Thursday 22 Spent at Bramfield with nephew John Beck & Smith when at work in the road 1s 6d.

Fryday 23 Spent at Tewin Jacks with Coz J Beck the elder, & Simon Worby & gave old Webster 1s 7d.

Saturday 24 To market on poney. Sold 5 load of wheat at 37s 6d per load. Dined at the Vine Momforts on stakes with Hanken butcher, Butterfield, 2 Claphams &c. Spent each 1s. Spent after at Bull 6d. The great shew of wild beast & birds at Bull. Gave the man that blowed the french horn 3d, hostler 4d. Markets much the same.

Sunday 25 To Tewin church a charity sermon preached by the Curat of Hardingfordbry (*Hertingfordbury*). Gave 2s 6d. Dined at Johns Tewin with Coz John Beck the elder. Spent after with him & one Mr Nickolds, a traveling linnen draper 2s.

Monday 26 Afternoon to Lord Cowper's Pansanger. Supt with Mr House the house stewrd. Gave the 2 boys 1s.

Thursday 29 To Hartford bells ringing mayr's fiest, Mr Kimpton maior.[293] Spent at the Cold Bath with Mr Cock 6d. From thence to Bramf[iel]d

---

[293] William Kimpton, mayor of Hertford [Turnor, *History of Hertford*, p130].

Vestrey, to appoint surveyors, myself againe, Mr Vaux, Mr Bourchier, Mr Derds, Jam[e]s Allen, all that was there besides Auston clerk.

Fryday 30th Afternoon to Tewin Jacks. Spent there with Mr Cock and gave my men some beer as cleening Husmer Pond. Spent 3s 6d.

Wotton Statute 19
Kimpton Statute 21
Codicot Statute 22
Wellwin Statute 26

This month cleaned the same Husmer Pond all over, as well as we could as being little water in it. So cleaned one part, & then let the water in & so other parts. Carted it out some in Husmer, other in Stable Field. Never known to be cleand before.

OCTOBER Saturday 1st To market on poney to pay Mumford at the Vine bricklayer £20 for & towards building Bramf[iel]d poor house. Spent there 1s. Gave 4d. Came home by Pansang[e]r Ld Cowpers. Staid late.

Sunday 2d To Bramfield church. Afternoon to Tewin. Spent at sons there 3d.

Monday 3d Evening to Tewin clubb. Spent over 3d.

Tusday 4 To Ware in little cart to carry sister Hasler 3 piggs. Dined there with Mrs Sissom. Spent 3d. Gave 6d.

Wednesday 5 Afternoon to Hardingfordy (*Hertingfordbury*) clubb 2 nights 1s.

Saturday 8 To market on poney. Dined at Bulls Head. Diner 1s 6d. Spent after 6d. Spent at Bull after 1s, hosler 4d. Gave Hall 3d. Markets wheat 40s, barley 24s, peas 27s, oates 25s &c.

Sunday 9 To Hardingfordbury church, a charity sermon. Gave 2s 6d. Afternoon to Tewin. Spent 3d.

Monday 10th To the Feathers Tewin Upper Green, Joseph Whittenburys, Esqr Macky's wood fieast. John Molding took the money. I paid for 1 rood £1 15s 0d. Spent each 2s. Spent at Jacks after 1s.

Tusday 11th Mixs (*Michaelmas*) day. In the afternoon to the Run[n]ing Dear, Port Hill. Spent 3½d. Gave 6d.

Friday [14] To Ware in Stewrds cart. Slept there. Spent & gave there 2s. Spent at Stewrds the 2 Brew[e]rs as came home at Hartford 1s. Spent at Medcalfs the Half Moon 3s. Gave to Rose Hudson &c 2s.

Saturday 15 To St Albans Town Hall to appoint surveyors of the highways, and to appoint assessors of the new taxes. Dined at the Redhouse. Diner 2s. Spent after 1s 6d, ostler 6d. Came home by Stanborough. Spent 4d.

Sunday 16 To Bramfield church, Mr Newton of Tewin preached. Afternoon to Tewin. Spent at Jacks 3d.

Monday 17 Afternoon to Bramfield after taxes. Spent at Wd Derdses with John Sheath &c 9d.

Tusday 18 Round Bramfield to deliver papers on the new taxes. Spent at Derdses 6d.

Wednesday 19 To the clubb in the evening at the White Horse, Hardingfordbury 7d.

Fryday 21 To Bull at Ware to pay taxes, paid all taxes for 1802, and £15 towards this year 1803. Onely Byde & Pierson. Dined at Eagle with Mr Elstone of Diggswell, Samms from Hoddesdon, Iardale from Wormley, baker. Spent each 3s. Spent as came home at Hartford with Elstone 1s at [Green] Dragon.

Saturday [22] To market on poney. Put up at the 2 Brewers by the Blucote Buildings one Stewards, diner 1s.[294] Spent after with Gear & Thos Smith 1s,

[294] Christ's Hospital, or the Blue Coat School, was founded in 1553 by Edward VI as a hospital for orphans in the Greyfriars' buildings in Newgate Street, London. The distinctive uniform of long blue coats and yellow stockings, still worn by the pupils, gave the school its name. The girls moved to Hertford in 1704 to new buildings at the end of Fore Street, while the boys remained in London until 1902 when they moved to Horsham, Sussex, the girls joining them there in 1985. The Hertford buildings were partly demolished and those remaining are now both residential and office accommodation [Weinreb et al, *London Encyclopaedia*]; The Two Brewers public house next door was the brewery tap for Young's brewery [Whitaker, *Brewers in Hertfordshire*, p117].

hostler 4d. Spent after at the Run[n]ing Dear Port Hill with Butterfield & Colley 1s.

Sunday the 23 To Tewin church the first sermon, Hamelton there. Afterwards to Woolmer Green the Redlyon Mrs Crowes, recd my rent. Mr Cock went with me. We dined there & drank tea, & Butterfield & Thos Smith was with us. Dinner & tea &c and the ostler &c, home by 9 clock 12s.

Wednesday 26 To London in Hartford Cambells Coach from Angell, fair innside 4s 6d. Came home on the Saturday 29 in the same coach ½ inn, ½ out, for 3s. On Fryday 28 saw the great revew in High (*Hyde*) Park by the King, 27 thousand vaulentiers in and about London, and supposed to be 500,000 spectators, and on the Wednesday the 26 before there was the same number revewed by his Majesty in High Park about 54,000 on the both days all vaulteers (*volunteers*).[295] I never saw such a sight all my days. Saw the hopmerchant Mr & Mrs Bulbey & Mr Smith there, Mr Nickolds, & Mrs King &c. Came home the 29th. Slep at Coz Becks. Spent in all 7s besides coach.

Sunday 30 Not to church, the afternoon Mr Cock & I to Tewin. Spent at Jacks 3½d.

> The Begining of this month & the latter end of last, cleaned Husmer Pond, as little or no water in it & the springs never known so low, it was never known to be cleaned out before. The middle very deepe, mirey bottom, could not git all out.

NOVEMBER Tusday 1st To Ware. Dined at Eagle. Spent & gave 1s 1d.

Wednesday 2d To the Rose & Crown, Tewin to the Association Fiest for Prosecuting Fellons for depredations held there. Diner mock turtle, fine lyne (*loin*) of rost beef, pudings &c. Mr Dean, Mr Pallett, Mr Webb, Mr Humfield, Simon, Brux, Rowley baker, Bowley, Elston, Hanken, Johnson, Ben Sqr (*Squire*), Mr Patient, my self, Mr Preston, Mr Edmans. No wine, plenty of punch. Each paid 7s.

November 5 Saturday Jorney to St Albans to swear to the returns of the overseers, & to sighn the same returns of all my parishes, the 2 Rows from

---

[295] It is reported that on the two days 26 and 28 Oct, 27,077 troops were reviewed [*The Annual Register,* 29 Oct 1803].

Shephall which was sumond as did not make their returns.[296] Dined at Red House 2s. Spent after & horse 1s 6d. Spent at Stanborough 3d. D[itt]o at Tewin as came home 6d. Markets, the best wheat 40s.

Monday 7th To tythe fiest at Bramfield. Mr Bourchier dined with us in landrey (*?laundry*). Diner 3 fowls, bacon, & ribbs of rost beef, pudings &c. Dined my silf, Derds, Whittenbury, Smith for Mrs Hunsdon, Hornat, Allen & son Will[ia]m Carrington which was all. Plenty punch, good beer & good comp[a]ny. Gave Webst[e]r 1s.

Tusday 8 To Hartford Fair. Dined at Richardsons & spent 1s 4d. Spent at Cold Bath as came home one Winters, with Molden, Burr, son John, Ben Sqr (*Squire*), & Lowin 1s.

Saturday 12th Jorney to Town Hall [St Albans] on poney to carry in returns for the Income Tax on property, but not settled, must go agine on 3d of Dece[m]b[e]r. Dined at Redhouse with Pierce, Mathews, Simkins, Woodfield, Parker, &c. Dinner 2s. Spent after, horse & ostler 1s 6d. Went by Stanborough & came [home] the same. Commissioners, Howard, Gape, Kentish, Cowper clerk.

Sunday 13 To Bramfield church. Afternoon to Tewin Jacks. Spent there with Bowley, butcher &c 1s 6d.

Tusday 15 To Ware on poney, bought 10qr malt of Cadmore at 60s. Dined at Haslers. Spent 1s 2d. Home erley.

Fryday 18th To Tewin to rceive rent of Day, North, Ward, Canfield, & Thos Sheath. Receivd all their rent up to Mxs (*Michaelmas*) last. Gave supper and spent in ginn & beer 12s.

Saturday 19 To market on poney. Went by Esqr Emmotts to recive bill. Dined at Bull. Dinner & spent 2s 6d. Spent at Gears and gave away 2s.

Sunday 20th Not to church but writeing warrants and the afternoon to Wellw[in] to put in the post for making Speciall Constables. Spent at Tewin as came back 3d.

---

[296] Possibly returns of vagrants failing to secure settlement in their new parishes and sent back to their old ones. This would require both overseers to secure authorisation for removal and constables to carry removal out.

Wednesday 23rd To Hartford. Spent at Blackbirds with Gilbertson grocer 9d. Spent at Shipp with Gripper 9d. Gave 2d.

Saturday 26 Jorney to St Albans Town Hall to appoint Speciall Constables, for the parish of Bramfield, & other d[itt]o against an attempt of the enemy.[297] Dined at Redhouse. Dinner 2s. Spent after & at Stanborough 1s. Wm Adams & John Hart was appointed for Bramfield.

Sunday 27 To Bramf[iel]d church. Afternoon to Tewin. Spent with Mr Dean, Mr Hanken, Brux & Pridmor 1s.

Wednesday 30 To Hartford with Cock. Gave hamm to Medcalf, puttatos (*potatoes*) to Hall, after to clubb Hardfordby (*Hertingfordbury*). Spent over clubb with Hanken when sold turnops at £3 per acre, 9d.

> Now the rain so much wanted came Tusday night 8th & Wednesday 9th of this month as being dry since the 20th day of June last.

DECEMBER Saturday 3d Jorney to St Albans on poney with Wm Smith to deliver in papers on the New Taxes. Smith & Preston was sworn in Speciall Constables. Dined at Redhouse. Dinner 2s. Spent after & ostler 1s. Spent at Redlyon at Hatfield as came home 1s.

Sunday 4th To Ware. Staid all night, paid Cadmore for 12 quarter of malt at 60s per qr. Spent with Aylon & him 2s. Gave Will Francis 6d.

Monday 5 To Tewin clubb. Spent over & gave Chapman & little boy 4d.

Saturday 10th To mark[e]t on foot. Dined at Bull second table. Diner 1s 4d. Spent after in little room with Gripper 1s. Spent after at [Green] Dragon with

---

297 A letter was sent to the Justices by Charles Philip Yorke, one of His Majesty's Principal Secretaries of State, stating that 'in the Event of the French making an attempt to invade this Kingdon, it would be of importance to provide for the internal good Order and Tranquility of the Country' and proposed that 'it should be recommended to the Magistrates of this County to enquire in their several Districts what Trust Worthy Housekeepers or others, who are not enrolled in any Volunteer Corps or liable to Military Service from being included in the first and second Classes under the General Defence Acts, would in the Event above mentioned engage to come forward and to act Special Constables'. The responsibility was given to the High Constables to make out a list of eligible men for this purpose [*HCR* vol IX pxi-xii and 52-3].

Shadbolt 6d. Spent after at Cold Bath with Pridmore school master at Tewin, and Harrington of d[itt]o 6d. When Pridmor & Harington left me with torch.

Tusday 13th Spent at Mrs Derdses, Bramfield with Rich[ar]dson from Bulls Head, Hartford, & a Sergant of the Hartford Volunteers, 9d.

16th Fryday Spent at Tewin by my self 3d.

Saturday 17th To market in little cart with Cock. Dined at Richardsons Bulls Head on tripe. Spent & gave there 1s 2d. Spent at Bull after 7d, gave ostler 5d. Spent at Cold Bath 6d. Came home with us, Sqr (*Squire*), Wm Smith & Sheath &c.
Sunday [18] To Bramf[iel]d church.

Monday [19] To Hallords (*Hollards*) Farm to see Mrs Hunsdon. Came home by Tewin. Stopt at son Johns. Was well treated with elder wine with maney others as being my grandsons Johns birthday. Deaff Jimmey came to Bacons with me.

Tusday [20] To Tewin to Jacks. Spent 3d.

Fryday [23] Spent at Tewin sons, with Day & Cheek from Hartford, & after with the vestry held there Thos Whittenbry, Brux, Simon, Warby and John Sheath, 1s 3d.

Saturday 24th To market in little cart with Mr Cock. Dined at Bulls Head on stakes given by Hanken. With him & Cock & young Clapham spent each 1s. Spent after at Bull 1s. Gave ostler 6d.

Sunday 25 Christmas Day To Bramfield church. To Hunsdons after noon. The great high wind this Christmas Day.

Monday 26th To Jos Whittenbrys Tewin Upper Green, the Feathers, according to custom, with son John, Simon Warbey, Thos Whittenbry, old Webster, John Squier, Thos Watson, Grims, they spent each 1s. I spent 5s.

Wednesday 28 To Lord Cowper's rent fiest, at Cole Green at Mr Thos Palletts, his stewards. Round of beef lyne (*loin*), rost veal & hamm, pudings &c. Good beer, plenty of punch, home by 5.

Thursday 29 To Ware with sister. Staid all night, spent 1s. Walked home next day Fryday 30th and from home to Tewin to ven[i]son fiest at Jacks. 8 in company, each 5s 6d, my self, Harrington, Simon, Pridmore, Whittenbury, a gentleman at Simons, Moulding, & Geo[rge] Hasler.

Saturday 31 Jorney to Town Hall St Albans apeall day about the Income Tax. Burges, & Jos Derds & Mrs Hunsdon went. Dined at the Red House, a turkey, leg mutton, spearibb &c. Dinner 2s. Gave the girll 6d. Spent after 6d. Spent at Redlyon, Hatfield 6d. Gave ostlers here & St Albans 7d.

Thus ends this year, at the latterend wet & a flood, as the finest harvest ever known and the greatest for barley ever known, as being dry wather since 20th of June to the 9th of Nov[embe]r. And a flood at the end of the year. And the want of water never known so bad, as most ponds dry. I was forsed to fetch water from the river at Poplar Green to brew with, as Husmer Pond Dry. And I cleand it out, as never known to be cleaned before. Wheat about 34s per load the best, barley 24s per qr the best, peas 24s per load, oates 26s per qr, malt 64s per quarter as a duty of 35s per quarter, hopps 16d per pound.

And Ginnings Burry (*Jenningsbury*) great house pulled down near Hartford, by Lord John Townsend of Balls.

And this year Esqr Cashwell (*Caswall*) of Sacomb, bgunn bilding a new great house in his park some distance from whear the old house stood as was puled down about 20 years back, whear one old Roult lived, Cashwell's grandfather.

The greatest flood ever known in England was Monday 9th, Tusday 10, Wednesday 11 February 1795.

The first that was buried in a coffin was Joseph the last virce of Ginnises.[298]

In the midle of the day or 12 clock at the eaquanox, a stick 3 foot the shaddow will be 3 foot 7 inches.

[298] Genesis ch 50, verse 26: 'So Joseph died, being an hundred and ten years old: and they embalmed him, and he was put in a coffin in Egypt'.

Deaths, marriages & other events for this year 1803

Fryday 14 January was buried at Hardingfordbury church Mr Ewd Polter formerly servant to the 2 Miss Searanks at Hatfield. Was found dead in the bed whear he lodged at Hatfield aged about 60. No nails or plate on his coffin.

Skeggs plumer & glaiser at Ware found dead in his hoggs coart, supposed went to feed them & took in a fitt this **January**.

Fryday 11 [February] Blewitt from Tewin workhouse buried, formerly a Light Horse Man and in the wars in Germaney with Generall Ellett he gained his settlement at Tewin by living horskeepr with one North, miller at Tewin Mill, about the year 1755.[299] I ground there then.

Monday 21st Feb in the morning died Mr Thorowgood, butcher at Ware.

This month was buried at Bramfield Dame Brux wife to old Brux of d[itt]o age 88.[300]

Fryday 4 [March] Died at Hartford Mr Samuall French, chieff constable there age 60.

Tusday 8 Died the Duke of Bridgwater. He latley purchased Woolmers for £15,000 of Esqr Whitebread and was making great addition to the house, and all new out buildings.

Old Mr Claile of Hartford Heath farmer & carpenter, he was one that hope (*helped*) build the two wings to one Mr Scott's house at Amwell End about

---

[299] James Blewitt was buried on 11 Feb at Tewin [HALS: DP106/1/2]. George Augustus Eliott, 1st Baron Heathfield (1717-1790) was the Colonel of the 1st Light Horse raised on 10 Mar 1759 and fought campaigns in Germany during the Seven Years War. After the war his regiment was renamed the 15th or King's Own Royal Light Dragoons. He was made a Major General in 1759, Lieutenant General in 1765 and Governor of Gibraltar in 1775. With his troops he successfully held Gibraltar against the Spanish during the siege of 1779-1782 and in 1787 was created Lord Heathfield, Baron of Gibraltar [James Falkner, 'Eliott, George Augustus, first Baron Heathfield of Gibraltar (1717–1790)', *ODNB*, Jan 2008].

[300] 'Ann Brooks, wife of Brooks, labourer' was buried at Bramfield on 17 Feb 1803 [HALS: DP22/1/3].

the year 1766. Buried at All S[ain]ts Hartford **Sunday March 13th** this year 1803.

John Crow of Hartford buried at All S[ain]ts Hartford **Sunday 13** aged 29. He was son to one Roger Crow wich formerly kept the Vine.

Sunday Night March 13 Died Eliz[abe]th Day wife to Thos Day of Bramfield. Buried the Thursday following at Wormley, a herce and 2 horses and 2 little carts.

Thos Prockter Esqr at Bengeo Hall, & brewer at London buried in Bengeo church **Wednesday the 16 of this month.**

John Wellingham, tanner at Whitwell died this month, buried **22d** at Pauls Walding church ag[e] 65.

Dr Oldmeadows of Wellwin died **22** of this month aged 35. Left a large family.

Sunday 27 Died Nancy Pierce at sisters Hasslers at Amwell End, Ware. Buried at Tewin on the Thursday following about 2 clock by Mr Thos Lloyd, for Mr Newton.[301] A good dinner at son Johns the Rose & Crown. A herce & pair, a morning coach & pair, from Mr Flack Hartford, Mrs Barnatt of Ware undertaker. Aged 54. The coffin covered with black cloath, & plate, 4 men bearers and was carried on the bier from the herce. She was first Coz to my late Dame, & sister [in law] Hassler and she had lived servant maney years with Mrs Goodall, Spittle Square, and at her death which a bout a year back left her £500 which she has left to my children and brother Haslers & honest & faithfull servant.

Tyler's wife of Waterford hanged her self this month.

Mr Field of Colsfoot Farm, Datchw[o]rth died the **3d [April]**. Buried at Datchw[o]rth church.[302]

---

[301] 'Ann Pearse from Gt Amwell' was buried at Tewin on 30 Mar 1803 [HALS: DP106/1/2].

[302] 'William Field, farmer' was buried at Datchworth on 7 Apr 1803 [HALS: DP33/1/24].

Mr Edmond Edmonds of Margate (*Kent*) died on the **5th** he belonged to the Green Dragon New Union Society, Hartford. He formerly lived at Mr Hunsdons at Bramfield West End Farme as border. Worthy man.

On Wednesday evening 7 clock the **6th** was shott dead Col[onel]l Montgomery, by Capt[ain] Macknamara in a duil near Chalks Farme, Primrose Hill near London. This unfortnate afare happned as thus the Coll & Capt the same day was both riding in High (*Hyde*) Park & each with a Newfoundland dogg, the doggs fell to fighting, which caused them to have words, which ended by the death of the Colln & the Capt wounded, for both shots hitt. They appointed to meet in 2 [h]ours after they had words which they did. The Colln was had to Chalk Farme but died instantly, the Captain was much wounded but on tryall after, was acquitted.[303]

Capt William Jackson buried in a vault in the midle of St Andrews church yard Hartford **Sunday 24**. He lodged in part of a house belonging to one England in Maiden Head Street, Hartford. He was in the navy servis but on half pay. A very worthey good man aged 57.

Monday 9th [May] Mrs Pinnaks plowman of Diggswell Lodge runn over near Walken (*Walkern*) as been to fetch a waggon load of hurdl[e]s. Died the 15th at Walkorn.

Monday 23 The Hartford morning coach overturnd at the bottom of the hill at the entrance of Newington agoing to London. One man from Stanstead killed nown by the name of Lowder, Mr Usborn's son legg broke, Mr Pollard's daughter's arme broke, of Hartford, Mr Hanken butcher of Hartingfordbury very much brused, & others much hurt as 14 passingers, one more since dead.

Wednesday 25 Was buried from Hoddesdon Mr Wm Whittenstall, a hers[e] and six, 3 morning coaches in four & his own cariage &c &c at Hitchen. He lived at this end of Hoddesdon whch is in the parish of Great Amwell, and died in a fitt at Amwell Church at a vestrey there, Tusday evening the 17th. He came there in his own chariott very well, and in about 3 [h]ours was caried

[303] This duel fought between Colonel Robert Montgomery RN and Captain James Macnamara (1768-1826) about a dog was reported in *The Times*, 7 Apr 1803 [*The Times* Digital Archive, 1785-1985].

home in a herce & shell coffin to his own house. He was a man in Great Brewery at Hodesdon & mealing (*malting*) aged about 55.[304]

On Wittson Tusday in the morning about 4 clock, **the 31st** was found dead in their bed, John Ramsey's, wife and child, which lived in St Andrews church yard, Hartford. The affair was as thus, she had a vollent paine in her face & teeth, and sent to Dr Bradleys in the town, for something to ease her, they sent her some lodnahm (*laudnum*) to put to a poltess to lay on her cheek, but she took it inwardly and the child about 6 month old sucking recived the same. Mr Ramsey had been on the Whitson Monday with maney others the boundarys of St Andrews parish, and dined at the Maidenhead with the companey, & staid late so knew nothing of the matter. I saw Mr Ramsey on horseback in good spirits, as we met them at Maple X (*Cross*) Hill in the road going to Goldings, as Bramfield people was going their boundreys at the same time, and we went togather from thence to Hooksbushes Corner into Gilbirds Pikel (*Pightle*), oppsate Bacons, then they turnd to the left X Tewin Road, & Bramfield to the right down by Bacons orchard.

On Whiston Wednesday earley in the morning the **1st of June** was burnt to death Mr Williams & wife & 3 children and one other person at the Three Cranes near Mile End Turnpike, London. His house was discovrd to be all on fire below so could not come down, & his windows was all iorn bard (*iron-barred*) that he could not git out at the top so they instantly perished as the chamber floor fell.

Thursday the last of this month **[30th] June** was found dead in her bed Mrs Walker of Hartford, widow in Castle Street between the market & the Blackbirds where she had lived maney years and kept a school for small children to read.[305]

---

304 'William Whittingstall of Hodsden' was buried at Hitchin on 25 May 1803 [HALS: DP53/1/5]. He owned maltings in Hoddesdon and Stanstead Abbots. His brewery was subsequently purchased by William Christie and George Cathrow [J A Tregelles, *A History of Hoddesdon* (Hertford, 1908), p262; Whitaker, *Brewers in Hertfordshire*, pp149-157].

305 Lydia Walker was buried at All Saints, Hertford on 5 July 1803 [HALS: DP48/1/25].

The **9th [July]** in the morning died old Mr Godfrey of Rickneys, parish of Bengeo aged 97 years. Buried at Little Munden.[306]

Born of a Wednesday, died of d[itt]o, buried d[itt]o. **Wednesday 13th** died Mr Henery Hunsdon of Bramfield West End Farme. Buried the Wednesday following at Great Amwell.[307] Herse and pair, coach and pair, my self, Mr Webb, Preston, Burges, Bowley, Sheath, Whittenbury, Derds, Richardson, John Carrington. We all on horsback & my little cart, & Mr Odall with his little cart, and cloaks, silk hatbanks & gloves. The great thunder storme while at church. Aged 37.

Mr Parnall of Wotton, schoolmaster there died **Fryday morning the 15th** aged about 40.[308]

Wednesday 24 [August] in the morning died Mr Neall, atturney at law at the Great House oppiset the Black Swann, Castle Street Hartford. Buried on the Satturday the 27 at All Saints Church, Hartford aged 59.[309] Left a widow & one son about 18.

Thursday 8 [September] died Thos Kinder, great brewer at St Albans & one of the Justices of the Peace there. Died almost sudingly, a good man, aged about 60.

Thursday 15 died Mrs Chapman, wife to Mr Chappman St Andrews Street, Hartford, in an apperplective fitt.[310] Most aimeable good woman, aged about 60.

The same day died Mr Atkins the wheeler at Hartford up Castle Street.

Josua Parish buried at Tewin church **Fryday 30th Sepr** aged 55. A native of Tewin and lived in the little house by the upper alehouse.

---

306 'Thomas Godfrey of Bengeo' was buried at Little Munden on 13 July 1803 [HALS: DP71/1/1].

307 Henry Hunsdon, aged 37, was buried at Great Amwell on 20 July 1803 [HALS: DP4/1/11].

308 'John Parnell' was buried at Watton at Stone on 17 July 1803 [HALS: DP118/1/2].

309 'John Neild, attorney' was buried at All Saints, Hertford on 27 Aug 1803 [HALS: DP48/1/25].

310 'Ameialea Chapman' was buried at St Andrews, Hertford on 20 Sep 1803 [HALS: DP49/1/4].

Widow Aylott married at Bramfield to Joseph Mobrey this **October Monday the 3d 1803**.[311]

Wednesday morning 12 of Octr 1803, about 2 clock in the morning a great fire broke out at the White Hart Inn, St Albans, which burnt all the offices belonging to the s[ai]d inn & 9 horses & dameged the house to a great loss. I saw it on the Saturday following not out.

Sunday Octr 16th old Thos Wells buried at Hartford first church.[312] He lived at the Crown ale house at the entrance of Hardingfordbury, tho in Hartford parish, maney years aged 83. The house was built new while lived there as being a little old huse before.

Novr 12th 1803 in the morning died Mrs Mullett wife to Mr Thos Mullett, Hardingfordbury.[313]

De[cem]b[e]r Monday 12 1803 was married at Hardingfordbury, Mr Thos Pallett, Lord Cowper's stewrd to Miss Titmuss.[314]

Wednesday 14 died suddingly Mr Scate at the Bell at Puckeridge.

Likewise Mr Rogers about the same time near the 6 Bells Broxborn formerly stewrd to Lord Munstton at Broxbourn Bury.[315]

E[d]w[ar]d Lilley died this **Decbr 25 1803** at the Alms Housen Tewin.

---

[311] Sarah Aylett, widow and Joseph Mowbray were married at Bramfield on 3 Oct 1803 by H[enry] Purlewent, vicar of Bengeo [HALS: DP22/1/4].
[312] Thomas Wells was buried at St Andrews church, Hertford on 16 Oct 1803 [HALS: DP49/1/4].
[313] 'Elizabeth Mulet' was buried at Hertingfordbury on 16 Nov 1803 [HALS: DP50/1/7].
[314] Thomas Pallett and Mary Titmus of Little Munden were married at Hertingfordbury by licence on 12 Dec 1803 [HALS: DP50/1/5].
[315] John Rogers was buried at Broxbourne on 20 Dec 1803 [HALS: DP24/1/2]. Dowager Lady Monson and her son John Lord Monson sold Broxbournebury to Jacob Bosanquet in 1790 [*VCH Hertfordshire* vol 3, p432].

1804 (*HALS: DE/X3/7*)

JANUARY Monday 2 To Tewin clubb & supper round beef.

Wednesday 4 To Hartford to pay Mountford £20 on poney. From thence to Goldings to dinner, after to Widow Gears, Windmill Waterford. Spent there with one Baker a builder, carpenter of the dogg kinnell, Bulls Mill, and Samms of Bengeo, & gave in beer, & rum to the huntsman &c 4s.

Fryday 6 To Wotton the Bull Wiltshiers to recive tax & poor rates as being Bentfield's rent fiest, they paid all rates & tax … & gave me a good dinner.

[Saturday 7th] To market on poney. Dined at Bull … wth Baker, Chamberlin, Parker etc, dinner 1s 4d and gave ostler 1s 6d. [Then to] Blackbirds as recived money for 5 load of wheat. [Spent at] the Blackbirds common shop, 3s … . Spent & ostler 1s 3d. Markets wheat best 38s per load, barley 24s d[itt]o, peas 24s per load.

Monday 8 To the Quarter Sessions, Hartford on poney. Mr Robarts of Hunsdon prosecuted a woman name Turner for steeling in his house things, to be imprisend 1 year & discharged.[316] Spent 6d.

Wednesday 10 To Hardingfordbury the White Horse Sewills, clubb fiest. Dinner spent each 2s 6d. Spent after 1s. Cheester church clerk & his son, Hanken, 2 Hickmans, Mullett, 2 Phipps, Moore, Peck & Johnson. Rost beef, leg mutton, pudings. Chapman the boy came for me on poney. Home 11 clock, lost my hankerchieff.

Fryday 13 Spent at Tewin with Willm Worby who came from London to see us, with his father George, & uncle James & Simon, & Thos Sheath & young Patient in ginn & water 1s 6d.

Sunday 15th To Bramfield church. Afternoon to Tewin Johns. Spent with T[h]os Whittenbury, Sheath, Will Worby from London &c 1s.

---

[316] Mary, wife of John Turner of Stanstead Abbots, gardener was prosecuted for stealing a linen sheet (1s), a pair of childs half boots (1s), three pieces of carpeting (1s 6d) and a pair of white silk stockings (5s) the property of her master, John Roberts esq, of Bonningtons, Stanstead Abbots. She was given a year in the Bridewell and fined 1s [HALS: *HCR* vol IX p56].

Tusday 17th To Ware on poney. Staid all night. Came home next day by Bengeo church Purlivents. From thence to Thos Lloyds Hartford, recd £5 of him, thence to Medcalfs Half Moon. Spent there along with Wiseman from Wormley &c being the day of carring in the Millitia List 1s 6d. From thence to Bramfield Vestrey. Home 7 clock.

Fryday 20 To dinner at son Johns Tewin with Bassett, Waller, and Sheath my tenant. When I paid Basset £38 19s and Waller £23 for making or altring a stable into a shoomakers shop for Sheath at Tewin Upper Green. They treated me & so they ought for their imposition. Leg moton rost, 25s punch.

Saturday 21 To market on poney. Geo[rge] carried grist to mill & Bolts malt to Blackbird and Cock and I dined there on poork stakes from home. Spent & gave hostler there at Black Birds 1s 6d. Home forward. Markets cheeper, wheat the best at 35s per load, barley 22s per qr, oats 24s, peas 24s load.

Sunday 22 To Bramfield church. Afternoon to Tewin. Spent with Baker's man 3d.

Monday 23 To Woolmer Green Red Lyon on poney to meet Bassett carpenter about maken a poarch to the barn. Dined there on a hear (*hare*) rost with sone John and Bassett. Spent there & hostler 6s. The Dutches of Ankesters corps stoped there at Mrs Crows Red Lyon while we there a going to be buried at Greenthropp in Lincolnshire. Herce & 3 coaches.[317]

Wednesday 25 To Tewin Great House, a sale of some of the household goods there by Driver from Hartford by auction, as Esqr Schribier leeving the place, as sold to Lord Cowper for 30,000 guineas and now mooving himself and family to Suffolk. Spent at Tewin with Mr Jones from Knaboth (*Knebworth*) Lodge as came to the sale &c 2s.

---

[317] Mary Anne Layard, born 5 Mar 1733, married Brownlow Bertie, son of Peregrine Bertie, 2nd Duke of Ancaster and Kesteven, on 2 Jan 1769 at St James, Westminster, London. She died on 13 Jan 1804, aged 70, and was buried at Grimsthorpe, Lincolnshire. [G E Cokayne et al, (eds), *The Complete Peerage of England, Scotland, Ireland, Great Britain and the United Kingdom, Extant, Extinct or Dormant, new ed.*, 13 vols (1910-1959), vol I, p128]. In August 1782 and January 1783, Thomas Green was paid by the housekeeper of the Duchess of Ancaster for tuning a harpsichord at Sacombe Park [G Sheldrick, *The Accounts of Thomas Green, 1742-1790* (HRS, vol VIII, 1992) pp57-8].

Saturday 28 To market on poney put up at Black Birds, one Wrights. Dined there. Dinner 2s. Spent after & gave ostler 1s 4d. Markets full of all sorts. I bought 4 load of peas of Russell at 22s per load & 2 load of beands & peas at £1. Sent qr barley to Griper killn to make in malt today. A very wet day, home forward.

Sunday 29 To Tewin church, to Pansanger afternoon.

Tusday 31st To Ware dined at Eagle on hare. Spent after home 5 clock & gave 1s 1d.

> Thus ends this month the mildest and finest ever known, onley 5 frosty mornings.
>
> The 3 of this month was shot dead Thos Milward at Ham[m]ersmith. Some person was foolish to apear as a ghost in the church yard and had fritned severall and one Frances Smith, which was born at Cole Green, his father was the late L[or]d Cowper's steward who lived there, shot him suposing him to be the ghost. He was tryed, cast, condemd but got off for 1 years imprisinment. Milward was a bricklayr and had white frock & trousers.

FEBRUARY 1st Wednesday To Bramfield to carry orders to Burges constable to make a list of all poor men with children and to carry or send it to Grover of [Hemel] Hemsted.[318] Spent there with Basset & the cryer of Hartford 6d. Basset was arrested at the same time by the cryer by order of one Hill from Hartford & went to goall.

Saturday 4 To market on poney. Dined at Bull with King wich paid me 1 years rent for Whitbury Hill £7 10s. Diners both 2s 4d. Spent after with him 1s. I paid Stoton for 5 qr malt there. Spent after at Angell, Kambells 1s. Spent after at Cold Bath with Sheath & Ewington 6d, ostler & gave away 1s. Full markets & plenty of all sorts.

Sunday 5 To Bramfield church, afternoon to Tewin. Spent by self 3½d.

---

[318] Men who were infirm, or had a large number of children, were listed but not liable for the militia ballot as their families could become an increasing burden on the poor rates.

Tusday 7th To Bramfield. Spent at Wid Derdses 6d. Mr Bourchier married today.[319] Gave Burges 1 guinea.

Wednesday 8 To Hardingbry clubb, ostler 7d. Spent on Phipp when paid me for wood 1s. Spent more 3d. Gave Chapman 2d.

Thursday 9 To vestry at Bramfield Mr Bourchier, Mr Preston, Derds & Burges there & Auston the clark.

Saturday 11 To market on poney. Dined at Mr Archers when paid his butcher's bill. Spent with him after at Turks Head 6d. Spent after at Angell when went to see Casses 100 qr malt sold by Driver for duty 6d. Spent after at Bull with Baker from the Hide 1s. Wheat best 36s, barley 22s, peas 24s, oats 24s. Great markets. Ostler & gave 8d.

Sunday 12 To Br[amfield] church, after to Wid Derdses to drink with Butterfield who officid (*officiated*) as church clerk for Richardson. Spent 6d.

Tusday 14 To Bramfield wood sale of 3 acres in Simons Spring. Bought none as asked six pounds per rood - £24 per acre. Sold by one Crew from Luton. The wood no better than comon. Hartford people bought none. Onley Joseph Derds ½ rood 3 guines. Spent at Widow Derdes with Hartford people, Ramsay, Chapman, Handley &c 2s 6d.

Thursday 16 To Tewin. Spent at Johns 3½d.

Saturday 18th To market in afternoon on poney with 2 carts to bring my malt from Griper kill in Back Street. Put poney up at Chapmans. Had 10 qr 1 bush[el], I think they cheeted. Gaven (*gave*) the malt maker & my men 1s. Spent at Richardsons Bulls Head 10d. Gave Widow Camp wood today, gave for horse 3d. Best wheat 35s per load, barley 22s. Gave Forster 3d.

Sunday 19 To Br[am]f[ie]d church. After dinner to Esqr Bakers to see the Bayford Volunteers. They marched from the house to Hartingfbry (*Hertingfordbury*) and there in a meadow fired, about 80 of them. Was well entertained by Mrs Baker with wine. Spent after at Hartingfby Sewills 1s. Baker's son is Capt[ai]n and Vaux ensigne.

---

[319] The Revd Edward Bourchier, rector of Bramfield was married at St Giles in the Fields, London, to Harriet Jenner on 7 Feb 1804. 'Thomas Lloyd, minister' performed the ceremony [LMA: Bishops Transcripts, St Giles in the Fields, 1804].

Tusday 21 To Ware on poney. Dined at Eagle, brother Hasler very ill. Spent 6d. Stopt at Onwins the Plow, Hartford to see the Hartford Volunteers fire in his mead[ow]. Spent 1s.

Wednesday 22 To clubb Hartingbry (*Hertingfordbury*). Spent after clubb with Auston printer 6d. Chapman & little boy came for me.

Fryday 24 To Tewin afternoon. Spent 3d.

Saturday 25 A court at Tewin Bury hild (*held*) today to convey Tewin Great House & estate from Will[ia]m Schribier & his son, to Earl Cowper, which purchased it for 30,000 guineas. Onley Wm Schribier & his son & his lawyer, and Mr Nicholson, the stew[a]rd of the court, & Mr Pallett, Ld Cowper's stewrd, and Mr Dean and my silf the 2 hommages there. A good spribb (*spare rib*) for dinner, and ½ crown each, Dean & I.

Sunday 26 To St Andrews church Hartford, from thence to Ware to see brother Hasler, found him very ill, not like to live. He had 2 very bad fitts while I was there, but survived againe. I went on poney home 6 clock. Gave Frances & spent 6d.

Wednesday 29 To Esqr Baker's park of Bayford to see the review of the Hartford & Ware, Bayford, Esington (*Essendon*), [Little] Barkhamsted, & Hartingfordbury Volunteers revi[e]wed by Generall Fox, about 300 in all.[320] Baker gave the Bayford &c Volunters a good hot dinner down at the Burry Farm. The Hartford & Ware dined at the Town Hall, Hartford, a cold diner & 1 q[ua]rt of ale a man given by their officers.

MARCH Thursday 1 Went to Esqrs Plumers at New Place, Gilston on poney, & Mr Thos Cadmore of Ware went with me to ask Mr Plumer if he had a small farm to let, for old Mrs Hunsdon. Found Plumer very ill of the gout. Was kindly & well entertained by his desire, but no farm. Mr Buckland his buttler, & Mrs Buckland his wife housekeeper. Slept at Ware as came back. Spent & gave away 3s.

---

[320] In late 1803-4 Henry Edward Fox (1755–1811) briefly took Lieutenant-General Cathcart's place as commander of the London district of Supplementary Militia before returning to the Mediterranean in Dec 1804 as Lieutenant-Governor of Gibraltar (appointment dated 2 Apr 1804) and was promoted local general on 23 Nov 1804 [R N W Thomas, 'Fox, Henry Edward (1755–1811)', *ODNB*, 2004].

Saturday 3d To St Albans to draw Millitia at the Town Hall. Drawd onley for the Armey of Reserve, 1 for Codicote, 1 for Hexton, & 1 for Bramfield. Grover the clerk & Vandermulen & Justinen Casmajer there. Dined at Redhouse Plumers. All my constables, but Br[a]mf[iel]d there. Dinner 2s, corne for horse & hostler 1s. Spent after 1s. The great snowey afternoon. Spent at 3 Horshoos as came home, 6d. Cold.

Sunday [4th] Not to church but to Tewin in the afternoon, to receive presentments for the Assizes. Staid late with Sheath, Pridmore, Burges, & Mortimore. Spent in all in beer, ginn & water 4s.

Monday 5 To the Assizes at Hartford, Judge Heath, and Sergant Shephard, and Sergant Best there, High Sheriff, Ewd Garraw (*Garrow*) Esqr from Totteredge, near Barnet, foreman Grand Jury the Honble Peniston Lamb. The Assizes over on Tusday, 5 to be transported and 1 left for execution.[321] Spent & gave 3s.

The great law cause this Assize between Whittingstall of Hod[de]sdon brewer there, and Admir[a]l Pear Williams at the White Pinckl House at the end of Hodsdon town, about water in the brook on the back of Hodesdon. Whittenstall haven engrosed the s[ai]d water by building an engin reservoir to serve his brewhouse on the said brook, which been built about 18 years from this time, but this being the driest summer ever known caused this law sute. Therefore he is to have no water from his engin, when the brook don't runn over a serten place.

Thursday 8 To dinner at the Rose Crown Tewin sons on a fine turkey w[eigh]t 18 pounds given by John Moulding bayliff to Esqr Mackey at Marden, & pork & greens. Dined - John Molden (*Moulding*), my self, W[illia]m Watson the baker, 2 Paitents, Rob[er]t Grimes, John Lenard, tayler Paddy, Mr Pridmore school master and after dinner came Tho[ma]s Sheath & sone Will Carrington, & Clapham. Plaid at roley polley in the parler, and

---

[321] There were six people given transportation sentences: William Baker, Joseph Bumstead, William Clark, John Long, Henry Marks and John Pryor. Five served their sentence of seven years on the Hulks while Baker was pardoned in 1809. There were three people sentenced to death, namely Henry Baldwin, Berwick Marshall and John Robinson, all of whom were repealed to life transportation. Baldwin was sent to the army, while Marshall was sent to Australia [TNA: Hertford Assize records information from Ken Griffin].

spent over all the luseings, 3s each & gave 18d to the maid.[322] Ginn & water & beer, till 12 clock.

Saturday 10 Not to market but to Esqr Bakers Bayford to carry 2 ginea fowls as I promesd to give Mrs Baker. Was well entertaned by Mrs Massey the houskeeper, for Mr Baker & Mrs Baker, was gon a rideing, & Bigg the buttler. Came from thence to the Black Swan Hartford, one Taylers. Spent there with Isaac Taylor blacksmith, Newgate Street, & Rob[e]rt Raper the phospross (*phosphorus*) man 2s. Gave at oyle mill & spent 1s.

Sunday 11 To Bramfield church afternoon. From thence to Tewin with Richardson to son Johns. Spent there with him, & Mortimore, Simon Warby was there, 14d.

[Wednesday] 14 Went to Ware on poney, found brother Hasler very ill. Came home to the clubb Hartford. Spent & gave 15d.

Thursday 15 Afternoon to Mr Webbs Tewin Hill for seed barley, to have w[ha]t I liked at 24s per qr, but he wanted white oates, I having some so we [ex]changed. Found them all well. Smoked 2 pipes with him.

Fryday 16 Dined at sons Tewin on salt fish given by Mr H Cock, onley Cock, Pridmore and my self. I spent 6s, Pridmore 2s 6d. Cock nothing.

Saturday 17th Journey to the Town Hall St Albans to swear in for Militia & Armey of Reserve. James Adams went as being chosen for the Armey of Reserve from Bramfield. He offerd a man 30 guineas but he would not take it, therefore he was given another fortnight. Went in cart with Smiler, mear (*mare*). Carried Sall Carrington & children. Dined at Plumers Red House 2s. Spent after, corne and ostler 1s 6d.

Sunday 18th To Bramfield church. After diner to Tewin church to the funeral of Eliz Sheath, wife to John Sheath, at Archers Green, church clerk of Tewin buried on the right of the church poarch as you enter, aged 72, from thence home.

322 Roley-poley or Half-bowl: Joseph Strutt describes this in detail and specifically cites Hertfordshire as a location where it is still played. See Glossary for more detailed information [Strutt, *Sports and Pastimes of the People of England* (1845 edition), p274].

Monday 19th To Wotton Turnpike meeting at Crawleys White Horse. Paid 1 years duty for Bramfield £2 18s 0d for the road begining at the front of Goldings House to Maple Cross Hill. Commisioners there, Dickenson, Byde, Cobham, Kitchener, Kimpton, Alington clerk. Dined with me, Bush, Crowley, Vigus, Fustead, Stockbridge, Auston, Cock &c. Diner &c 3s. Spent after with Buterfield 6d, ostler 6d. Spent at Widow Pecks Stapleford with Buterfield 6d.

Tusday 20th To Ware on poney to see brother Hasler. Found him very ill. Spent 6d. Gave away 5d.

Wednesday Evening [21] To clubb Hardingfordbry on foot. Little boy came for me on poney. Spent over the clubb with Chesher & Rob[e]rts 6d.

Fryday Afternoon 23 To Bramfield to settle parish buisness, onley Derds and Burges. Had on the account 3 pots beer.

Saturday 24th To market on poney. Dined no whear but settled with Griper and paid him £40 for making 20qr barley into malt. At the Bull he treated, & likewise paid Canning & Pollard bills for the parish. Spent other places as Vine and Bulls Head, with Baker at the Hide & Kent carpenter 1s. Gave ostler at Bull 6d.

Sunday 25th 9 in morning to London on poney by Ware. Stopt at Tinners at the Kings Arms, Endfield Highway refreshed & poney 1s. Gotn into London ½ pst 3 clock. Put upp at the Bear & Ragedstaff the east corner of Smithfield. Spent at Land[lord] Nickolds the Puter Platter St Johns Street with Coz T Beck 1s. The Sunday evening slept at nephew Becks. To the bank Monday, bought inn for son Will 1 hund[red] 3 per cents consolls for £57. Home the same afternoon. Saw Cooks & dined at Mr Sissim, John Hasler's marster's tayler. Spent at Mrs Kings at the Bear & Staff as I took my poney 1s. Gave ostler for corne & hay & self 3s. At Ware 7 clock. Slept there. Home next day. Gave away to one & others 4s.

Thursday afternoon 29th To Wotton in little cart with Betsey Warby to her sister Derds there coller maker's widow. Turnpike at Stapleford 5d. Spent at Widow Pecks Stapleford as came back 6d.

Fryday 30th Good Fryday To Bramfield church 2 clock. Stopt at Widow Derdses with Geo Richardson. Spent & gave &c 7d.

Saturday 31st To market on foot. Dined no ware. Spent at Richardsons Bull Head & gave to Wells 1s. Came home by Goldings Esqr Emotts from thence to the Windmill Waterford Wd Gears. Spent there 5d. Gave old Dickinson &c at Hartford 6d.

APRIL Sunday 1st Easter Sunday To Tewin church, the sermon preached by Mr Mays of Diggswell.[323] Text last of Luke 32 virse,[324] after diner to Jacks Tewin. Spent there with Hary Lawrance 6d.

Monday 2d Attended the Easter vestrey at the Grandisons Arms Bramfield, Widow Derdses. I stood overseer againe, Jos Derds churchwarden, Richd Burges constable. Diner 2 ribbs rost beef, leg of mutton, leg of pork, pudings &c. Mr Vaux, Mr Preston, Allen, Derds, Burges, Richardson, & Thorowgood. Paid for dressing, drink & bread, cheese &c besides the bill for the meat £2 1s 0d.

3d Easter Tusday To Codicot on poney to give warrants for overseers. Stopt at Hallards (*Hollards*) to Mrs Hunsdon, no were else but at Tewin Jacks. Spent there with Pallet of Eason Green (*East End Green*), & Ben Sq[ui]r[e] & Sheath, church clerk, & Bob, blacksmith & Wells with fiddle [blank].

Thursday 5th To Mr Browns Amwell Bury on poney to receive money of him as overseer for Great Amwell. Paid to Day's wife at Bramfield as her husband went substitute for a person at Great Amwell. Dined at brother Haslers the Eagle, Amwell End. Spent after at [Green] Dragon Hartford, and at Bramfield with Pridmore & son John & gave away & hostler all together 2s 8d.

Saturday 7th To St Albans on poney Town Hall to appoint overseers, my self for Bramfield, Boys & Cowper clerks, Justices Donvell, Searanke, & Baskerfield may[o]r.[325] Dined at Redhouse dinner 2s. Spent after with Simkins, Woodfield, & Parker, from Newnham, Hexton & Sheephall 1s, hay

323 Nathaniel May, rector of Digswell, 1797-1811 [Clergy database, CCEd Person ID: 2001].

324 Luke ch 24 verse 32: 'And they said one to another, did not our heart burn within us, while he talked with us by the way, and while he opened to us the scriptures?'.

325 Thomas Baskerfield (1751-1816), mayor of St Albans and Chairman of the Quarter Sessions, 1803-4, was also a noted Hertfordshire artist [Gibbs, *Corporation Records of St Albans*, p294; G Cox, 'Thomas Baskerfeild, Hertfordshire antiquarian and topographical artist' in *Herts Past & Present* no 25, Spring 2015].

& ostler 6d. Came home by Stanborough the Horse & Groom, Jonas Langtons, spent there 6d. Gave for hay & man 3d.

Sunday 8 To Bramfield church Revd Mr Johnson of Datchworth did duty for Mr Bourchier. After dinner to son Johns Tewin Rose & Crown with Mr Cock. Had 2 pots 6 p[en]ny so home to tea. Spent 6d.

Monday 9 Went to Witford (*Widford*) on poney, with Wm Hunsdon from Hollards Farm, Codicote, John Lawrance & George Richardson, to look of a farme called Cuttlers in the parish of Much Hadam, near Witford. Dined at Bell, Witford one Dunns.[326] Dinner leg muton, turnops &c one Mr Swaller is the tenant, & going to leeve. The farm belongs to Rob[er]t Dimsdall, Hartford, and much out of repair. So we appointed to meet againe at Hartford the 21, after seeing the landlord. The farme £70 per year. Horses & dinners 15s. Spent my part 5s 6d.

Tusday 10 Evening to Tewin Jacks. Spent there with Simon Warby & the Brewers 6d.

Wednesday 11th To Bramfield wood sale. The Hartford people met & we drawd for it, went into the wood but the price as £8 per rood or more, so all gave inn our tickets & had none. Allen sold it. Dined legmutton &c. Spent each 2s 6d.

Thursday 12th To St Albans Quarter Sessions on poney by Stanborough. Baskerfield may[o]r chearman but Donvell did the buisness. No great buisness - 1 boy for steeling of linnen to be transported for 7 years.[327] Dined at Redhouse with Pierce, Lane and Morgin. Diner and spent & horse 2s 6d. Stopt at Stanborough, spent there as home 3d. To day was a great inspection of Voulenteers in Hatfield Park.

Fryday 13th Dined at Rose and Crown, Tewin. Mr Deans treat of Tewin Bury, leg of moton rost & puding &c. Mr Dean, Mr Rowley baker, Mr Thos Whittenbury of Quino (*Queenhoo*) Hall, Mr Brooks, Mr John Moulding

---

326 Arthur Dunn kept The Bell, Widford from 1806-17 [HALS: QSVR1806-17]. Carrington's diary entry suggests that Dunn was there earlier.

327 The boy was Thomas Henton, aged 16, convicted of stealing three tablecloths valued at 20 shillings. He was sent to the prison hulk *Retribution* in May 1804 and from there to the army in Dec 1804 [*HCR* vol IV p104 and information from Ken Griffin].

bayleff to Esqr Mackey [at] Mard[e]n, Mr Thorrowgood blacksmith Tewin Upper Green and my self, & Simon Warby after diner and my son John. Spent over after Dean paid 1s each. Staid late, fell of my poney & fell down in the yard. O for Shame.

Saturday 14 To market with Wm Hunsdon on poney to speek to Mr Hagger about Cuttlers Farme, but did not stop as not well from my fall the last night, but went to Tewin, Ma[c]k[e]y's wood sale. Drawd for 1 rood and spent 1s 6d. Came home.

Sunday 15th Not to church. Afternoon to Tewin. Spent there with Mr Dean, Mr Gillman, Mr Wilson, Mr Daviss from Hartford in brandy, ginn, water & ale 2s.

Wednesday 18th Afternoon to Hartford, after to the clubb Hardingbry (*Hertingfordbury*) Sewills the White Horse, and saw the sighn, as had been new painted hung up. Drawd up by ropes, E[dwar]d Mumford bricklayr, Millers, & Chesher shoomaker &c there. 5 clock at clubb 2 Hickm[an]s, Moor gardner, old Chesher church clerk & son, Hanken butcher, Mr Mullet, Rob[e]rts Ld's groom & Phipp labourer there. Clubb & gave for poney 8d.

Fryday 20th To St Albans Town Hall on poney through Lord Milburn's (*Melbourne's*) park, to meet Commisioners of Taxes, & to take the Oath of Illeagince (*Allegiance*), & to receve papers from Sidgwick the survyor (*surveyor*), of Rickm[answor]th for the year ensuing. Dined at Plumers Red House, with Pierce & Matthews of Codicote, & Simkins of Newnham, & young Kirkby of Norton, Parker of Sheephall, & Woodfield of Hexton. Dinner & spent after 3s. Spent at Stanborough with Mr Briant 8d.

Saturday 21 To Hartford on poney, left him at Chapmans. Spent at Bulls Head with Bones from Witford (*Widford*) & Lawrance from Codicote 6d. Came home by Goldings to receve tax, from thence to Mrs Gears at Waterford. Spent there with Datchworth people 6d. After thence to Green Hall, Esqr Vaux for tax, from thence to Wd Derdses. Spent there 1s. Gave away to different persons 7d.

Sunday 22 Not to church but Hardingfdbry (*Hertingfordbury*) to Mr Johnsons, from thence to Ware, brother Haslers to diner. From thence to Bengeo church to Mr Thos Dew's funerall from the French Horne, Ware. A vass number of people. Aged 49. From thence to the Run[n]ing Deer,

Rich[ar]d Gears, Port Hill. Spent there with Mr Hanken butcher & Butterfield 1s.

Wednesday 25 To Tewin afternoon. Spent at Jacks by self, Lowin, Thos Sheath & Lenard, Pridmore & Will Watson at shuffell ½.[328] I went to enquire after Mortemore who lodges at Simons, & the baylys (*bailiffs*) after him. Spent 3d. Sent Will to Bennington to the sale of Hollingsworth of Box Hall deceased.[329]

Fryday 27 To Bramfield after taxes & rate on the Solger, from thence afternoon to Tewin. Spent there & dined with a stranger, & Babb 6d. From thence to Mr Pallett's Cole Green, called on clerk.

Saturday 28 To market on the Soldier. Put up at Bull & dined there at second table with Chamberlin, young Baker, Parker from Sheephall &c. Spent after & dinner at Bull. Dinner 1s 4d. Spent 1s. Spent at Blackbirds with Harry Bush 6d. Spent at Cold Bath at the end of the town as came home with Thos Harding when I lost my horse while drinking, so walked home on foot with Harding, but my horse was found in the morning by Radfield Wood by Shok Godfrey 6d.

Sunday 29 Not to church but evening to Tewin. Spent there with Mr Dean, & Mr Eylott, &c. The Genmn (*Gentlemen*) came to look of Tewin House with Mr Pallet his servant. Dined at Jacks. Rowley & Brooks came in but I left them 1s.

> This month Esqr Cashwells new house of Sacomb begins to make its appearance, as a number of workmen. The Roults formerly lived at Sacomb Bury and owned the estate, lords of the manner there but this presant Caswell's father married old Roults daufter (*daughter*) for Rolt had a son but he was killd at the Battle of St Cass,[330] and this old Caswell was with him & was wounded & wen he came home he

[328] Shuffell ½ = Shove halfpenny (see Glossary for more detailed information).
[329] Daniel Hollingsworth had been buried at Bennington on 17 Feb 1804 [HALS: DP18/1/2].
[330] The battle of Saint-Cas, Brittany, on 11 Sep 1758, was a major defeat for Britain during the Seven Years War. Britain's naval forces under Admiral Lord George Anson (1697-1762) together with a land force led by Lt. General Thomas Bligh (1685-1775) were routed by the French coastal defence forces [See N A M Rodger, 'Anson, George, Baron Anson (1697-1762)', *ODNB*, 2004].

maried the daughter as being the heir, so came by the estate & he pulled the old house down as Roult formerly lived in & sold it pease meele (*piecemeal*), & went to live at Cold Harber but now he is dead, his son is building a new one near whear the other stood.

Good wheat 35s per load.

MAY Wednessay 2d To Hardingfbry (*Hertingfordbury*) the clubb afternoon. Gave some hopps to Johnson. Saw the funarall of Whrenn's daughter Mary buried aged 30. Clubb & horse, home forward 7d.

Thursday 3 To Prestons & Goldings after taxes, from thence to Waterford. Treated Sarah Carter from Totnam (*Tottenham*) a going to Sheephall 1s. From thence to Vaux Green Hall, from thence to Quino Hall, from thence to Jos Whittenburys at the Ploome & Feathers Tewin Upper Green. Spent 1s with old Squier & Thos Whittenbury of Quino Hall there.

Fryday 4 To Ware to the Bull to pay taxes. Paid £90 and £15 being paid before, which is all that's paid for 1803. Dined at Eagle, leg moton rost, pye & pudings, with Iardale [from] Wormley & Sams from Hodesdon, Campkin from Datchwith, & Elston of Diggswell. Diner & spent each 3s 6d. From thence to Tewin with Elston, a fiest given by Gillman brewer, Kimpton may[o]r of Hartford & Mr Archer & maney from Mr Dean of Tewin & Rowley, Pallett of Colegreen &c spent 9s each. I spent 2s.

Fryday 4th The great dinner at the Roas & Crown, Tewin, son Johns, given by Mosey Gillman of Hartford brewer, who serves the house with beer. Salman (*Salmon*), hamm, veal & qr of lamb, pyes, pudings &c for dinner. Drink, nothing but wine. For drink each person 9s. Companey, Gillman, alderman Kimpton mayer of Hartford, Mr Alderman Archer, butcher, & Mr Pallett, Lord Cowper's stew[a]rd, Mr Frances Dean of Tewin Burry, Mr Guttredge, Mr Gilbirtson grosers & Willson goaler of Hartford,[331] Mr Preston, & Mr Hanken butcher who fell from his horse a going home, Mr Ramsey c[hief] constable & others, & Mr Elston of Diggswell, & my self we came late. Charge 2s each.

---

[331] Charlotte Willson was gaoler and bridewell-keeper in Hertford from 1795-1813. Various members of the Willson family held this office from 1756 until after 1825 [*HCR* vol IX pxxii].

Saturday 5 To market on poney, left him at Chapmans. Dined at Mosey Gillmans. Spent at Bulls Head after. Wm paid him for ashes & Thos Insom for catching molds (*moles*) with Watford & old Squir & Clapham &c 6s. Gave old Hall 6d. Spent at Cold Bath & gave for poney 6d. Good wheat 35s per load.

Sunday 6 To B[ramfield] church, Datchworth minister Mr Johnson did duty for Mr Bourchier as his house is new building, a making it higher & larger. Went to Tewin in afternoon. Spent at sons by my self 6d.

Bramfield Rectory by H G Oldfield, *c*1800 (*HALS: DE/Of/2/250*)

Patmore of Ayott Farm where Field formerly lived lost 10 sheep in clover this week bustead.

Monday 7th To Tewin clubb. Spent & gave to Kent, & gave old widow Chalkley 1s 6d. Spent 6d.

Wednesday 9th To Tewin clubb fiest, nephew Thos Beck dined with us, which came from London to day by coach. After clubb, Sall treated him & my self with a bottle of her wine, home 12 clock.

Thursday 10 Evening to Tewin, Coz Beck & my self. 1 bottle of curant wine & 1s ginn & water.

Fryday 11th To Lord Millburn's (*Melbourne's*) races Brockett Hall Park, to day and to morrow. Saw the Prince there and a vass number of people. Went on poney. Spent at Elstons Diggswell as came home with nephew T Beck, Mr Young & Webb &c, 2s. The nex[t] day not there, but I herd that there was 5 races, and one Mortimor which lodged at Simon Warbys at Tewin Lower Green woon a race with his mare, and after sold her for 100 guineas.

Saturday 12 To Hartford May fare. Had my colt Ball there, which I baught of Mr Randall of Bramfield Place for £9. Sold at the fair to one Charles Benn at Cranford near Hounslow (*Middlesex*) for £18. Dined on sassages with coz T Beck, & Mr Cock at Bulls Head. Spent & gave away at the fair & poney at Chapmans 4s. Wheat 35s per load.

Sunday 13 Not to church but afternoon to Hartford on poney. Left him at Chapmans, and went with Chapman to the quakers meeting to the funeral of Mr Thos Hagger's wife, a young woman who died in child bed of the first child. Buried in the meeting house yard.[332] They lived at the Seal Mill, one Speciall West was speaker on the occation. Saw the French prisioners in a

[332] Hannah Hagger, aged 26, had died on 8 May and was buried on 13 May 1804 [HALS: NQ1/5D/1]. Thomas Hagger was the son of Stephen Hagger and his wife Susanna, née Dimsdale, sister of Baroness Elizabeth Dimsdale. Thomas was bequeathed £20 in Elizabeth's will [Falvey, *Dimsdale Receipt Book*, family tree and Appendix 3]. The Quaker meeting house and burial ground in Railway Street, Hertford is the oldest purpose built meeting house in the country still in use. It was built in 1670 at a cost of £243 [D M Butler, *The Quaker Meeting Houses of Britain vol 1* (Friends Historical Society, 1999) pp256-8].

barn at the back of the Blewcoat Buildings, and saw Allington's Band of Musick. Spent at Spratts Little Bell, 1s 4d.

Wednesday 16th To clubb Hardingfordby (*Hertingfordbury*). Was in companey with Mr Dove formerly his father of Chipping by Buntingford which came to day with his horses to take possession of Phipps Farme, Hardfordby Street. But Phipp would not grant leve for his horses in the farme stable, therefore he put them at the White Horse stables. Clubb &c 7d.

Fryday 18 Afternoon to Tewin. Spent with George Hasler, Will Frances & Cock at Jacks 6d.

Saturday 19th To market in little cart & Dimon (*Diamond*). Put up at Falkorn Mrs Ramseys. Dined there with Cock as he going to London by the coach & Carter that hanged Shock Oliver, & Clerk of Had[h]am & 1 other man. Second table dinner each 2s. Spent after there with Preston & Butterfield 1s 6d. Spent at Bulls Head & gave & ostler 1s 2d. Markets good, wheat at 32s per load.

Sunday 20th To Tewin church Mr Mays preached of Diggswell. After to dinner at sons Rose & Crown as being a wedding dinner for Geo Hasler and Mrs Barnad as married this morning at Amwell.[333] Fillet veal, ham, qr lamb, pudings & pyes &c and plenty of good curant wine al free.

Monday 21st Was schoorer (*scorer*) at Tewin Upper Green to cricket match for a fiddle. After came down to son Johns and spent with Ipgrave shoomaker, which won the fiddle, Thos Sheath, & tayler Paddy, as being Whittson Monday 1s 3d. Gave old Webster & Leever 10d.

Tusday 22th To Ware on poney. Spent at Wheat Shieff one Burrs, with John Aylon & Parker, Cadmore, & a Mr Page 1s. Staid all night as Mrs Barnat George's wife gave their workmen all supper at Eagel. Went to Mrs Clales buring at Ware church.[334] Gave for poney &c 1s.

Saturday [26] To market on poney, left him at Chapmans. Went late, dined at home. Spent at Angell 3d. Spent at Richardsons Bulls Head with Waller

---

[333] George Heasler, bachelor of Great Amwell, married Anne Barnard of St Johns Hertford, widow by licence on 20 May 1804. Witnesses were James Clapham and Mary Carrington [HALS: DP4/1/15].

[334] 'Ann Cleal' was buried at Ware on 22 May 1804 [HALS: DP116/1/5].

3d. Spent after Great Bell Beacrofts with Fletcher bricklayr down Cowbridge Lane over right the great house whear Barron Dimsdall liveth, 6d.[335]

Sunday 27th To Bramfield church afternoon Johnson parson of Datchw[or]th preached, as Mr Bourchier not at home, his house all to pieces as making great addition to it by Green, carpenter of Bengeo and Fletcher, brickl[ay]er of Hartford. Afterwards went to Wellwin to see the Bayford & Little Barkhamsted, Esington (*Essendon*) & Hartingfordbury Voulenteers, in quarters there. Baker's son of Bayford Burry is capt[ai]n & John Vaux of Bramfield lieutenant. Was made welcome at the White Hart their quarters by order of the officers given to their corproll Cowper. Took the corprall after to the Checkers and treated him with bottle syder 1s. Came home from thence with Stratton from Hartford, brewer, who had been to see some of them. Came threw the Warren. Stopt at Tewin. Spent each 10d there. Lent Mr Waller of Diggeswell Hill, brick man my horse the Sager (*Soldier*), as he is one of the yemondry in Capt[ai]n Lamb's troop, as they are all cal[l]ed out in quarters at St Albans for 2 weeks & so are some to one place, some to others. The Bayford etc are quarterd at Wellwin.

Tusday afternoon [29] To Ware on poney to see after Aylon & Richardson to way (*weigh*) the w[eigh]ts. Ostler & spent 8d.

Wednesday 30th Dined at Rose & Crown Tewin when took Levy Money. Onley Rooe from Sheephall, & Alvey for Codicote, & Mr Rowley for Camp of Pauls Walden there. Dinner and spent 3s.

Thursday 31 Went with Mr Aylon, Richardson & son Will, they in little cart Smiler mare, I on poney to Codicote & Pauls Walden to way (*weigh*) the w[eigh]ts. Took 1 qrn (*quartern*) lofe away at Bendage (*Bendish*), Kimpton baker, & Warbys w[eigh]ts at Whitwell 2 light, others all well. Expences in other book. Dined at Bull, Whitwell Dixons, home forward.

JUNE Saturday 2d To market on poney. Dined at home, put up poney at Chapmans. Went to the sale at the Falkorn of Mold Round Wood about 8

---

[335] Cowbridge House, Hertford, had been the home of Baron Thomas Dimsdale. Thomas died on 30 Dec 1800 and in 1804 his widow, Elizabeth was in residence. For more information about this family see the Introduction in Falvey, *Dimsdale Receipt Book*. The house was amongst the properties bequeathed to Baron Nathaniel in Thomas's will; perhaps he lived there as well; he did not marry.

acres ½ by Mould Wood Mill. Sold for 211 guineas by Ramsay auctineer. Spent there, and Bull &c & gave away 2s 3d. Sent Will to Town Hall St Albans to day to deliver in to be signd 3 Land Tax papers & 2 House & Windows & Serv[a]nts &c Tax, & to carry a qrn (*quartern*) loaf as taken away at Bendage (*Bendish*) Smith's shopp as wanting 4ozs of w[eigh]t. A summonds for the shop keepr & the baker from Kimpton Peter Windgrove to appe[a]r next Saturday, & Will must be there likewise.

Sunday 3d To Bramfield church Mr Bowger (*Bourchier*) preachd. After dinner to Tewin son Johns. Spent there with Thos Sheath, tayler Paddy, & Burges from Bramfield each man 6d.

Monday 4th To Tewin clubb. Spent & gave over the clubb to Mrs Pallet, widow 10d.

Thursday 7th Afternoon to Bramfield. Spent at Mr Derdeses with Mr Cock. I treated, he had been to see old Clibbons 1s 6d.

Fryday 8th Afternoon to Mr Bowger's (*Bourchier's*) Bramfield, from thence to Tewin. Spent at sons Rose & Crown by self 6d.

Saturday 9th To market on Solder Bobb. Dined at Bull second table. Dinner and spent after with Williams 1s 4d. Spent 8d. Spent after at Geo Richardsons Bulls Head with Williams 4d. Spent after at Bell with Aylon & his son John 9d. Spent after at Bull with d[itt]o 6d. Ostler 6d & gave away 3d. Home 8 clock. Saw the chaff cutting mescheene in the market place & grind malt & beens & barley.[336] Saw it work, the whole for grinding & cutting togather 12 guineas. Markets little dearer but wheat 35s.

Sunday 10th To Bramf[iel]d church, from thence afternoon to Claphams, Bulls Mill. Staid, drank tea, gave boy 2d.

Monday 11th Evening to Tewin. Spent 2d.

Tusday 12 To Ware on poney. Dined at Eagle. Spent and treated Thos Hartford, & gave old Bridges 2s.

---

[336] A chaff cutting machine was first mentioned in 1772 [*OED*: Source William Bailey, *The advancement of arts, manufactures, and commerce; or, descriptions of the useful machines and models contained in the repository of the Society for the encouragement of arts, manufactures and commerce* 2 vols, 1772].

Wednesday 13th To Clubb Hardingbry (*Hertingfordbury*). Stopt but a short time, but from thence to the clubb at [Green] Dragon as being qrtly (*quarterly*) night. Spent & poney 5d. Brown hurdle maker married & ruff (*rough*) musick about town.

Thursday 14 To Mr Palletts, Lord Cowper's steward at Cole Green to pay rent. A great company – sr lyne (*sirloin*) beef, lyne of veal, lamb buttock, beef, pudings &c. Plenty of good punch, some good songs. Mr Dooe was there which just entred Hardingfrby (*Hertingfordbury*) Street Farme. Capt[ai]n Spence &c. Drank tea. Chapman boy came for me. Home 9 clock. Gave for my poney 6d. Gave maid 6d.

Fryday 15 To vestrey at Bramfield 4 clock.

Saturday 16 To market on poney, put up at Chapmans. Dined at Bulls Head on stakes with Mr Cock & old Clapham. I gave stakes & spent 6d. Spent after at Ramses Falkron at grass sale 7d. Spent after at Running Deer, Port Hill 2s. Gave for poney & gave away 1s 2d.

Sunday 17th To Bramfield church Mr Vauxe's brother in law preached the sermon, Mr Bowger (*Bourchier*) red the servis. Afternoon to Tewin. Spent at sons by self 3½d. Called to old Gass, gave him 1 pt of beer 6d. Gave the nurs cord[i]al 3d. Gave to a brieff, loss by fire 1s.

Monday 18th To Quino Hall to acquaint Mr Thos Whittenbury of the tax on property. They was sheering his sheep. Gave his lame sheephard Hart 1s.

19th Tusday Shoore my sheep, Sowell, Currell, & Mardall, sheerers. 65 sheep, fine wather. Shoore them by the schoore (*score*).

Wednesday 20th To London with sone John, in my little cart. Put up at Beer & Ragged Staff, Smithfield. Went to Ld Cowper's, Geo[rge] Street, from thence to Pickadily Black Bear, Mary Scotts. I slept there. Next day home by Southgate. Went to bank, took ½ q[uarte]rs dividends of the 4 due Lady Day (*25 March*) last. Spent going up at Tinners, Kings Arms Endfield Highway, & in London, & horse and at Days, The Crown Southgate as came home all to gather 12s.

Fryday 22 To Tewin in afternoon to the shepsheers fiest at the Rose & Crown. Paid the shearers for sheering 65 sheep 15s 6d. Spent with them there 1s 2d.

Saturday 23 To Ware on Soger (*Soldier*) with 5 schoor (*score*) faggotts in carte with George, to baker Pages. Brought home 5 qr of malt from Cadmors. Dined at Ware on mackerall. Gave men 1s. Spent and ostler there 6d. Stopt at Bull Hartford. Spent there 8d. Spent at Bell & gave at Richardsons & ostler 8d.

Sunday 24 or Midsumer Day To Tewin church, after dinner to Bramfield Church. After spent at Mrs Derdses, with Butterfield, church clerk of Bengeo, who officieated for Geo Richardson, church clerk of Bramfield & Mr Mash of Ware 8d. Home then directly as being thunder, but not great nor much rane.

Monday 25 To hay cart in Bansleys as made the stack there, Rich[ar]d Gear came to help. Very hot day. Finished the next day but thin cropp.

Wednesday 27 Evening to Hartingbry (*Hertingfordbury*) club, paid for three nights. Staid late but few there 1s 6d.

Thursday 28 To clubb fiest Hartford, went on foot. Good dinner, good company. Came home in Watson's cart with son John, Simon Molding, home ½ past 9. Colected some money for Hunt. Gave away 9d.

Fryd[ay] Evening 29 To Bramfield on Springam's acpt (*account*). 1 pot at Mrs Derds on parish, from thence to Tewin about old Mr Gasses funeral. Spent at sons 6d.

Saturday 30 Jorney to St Albans town hall, to the appeal of the property tax. Dined at Plomers Red Hous, diner 2s. Spent after there with Ipgrave from Gusterd Wood (*Wheathampstead*) 1s. Spent at Stanborough Hors & Groom with Nickolds blacksmth, Mr Stepenson, Mr Marchant & Chipperfield 2s on poney, home late.

> An account of old Rob[er]t Gasses funeral who died the 29th of this June aged about 90. He & his wife lived in a room at Tewin Lower Green. For maney years past he worked at Tewin Mill when a glass mill in pollershing glass & making spectacles. He belonged to Little Batholamew, London, and that parish allowed him 45 shillings per quarter & paid rent.[337] He, with one Mr Joseph Strutt was the beginer

[337] St Bartholomew the Less, West Smithfield, London. Presumably these payments represent an agreement with Tewin parish under the Settlement Laws.

of the Sundy School at Tewin, and attended the children to church, 80 girls & boys or better in the year 1790.

Clerk feese	0	6s	0d
Parsons	0	3s	0d
Kent for coffin	£1	8s	0d
For shrowd & pillow	0	10s	0d
To beer & ginn &c had at funerl	0	11s	9d
To 2 women atending at his funerall & before	0	9s	0d
To bread & cheese	0	5s	0d
	£3	12s	9d

JULY Sunday 1 To Bramfield church. After to Tewin to old Mr Gasses burieng. Spent at sons with Mr Cock, & Sheath, church clerk, 1s.

Monday 2d To Tewin clubb in evening.

Tusday 3d To Esqr Emmotts at Goldings for poor rates, from thence to John Vauxes Esqr, Green Hall. Emmott paid but Vaux promesd. Spent after at Wid[ow] Derds, Bramfield 5d.

Thursday 5th To Midsumer Fair Hartford on foot with Mr Cock. Spent there and gave away with Cadmore of Ware, Kirby baker at Puckridge, Mr Grifeth, & Cock at Winters Cold Bath 4s.

Fry 6 Evening To Tewin to pay Kent for coffin and shrowd for old Gass, & son for beer &c &c. Herd that Rob[er]t Wray of Ayott Green sackcarer (*sack carrier*) yesterday fell of a cheratree (*cherry tree*) & died directly.

Saturday 7th Carried my wooll, 6 todd 12 pound, in little cart the Solder horse to Mr Scate of Hoddesdon neare the market house. Rec[eive]d 35s per tod & to receive more after if market will afford. A very wet day. Staid & dined with Mr Scate. Gave him & something for man 2s 6d. Spent at Bell there Wd (*Widow*) Watmans, with Mr Paul fr[o]m Hadham & Scate, 1s 6d. Came home by Ware, paid Cadmore. Spent 6d, gave 3d.

Sunday 8th Not to church. Afternoon to Cole Green to Mr Palletts, but he not at home. Came to Tewin son Johns. Spent there with Mr French, smith from Hartford, one Bowyer from London, & Mr Moulding, Esqr Mackey's bayliff &c 1s 6d.

Wednesday 11 To Tewin fair. Spent in companey with old Mr Rowley & his son baker at Tewin, Wiltshire of Wotton, from the Bull, Mr Cock, John Molding Esqr bayliff, & Geo Richardson from Bulls Head, Hartford 2s. Gave away to Miss Barnatts & others, 1s.

Thursday 12 To St Albans Quarter Sessions, Donvell chairman, on Bob. Went by Ayott Green & Water End. Paid Mr Boys £40, other paid befor by Will. A full Sessions. Dined at Plumers Red House by self on stakes. Diner &c 2s 6d. Came home by Stanborough. Drank at Chipperfields. Stopt at Tewin Bury & drank there & Frances Dean came to Tewin with me. Spent togather there 4d.

Fryday 13 To Wotton the Bull Wiltshiers to Pall Bentfield's (*Paul Benfield*) rent fiest taken by Mr Arnold for Lady Rumbold. A good dinner given to us with the tenants and punch, and all our rates & taxes paid to the different parishes. Pallet of Aston End was our clerk. Spent over wat was given 1s, ostler for poney 6d. Home 11 clock.

Saturday [14] To market on poney. Left him at Chapmans. Dined at Bulls Head Richardsons. Diner & spent there 2s. Went to Bull after. Gave Gripper a draft of £40 for making 20 qr malt. He treated, spent after with Cannon when he paid me for 7 load wheat at 33s load, 1s and Mr Brown the seeds man. Spent after 6d at Cooks Maidenhead with Harry Bush. Gave away 3d.

Sunday 15 To Bramfield church Mr Johnson from Datchw[or]th preached. Afternoon to Tewin to meet my constables for presentments for the Assizes to morrow, onley Chalkley from Whitwell there. Spent there [blank] shillings each, and Taylor there from Hartford, Gillman's clerk.

Monday 16th To the Assizes on poney. Left him at Mr Chappmans at the entrance of the Town. Judges Hothom & Mack Doneld, foreman of Grand Jury, Spencer Cowper, Member for Hartford. Judge came inn St Andrews Street. The assizes over in six hours both law & fellons from the time they came inn which was 11 clock till 5 before dinner.[338] Spent at Richardsons & at Spratts & gave for poney 1s 8d. Gave away 4d.

---

[338] There were just six cases involving five people resulting in two being transported for seven years and three acquittals. Both Joseph Norris and William White served their sentence on the hulks [TNA: Hertford Assize records; information from Ken Griffin].

Tusday 17 Spent at Hardingfordbury when p[ai]d Hanken for cow £11, & sold him 2 calves for £4 5s. Spent & gave for poney 10d.

Wednesday 18 To Bramfield afternoon to settle Thos Tylers, who lives at Cheshunt who had three asses stolen. He has but one hand, & belongs to Bramfield, by consent of Derds & Burges, gave him 10s 6d. Wid[ow] Crouts man & Mumford there. Spent on parish acpt (*account*) 1s 8d.

Fryday 20 Afternoon to Tewin. Spent there with Mr Dean of Tewin Burry, & Mr Willson from London coach maker, brother in law to Dean by marriage. Very bigg man 1s.

Saturday 21 To market on poney, put up at Chapm[an]s. Spent at Richardsons Bulls Head with Clapham jnr, 3d. D[itt]o at Bull with Aylon & Sanders, church clerk, 5d. From thence to Rooe buck Port Hill, Aylon, Sanders & Pennyfather, spent each 1s. Markets cheeper, good wheat about 38s per load. Ostler 3d.

Sunday 22 Went to church but was none. To Tewin in afternoon. Spent at Johns with Mr Bloom, & his brother, John Sheath church clerk, Thos Sheath shoomaker & Bowyer plastrer from London, at work Tewin Water, 1s 3d.

Tusday 24 To Ware on Solder Bobb by Bengeo. Spent there 8d. Came back the same way. Stopt at Purlivents near the church. Drank 1 bottle of wine with him.

Wednesday 25 Jorney to Brighton from Bacons on horse back on Solder Bobb. Stopt at Crown South Gate one Wm Days. Spent there 1s. From thence to London the Bear & Staff Smithfield. Slept there Mrs Kings, horse & self 5s. **Thursday 26** over Blackfryers Bridge for Brighton, first place Clapham Common, & Bellam (*Balham*), Upper Tooting, Lower Tooting, Mitcham, Sutton. Stopt there and had a glass of gin with George Randall, Mr Pedder's servant which I overtook on the road going to Brighton so we went togather, 3d. From thence X (*cross*) Banstead Downs or Walton Heath to Rygate (*Reigate*). Refreshed there a q[uarte]r of [h]our 8d. From thence to Horley, and then to Crawley in Sussex, there we slept togather. Horse and spent alltogather, hossler, waiter & boot 6s. Nothing in morning but off by 7 clock. The third day **Fryday 27th** to Hand X, to Cuckfield which is a large church & the Bishops confirming as we went through, thence to Clayton, &

Patchon (*Patcham*), and Preston. Stopt and refreshd there at Preston & gave the horses some hay 9d. From thence to Brighton by 4 clock.

Saturday 28th Saw the town & sea in morning, then to Brighton rases on the hill by the town. Dined at the Golding X after, spent 2s 6d. Then saw the Prince and other great people walk the Steyne.[339]

Sunday 29 to Brighton church.[340] Never saw so maney people at a church in my life & not a very large church nither but so well contrived to hold 2 minesters & reed the law at the communion table. The text 16 Luke part of the 2d Vers, 'give an account of y[ou]r stew[a]rd ship, for thou maint be no longer steward'.[341] Dined at Mr Randalls & we spent the aftenon at his house in North Street.

Monday 30th to the raceses againe. After dined at Esqr Emmotts from Goldings near Hartford who was at Brighton & in lodgings in a great hous froonting the Steeyne.

Tusday 31 Washed in the sea & drinked the water, then after breakf[a]st rode 6 mile to see that large high hill, with the great hollow in it, called the Devels Dike, by Fulckstone (*Fulking*), & pyoneis (*?pines*) and new timber, and rode back to the raceses againe. After over dined againe at Esqr Emmotts, with Mr Yale, & Mrs Yale, the upper servants to the Squier, and with Benj[ami]n Squier of Tewin, farrier who was down there for his health, then walked to the sea, & the Steeyne & herd the bands of musick, then home to Randall in North Street to sleep.

Wednesday August 1 Waded in the sea in morning & drank some water. Then saw 1,000 Hanovarons (*Hanoverian*) soldiers come in 2 bands of musick. They pitched their tents at the end of the town instantly, and the Prince of Wales gave them 6 hogheads of beer. I saw them, then dined at Mr

---

[339] The Prince of Wales, Regent and later George IV (1820-30), did much to develop Brighton into a fashionable resort. The Old Steine, to the east of The Lanes, was at one time the village green of Brighton and during the Regency period it became the place to promenade and be seen.

[340] The parish church of St Nicholas, Brighton. A church here is recorded in Domesday Book; the font dates to 1170.

[341] Luke ch 16 verse 2: 'And he called him, and said unto him, how is it that I hear this of thee? Give an account of thy stewardship; for thou mayest be no longer steward'.

Randalls and spent the afternoon at his house. Smoaked & drank 2 bottles of Dorchester Ale, then walked to see the soldiers p[a]rade. Herd the 4 bands, the Princes, the Sussex and the 2 Hanoverans, then walked the Seeyene (*Steine*) with the nobility. Then after spent at the Golden X (*Cross*) with Ben Squier 2s 6d.

Thursday Augst 2d Walked to the sea with Ben Squier. Drank the water and left Brighton about 10 clock. Gave the 2 maides 4s, the ostler or man of Randalls 2s 6d, Mr Randall's 3 children, Fanney, George, & John, new crown each 15s. Came over the Downs to Lewis, a large market town 8 miles from Brighton in Sussex. Drank 1 pint of beer there, then over Ashdown Forrest to which X (*cross*) to East Grinstead, whear I slept at the Swann. Horse & self 7s.

Fryday 3d Set off from Grinstead, to Croydon which is 20 mile through Godstone. There refreshd horse & self at the Anker, one Palmers near the turnpike. Croydon is a large market town & pleasant. Spent there 1s. From thence to London 10 mile. I saw at Croydon the new iron road making from London a going to the West, was finished to Croydon.[342] Came into London over Blackfryers Bridge to the Bear & Staff Smithfield 5 clock. Slept there, horse & self 7s.

Saturday August 4th Set off for home by St Albans 21 mile. Dined there at Redhouse after done my buisness with commisioners with Coz E[d]w[ar]d Pierce from the Noade at Codicot. Diner spent & horse 3s 6d. Left St Albans about 5 clock. Came by Stanborough. Spent there with Jonas Langton's father in law, from the Buildings St Albans 1s 2d. Came home through Woodhall Woods to Grubbs Barne, home by 10 clock. So there's an end of my jorney, but my jorney to Brighton was to see Mr John Randall & his wife which about 4 yrs back lived at Bramfield Place Farme, he formerly lived servant with Lord Grandison so he came into the farme. But Ld Grandison dying he was put out of the farm, and sold his cropp standing at the beginning of harvest, his wheat at £16 per acre, barley & oates at £12 d[itt]o and peas at 8 and made sale of his other things, & purchased a place at Brighton and settled there as cole merchant. Brighton is a large well built town much

[342] The Croydon or Surrey Iron Railway was the first public railway to be statutorily incorporated in 1801. It ran from Wandsworth to Croydon and Carshalton and was used for the carriage of goods at a cost of between 1d and 3d per ton [Plans of the railway are held at the Parliamentary Archives: HL/PO/PB/3].

resembling London. It is remarked for its narrow alleys. Has market every day for fish, &c but no corne. There is a pleasant green plaine called the Seeyne (*Steine*) wheer the nobillity walk. The Duke of Malborough [has] a noble house there, and the Prince of Wales a very noble palles, and gives life to the town.[343] Brighton is washed on the south by the sea, has a battrey of 9 42 pounders to the sea.

Markets: wheat 46s best per load.

Sunday 5 Not to church but went to Goldings with letter from the Squier from Brighton. After to Tewin. Spent at sones with Cantelope when p[ai]d him £10 for Moumford, & with John Sheath, church clerk of Tewin &c, 1s 2d.

Wednesday 8 To Ware on Bobb. Dined there & spent with John Aylon and gave Will 8d. Came back to clubb Hartingbry (*Hertingfordbury*). Clubb 2 nights, 1s 2d.

Saturday 11 To market in afternoon on Bobb. Spent at Bull with Chapman, & Smith of Nobles and one Mr Reed, 3 pintes & hostler 1s. Fine day buisey at wheat cart out of Husmer & filling the new wheat hovell.

Markets: wheat 46s best per load.

Sunday 12 To Bramfield church morning. After dinner to Tewin sons John. Spent there with Mr Dean Tewin Burry, and Mr Rowley baker & Mr Molding Esqr Mackey's bayleff, and Thos Sheath shoomaker Tewin Upper Green, 1s 6d.

Tusday 14 afternoon to Green Hall Vauxes to settle poor rates. Recivd of him a drauft of £30 to be paid in 6 weeks, which I dont undrstan[d], & he owes 17s 6d besides. Spent after at Mr Derds, 6d.

Fryday 17th Spent at Tewin evening when went to settle with Rowley baker for 7 load of wheat at 35s load but he did not come, 6d.

---

343 Brighton Pavilion, the Prince of Wales' palace, was built as a seaside retreat in three stages beginning in 1787. It has an exotic exterior and Chinese inspired interiors conceived by architects such as John Nash, Henry Holland and Augustus Charles Pugin [http://brightonmuseums.org.uk/royalpavilion/history/history-of-the-royal-pavilion/].

Saturday 18th To market on poney. Left him at Chapmans. Dined at Bulls Head Richardsons. Diner 1s 6d. Spent after on Insom when paid me for 7 load of wheat sold to Farr, at Burleys Mill 6d. Sold for £2 9s 6d per load. Spent after at Bull with French, blacksmith at Old X (*Cross*) 1s and after with him at Woollpack with Phillips from Stanstead blacksmith, 4d. Gave for poney 3d. In all 3s 7d.

Markets dearer, best wheat at 52s per load on account of being very whet or wet wather. Sold French, blacksmith 1 load of wheat for 49s.

Sunday 19th To Ware church. Dined at brother Haslers with Coz Cooks from London and Capt[ain] Davis & wife. About 5 clock they set off for London in shays (*chaise*) from Mrs Ramseys the Falkron Hartford, and I came home with Mary Ann & Clapham in my little cart with Bobb. Spent with Aylon & Cadmore & gave &c 3s 6d.

Wednesday 22 Evening to clubb Hartingbry (*Hertingfordbury*). Clubb & spent over with Cadmore from Ware & Godfrey, his brother in law, & ostler, 1s 1d.

Thursday 23 To Tewin in evening. Spent the evening at son Johns, & supt there, as having 2 of the 3 acres of barley & wheat. Mr Rowley baker brought it home for him, so he gave the supper, & to 3 Londoners there which lodged at his house, one Clay, & Bowers &c which worked at Henery Cowper's, Tewin Water, & Townley which came to see me at Bacons, formerly Mr Strutt's [ap]prentice. Several songs and good company. Townly had gin & water & my self spent 1s.

24 Fryday To Tewin againe in evening with Mr Townley. Spent in rum & water, & Rowley baker paid me for 7 load of wheat sold him 6 weeks back at 35s per load. He spent 1s, Townly 2s 6d, I 3s.

Satturday 25 To market on poney. Chapman went with cart 7 load of wheat, but markets cheeper - not sold. Dined at Bull. Dinner & spent after 2s 2d. Spent after at Baxters, Green Dragon with Akers 1s 6d. Markets cheeper, best wheat not 50ty as being a fine week.

Sunday 26 To Tewin church with Townley. After dinner to Tewin with Parson Nickoldse's son who came to see me which had left sea. Spent 9d. His father is c[u]rate for St Andrews Hartford.

Monday 27 Finishd harvest, Husmer wheat, Houses & first Park & 3 acres in Cherretreefield barley, Six Acres & most of Cheretree Field oates & peas Crabtreefi[e]ld & Middle Park. Geo Burton of Tewin and Bray of d[itt]o month men Burton 50s, Bray 40s filled the hovell with wheat, barley barn of barley, & wheat barn of wheat, the oats set abroad. Son John & one Parker at supper, as strangers. Fine harvest, some rain about the mid[d]le, some wheat indifer[e]nt, fine latterend.

Wednesday 29 To Bramfield afternoon. Spent at Wd Derdses with Dimsey from the Queens Head Hartford 4d. After to Tewin. Spent there with Tow[n]ley & son Wm as Townley going next day 4d.

> **24 of this month** Mrs Baker of Bayford & her sister, & 2 of Mrs Baker's daughters came to Bacons to see us, in their open car[r]iage. Gave Poll 2 large fine old chiney (*china*) dishes. Stopt some time. Drank glass of grape made wine each & returned.

SEPTEMBER Saturday 1 To market on poney. Left him at Chappm[an]s. Dined at Bull second table. Dinner 1s 4d. Spent after 2d. Spent at Richardsons Bulls Head 6d. Gave old Hall 6d, Chappm[a]ns girll 3d. Home forw[a]rd to spend larges at Tewin. Spent 1s 8d.

> Markets cheep[e]r. I sold 7 load at 44s per load.

Sunday 2d To Bramfield church afternoon, from thence to the Feathers Tewin Upper Green Jos Whittinburys. Spent with Thos Sheath, & R[o]b[er]t Grimes, & one Mortimore which lodged at Simon Warbys, Tewin Lower Green butcher 1s.

Monday 3 To Pansanger to dinner, afternoon to Tewin clubb. After supped with them on shoulder of moton & ducks given by Esqr Millses servants, at Tewin Great House whos[e] master has just came to live there. Spent each in brandy, rum & water &c 2s each.

Wednesday 5 Yearly meeting of my constables at Tewin, all there. Dinner ham & eggs. Spent each 3s 6d.

Bramfield	Richd Burges
Newnham	Wm Simkens
Norton	Thos Street
Hexton	John Day

Sheephall	Jos Parker
Pauls Walden	J Chalkley
Codicote	Wm Smith

Fryday 7 To Bramfield in afternoon to vestrey. Preston, Derds & Burges there, Mr Vaux came late. Vestrey to grant rate, and for Crane for cloaths for his children. The woman came in, her husband beat her & left her. I gave her 6d.

Saturday 8 To market on cart with 6 load of wheat. George drove it so left Solder Bobb horse for me to ride home. Dined at the Vine Moumfords on stakes with Mr Smith of Munding (*Little Munden*) Dane End and Hankin butcher of Hardingfordby (*Hertingfordbury*). Spent each 1s 6d. Sold the wheat for 46s per load. Spent at Bull & gave 2s.

Sunday 9 To Bramfield church morning, afternoon to Hartingfordby (*Hertingfordbury*), Wm Johnsons. Met there one Mr Wiffin from Quakers Street, Spittlefields & one other gentleman on visit there. From thence I went to Esqr Emmotts to see Geo Randall who went to Brighton w[i]th mee.

Monday 10 To Bush Fare with Mr Hankin butcher of Hardingforby (*Hertingfordbury*) on my Solder Bobb. Bought 5 calves of one Mr Robarts Welchman (*Welshman*) at £4 14s 0d each. Brought home by Deavonshere at the Crown & Thistle Hartford, Back Street. Expences at the fair: horse 6d, saddle 2d, spent 9d. Slept at Eagle Amwell End, spent & gave 8d.

Wednesday 12 To Bramfield to give Mrs Derds her certivicate (*certificate*) for Licensing. The evening to Green Dragon Clubb Hartford on poney. Spent nothing besides clubb. Home with Simon in cart, tied poney to his horse. Thorrowgood with his cart came with us. Gave 3 pence for poney at Chapmans as left him there. Home ½ past 10 clock.

Thursday 13 to the White Horse, Sewills Hardingforby (*Hertingfordbury*). Statute, John Ramsey chi[e]ff constable, 26 at dinne[r], fowls & hamm, geese pudings & pyes, no beefe, mutton &c. Mullet, Phipp, Smith, Mr Pallet, Mr Hill, Mr Evens, French, 2 Hickmans, Woodards &c, there. Chapman & little boy came for me. Plenty of wine &c, a good attendance. Spent each 11s. The dearest Statute I ever at.

Saturday 15 To Hartford market on Solder Bobb, & Ben with cart 6 load of wheat. Emtied the wheat & he went to Ware for load of dung, Ensom the sackcar[ri]er. Sold the wheat to one Hudson at Town Mill at 48s per load, but he thinking they was not so good as the market sack, wanted me to bate him. Therefore he left them at the mill for me to sell another market day. I dined at the Bull first table 2s 6d. Gave old Hall 5d & horse 6d. Spent after at Bull and Crown & Thistle Devonshires when I paid him 5s for bringing 5 calves from Bush fair, all 4s. Borrowd Mr Chapman's cart & put Bobb in & brought Coz Cooks to Bacons to sleep, 3 daughters, & 1 sone in law, & 2 children as came from London this evening to Hartford in shaises. I sold 6 load of wheat to day for 48s per load.

Sunday 16 Not to church but to Tewin with Coz Cooks & their children & chaises came from Hartford to Bacons to fetch them to dinner at Falkern Mrs Ramseys, and to take them to London. Will went to Hartford with them in Chapman's cart so left his cart & brought Bob home. I went afternoon to Pansanger. Lord Cowper came wile I was there from London in 2 hours ½, coach in 4 bays.

Monday 17th To Wotton Stattute on Bobb. Horse put up at Wilshers the Bull. Dined there, dinner 2s. Spent after there with Mr Chappman & Cock 9d, ostler & gave away 9d. Home 8 clock.

Wednesday 19th Afternoon to Hartford with great cart to fetch tears (*tares*), afterwards to Hardingfordy (*Hertingfordbury*) the Clubb. Mr Doo there, Coz Thos Beck, Mullett, Phipp, Hanken, Chesser, church clark & Peck &c there. Clubb 1s.

Thursday 20th To Codicote Stattute on poney with nephew Thos Beck. Went by Robliheath (*Rabley Heath*), and left the poney there at the Robin Hood alehouse one John Males, and walked to Codicote, to the George as the Statute kept there. 24 at dinner. Spent each 7 shilings. Batten from White Hart, Wellw[y]n, alderman Evens Hartford &c &c there. Claranett (*clarinet*), fidle, french horne. I came away ½ pst six & Coz Beck took the poney at Robleheath, through Ninns Wood, Burnaham Green, to son Johns Tewin. Spent there in curant wine & ginn & water 1s 6d. Gave at Robleheath 1s 2d. Gave away 3d. Gave musick 1s.

Saturday 22d To market on Soldier Bobb with 5 load of wheat to mill, & 2 to market to sell with the other 5 left unsold last market day. With Benn & great cart. Sent 3 load of tears home bought of Pallet of Aston at 20s 6d load & 3 load of beens & peas at 23s load. Dined White Hart Camps. Nothing dinner.

Spent there 9d. Spent at Bull after with Parrott of Wheatamstead 1s 3d. Sold the wheat for 48s per load. Gave ostler 6d.

Sunday 23 To Bramfield church morning. After dinner to Tewin son Johns with Mr Johnson, & Mr John Hickman from Hardingfordbry (*Hertingfordbury*) who came to Bacons about my horse Soldier Bobb which I sold him to Mr Johnson, for 18 guineas. Spent there with them & Mr Dean, Rowley & Moulden 18d.

Monday 24th Begun taking up puttatos (*potatoes*) 1 acre ½ at this first end of Stable Field as they was planted in roose (*rows*), so we plowd them out. Had Ann Templemn & her children & som others from Bramfied to pick them up – had near 400 bushell. The ground very dry as had no rain since the 15th of last month, yet such a great cropp and taken up so cleane.

Tusday 25 At home & Mrs Baker of Bayford came in her carriage & brought us a fatt ghoose as a present for Mixs (*Michaelmas*) Day, her daughter with her.

Fryday 28 To Bramfield, from thence to Pansanger carry geese, from thence to Tewin. Spent at sons 3d.

Saturday 29 To market on poney. Dined on stakes with Mr Hanken at the Vine. Spent there & paid Mumford £10 for workhouse, 1s. Spent after at Bulls Head Richardsons 9d. Spent after at [Green] Dragon Baxsters when took money for 4 load of wheat of Ensom at 47s per load, 6d. Carried 10 qr barley to day to make malt at Gripers Mill by Old X (*Cross*). Came home by self 8 clock. Gave for poney to Chapman's girll & gave old Hall 9d.

Sunday 30 To Bramfield afternoon church. Spent at Mr Derdses when eat some mutton before church 6d. After church evening to Tewin. Spent there with Mr Dean & one other man with him from London, & Thos Whittenbury 8d.

OCTOBER Monday 1st Evening to Tewin Clubb. Spent 3d.

Tusday 2d To Baldock fair in cart with Smiler mare, son John & Grimes blacksmith Tewin. Put up at Anker as go inn. Bought 2 qrn (*quartern*) of cheese, 2 meal at 23s qrn, the best cheese 40s. Dined at Anker diner & spent togather 2s 3d. Brought E[d]w[ar]d Andrew to Broadwater (*Knebworth*) his home. Spent at Woolmer Green 6d, at Tewin son Jons 6d. Home at Tewin 7 clock.

Thursday 4 To meeting of vestrey at Bramfield at Wd Derds the alehouse to settle surveyors' acpts (*accounts*). Onley Jos Derds & Burges there. Spent on parish acpt (*account*) 3s.

Fryday 5th To Whitwell Statute with Geo Richardson in little cart, the mare Smiler. Waid the w[eigh]ts at Codicot as went, and waid the waits at Whitwell. Took 3 away from Reed, small wts. Then dined at Bull Dixens, a good companey about 25 at dinner, Mr Crabb, Mr John Hill &c & from Hitchen Wm Ramsey & Dimsey from Hartford. I left them forward about 5 clock paid for Richardson & self 16s. Stopt at Tewin as came home, found Mr Carr & Ashley there.

Saturday 6 To market on poney. Dined on stakes at Blackbirds with Mr Cock. Spent there 1s. Spent after at Bulls Head Richardsons 1s. Gave for poney at Chappmans 6d. Gave away 3d. Markets about 50s per load, barley 36s qr.

Sunday 7 To church at Hardingfordbry (*Hertingfordbury*) charity sermon by the Revd James Hook the Rector, the first sermon he preachd there, as just came to the livens of St Andrews of Hartford. Likewise latley held by the Revd Mr Chumndley for maney years.[344] Dined at Mr Hankens butcher. Gave 2s 6d, gave his boy 6d.

Tusday 9 To Ware from Hartford with Mr Cook, Woolmers' steward. Dined at Eagle togather & came home togather as far as Hartford. Spent &c 1s 9d.

Wednesday 10th Dined at son Johns Tewin with Mr Dolling & Mrs Howerd from Codicote which came to see us - they treated. After they left Mr Webb, Mr Waler & Mr Rowley & my silf staid & spent in brandy & water & curant wine each 2s. Gave my men 1s wich came for me. Home ½ p[a]st 10 clock.

---

[344] Revd James Hook, rector of Hertingfordbury 1804-1817 and rector of Hertford St Andrew 1805-1817 [Clergy database, CCEd Person ID: 7479]. Revd Mr Chumndley: Robert Cholmondley, rector of Hertingfordbury 1755-1804 and rector of Hertford St Andrew 1755-1804 [Clergy database, CCEd Person ID: 48097]; Cholmondley died at Bath in June 1804 (see Carrington's list at end of 1804 below).

Saturday the 13 Jorney to St Albans Town Hall to appoint surveyors & new assessors on the prope[r]ty Tax &c. Dined at Red House with Simkins, Parker & his son of Sheephall, Woodfield of Hexton, Street of Norton, and Matthews of Codicote &c. Dinner 2s, spent after 6d, ostler 6d. Spent coming home at Jonas Langtons Stanboro (*Stanborough*), 1s. Went on poney by Stanboro.

Sunday 14 To Tewin church, afternoon to Bramf[iel]d church, after to Tewin son Johns with Benj[a]m[in] Winn, Mr Vauxe's stew[a]rd or bayliff of Green Hall. Spent there in ginn & beer, home 7 clock 1s.

Wednesday 17 To Hardingbry (*Hertingfordbury*) Clubb. Spent over 6d. Bought a cart as being Mr Phipp's sale as leaving the farme. Sold by auction by John Ramsey, as one Dooe taketh possesion. Cart £4 13s 0d, a dray plow 10s 6d, 3 harrows & draufts £1 8s 0d. Little boy came for me.

Thursday 18 To Hartingbry (*Hertingfordbury*) to fetch the things. Spent at Sewills White Horse when bought all the trimins in the road to Hartford for 10s. Dined at Hankens 6d. Bought of Crawley the younger.

Fryday 19 To Esqr Emmotts after taxes & Mr Preston of Broadoak End Farme. Drank plenty of the sq[ui]r[e]'s beer & so home 5 clock on poney.

Saturday 20 To market on poney. Dined at Bulls Head on stakes with Mr Cock, young Clapham, my son Willm, & Mr Hanken butcher. Spent 3s. Spent after at Bull when took money for 4 load of wheat of Ensom sackcarer sold at 54s per load, 6d. Spent at Cold Bath as came home & gave for poney, 6d. Came home part of the way with Vauxe's bayliff.

Sunday 21 To Bramfield church morning. After diner to Tewin sons with Night the blacksmith of Diggswell which brought a poney for me which I bought for £4 14s 6d but if he proved according to his word, in 2 weeks, then I was to give him 10s 6d more. Spent there with him & Mr Cock 1s 9d.

Tusday 23 To Hartford with 2 carts to carry 16 qr of barley to Gripper's killn to make in malt & to bring the other 10 back that was made. Gave Pinnack the malt maker & my men in beer at Shipp 1s 3d. Had 10qr 6 bush[el] back increese.

Wednesday 24 To Woolmer Green by self on black poney to recive 1 yrs rent of Mrs Crow at Red Lyon. Dined on stakes & inoins (*onions*). Spent there with Shelford butcher & Mr Saingfile 3s 6d, ostler 6d. Came from thence to Tewin son Johns. Spent there with Rowley baker, Bowley butcher, Thos Sheath shoomaker, John Molding, Jos Lowin, Pridmore schoolmaster &c as being at dinner there. Home 11½ clock. Spent 1s.

Thursday 25 To Esqr Emmotts of Goldings after taxes in the morning, paid all & made welcom. Afternoon to Quino Hall Whittenburys, none, to Esqr Vauxes Green Hall, none. Spent at Derds 4d.

Fryday 26 To Ware to Bull to pay taxes. Paid £89 for all taxes due for 1803, and £50 towards the taxes for this year 1804, onley Byde & Piercen there. Hudson for Ware & Walker for Amwell was there when I paid. Dined at Eagle on rost beef & poork and rist (*rice*) puding &c. Smith of Roxford, Field of Colegreen, Elsom of Diggswell, Walker & Samms. Spent each 3s 6d. Spent at [Green] Dragon at Hartford as came home 6d.

Saturday 27 To market on black poney, put him up at Bull. Dined at Vine on stakes with Chalkley my constable from Pauls Walden which came about a man to serve in Army of Reserve. Went to Capt[ain] Rowen at Angell, and a further time is given to 15th of next month, and Smith of Roxford & Mr Cook bayleff at Woolmers & Hanken butcher, spent each 1s 6d. Spent after at Bull & gave ostler, 1s 4d.

Sunday 28 To Tewin church, after noon to Tewin son Johns. Spent by my self 3½d.

Wednesday Evening [31] to Hardingbry (*Hertingfordbury*) Clubb at the White Horse Sewills. Clubb & gave 2 boys, little Will groom & Sparks, which came for me, 10d. Staid late with Mr Dooe the new farmer which entred on the Street Farme this Mxs (*Michaelmas*), late Phippses, & Mr Johnson from Stanborow, who came there about tythes for the new minister & Chester church clark, & Peck baker. The great raine the last 2 [h]ours of this month which stopt us.

NOVEMBER Thursday 1 To Bramfield evening to settle parish buisness, Derds & Burges met me. Spent at Wd Derdses 15d on parish acpt (*account*), Kitty very ill.[345]

---

[345] Katherine or Kitty Leever was buried 6 Dec 1804 (see diary entry for that date and list at end of 1804 below).

Fryday Evening 2d To Tewin. Spent at sons 3d.

Saturday 3d To market on poney. Dined at Blackbirds one Whrights on sasages with Mr Cock & Baker from Hatfield Hide 1s 6d. Spent after at Angell enquiring for Vaux 6d. Home forward. Markets wheat £3, barley 50s. Horse 3d. Saw the otter catched by Stanstead in a ditch, by some of the Ware bargemen alive. G[ave] 1d.

Sunday 4th Not to church, to Tewin after dinner. Spent with Mr Winn & Mr Cock 6d.

Monday 5th To tythe fiest Mr Bourchier's Bramfield. Dined in the landrey (*?laundry*). Mr Bourchier dined with us. A good round of beef & pudings &c. My self, Derds, Burges, Whittenbury, Allen, and Benj[ami]n Whinn, Mr Vauxe's bayliff there. Good ale & plenty of rum punch. Broak up 6 clock. Gave Webster 1s. Saw Templeman, & Wm Derds fighting at the fire.

Wednesday 7th To the Association fiest at Tewin. Dinner lyne (*loin*) of rost beef, & mock turtle, & turkey &c &c. Bill for dinners & beer & punch &c £5 10s 9d. Spent each 6 shillings. Members there was my self, Mr Pallet, Mr Gillman & Guttredge, Mr Dean, Mr Field, Mr Webb of Tewin Hill, Mr Rowley baker, Mr Elsom of Diggswell, Mr Bowley butcher, Mr Webster, Mr Patient, & Whinn for Vaux bayliff.

Thursday 8 to Watchard (*?Hertford*) Fair with 2 poneys. Dull trade of all sorts of cattle, sold none. Came home forward. Spent with Boden at Bull 3d. The finest day & cleere as ever known.

Fryday 9 To Hartford with great cart to fetch peas bought the Saturday before, & 3 qr of oates of Brown at 27s qr. Gave at Blackbird[s] 3d, at White Swann 6d. Wheat £3 10s per load.

Satturday 10 To market on black poney, put up at Bull. Spent there with Usborn, French & Keep when French paid £2 9s for 1 load of wheat, 1s. Spent at Bulls Head with Aylon & Bull together 1s. Spent after at Cold Bath as came home with Hanken of Tewin Gate when sold some wheat to one Chapman for £3 6s per load, & ostler 1s 4d.

Sunday 11 Not to church but to Pansanger, Lord Cowper afternoon. Staid tea & supper with Mr House, house stew[a]rd, & Mr Daviss Lord's gentleman, &

Mr Langell, Spencer Cowp[e]r's gent[lema]n.[346] Gave young Patient which lives there for poney 3d.

Tusday 13 To Ware market. Was bid 55s qr for barley but refused. Dined at Eagle, found brother very bad a bed. Diner & gave 8d. Stopt at Hartford & gave Baldwinn at Angel for placeing the assessment on property tax for Bramfield. Called at Prestons for his paper 1s 4d.

Wednesday 14 To Bramfield wood fiest, the money taken by one Mr Crow, Lord Henry's stew[a]rd, woodard (*woodward*) at Luton Hooe. He gave the dinner rost beef, boyled leg muton & puddings. Spent 18d each. Went from thence to Hartingbry (*Hertingfordbury*) Clubb. Spent there with Mr Dooe as being a vestry and Smith, Field, Mullet &c, 1s.

Thursday 15 To Hartford with 2 carts to fetch malt, 10 qr from Gripper's killn, had 10 qr 5 bush againe. Gave putting upp 6d. Spent on the men at the Shipp, one Cooks, Old X (*Cross*), by blacksmith's shopp, & Brown's man seedsman, as had 3 qr oates, 1s 8d.

Fryday 16th To Tewin afternoon, to son John's daughter Ann's christning. They had had a good [blank] & so had I after & plenty of good punch & curant wine. Staid supper & 2 companys at cards. Broke upp at 1 clock, with God Save the King with 3 cheers. G[ave] Nurs Ambrose 1s & Grant the maid 1s. Mr Dean, godfather, Mrs Webb, Mrs Rowley, godm[othe]rs, Webb, Rowley old, Rowley young, Pridmore & wife, Otway, & Clay, &c &c there.

Saturday 17 To St Albans Town Hall to return the papers on the tax on property. Dined at Plumers the Redhouse, with Pierce & Matthews from Codicote, Woodfield from Hexton, Parker from Sheephall &c. Dinner & spent 3s. Went on black poney through Ld Milbrons (*Melbourne's*) parke to pay W[i]d[ow] Bassett's money. Came home by Stanboro. Stopt at Mr Johnsons there the farme to tea, home 7 clock.

Sunday 18 To Tewin church, a charity sermon preached by the Revd Arther Bush A M and chaplain to his Highness the Duke of York.[347] Gave 2s 6d.

---

[346] Langell, Spencer Cowper's gentleman is mentioned again on 18 Nov and 16-17 Dec with varying spellings: Langden, Langwell.

[347] Revd Arther Bush A M: Perhaps Edward Arthur Bush, known to be curate at Bayford Chapel, Essendon, in 1802 [Clergy database: CCEd Person ID: 46444].

The text Matthew 6 Chaptr 22 & 23 Verse, of Lite & Dark.[348] After to Tewin afternoon with young Nichelson which had been at sea, his father curate at St Andrews Hartford. Spent at sons each & Langden with us, 1s. He treated.

Tusday 20 To Ware market on black poney. Dined & slept at Eagle, went into market. Spent at Wheatshief with Aylon one Burrs, 9d. Was bid 50s for my ba[r]ley. Did not sell. Spent after at Eagle with Aylon, Wand, & Auston stone mason Hartford, 1s. Gave to ser[van]ts 1s. Barley £2 15s 0d.

Thursday 22 Afternoon to Tewin. Spent at sones with Pridmore schoolmaster at Tewin 6d. Welch from Codicote, Waller brickman & Woodards carpenter from Cole Green there, & Wm Johnson.

Saturday 24 To market on poney with Mold. Cart 1 load of wheat to mill, 2 bush[el] barley & 3 load for market. Sold them to Carter the coach man at £3 3s per load. Dined Bulls Head on a stake Archer gave me. Blott the shoomaker took part. Spent after with Smith & Blott 1s. Gave Hall & for my poney at Chapmans, 6d.

Sunday 25 Not to church, but to Tewin afternoon to meet Whittenbury ab[o]ut his rates which he paid. Spent after with him and Winn Vauxe's bayliff, Thos Sheath & Johnson from Hartford, 1s 6d.

Tusday 27 To Tewin to blacksmiths. Spent at sons with Spencer postman 3d.

DECEMBER Saturday 1st Not to market but at home inning part of old barley reek (*rick*). In the evening to Tewin sons, to pay Tingey & Brounsell for faggotting. Gave them 18s & 3 potts of beer 1s 3d.

Sunday Second To Bramfield church, after dinner to Mr Palletts Cole Green and from thence home. Gave boy for poney 2d.

Tusday [4] To Ware market. Dined at Eagle. Sold 5 qr of barley at 49s qr to Smith at Hartford. Spent at Ware with Aylon & bricklayr & horse 15d. Spent at Hartford the 2 Brewers one Stew[a]rds with French blacksmith, & paid Corage for hops, 1s.

---

348 Matthew ch 6 verses 22 & 23: 'The light of the body is the eye: if therefore thine eye be single, thy whole body shall be full of light. But if thine eye be evil, thy whole body shall be full of darkness. If therefore the light that is in thee be darkness, how great is that darkness!'.

Wednesday 5th To tythe fiest at White Horse, Sew[e]ls Hartingf[or]dbury, the fiest taken for the Revd Mr Hook taken by Johnson, land surveyor of Stanboro. St Andrews & Hartingfordbury both parishes there, the Revd Nickelson & Mr Pallet there. A good dinner & plenty of punch & musick &c &c. Gave Hore fidler 8d. Gave for poney 6d. Wheat £3 6s.

Thursday 6th Spent at sons when went to carry a hamm & smale legg of mutton 3d. Afternoon spent at Mrs Deardses Bramfield when went to Kitty Leevers buriall, 3d.

Fryday 7th To diner at Tewin when my tenants paid rent, a hamm, small leg of mutton & puding &c, Sheath, North, Day & Ward, there. Spent in beer & ginn & water 15s & 10d. Paid the Property Tax for Sheaths 8s, Norths 5s & Wards 5s.[349] Little Boy came home with me 10 clock.

Saturday 8 To market on poney. Dined at Bull. Dinner and spent after there & ostler 3s 6d. Markets much the same. I took money for 3 load of wheat sold to Carter coachman £9 9s. Samuall Baker Esqr of the Park Hartingbry (*Hertingfordbury*) buried there today a wa[l]king buring.

Sunday 9th Not to church, afternoon to sons Tewin. Spent there by self 6d. Gave away 1s.

Wednesday 12 To Hartingfordbury to see Mr Geo[rge] Hankin butcher there who has been very ill, but now better. From thence to Green Dragon Clubb Hartford, as q[ua]rt[er]ly night, paid for Mr Dolling 8s 8d. Came home on poney with Simon Thorowgood, taylor Paddey, & son John, ostler 3d.

Tursday 13th To Tewin. Spent there with Mr Pridmore schoolmaster, Mr Dean, Rowley & Esqr Millses buttler at Tewin House 6d.

Saturday 15th To market on black poney. Dined at Richardsons Bulls Head. Sold 2 sheep & 9 lambs to Lame Rickat. Lambs 19s 6d each, ewes 13s each, old ones. Dinner &c 2s. Spent after at Cold Bath with Wm Smith 2s. Gave Chapman's girll & gave away 8d. Markets cheeper, best wheat £3 3s, barley 45s qr.

---

[349] Carrington is here paying the tax on his own properties in Tewin let out to tenants Sheath, North and Ward.

Sunday 16 To Bramfield church. After dinner to Pansanger Lord Cowpers, staid & supt there, in stew[a]rd's room with Mr House, cook, & Davis, lord's man, & Langwell, Spencer's d[itt]o.

Monday 17 To Tewin with Lord Cowper's man Davis, & Langden Spencer's d[itt]o. After noon spent at sons with them, 1s.

Wednesday the 19th To Lord Cowper's rent fiest at Mr Pallett's his stew[a]rds Cole Green. A good dinner, buttock & sr loyn rosted, veal & ham &c, plenty of punch. About 50 at dinner, gave the ser[van]ts 2s. Came home with Grimes, & Ewington, & my 2 boys 8 clock.

Thursday 20 To Tewin to meet Winn Mr Vauxe's bayleff of Bramfield, to buy 10 piggs & a hiefer. Delt not, spent 1s.

Fryday 21 To Bramfield. Baught the pigs & heiffer for £17 5s. Spent on him at the Grandisons Arms Mrs Derdses there, 1s. Home 5 clock.

Saturday 22d To market on foot as frost. Dined at Bull diner 1s 4d. Spent after there with Winn 8d. Spent at Richardsons Bulls Head 7d. Gave old Hall &c at [Cold] Bath 6d. Bought 5 load beans & peas J Palmer & 1 load of Wm Bull all at 30s 6d. Came home with Winn 7 clock.

Sunday 23 Not to church, afternoon to Tewin Johns. Spent there by myself 3d.

Monday 24 To Bengeo church to settle with the Revd Mr Purlivent which lives in the house the south side joyning the church yard. Was made welcome. Gave maid 1s. Spent after at the Buck, Port Hill kept by one Blane as came back with Parker, 6d.

Tusday 25 Being Christmas Day to church at Bramfield. Gave all the poor a dinner. Fetched in the cart except old Brux. Gave him &c 1s. After they gon, went to Mrs Hunsdons, spent an oure there with Thos Ensom.

Wednesday 26 To Clubb Hartingbry (*Hertingfordbury*), clubb 1s 6d as 3 nights. Gave little boy & Thos as came for me 6d.

Thursday 27 To the Feathers, Tewin Upper Green kept by Joseph Whittenbry according to my yearley costom, onley son John & Thos Whittenbry of Quino

Hall & Mr Wing, Mr Vauxe's bailiff. Spent my part 5s, they 6 pence each. Stopt at sons Lower Green as came home. Spent there with Wing 2s.

Fryday the 28 To a meeting at Bramfield on Rich[ar]d Tyler's account, which returnd from Iarland. Spent there on parrish account 2s 6d.

Saturday 29 To market on foot with Richd Tyler which returned from Iarland, as been a soldier 12 yrs there and lived with me when listed, & now discharged so belongs to Bramfield. Cloathed him and the next day gave him 10s and he returnd to Iarland, as he said to his wife and 4 children. Dined at Bulls Head on stakes with Hale, woodman. Bought 6 load of beens & peas of Jery Palmer at 30s 6d load, paid him at Bulls Head £9 3s. Bought 2 load of peas of Insom & 1 load of boyling [peas] of Palmer. Spent in all and gave Hall 3s.

> Thus endes this year 1804. Markets now best wheat 65s per load, barley 50s per quarter, oates 35s d[itt]o, peas 33s load. Great plenty of hopps this year. Baught the best by the pocket at 9d per pound, malt dear as £4 16s quarter, as duty and making 40s qr. The cropp of wheat lookd great & promising at harvest but when we came to thrash, the yeald is found so small that a man must work hard for ½ load per day, and the wheat thin like rye. A great deal hardly pay for thrashing. Barley yealds midling but a short cropp was sown last season, as being so cheep last year, which makes in bear (*beer*) the prise.

Deaths & Marriages &c 1804

JANUARY: Old Mr Abr[aha]m Batten of Wellwin barber died **the 24** aged about 80ty.
The Dutches of Ankester buried at Greenthropp (*Grimsthorpe*), Lincolnshire **25th**.
Revd Mr Grayham rector of Wotton & Aston, formerly curate of Hartingbry (*Hertingfordbury*) died at Aston whear he lived the latterend of this month.[350]
Mrs Raymond at the George, Codicote died **30**, buired at Diggswell.[351]

[350] Charles Graham, rector of Watton-at-Stone and of Aston, 1798-1804 [Clergy database: CCEd Person ID: 61088].
[351] 'Mary Rayment from Codicote' was buried at Digswell on 3 Feb 1804 [HALS: DP34/1/2].

FEBRUARY: On the 7th on Tusday was married at London the Revd Ewd Bourchier rector of Bramfield. Came to Bramfield the same day in shaies in 4. Gave the 2 boys a pound note each, & the ringers 1 guinea.
Brown upholster[er] next door to the Little Bell, St Andrews Street Hartford, and formerley did keep the Bell died **Monday the 13th**.
14th Died Samuall Hide of Ware, a vass (*vast*) man to buy & puff at auctions. There was a sale at Tewin House when Schribier left, & he was there 4 days before his death and bought severall things.

Thursday 16 Mrs Crow of Hartford buried.[352] She was formerly wife to Roger Crow at the Vine Inn Hartford.

MARCH: Sunday 18th was buried at Wotton (*Watton at Stone*) Mrs Emott wife to Wm Emott there.[353] About the year 1755 was deary (*dairy*) maid to old Lord Cowper of Fidgon Hall or Cole Green House which house is now pulled down, & her husband was my Lord's footman there.[354]
Sunday 18th d[itt]o was buried Eliz Sheath wife to John Sheath church clark of Tewin aged 72. She was former[l]y a Wilkinson, native of Tewin. She lived at Archers Green. Buried on the right of the church poarch as you enter in.
Mr Bigrave, farmer Sheephall Green died **Satturday morning 9 clock 31 of March.** Buried the Wednesday following at Sheephall aged 54.[355]

APRIL: The 2d of this month being Easter Monday died Peter Harding of Tewin. He came home to his fathers at Tewin on the day before Easter Sunday from Hartford as being prentice to one Blott shoomaker there and died the next day aged 15 yrs.

---

352 'Hannah Crow, aged 48' was buried at All Saints Hertford on16 Feb 1804 [HALS: DP48/1/25].
353 'Susan Emmett' was buried at Watton at Stone on 18 Mar 1804 [HALS: DP118/1/2].
354 William 2nd Earl Cowper (1709-1764) was a Lord of the Bedchamber from 1733 to 1747, became lord lieutenant and custos rotulorum for Hertfordshire in 1744, and was a Fellow of the Royal Society. He died at Cole Green. His grandson, 5th Earl Cowper demolished Cole Green House in favour of a new house at Panshanger [*VCH Hertfordshire* vol 3, pp468-472 (1912) and diary entries in 1802 above].
355 'James Bygrave, farmer 54', was buried at Shephall on 4 Apr 1804 [HALS: DP100/1/2].

Arther Warren Esqr died at Graveley whear he lived and buried there the **7th of this month** aged 74 yrs. This was the onley son & child of old Rich[ar]d Warren Esqr of Marden in the parish of Tewin, which was High Sheriff for the County of Hartford in the year 1727 and proclamed George the 2d at Hartford, but he married his owne cozen contrary to his father's consent, which so offended him that he left all from him that he could and his father dying in the year 1768, he came to live at Marden, as came to him as his mother's jyonter (*jointure*) as his father could not hinder, worth about £12,000 with the timber, but he keeping a pack of hounds and living at a great rate soon got into dept (*debt*) in about 16 years. So sold Marden to Esqr Mackey of Tewin House near the church for £7,500 so paid his dets, & saved him self about 100 per anam, and went to live at a place called Charlton near Hitchin. He lived there about 5 year, & his wife dying, he then married his maid which had lived with them maney years and then purchased a pleasant little place at Graveley near Stevenage, whear he ended after liven about 5 yrs more. He had 3 children by his former wife, which them & their mother lye in Hardingfordbury church yard in a little spot paled in, near the chansell door. He formerly was Lieutenant & Quarter Master in the Hartfordshire Millitia when first rased 1757.
Riddle of Bayford died **the 14**. He was the driver of Esqr Baker's carriavann from the country to London &c with things for the town house.
17th Two boys drowned at Wemstead (*Whempstead*) near Wotton belonging to one Willmott gardner, one 7 years the other 10.[356] The mother had sent them to the pond to fetch a pail of water as she being ill, and the father not at home. But when he came home she told where she had sent them supposeing they at play, but the father found them both in the pond drownd. The wind was very high that day & pond deep.
Nickolds of Bayford buried **22d** aged 79 yrs.[357] He was a very stout, strong labouring man formerly used to catch molds (*moles*) for me & others.
Mr Thos Dew buried at Bengeo **Sunday 22** from the French Horne, Ware. He had lived there maney years, a herce & pair, 2 morning coaches, & shaies &c. Supposed to be 1,000 people at the church from Hartford & Ware or more. Aged 49. They sung when the corps entred & after the servis an antham. I was there in the church.

---

[356] The two boys were George and William Willmott, 'accidentally drowned', buried at Watton at Stone on 20 Apr 1804 [HALS: DP118/1/2].
[357] 'John Nicholls, buried in woollen aged 79' at Bayford on 22 Apr 1804 [HALS: DP37A/1/4].

Geo Ginn a carpenter buried at Tewin the **31**. Worked at Ld Cowper. Native of Braffen (*Braughing*).

MAY: Mary Wrenn buried **Wednesday 2d** at Hardinbry (*Hertingfordbury*) church, spinster aged 30. Her father is gardner to Mr Baker at Hardingfordbury Park.
Mr Watman at the Bell Hodsdon burried at Broxburn (*Broxbourne*) church **Sunday the 6th**.[358] He was clerk to Mr Whittingstall brewer there. He formerly kept the Bull Inn Hartford as married the widdow of Mr Morley which kept the s[ai]d inn. He was bread (*bred*) to the Excize.
Tusday 15th the great fire at Stevenage at the White Lyon, accasiond by the woman's son shooting at ratts (or leting of squibbs) among the straw, burnt 6 houses and vas[t] quantity of goods. Brok out about 2 clock in day time.
Sunday 20th was married George Hasler at Amwell Church, to Mrs Barnet of Amwell End, Ware, widow carpenter & undertaker. She about 35 years, George about 22.
Tusday 28 Wm Gaylor buried out of Tewin workhouse, aged about 65. He had been a strange man for harrowing at Tewn Bury, would go over 30 acres per day, 4 horses.

JUNE: The Hon & Revd Mr Cholmndy minester and rector of Hartingfordbury, & St Andrews Hartford, both livings 50 years & upwards, died at Bath the **beginning of this month** aged 84 or thereabots. He was in the rebellion in Schotland in 1745, but acted faint harted, so made him a parson.
Denness at the George, Amwell End, Ware buried at Amwell church **Tusday 12 of June**.
Thos Squier whitesmith at Hartford jurniman (*journeyman*) died **Wednesday 22**. Brother to John Squier, farrier at Tewin.
Samuall James at the Earl Cowper's Arms Birch Green died **27**, buried **Saturday 30th** Hartingbry (*Hertingfordbury*) church aged about 65.
29th of this month died Rob[er]t Gass of Tewin. Buried on the Sunday following at Tewin church opposite the porch by the path from the stile, aged about 90. He was a native of London, and belonged to Little Ba[r]thol[o]mew by Smithfield, and that parish allowd him his latter days, 45s per quarter and paid for a room for him, he was brot from London by one Thos Righbright an

---

358 'Thomas Watman from Amwell' was buried at Broxbourne on 6 May 1804 [HALS: DP24/1/2].

optision (*optician*) about the year 1760, who took Tewin Mill which was a corne mill and at a great expence alterd it into a glass mill for pollishing convix and concave glasses & spicticles glasses &c &c and no addmittince for aney to see the same for years, and this Gass was in the same line & worked at the mill for Righbright maney years, but Righbright & his wife dying, one Flindall his fore man took it, but old Mr Schribier the landlord dying, the son wanted more rent. Theerfore Flindall left it, and in the year 1803 it was taken by one Cannon of Wellwin and made a corne mill againe, after upwards of 40 years a glass mill. This Rob[er]t Gass, with one Joseph Strutt, an engraver from London, which boarded at Bacons Farme, whear the first beginers of the Sundays School at Tewin, which taught the children and braught them to church in 1790.

JULY: The 5th of this month Mr Robt Wray a small farmer & sackcarrier at Hartford, which lived at Little Ayott Green near Ld Milburns (*Melbourne's*) Park fell from a cherretree & killed immeadeatly. A man of good carrector, aged about 60.
Lady Salsbury of Ofley died the **latterend of June last**, buried at Ofley.[359] She was the onley child of Sr Henery Penrist, Judge Advocate of England, which lived at Great Ofley and in Sr Henery's time he chose one Salsbury a man of small fortaine for her husband about the year 1750 for she was deformed in body but the richest aires (*heiress*) in England. And at her death left great legeseys.
John Bentley shopkeepr & butcher in St Andrews Street, Hartford died **the begining of this month**. Buried at Little Munding (*Munden*) aged about 45.
Mrs Hall wife to Mr Hall barber Fore Street, Hartford di[e]d this month.[360] She was a native of Tewin, one Cates bricklayr daughter aged 80.

SEPTEMBER: Mrs Green at the Globe & Compases, Bengeo died this month.[361] She & her husband, who died some time back, had kept that house 50 years or upwards, aged 83.

---

[359] Dame Sarah Salusbury died at her house in Harley Street, London, on 24 June 1804 and is buried in the chancel of Offley church. She was the second wife of Sir Thomas Salusbury who had married firstly Anna Maria only daughter of Sir Henry Penrice (1677-1752), Judge of the High Court of Admiralty on 20 Nov 1751. It is Anna who apparently had a stammer and was an epileptic [D C Baines, *'Two Coats Colder', Chronicles of Offley in Hertfordshire* (Offley, 1994), pp42-45].
[360] Sarah Hall was buried at All Saints, Hertford on 2 July 1804 [HALS: DP48/1/25].
[361] Sarah Green was buried at Bengeo on 30 Sep 1804 'aged 77 yrs'

Cotton, barber at Ware, near the Bay Horse alehouse died this month.[362] A good man ag[ed] 68.

OCTOBER: Mrs Mann, braiser (*brasier*) & broker in Hartford market place buried at Hardingfordbury **Sunday 7 of Octr** aged 74. She had lived a widow upwards of 40 years since her husband death & kept on the buisness.
On **Wednesday the 10th** in the morning was found dead on a stack or clump of bricks that was burning at the brick ground at the entrance of Hartford near the Seall Mill, a soldier which quarterd at the White Hart Hartford, about 25 years of age. A fine young man. He had been drinking at the Cold Bath, but went home to his quarters, but late & locked out, so it was supposed for warmth went up on the clump and was stifled, as he had set a lader to get upp.
Charles Nightingall, tanner who worked in the tann yard at Hartford, formerley Grippers and others upwards of 60 years, died this month aged 80 old.

NOVEMBER: Burr farmer at Perrywood Farme near Wotton buried at Anstey **Sunday 18** of this month.[363] A young man left a wife & familey aged about 35.

DECEMBER: Thursday 6 of this month was buried at Bramfield Katherine Leever. She was a Clerke from London and the Widow Derds at the Grandisons Arms Bramfield alehouse was her aunt, but she married one of Thos Leevers sons of Tewin, & he left her, & went for a soldier, so she lived with her aunt at Bramfield aged 28 yrs.
Samuall Baker Esqr of Hartingbry Park House near the church & brother to Wm Baker, of Bayford, died **Sunday morning the 2d** of this month. Buried the Saturday the 8 following in the church, a walking funarall. The pall held up by six Sqrs (*Squires*), a good hous keepr. Single Man aged about 56. Very rich.
Monday 17 died Wm Field some time back master carpenter at Datchworth & lived at that neat little bricked house on the middle of the Green, but lately allowd by the parrish aged 69. I lost by him.
A very extrordany accident happned the **26 of the month** or evening after Christmas Day. Mrs Hunsdon's maid of West End Farm, Bramfield went to the well for some water out of the bucket supposing to be standing on the well

---

[HALS: DP17/1/15].
[362] James Cotton was buried at Ware on 16 Sep 1804 [HALS: DP116/1/5].
[363] James Burr was buried at Anstey on 18 Nov 1804 [HALS: DP5/1/3].

lidds in the dark. The well was open & the bucket at the bottom. She fell to the bottom unhert & was drawn up hanging by the chane 98 feet deep, about 17 years of age. One Sparks from Tewin, the other maid, went to draw but not performd it.

Thus ends this year 1804.

Esqr Cashwell of Sacomb, grand son to Roult, formerly of that estate is a building a very fine & large new house this year not yet finished not farr from ware the old house stood, which old Roult his grandfather lived, which old Cashwell his father pulled down 20 yrs back, & sold piesmeel (*piecemeal*) in lotts.

The Honable Spencer Cowper, brother to the present Francis Earl Cowper of Pansanger, late of Fidgon Hall or Cole Green House, but this pressant Earl pulled that noble house down about 4 years back which was build by their great grandfather Ld Chancler Cowper, about the year 1710. This Spencer I say is a building a new large house near the church at Digswell this year, not yet finished, Spencer is member for the Borough of Hartford, & singel man & his brother so at preasant.[364] There was a large old house whear Spencer is building this before built at differant times, and not reguler, formerly belonging to Esqr Shelcross. After his death to Esqr Williss and all Diggswell Estate, but Williss dying his daughter sold the estate and manner (*manor*) to the Cowpers, about the year 1788.

Still at war with the French, and the latterend of this year, the great Boniparte was made Emperer of France with great rejoiceings and eleuminations (*illuminations*) there. And our Millitia, & Armey of Reserve, and other forsces, are all on the co[a]st round the kingdom, to prevent their landing, and our shiping looking out at sea, and the inland Associations, & Yomendry so plenty of soldiers, seamen, shipping & loaded with taxes, a looking at each other, for this 2 years past.

[364] The Shalcross family had held the Digswell estate from 1656 and it descended to Elizabeth Willis wife of Captain Barkley RN in 1785. The Barkleys lived in London and sold the estate to the 3rd Earl Cowper in 1786. Spencer demolished the old medieval house and rebuilt it partly on the same site [*VCH Hertfordshire* vol 3 pp81-85; D Ward, *Digswell from Domesday to Garden City* (Welwyn, 1953)].

This year and part of last year Bayford church taken down as an old and decaid building, and new built with brick from the ground on the same spot, by one Mr Simpson, marster carpenter of Esington (*Essendon*), and finished and opened this **Christmas Day or Decbr 25 1804**. Wm Baker Lord of the Manner (*Manor*) gave towards it £500. The old church had 3 bels and a dove steeple the same as Barkhamstead of wood, or Bramfield, but now but one bell.

Cole Green House, undated sepia wash (*HALS: CV/Herting/39*)

THE ARITHMETIC BOOK

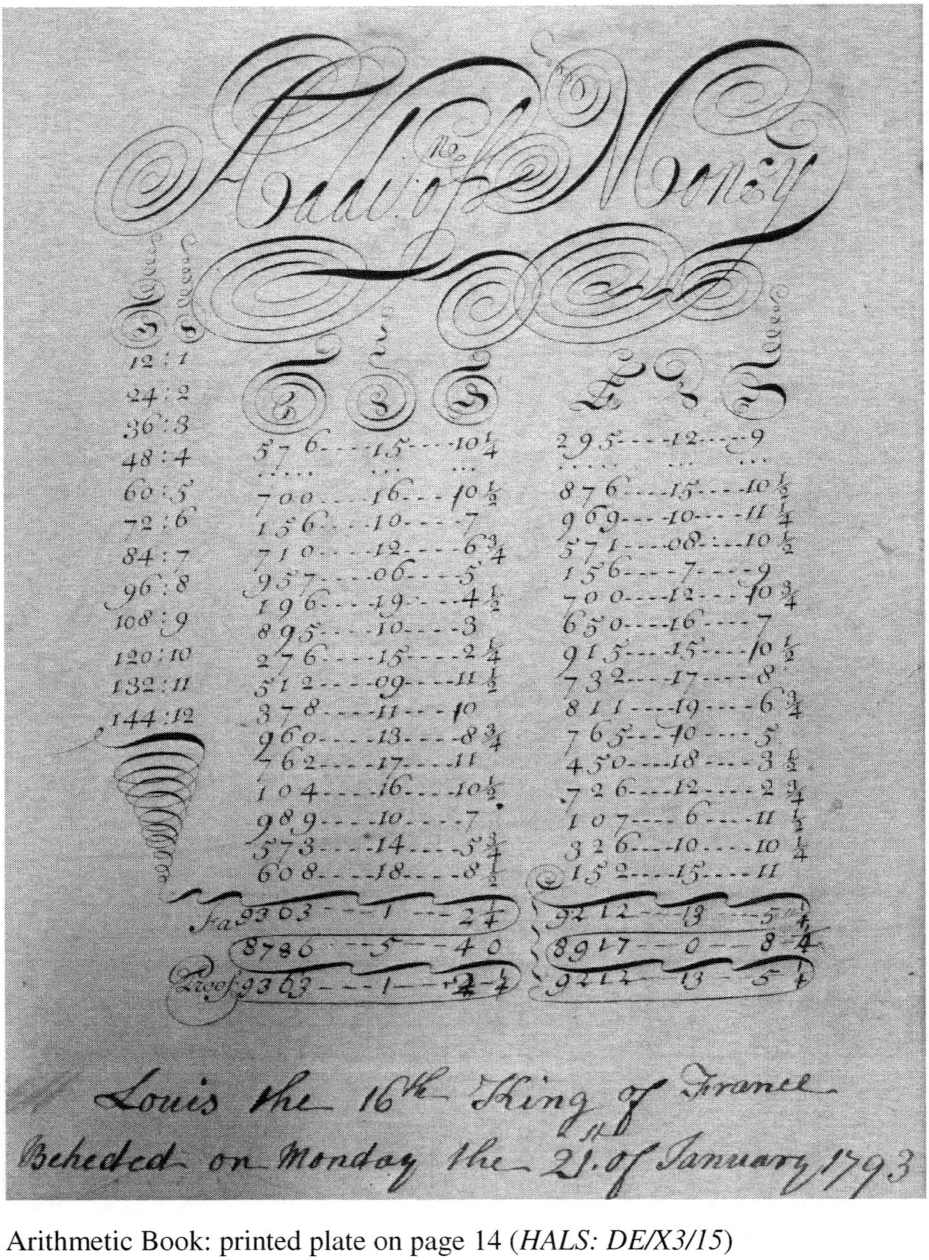
Addition of Money

	£	s	d	£	s	d
12 : 1	576	15	10¼	295	12	9
24 : 2	700	16	10½	876	15	10½
36 : 3	156	10	7	969	10	11¼
48 : 4	710	12	6¾	571	08	10½
60 : 5	957	06	5	156	7	9
72 : 6	196	19	4½	700	12	10¾
84 : 7	895	10	3	650	16	7
96 : 8	276	15	2¼	915	15	10½
108 : 9	512	09	11½	732	17	8
120 : 10	378	11	10	811	19	6¾
132 : 11	960	13	8¾	765	10	5
144 : 12	762	17	11	450	18	3½
	104	16	10½	726	12	2¾
	989	10	7	107	6	11½
	573	14	5¾	326	10	10¼
	608	18	8½	152	15	11
Fa	9303	1	2¼	9212	13	5¼
	8786	5	4 0	8917	0	8¼
Proof	9363	1	2¼	9212	13	5¼

Louis the 16th King of France
Beheded on Monday the 21. of January 1793

Arithmetic Book: printed plate on page 14 (*HALS: DE/X3/15*)

APPENDIX ONE

The Arithmetic Book

(*HALS: DE/X3/15*)

Page 1 (*stuck to inside of front cover*):
Bramfield died July 26, 1792 Wm Derds at the Erle of Grandisons Arms.

8 new bells for Adderbury in Oxford Shire within 2 miles of Banbury cast by Bryant Hartford April 1790. Tener w[eigh]t 26 Hundred.[1]

Swalecliffe nere Whitstable the living of V Warrons, Kent.[2]

July 10, 1792 the great meeting at the Town Hall, Hertford of the gentlemen, clergy, freeholders etc to send address to the King for his kind procklimation for the care of his subjects w[hi]ch was agreed to.[3]

Page 2: (*Writing practice numbers 1-10, 20 etc to 90 repeated down the page*).

Pages 3-4: (*Multiplication tables 1-12 and a pence table from 20 pence is 1s 8d, then in tens to 120 pence is 10s*).

3 Barley Corns	1 inch
6 inches	one ½ foot
33½ feet	1 pole
40 pole	1 furlong
8 furlong	1 mile
3 mile	1 League
20 Leags	1 Degree

[1] A new peal of eight bells was cast by John Briant of Hertford in 1789 and the first peal was rung in 1790. The *Northampton Mercury* dated 26 Jun 1790 reports on the event and states that the tenor bell weighed 26 hundredweight. The bell actually weighs 24 cwt and 14 lbs [Dodds, *Hertfordshire Bellfounders,* pp213-5].
[2] Vincent Warren, rector of Swalecliffe, Kent, died on 7 Dec 1791 [Clergy database, CCEd Record ID: 309106].
[3] On 21 May 1792 George III issued a Royal Proclamation against seditious writings, banning *The Rights of Man* and charging Thomas Paine with sedition.

APPENDIX ONE

Page 5:
The barometer is for whet and dry; the thermometer is for heat & cold.

Clover about 10 pound, turnip about 3 d[itt]o to 1 acre.

Some have died young,	I have often done well
While others old have fell.	That I herd never.
Yet those lived long enough,	I once did ill,
Who lived well.	That I herd ever.

For Rumatism: Take 1 q[ua]rt of good gin, 1 ounce of Almonac Almoniac. Mix them together in the bottell shaking it well & take ½ quarten in the morning fasting & lie in bed one hour after.

Page 6:
June 26, 1787 measured the Great Field at Panshanger by the garden for Esq Law: 24 acres 13 pole.

Measured the other Grass Field below the wood or garden: 8 acres 52 pole.

Pages 7-10: (*Mathamatical calculations involving money, using addition, subtraction and multiplication*)

Page 11:
The Hair Powder Act took place this May 1795, that whoever chose to wair powder must pay one guinea per year.

Jurney to London in little cart with Poll & Mary Scott on Sunday February 28, 1796.

In this year 1797 the Provincial Cavelry was raised and the Supplementary Millita. But the cavelery was soon dismist onley had a few meetings to inspect the men & horses by the Marquess of Salsbury & discharged, but the Supplementrey Millitia continued.[4]

Page 12: (Printed plate: '*Addition teacheth to Add several sums into one Total summe' with calculations in columns*)

---

[4] The cavalry was to be a levy of one horse in ten on all of those who paid the horse tax and was intended to strengthen the Supplementary Militia authorised by 38 Geo 3 c19. It proved impossible to levy or train and it was wound up in 1798 [J R Western, *The English Militia*].

APPENDIX ONE

Thos Pennyfather gent[lema]n farmer which lived at Harmer Green Farme in the parish of Wellwin, set out on horsback about 10 o clock on Tusday the foornoon 4th August 1789 to Diggswell Place Farme by the church to see his late brother William's widow & children to advise them when to begin harvest & had been riding about to see their cropp & a coming down the valley oppisit Diggswell church his horse hind foot twas supposed catched the fore foot and fell on him & chrusht him allmost to death. He lived till the Thursday following about one clock he died, buried at Wellwin church the Munday following, aged 53 years, from Diggswell a walking burial. I was there.

Page 13: (*Blank*)

Page 14: (Printed plate: '*Addition Money' with calculations*)

Louis the 16th King of France was beheded on Monday the 21st of January 1793.

Page 15: (*Blank*)

Page 16: (*Multiplication calculation*)

Page 17: (*Blank*)

Page 18: (Printed plate: '*Avoirdupois Weight. Note that 8 drams is 1 ounce, 16ozs 1 pound, 28lbs is a quarter, 4 quarters a Cwt, 20C a Tun, 19½C a Fodder'*)

Hertford new goall built this year 1777 at the end of the town as you go to Ware and the old goall in the midle of the town converted into tinnements on electtion business, as made 14 dwellings, but after the electtion was totally puled down and made a butcher's market on, as tis at the preasant 1804.[5]

Page 19: (*Blank*)

Page 20: (*Multiplication calculations*)

Page 21: (*Subtraction calculations*)

---

[5] The site of the old goal in Fore Street, Hertford is occupied by the Corn Exchange built in 1858, now used as a public hall with shops on the ground floor [C Heath, *The Book of Hertford* (Chesham, 1975) p92].

APPENDIX ONE

Page 22: (Printed plate: '*Addition of Troy. Note that 24 Grains 1 Pennyw[eigh]t, 20 Pwt 1 ounce, 12 ozs 1 pound Troy'. With explanatory calculation)*

A little free hold estate between Bulls Green and Hoppersend in the parish of Datchworth consisting of 3 tiniments, orchard and 2 little fields, about 3 acres, belonging to the widow South, was sold by auction at the Horns, Bulls Green, by E[d]w[ar]d Batton for 204 guinneas to one Hall on Wednesday the 11 of January 1797. I bid 203 guineas.

Page 23:
On Saturday 22nd June 1793 was brought to Hartford on a cariage made lowe for that purpose, drawn by 8 horses, the shipp called the *Adventure* from Henlow in Bedfordshire, built there, belonging to Geo Edwards Esqr of Henlow. It was lanced (*launched*) or drawn into the river at the bridge at the back of the Pryory Farm, so away to Ware, by London to Winsor to another of the said gentleman's estate there. It saled off the s[ai]d afternoon & the cariage returned back to Henlow.

1796 November Thursday the 5th from 11 to 12 at night and from 12 till 3 clock on the 6 Fryday morning happned the most terable highwind as ever was known. I think it was higher than that on Fryday night the 15th of February 1760. As to the damage I am not able to say, but the next day the whole country was nothing but a wrack (*wreck*). Some h[o]uses down, some stript and trees down &c. I had 15 trees splitt of and blown down in Bacons Orchard, cherres & apples & it almost destroyed the orchard. We all was up & stood under the hollebush for fear of the house falling. It was a westtlery (*westerly*) wind.

Page 24:
Rich[ar]d Turpin, highwayman was born at Helmpstead (*Hempstead*), Essex the son of John Turpin farmer there. After many depredations of house breaking and highway robing &c he was hanged at York the 10 of April 1739. Turpin shot dead a man near his den on Eppen Forist (*Epping Forest*) who went with a nother man together with a long gun to take him.[6]

[6] Dick Turpin: 'In February 1737, ostensibly upon the authorities learning of Turpin's intention to return home and rendezvous with friends, an ambush was laid at Puckeridge, Hertfordshire, and although Turpin eluded capture his wife, Elizabeth, and her companions were committed to Hertford gaol on suspicion of highway

Johnathon Wild the noted theeftaker & the receaver of stolen goods was executed at Tyburn May 24, 1725.[7]

The most sevear sharp <night> frost Christmas Eve Saturday the 24 December 1796, for one night as was never known in this part of the globe. The night was very clear & star light, no wind nor clowdy. Maney people was frozen to death. I came that evening with Mr Henry Hunsdon from St Albans in little cart. I was taken out all most dead and for weeks before the right use of my arme. The ice was clierd (*cleared*) in the day time in the horspond & frozen 6 inches this night measured by Bassett, carpenter.

Why should I deprive my neighbour
Of his goods against his will
Hands were made for honest labour
Not to plunder or to steele.

Tis a foolish self deceiving,
By such tricks to hope for gain,
All that's ever got by thieving,
Turns to sorrow, shame & pain.

Oft we see a young beginner
Practice little pilfering ways,
Till grown up a hardned sinner,
Then the gallows ends hos days.

Away from fools I'll turn my eye,
Nor with the scoffers go,
I would be walking with the wise,
That I may wiser grow.

Page 25: (*Multiplication calculation)*

Page 26: Printed plate: '*LIQUID Measure'*. *Note that:*

2 Pints	*1 Quart*
4 Quarts	*1 Gallon*
8 Gall[on] Ale, 9 Beer	*1 Firkin*
2 Firkens	*1 Kilderkin*
2 Kilderkins	*1 Barrel*
18½ Gall[on] full guage	*1 Runlet*
42 Gallons	*1 Tierce*
63 Gallons	*1 Hogshead*

robbery, but afterwards released.' He was tried and convicted, and executed at York on 7 April 1739 [Derek Barlow, Turpin, Richard [Dick] (1705-1739), *ODNB*, 2004].

[7] Much popular literature about the thief taker Jonathan Wild was in circulation during the eighteenth and nineteenth centuries, including, for example, Henry Fielding's *Jonathan Wild the Great* (1743) [Andrea McKenzie, 'Wild, Jonathan (1683-1725)', *ODNB*, 2004].

84 Gall[ons]	*1 Pipe or Butt*
252 Gall[ons] or 4 h[ogs]h[ea]ds	*1 Tun of Wine*

Lord How's victory over the French fleet June 1, 1794.[8] Beat them and took 2 ships of 80 [guns], 4 of 74.

Page 27:
15th of Sepr 1784 Lunerday assended in a boolone (*balloon*) at the Attillery Ground, London to a great hithe over Barnat (*Barnet*), North Hall (*Northaw*), then went for St Albans, then took his course east over Codicote, Wellwin, Tewin, Bengeo & landed him self in a little meadow at Standon Green End.[9] He throwd his line out & was pulled down by a young woman in the meadow who was fritned at first and runaway, thought it the Devell, till he made her sencable and gave her 5 guineas. It was a very fine hot day. I saw him plane as he came over Bacons, he was at a great hight for his boloon was 30 feet round but appeared no biger than a boys kite. Maney people followd him on horsback & foot & was up soon after he fell, and Wm Baker Esqr of Bayford Bury took him home in his carriage to the Bury and his boloon and was there some time, a weak or more. Baker had a great pibple (*pebble*) stone which had lane in Bengeo Street, no one knows how long, remoovd to the place he fell & a brass plate put theiron with the account. I suppose the stone to way 30 hund[redweight], people used to sit on it in the street as it was by the path side.

Page 28:

---

[8] See the report of the battle in the *ODNB* entry for Earl Howe (1726-1799) [Roger Knight, 'Howe, Richard, Earl Howe (1726-1799)', *ODNB*, 2004].

[9] Vincenzo Lunardi (1759-1806), Secretary to the Neapolitan Embassy in London, made the first ascent over England in a hydrogen-filled balloon on 15 Sep 1784 from the Artillery Ground, Finsbury, London. The stone at Standon still stands and its inscription reads: 'That Woundrous Enterprise Successfully Atchieved By the Power of Chemistry And the Fortitude of Man, That Improvement in science which the Great Author of all Knowledge, Patronising by His Providence The Improvement of Mankind, Hath Graciously Permitted To their Benefit And his own Eternal Glory' [Elizabeth Baigent, 'Lunardi, Vincenzo (1759-1806)', *ODNB*, May 2009; See also Lunardi's own account in *The Gentleman's Magazine*, Oct 1784, reproduced in Jones, *Hertfordshire, 1731-1800,* pp67-8].

APPENDIX ONE

I demand how many inches it is from London to Hartford which is 21 mile, 2 furlongs & 16 pole (*with calculation*). (*Signed*) Wm Carrington.

Oates and barley ground together and dressed, the flower boyled in water like gruil and given to calves milk warm. Very good when short of milk. This for calves that are wheaning.

Page 29:
I desire to know how much Timber there is in 24 foot long and 24 inches girth (*with calculation*). Now how much feet in 24 foot long and 6 inches girth (*with calculation*).

Page 30: Printed plate: '*Dry Measure'. Note that:*

14 Ozs Avoirdup[ois]	*1 Pint*
2 Pints	*1 Quart*
2 Quarts	*1 Pottle*
2 Pottles	*1 Gallon*
2 Gallons	*1 Peck*
4 Pecks	*1 Bush[ell] of Wheat*
2 Bushells	*1 Strike*
2 Strike	*1 Comb*
2 Comb	*1 Quart[er] or Seam*
10 Quarters	*1 Last*

Page 31:
County of Hertford, Hund[red] of Cashio or Liberty of St Albans. In the year 1331 the 4th year of King Edward 3d and in Rich[ar]d Wallingford time the 2d and 28th Abbot of St Albans. About October in the same year was a sessions of Gaol Delivery held at Brantfield (*Bramfield*) in this county of Hartford upon a disagreement between the abbot and monks of St Albans and fryors &c of St Albans and the towns people of St Albans. Which was one Tavenner of the town had so highly offended the abbot that he was fully deturmined to punish him. Whereoff the abbot sent two monks and one Walter Amersham the abbott's mareschell to take him up. A desperat fray ensued and Taverner struck Amersham whereoff Amersham struck Taverner and killed him, which so enraged the towns people that a great mobb ensued and they killed Amersham & the other two monks fleed whereoff they was all summoned by

Rich[ar]d Pereres High Sheriff to attend at Brantfild to try the murderis and to answer the complaint.[10]

Page 32: (*Multiplication and subtraction of money calculations*)

Page 33:
Some people then talk so much about Kings,
And call out for Liberty and such things (Repe[a]t this line)
And say that our land it doth decay,
And so loded with taxes that they'l run away.

God send us peace in our land that wee live in,
Showe tis the same as was Adam and Eve in,
And let us not do then as Cane did they say,
Who killed his brother and then run away (rep[ea]t this line)

For we have women to wash and keep us then cleene,
To lye by our sides and dance on the Green,
To cook our provisionand with us to play,
And they that don't like them I hove go away

We have butchers our meat then for to kill,
And bring it home our belleys to fill,
We have excellent bread & strong beer I say,
And they that don't like it I hove go away.

We have parsons to preach our solds for to love,
And attend on us then when we go to the grave,
And if we are in danger they for us will pray,
And they that don't like them I hove go away.

May fortaine protect our Great Men in command,
That fights our battells by sea and by land,
And send them success & I hallow huzza,
See yonder our fows how they run away.

---

[10] Richard Perers was sheriff of Hertfordshire from 1314-1317 [Austin, *List of Sheriffs of the County of Hertford*]. This episode is related in *The History of the Ancient and Royal Foundation called the Abbey of St Alban* by the Revd Peter Newcome, Rector of Shenley, Hertfordshire, published in 1795, pp221-2, a work Carrington may well have seen.

APPENDIX ONE

May God bless noble George that sits on the throne,
A better King shour never was known,
And so is the Queen as I hear them say,
And they that don't like them we drive them away.

And now to conclude and end my song,
Lets all live in peace then every one,
And be thankfull for the blessings we enjoy every day,
And then we no reason for too run away.

The chorus to each verce:

For the land that we live in,
Is the best then I know,
And they that don't like it,
Away let them go.
(Repet the 2 last lines over againe).

Page 34: Printed plate: *Cloth Measure. Note that:*

4 Nails or 9 Inches	*1 q[uarte]r of a yard*
4 Quart[ers]	*1 Yard*
5 Quarters	*1 Ell English*
3 q[uarters] of a Y[a]rd	*1 Ell Flemish*
6 q[uarters] of a Yard	*1 French Auln*

Page 35: (*Blank*)

Page 36: (*Multiplication and division calculations)*

Page 37:
The Borough election for Hartford was on Wednsday ye 16 of June 1790. Members chosen the young Baron Dimsdale and John Calvert of Albury Hall Esqr, and Wm Baker of Bayfordbury was thrown out. 1 days poole (*poll*). The nomination for members for the county was on Fryday folowin, the 18th, when Wm Plumer and Hale of Wellwin, son to Esqr Hale of Kings Walden, and William Baker, which lost the ellection for the Borrough, was nominated. Baker was called by the voice of the freeholders unexpected in the fi[e]ld, for Hale came with a great company to meet Plumer & we thought there w[oul]d be no oppisiton (*opposition*). Lord Grimston the late member with Plumer

was called to the House of Pears (*Peers*) and so he rickamended his brother in law Mr Hale of Lockley near Wellwin in his room, but he lost it.

The electtion for the County was on Wednesday the 23 followin <June 1790>. Each candidate came with their flaggs at their head of their companeys, Baker first, Plummer 2nd, Hale 3rd, & drew their companies in the field behind the goal. The show was great & all sides, and after

Page 38: (Printed plate: '*Substraction shews how to take a Lesser number from a Greater that the Rest or difference Between the two numbers given may be known'. With explanatory calculations*)

some time spent, drew of for the town for pooling about ½ after 11 clock. The pool was strong & noisey, as the cry was 'no Hale no lock up, small beer but Baker for ever', and continued so till 9 clock at night, when the acpt (*account*) of the pool being taken it was given in for Baker & he & Plumer was cheared about 11 at night with demonstrations of joy.

No of votes: Plumers 1830, Bakers 1301, Hales 1031.

The Marquis of Salsbury, Duke of Leeds, Duke of Bridge Water & most of the head nobillity was for Hale, but the freeholders shewed themselves independand and stood to Baker whome they nominated in the field. Baker gave entertainment the morning of the ellecttion and the next day at his house Bayford Burey.

Page 39:
Wheras Samuall Travers Esqr left by will bearing date July 16th 1724 £60 p[e]r an[nu]m to 7 gentlemen, that is £60 a piese yearly, and the 7 gentlemen to be added to the Poor Knights of Windsor and that a building should be erected near the Castle of Windsor for the habitation of the said 7 gentlemen who were to be superannuated or disabled old Lieutenants of English Men of War. And the said testator desired that the gentlemen so to be incorporated might be single men, without children, and inclined to lead a virtuos, studious and devout life. And that he would have them live in a collegiate manner in order whereunto he would have 26 p[oun]d p[e]r annum deducted out of their several allowances to keep a constant table. And whereas 21 such quallified Lieutenants of his Majesty's Navy are to be returned to the Lords of the Admiralty on the 1st day of Octr 1794, that out of the 21 the s[ai]d Lords are

to return 14 to his Majesty, that out of the 14 his Majesty is to appoint 7 to be the first persons appointed Poor Nights under the said will.[11]

Page 40: (*Mathamatical calculations)*

Page 41:
On the 29th day of June 1789, the large oak near St Mary Mgdalans College, Oxford suppose to have stood there six hundred years. The girt[h] of the oak was 21 feet 9 inches, height 71 feet 8 inches – cubic contents 754 feet. This tree fell down on the 29 above as by decay & luckily did no damage.

Wednesday the 1st day of Dec[em]b[e]r 1790 went with Mr Strutt & my son John to St Albans in little cart, the great snow as we went. Met Mr John Thane at the Red House, slep there that night & Mr Thane, Mr Strutt & myself the next morning whent to L[or]d Grimston's, Gorhambury, to take off som pickturs by his Lordship's permition. Dined there & was kindly treated with good wine & ven[i]son, his L[or]dship's servants that dined with us was Mr John Simkins butler or steward, Mr Darkins bailiff, Mr Hews cook, Mr Grayam gardner, Mrs Bond howskeepr. Sleep the next night at the Redhouse & came home the next day. Lord Grimston's house is a new one built about 6 years with stone.[12]

---

[11] Samuel Travers, a Windsor worthy, one time Member of Parliament for the Borough, died in 1728, and by his will dated 16 July 1724, left funds for the purpose of 'adding seven gentlemen to the present eighteen Poor Knights of Windsor'. They were to be 'superannuated or disabled lieutenants of English men-of-war'. There was a long delay in carrying out the terms of this bequest, owing to various counter-claims upon the funds and consequent law-suits. It was not until 1798 that a charter could be granted incorporating this new establishment as 'The Poor Knights of Windsor of the Fundation [sic] of Samuel Travers'. The first appointments were nominated in 1795. But according to the *Naval Chronicle* for the year 1803 it was not until that year that seven lieutenants of the Navy were to be installed Naval Knights of Windsor [E H Fellowes, *The Military Knights of Windsor, 1352-1944* (Windsor, 1944) ppxlvii-viii].

[12] The present house of Gorhambury was first inhabited on 20 October, 1784, and stands at no great distance north-east of the house which it superseded, that built by Sir Nicholas Bacon between 1563 and 1568. A fine portico on the main front of the house, reached by a broad flight of steps, leads to a large entrance hall from which the principal rooms open on three sides, the dining-room to the right, and a fine library in the middle, out of which small ante-rooms lead to larger rooms in the angles of the main block. There is a fine series of portraits, a number by [Peter] Lely and

APPENDIX ONE

(*Enclosed in this page: a separate small scrap of paper*):

Red House St Albans
Mr Strutt & I and Mr Thane

3 sup[p]ers	3s 0d
Brandy	9d
Do & water	5s 6d
Ginn & water	9d
Beer	1s 2d
Bacco?	3d
Tea for 3	2s 0d
Bedds	2s 0d
Tea for 1	8d
	16s 1d

Our bill at the Red House Dbr 1 & 2, 1790

Page 42: (Printed plate: '*SUBTRACTION Money'. With explanatory calculations*)

Page 43:
In the year 1738 the 25th of July St Jameses day was the most terable storme of thunder & lightening as in Hartfordshire naver known the like. The thunder was continual & about 1 clock the hale came so large & strong brake all the windows on the south side & killed fowls & hurt cattle. It came SW & went NE & destroyd the corne in its passage tho not above 3 mile wide. At Hartford all the houses on the south side windows broken & Ware & churches &c &c.

Page 44: (*Multiplication and Division calculations. Signed* William Carrington)

Page 45:
When God the foundation of this great fabrick laid,
And this world then first begun,
By his word was all things made,
And in an instant it was done.

[Anthony] Vandyck, but the most interesting include a picture by [Nicholas] Hilliard, presented by Queen Elizabeth to Sir Nicholas Bacon, and a full length of Sir Francis Bacon by [Paul] Van Somer [*VCH Hertfordshire* vol 2, pp392-405].

APPENDIX ONE

God said let there be light,
Which was all darkness then before,
And you infirnall spirits take y[ou]r flight,
And not come here no more.

The light then was the sun which now doth rule the day,
And the darkness God called night and ordered the moon and stars I say,
And the waters together in great lakes and that he then called sea,
And the instant then the word he spake dry land appeard to bee.

And from the dust of the earth so light then God he formed Man,
And breathed in him the breath of life and called his name Adam,
And Adam he gave names to all things God was pleasd to send,
And Man was made Lord of the same from the beginning of the world unto the end.

But Adam was yet alone as God then did concive,
Therefore he took from him a bone and made him a wife cald Eve,
And these two in the Garden of Eden was sent,
The same to dress and keep clean, and to obey God's laws and live content as happy as a King and Queen.

But old Saturn *(Satan)* did Eve beguile and causd them to be forlorne,
And so he did Cane their childe the first that ever was borne,
But God hath ordered since if men doth him but fear,
That when wer you from hence for the devil we need not hear.

For our Saviour Christ God did send tis eighteen hundr'd years or more,
That whoever on him doth depend will be for ever happy in serten shure,
For Matthew, Mark, Like & John they wrote his life which was so good,
And Paul & Peeter & every one sealed the same then with their blood.

For they well him new & to be sertain true
For they dayley attended on him till he did assend.
To them his blessing he gave which made them valent and brave,
And they preached the same unto their lives end.

Page 46: (Printed plate: '*Weight Avoirdup[ois]*'. *With explanatory calculations*)

Page 47:
Sunday March 20th <1796> went to London with Mr Chapman of Hartford to try what we could do for one Thos Witty now under sentence of dath in Hartford Gaol, and is to be executed on Thursday next the 24th along with one Watts for horse steeling, an old offender. The said Thos Witty stole a sheep out of a drove passing to London in Nov[embe]r last near Hatfield. Went to Wm Baker Esq, to Lord Grandison, to John Calvert Esq, to young baron Dimsdale. Got a reprieve through our application from the Duke of Portland, and it come down to me at Bacons about 3 ours before the hanging, and Watts was hanged by him self about one clock on Thursday 24 March. The said Thos Whitty was a bout 32 years of age, with wife an 4 children. Was borne at the sighn of the Horse and Groom, Stanborough near Hatfild, and his father is now living.[13]

Page 48: (*Subtraction and addition of money calculations*)

Page 49:
Memerandom, June 4th 1789 King Georges 3rd birth day there is now standing in Bacons orcha[r]d an ash tree which is 34 foot long 25 inches girt[h]. (*A mathematical calculation follows*).

The King George 3rd fell insane or went out of his mind in October last 1788 and continued at times outragous all the winter and spring. But he is now recovred & great rejoyecings this birth day as above. In April last one day as a fast was kept with a form of pray[e]r throughout England for his recovrey and now very great rejoyceings indeed as he continues better.
Great disputes and the Prince of Wales was to be appointed Regent but the King's recovry prevented it.

Page 50: (Printed plate: '*Troy w[eigh]t and Liquid measure' with explanatory calculations*)

---

[13] Thomas Wittey was found guilty of stealing a wether sheep at Hatfield, value 30s, the property of Richard York, Robert White and Joseph Langton at the Hertford Assizes 7 Mar 1796. His death sentence was respited on 22 Mar 1796 to transportation for 7 years. However records show that he remained in Hertford Gaol until 10 Oct 1797 before being taken to the *Lion* hulk moored at Portsmouth. He remained there until at least July 1799 but there are no records of his reaching New South Wales so he may have died in Portsmouth. See also Arithmetic Book p77 below for a fuller description [TNA: ASSI31/17; HO13/10 pp425-6. Information from Ken Griffin].

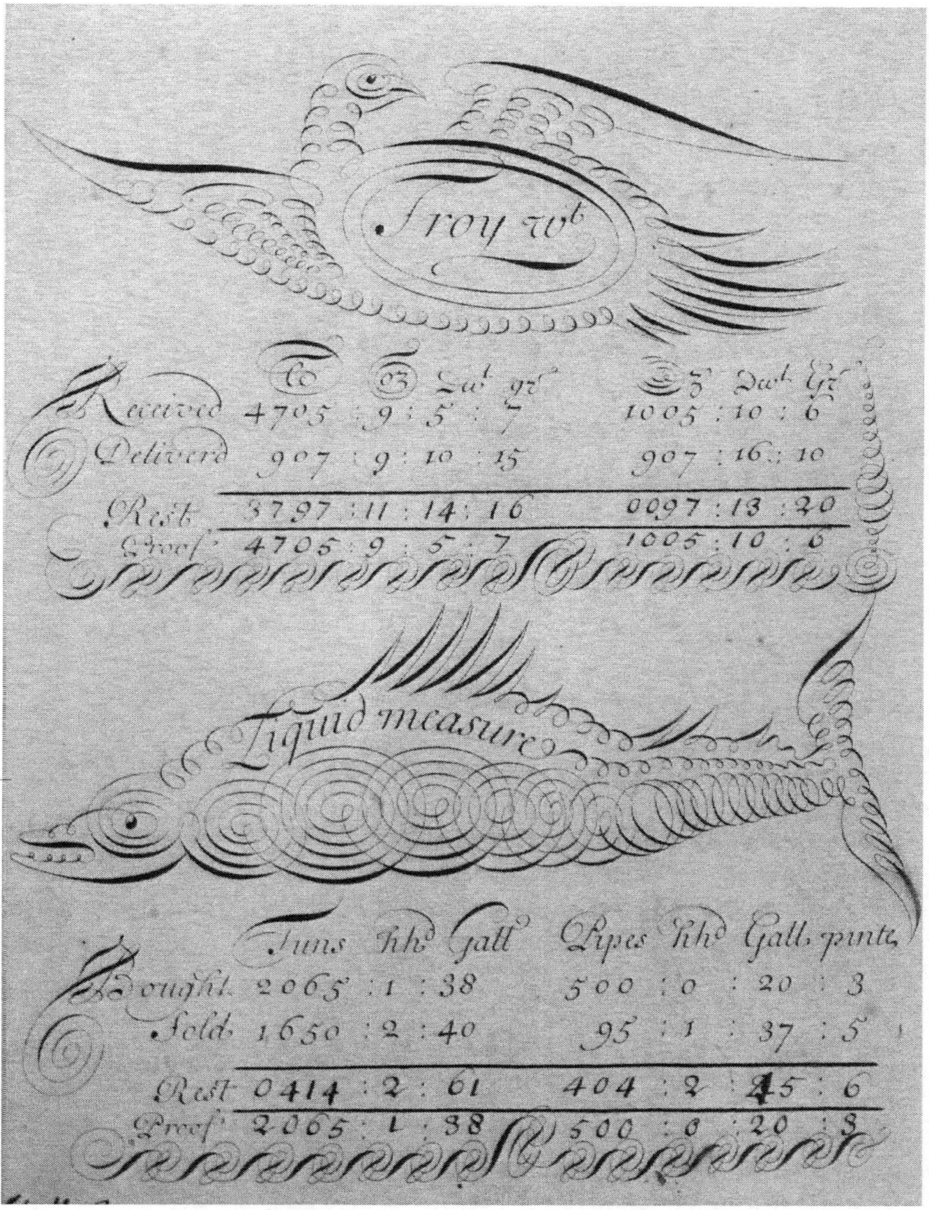

Troy wt

	lb	oz	dwt	gr	℥	dwt	gr
Received	4705	9	5	7	1005	10	6
Deliverd	907	9	10	15	907	16	10
Rest	3797	11	14	16	0097	13	20
Proof	4705	9	5	7	1005	10	6

Liquid measure

	Tuns	hhd	Gall	Pipes	hhd	Gall	pints
Bought	2065	1	38	500	0	20	3
Sold	1650	2	40	95	1	37	5
Rest	0414	2	61	404	2	45	6
Proof	2065	1	38	500	0	20	3

Arithmetic Book: printed plate on page 50 (*HALS: DE/X3/15*)

APPENDIX ONE

Sir Rich[ar]d Whittington, <knight and mercer>, twise Lord Mayor of London, first time in the year 1406, second d[itt]o in the year 1419. This was the poor lad Whittington that had the catt.[14]

Page 51:
O allass, alass we have lost Mr Strutt,
As worthay good man as ear was on foot.
For drawing or engraveing who could him then excel,
His works then will praise him he hes done them so well.
And for his antiquarin researches of things then of old,
His writeings will teach us what things are there told.
Full five years at Bacons he then there did live
With his sons and his prentice and no offence did he give.
And as the evening to spend as he constant took his walk,
How agreable as a friend and delightfull his talk.
He was founder of the Sunday School at Tewin I declair,
And on Wednesdays and Sundays he was constantly there.
And he hired a room for the same purpose I say,
And his sons and his prentice hope (*help*) teach them each day.
And old Gass at the mill * was his assistant as such,
And they was the first then that brought the children to church.
Full four schoor and ten girlls and boys then or better,
He taught to reed and write then which scarse new a letter.
And he found them in books in the same for to read,
At his own then expence none to their parrants indeed.
But as all things unsertain so it out fell,
He was cald then to London amongst his friends for to dwell.
And at Kirby Street, Hatton Garden at the Hole of the Wall,
On an evening you might find him if you then did but call,
Conversing with his friends on good subgects I say,
For he never kept bad companey to lead him astray.
He was true to his church and in the pathes of virtue he trod,
To his friends he was just and walkd humley with his God.
And on the 16th of October eighteen hundred and two,

[14] Dick Whittington was actually Lord Mayor of London three times (1397, 1406 and 1419). He was not a poor man, but from a wealthy family, and as a mercer he had a successful business and civic career before he became Lord Mayor [From a list of London's mayors at www.cityoflondon.gov.uk]

God was pleased to call him over to another world that is new.

*This old Rob[er]t Gass was an optiscion (*optician*) and worked at Tewin Mill, as then being a glass mill 1793 for convex (*convex*), concoves (*concave*) and other glasses.

Pages 52-53: (*Mathematical calculations by division*)

Page 54: (Printed plate: '*Dry Measure and Cloth Measure' with explanatory calculations*)

Page 55:
Waterford Mill and House and other offices burnt down by accident, supposing to be taking fire by the work of the mill on the morning of the last day of the year 1789. This mill is in the parish of Bengeo. This mill was rebuilt againe and fit for work in 15 months after.[15]

Burleys Mill and House near Lord Sailsbury's house or park in the parish of Hatfield burnt down by accident on the 7th Day of Dec[em]b[e]r 1790.

Page 56: (Printed plate: *Multiplication tables, 2-9 and 11-12*)
Recpt (*receipt ie recipe*) for cows that may be hoved by clover &c. Force one egg shell of tarr down the throat. Immeadet (*immediate*) cure.

Page 57
The account of the great fire at Marden in the parish of Tewin belonging to Robt Mackey Esqr: it broke out about 1 o clock <on the 11 of Sepr 1790> in the morning. Consumed 3 large barns full of corn and three reeks (*ricks*) of corn and a cart house, 2 carts, a waggon and a hogs courts and 2 sows and 16 pigs & a greatt number of geese and ducks and more. Dammage a great deel to the amount of 2 thousand pounds.

Page 58: (Printed plate: '*Multiplication: Is instead of many Additions And Teacheth how by two numbers given to find a third which shall contain either of the given Termes so often as the other of them contains Units'*)

---

[15] A slightly different version of the story about the fire at Waterford Mill can be found in *The Gentleman's Magazine*, Jan 1790, reproduced in Jones, *Hertforshire 1731-1800,* p94].

APPENDIX ONE

Mr Thos Handford of Bramfield Place Farme was buried at Bramfield Church on Monday the sixt of January 1794. Aged 59 years. On the north side of the church.

Page 59:
Monday May 31 1790 jorney to London with Mr Strutt in wiskey. Saw the British Museum.[16] Mr Townley, the prentis came Octr 25, 1790.
Thursday morning the 23 of December 1790 the turable storme of thunder and lightning highwind begun about 3 clock in the morning, was over about 6, held about 3 hours. Very shocking, dreadfull in deed, it came a bout S[outh] West. It went thorough the kingdom & did a great deal of damage. Went NE.

Page 60: (Printed plate: '*Multiplication' with calculations*)
On Satuorday night March the 2[d] 1793 the moast turable high wind about 12 a clock at the highest. It did a great deal of damage all over the Kingdom. At Huntingdon it blew down St Benedict church steeple after having standing 1200 years. No wind has been so high since the year [17]78 when it blew the old year out and the new in.

Page 61:
The great fire which happned at Mr Benj[ami]n Youngs farmer at the farm at the further Hatfield Hide neareist Hatfield was discoverd to be on fire a bout 3 oclock on the morning of the Fryday the 23 of Aug[u]st 1793. It burnt 3 barns full of corne, one wheat hovell of wheat. It was very unluckey for Mr Young as he had just finished his harvest, excepting 3 joggs or cart loads which was to be ind as the day above all his poultrey was burnt and his outbuildings. Luckely no horses in stable, the dwelling house was saved.

Page 62: (Printed plate: '*Multiplication' with calculations*)
The Hartfordshire Millitia returnd from camp at Warley Common in Esex and marched into Hartford with Lord Salsbury or Marques d[itt]o at their head on Munday about 1 clock the 21 day of Octr 1793 to winter quarters at Hartford, Ware & Hodsdon &c.

---

[16] The British Museum which had opened to the public on 15 Jan 1759 was then housed in Montagu House, Bloomsbury. The opening hours were restricted to three hours a day and only to a very limited number of people who were obliged to make application in writing to the principal librarian [Weinreb et al, *London Encyclopaedia*].

APPENDIX ONE

Page 63:
Memarandom of the great flood which happned on February Monday 9th & 10th & 11th in the year 1795 after the great frost from the 18th of December 1794 to this 9th day of February 1795, then a general thaw and such a flood for 3 days that ever was known in this part of the globe, and yet no rain, onley the melting of the snow that had fell. The continuance of the frost at times. Tewin River (*the Mimram*) was like the River Theams (*Thames*). I saw it and wanted to go to Cole Green from Bacons but could not cross it for 2 days not on horse back and most of the bridges was blown up on the rivers all over England. The newspapers was full of misfortains of this kind. The bridge at, or by, the Lockley garden up, the waggons went through the garden close by the house so into Wellwin by the Vine and Chequer end of the town, Tewin Water brige up, Tewin Bury brige up, Kingbrige up, Poplar Green up, Hertingfordbury up, Waterford up, Wotton up, Hertfords damaged, & Ware. I saw them repairing and workmen that set out on the Monday morning to work wear they crossed the rivers could not git home to their fameleys till the Wednesday or Thursday night following. I am a speaking of Tewin River, such as lived at Popler Green and worked at Marden and such as worked at Lord Cowper and lived at Tewin and at Grubbs Barn &c. And other rivers in proportion.[17]

Pages 64-72 and part 73: (*Manuscript essay 'Of Decimal Fractions' with various calculations*)

Page 73:
On Thursday the 12th of June 1794 between one and two a clock in the afternoon died William Clarke of Hatfield, taylor. Was buried the Sunday following on the south side of Hatfield church yard aged 73. He maried my sister Eliz[abe]th Carrington.

Page 74: (Printed plate: *'Division Teaches to Divide one Number by another to find how often one Number is contained in the other OR It shews how to Divide a Number into as many Equal parts as yow please'*)

---

[17] A lengthy description of the devastation caused by this flood in 1795 can be found in the Ayot St Peter parish register where Charles Chauncy was rector [HALS: DP/11/1/4]. It is also mentioned in *The Gentleman's Magazine*, Mar 1795, reproduced in Jones, *Hertfordshire 1731-1800,* p118. Carrington refers to it again on page 135 of the Arithmetic Book below.

APPENDIX ONE

Page 75:
Wednesday 8 clock evening May 13 1795 the great fire begun at Horwell (*Horrell*) Mr Youngs, farmer near Essington (*Essendon*). Was got under [control] about 11 that night, a good engin from the Marquiss of Salsburys and one from Hartford. Burnt down 2 barns and shedds and malting. It was accidential, his malting fired. Loss about 1 hund[red] load of wheat at £45 per load, and 1 hund[red] and 50 qr of malt at £53 per quarter, exclusive of buildings.

On the Thursday night May the 14 following was the great fire at Cheshunt near Turners Hill, one farmers Currall. Burnt all his barns and out buildings, but his house, a great deal of wheat, 2 calves, 4 hoggs, carts, waggons &c. Supposed to be set on fire.[18]

Page 76: (Printed plate: *'From Division Flows this proportion As the Dividend is to the Divisor so is the Quotient unto a Unit'*)

Page 77:
Sunday March ye 20th 1796 set of for London with Mr Chapman from Hartford, met him at Essington (*Essendon*) at the Kings Head about 9 clock Sunday morning, each of us on horseback. Went from thence to London with all speed to try w[ha]t we could do amongst friends for one Thos Witty under sentance of d[e]ath in Hartford Goal and was to be executed on Thursday next the 24 with one Watts, a horsesteeler. Got to London about 12 clock noon, put our horses up at Bear & Castle, St Gileses Pound. Went from thence to Hill Street, Wm Bakers Esqr member for the county of Hartford, from thence to Ld Grandisons at Carringtons Place near High (*Hyde*) Park Corner, and from thence to Esqr Calverts, Stable House Yard, St Jameses, member for the Borrough of Hartford. Made application to them all for the poor fellow and a repreeve come down to the goaler at Hartford the night before the execution and to me the next morning of the execution about 10 clock at Bacons that our request was granted for his life and likewise his sentance was to Bottinebay (*Botany Bay*) for 7 years onley. The said Thos Witty was borne at the Horse & Groome, Stanborough near Hatfield, a young man about 32 having a wife & 4 children, his offence was for steeling 1 fat sheep out of a drove passing to London, value 1 guinea, in Nov[embe]r last in that distressed time when corne sold at £3 per load.

---

[18] The fires at Essendon and Turner's Hill are both reported in *The Gentleman's Magazine*, May 1795, reproduced in Jones, *Hertfordshire 1731-1800,* p118.

APPENDIX ONE

Page 78: (Printed plate: *'Division' with calculations*)

Page 79:
Monday August the 18, 1794 set of for London in my little cart with Dame & sister Hasler. The next day left my Dame in London and sister Hasler and I set off for Beechworth (*Betchworth*) in Surry to see Mr & Mrs Jonson which formerly lived at Cheshunt, Hartfordshire and a great acquantance of brother & sister Hastler. Beechworth is about 25 miles from London. We went Rygate (*Reigate*) Road and came home Dorking Road as follows over Blackfryors Bridge (*A hand drawn map follows: see photograph overleaf*).

Page 80: (Printed plate: *'Division' with calculations*)
Mr Strutt and his son Wm Strutt & his prentice Townley left Bacons March 6, 1794 after being with us near 4 years. They were engraveers and worked at their buisness at Bacons and boarded with us. Mr Strutt was the person that begun the Sunday School with one Robrt Gass at Tewin about the year 1792 & 3 but he left as above & died at London Octr 1802, but the school his continued, but he was the first beginer of it at his own expence.

Page 81:
Memarandom – Sunday afternoon 22 Octr 1797 went to Shearness (*Sheerness*) with brother Hasler an[d] Mr John Aylon to see Mr Aylon's son on board the *Victory* shipp of 110 guns lying off Shearness at Black Stakes.[19] 3 clock afternoon set off by Hartford coach from Amwell End to London – sleept at Coz Cooks No 1 Billingsgate Sunday night. Monday morning 5 clock set off in a yatt (*yacht*) for Gravesend, arrived there wind being SW by 9 clock very comfortably being but five persons on board. Brakefasted there and staid in seeing the town and fortifications 2 hours. Set off at 11 clock for Chatham on foot being 10 mile through Milton, Chalke, Stroud, Rochester to Chatham. Came there about 2 clock. Went to Mr Boddingtons in the

[19] *HMS Victory* was launched in 1765 at Chatham Dockyard and was commissioned in 1778. She continued in active service for the next 34 years which included her most famous moment, the Battle of Trafalgar in 1805. In 1812 the *Victory* was retired from frontline duty and anchored in Portsmouth Harbour. For the next 110 years the *Victory* remained at her moorings there fulfilling a combination of practical and ceremonial roles. In 1922, amid fears for her continued survival, the *Victory* was moved into Portsmouth's Royal Naval Dockyard and placed in No 2 Dry Dock. Work then began on restoring her and continues today [www.hms-victory.com].

APPENDIX ONE

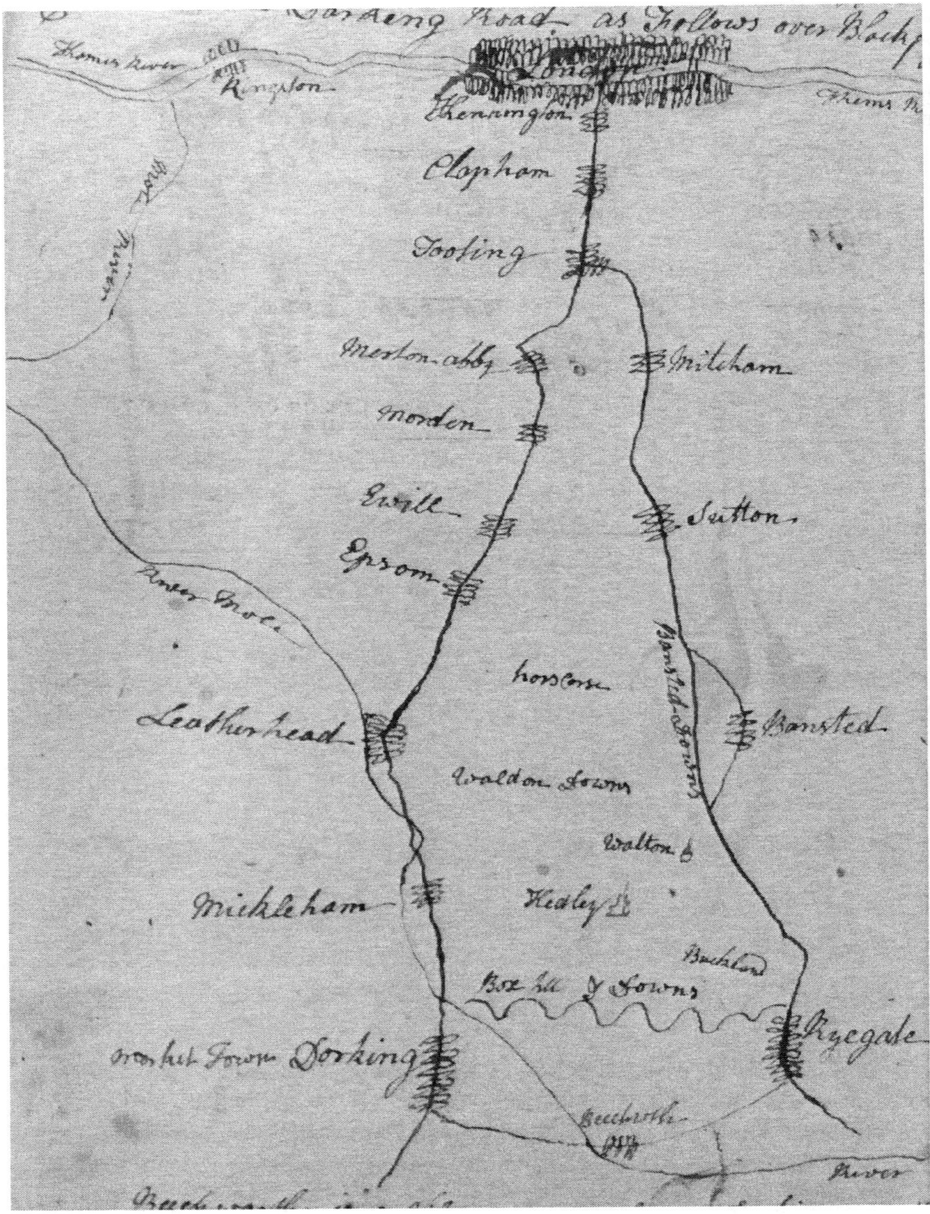

Arithmetic Book: map of the road to Betchworth, Surrey on page 79
(*HALS: DE/X3/15*)

dockyard but he being gon out we went to the R[o]yall Oak, Chattam by the water side and refreshed our selves, and then went on board a yatt for Shearness at 4 clock up the River Midway (*Medway*).[20] The same afternoon arrived at Shearness at half past 7 which is 20 mile by water. We was troubled to git lodgin. At last slept at a privet house. Man had been boatsman of a shipp for 1 shilling each. My bed was too short for me & indiferant. Shearness is a nasty place and is an island about 8 miles cross and badly off for fresh water. Next morning Tusday 8 clock we left Shearnasty, or Shearness, in a little boat to the shipp *Victory* which we came to about 9 clock at Black Stakes. We went a board & Aylon saw his son and they behaved very sivell to us and we breakfasted with them and staid about 2 ours with them in the shipp & we should have staid longer or all night but the same yatt that brought us over night, we saw of the shipp returning to Chattom. We called to them and we went in the shipp's boat to the yatt and arived at Chattom about 1 clock being a very fine day. And we saw Mr & Mrs Boddington, master of the works in the dock yard

Page 82: (Printed plate: *'Reduction. All Greater Names are Reduced into a lesser By Multiplication. All Lesser Names are Redused into a Greater By Division'*)
and we dined with them and he shewed us the works of the yard and we went aboard a new shipp that was just built, 98 guns was not lanshed (*launched*) but was quite ready, and to be called the Tumerear (*Temeraire*).[21] Then Mr

---

[20] Chatham Dockyard, located on the River Medway in Kent, was established as a Royal dockyard by Elizabeth I in 1567. For 414 years Chatham Dockyard provided over 500 ships for the Royal Navy, and was at the forefront of shipbuilding, industrial and architectural technology. At its height, it employed over 10,000 skilled artisans and covered 400 acres. It closed in 1984, and 84 acres of the Georgian dockyard is now managed as a visitor attraction by the Chatham Historic Dockyard Trust [See their web site at www.thedockyard.co.uk].

[21] HMS *Temeraire* was a 98-gun second-rate ship of the line of the Royal Navy, launched on 11 Sep 1798 at Chatham. She was named after the French 74-gun ship taken at the battle of Lagos in 1759, following the British custom of naming new ships after old prizes. At the battle of Trafalgar in 1805, under the command of Captain Eliab Harvey, she was badly damaged as she fought to relieve Nelson's flagship. During the battle, *Temeraire* helped force the surrender of the French ship *Redoutable* and captured the French ship *Fougueux*. She was converted to a prison ship in 1812 and finally sold and broken up in 1838 at Surrey Canal Wharf, Rotherhithe. She became famous as the subject of two paintings by J M W Turner,

Boddington directed us in a boat cross the river from the dock to a village called Queenbury (*Queenborough*), so left Rochester and Stroud on the left about 4 clock on foot to Gravesend which we reached about 8 clock the same evening. Went to the Three Bows and supt with Mr Merriott and Blear and then took the tide boat at 11 the same night and arived at London by 5 the Wednesday morning following and on the same afternoon came to Amwell End by the Ware coach all 3 of us. So there is the end.

Page 83:
On Thursday the 23rd of April 1789 was the day the King and Queen, George the third and Chorlot (*Charlotte*) whent in prosesion to St Pauls great church, London to return God thanks for the King's recovrey or his selfs recovrey from his insanity or madness which state he had been in for allmost a year past, and the sermon was preached by the Bishop of London and at night vast great illuminations at London and all over England, very great indeed.[22] Billey Pitt, his Prime Minister at this time.[23]

A cimey serkle canell (*semi-circular canal*) made or the river turned by the front of Tewin Water House and the water let into it about one clock Tusday the 13th March 1798, and it was filled in 1 hour ½ and run full over the tumblingbay at bottom. One Taylor was gardner, and the house &c was prepairing, or building, for Mr Henery Cowper to come to live at, who made these allterations, for whear the river is at front stood a very fine dove house & a large cannel (*canal*).

Pages 84-90: (*Various mathematical calculations*)

Page 91:

---

one showing her at the battle of Trafalgar, and the other showing her being towed to the breaker's yard in 1838 [Wikipedia].

[22] On 17 Feb 1789, three days before the Regency Bill was due to take effect, it was announced that the king was convalescent. A thanksgiving service was held at St Paul's on 23 Apr and medals were struck commemorating the king's recovery [John Cannon, 'George III (1738–1820)', *ODNB*, 2004]. Many pamphlets were printed and circulated, eg *A Form of Prayer and Thanksgiving to Almighty God; to be used after the General Thanksgiving, ... on Sunday the First Day of March 1789* [London: Printed by Charles Eyre and Andrew Strahan, Printers to the King's most Excellent Majesty, 1789].

[23] William Pitt, the Younger was prime minister from Dec 1783 to Mar 1801 and again from May 1804 to Feb 1806.

APPENDIX ONE

Rec[eive]d of Mr William Hunsdon the sum of £20 in full of all demands by me Wm Carrington £21 0s 0d. (*Signed*) W Carrington.

Note 12 inches is one foot in length & 144 inches is one Superfisial foot and 1728 inches is one Solid foot.

Sr John Mason served under 4 princes, Hen 8th, Ewd 6th, Queen Mary, Queen Eliz[abe]th and was Privy Counsellor to them all. He died at 63 years of age, single man, but notwithstanding all the grandger (*grandeur*) he has been in his life he says that seriousness is the greatest wisdom, temprance the best physick and a good conscience the best estate of all.[24]

Page 92: (*Mathematical calculations including* 'The Value of 48 q[uarte]r of Malt at £1 14s 6d per Q[uarte]r'. (*Signed*) W Carrington, 1782)

Page 93:
A list of the persons that gave towards the rilief of the French clergy that run away to England when the disturbances was in France & when they murderd their King Lewis the 16th in January 21st 1793. When a gathering was made throughout all the parishes in England this June 1793. This is for Bramfield parish:

The Revd Mr Thos Lloyd, Minister	£1 1s 0d
Mr Thos Lloyd Junr	£0 2s 6d
Miss Eliz Lloyd	£0 2s 6d
Miss Charlott d[itt]o	£0 2s 6d
Revd Mr Thornhill curate	£0 10s 6d
Mr Bryand Preston, Broadoak End	£0 2s 0d
Mr Geo Patterson, Green Hall	£0 2s 6d
Mr Hen Hunsdon, West End	£0 2s 6d

[24] Sir John Mason (1503-1566) MP and ambassador, became Clerk to the Privy Council in 1542 amongst other high offices. He was buried in the north choir aisle of St Paul's Cathedral, London, where his widow and his heir, his nephew Anthony Wyckes (later Mason), erected a monument; his son Thomas had predeceased him. 'The monument proclaimed that Mason had faithfully served four Tudor monarchs as ambassador and councillor, successfully weathering a succession of religious and political storms. His political longevity testified to his discretion in keeping his own counsel, and his adroitness in rendering himself indispensable to the crown. His diplomatic skill and personal affability were noticed by his contemporaries' [P R N Carter, 'Mason, Sir John (*c*1503-1566), *ODNB*, Jan 2008].

John Carrrington, Bacons	£0 2s 6d
Geo Richardson gardener to Lloyd	£0 1s 0d
	£2 9s 6d

John Carrington
Church Warden June 9 1793

Page 94: (Printed plate: *'Reduction of Coyne. Weight & Measure etc. In which Rule all Questions consist of two parts or Termes, the one Reall which is the Number proposed, the other Interogatory or required'.*)

Page 95:
Man's life is like a bubble,
So soon away doth pass,
And his days are full of trouble,
So push about the glass

CHORUS:
For wine doth wet the wit,
And why should we then fret
But drink and sing
Long live the King
And send us out of debt.

And womans then the same
As we then all do think
But often she doth us blame
For getting too much drink

CHORUS as above

Our children then you know
Whome we do take such care
Are often gon before they blow
Which makes us shead a tear

CHORUS:
But why should we then fret,
For wine will w[e]t th[e] wit
But drink I say ther gon away
And now they p[ai]d ther debt

At last when death doth call
To summons us away
May we be redy all
To go withy him I say

CHORUS:
But why should we then fret
Since wine doth wet the wit
But drink and sing
There's an end of him
For now he's paid his debt

Page 96: (*Mathematical calculations*)
And now he's paid his due
And nature that is free
So must I and you
And happy may we be

CHORUS:
Then why should we then fret
Since fate has orderd it so
But dring & be good company
Be merry before we go.

Pages 97-100: (*Mathematical calculations*)

Page 101: (*Mathematical calculations*)
Octr 30 1796 Sunday a charity sermon was preached at Tewin church by the Revd Mr James Moore of Hartford for the Sunday School at Tewin. Collected £16. Text Acts 20th chap 35 verce.[25]

Pages 102-109: (*Mathematical calculations*)

Page 110: (Printed plate: *'The Order of Deducting Tare & Trett'*)

Pages111-119: (*Mathematical calculations*)

---

[25] Acts ch 20 verse 35: 'In all things I have shown you that by so toiling one must help the weak, remembering the words of the Lord Jesus, how he said, 'It is more blessed to give than to receive.''

APPENDIX ONE

Page 120: (*Mathematical calculations*)
The ellection for the Borrow (*Borough*) of St Albans was on Thursday the 26th of May 1796 and a very strong contest accaishond by one Samuel Ferrand Waddington Esqr, cittison of London.[26] Though he lost it and he put up at Hartford for the county after, but he lost that also. Binghams votes 370, Byatt Bricknal for Lord Grimston 305, Waddington 206. So it was Bingham[27] & young Ld Grimston.[28]

Page 121: (*Mathematical calculations*)

Page 122: (Printed plate: *'The Rule of Three TEACHETH By Three Numbers given to find out a Fourth which shall bear such proportion to the second as the Third doth to the First. For the work You must Reduce your First and Third Numbers into one name and your second Number into the Least Denomination mentioned. Then multiply your second & third numbers*

---

[26] Samuel Ferrand Waddington (1759-*c*.1824), radical, was born at Walkeringham, Nottinghamshire, on 18 May 1759, the son of Joshua Waddington (1709/10–1781), vicar of Walkeringham, and his wife, Ann, daughter of Thomas Ferrand, vicar of Bingley. He was educated at a German university and trained for a life in commerce. He engaged in the hop trade, and resided near Tonbridge, Kent. He married, at Margate on 20 Apr 1788, Sarah, *née* Jarvis, with whom he had at least eight children. On the outbreak of the French Revolution Waddington strongly espoused the cause of the republicans, and in 1795 was chairman of several meetings in London held for the purpose of petitioning the crown and parliament to make peace with France. In consequence of his views he was expelled from the Surrey troop of light horse. In 1796 he attacked Edmund Burke in a pamphlet, *Remarks on Mr Burke's two letters 'on the proposals for peace with the regicide Directory of France'*, censuring him for applying the term 'regicide' to the Directory [E I Carlyle, 'Waddington, Samuel Ferrand)', rev Stephen M Lee, *ODNB*, Jan 2009].

[27] The Hon Richard Bingham (1764-1839), of St James's Place, Middlesex was MP for St Albans from 1790-Jun 1800; he owed his seat to his brother-in-law Earl Spencer, who gave him his interest at St Albans, thanks to which he headed the poll in 1790 and in 1796 [See his entry in R Thorne (ed), *History of Parliament: House of Commons 1790-1820*].

[28] The Hon James Walter Grimston (1775-1845), of Gorhambury, St Albans 'was expected to come into Parliament on the family interest as soon as he came of age and was duly introduced at St Albans in 1796, but the general election came sooner than anticipated, while he was still a minor. So he was not returned until 1802' [Thorne, *History of Parliament: House of Commons 1790-1820*].

together & divide the Product by the first the Quotient is the fourth Number sought in such denomination as your 2nd number was Reduced into')

Page 123: (*Calculation*: What will 75 quarters of malt come to at £1 12s 0d per quarter).

On Wednesday the 23 of July 1794 about 3 a clock in the afternoon a moast dredfull fire broke out at Mr Cloves, a barge builder at Stone Stares, Ratcliffe Highway. The fire was occaisoned by a pot of pitch boyling over. It was said to have burnt down 600 howses. I saw it and went through the rewings (*ruins*) on the Monday following and in severall places the fire was burning then. I came to London from Pla[i]stow, Es[s]ex.

On Wednesday morning January 6th 1796 about 3 clock a great fire was seen at Tewin towards London which was Lee Bridge Mills near Hackney burnt down and 1000 qrtrs of wheat supposed to be set on fire.

Thursday morning January 7th 1796 the next morning a bout 2 clock I saw from Bacons a great fire over Whear (*Ware*) which appeard as I saw in the morning 3 hay reeks of Mr Twinns, Amwell End, Ware being all burnt, supposed to be set on fire.

Pages 124-134: (*Mathematical calculations*)

Page 135:
An account of the hard frost after the dry summer and great flood Novembr 5 1794. The frost set in about 6 days before Christmas 1794 and continud very sever[e] till 27 January 1795. Mild & thaw 2 days, the 29th then sharp frost again till the 8th of February, then thaw and on Munday the 9th Tusday 10, Wednesday ll th was the greatest flood all over England that never was known to be the like. Maney people was drowned and all people that lived near the rivers & water courses where sufferers. It run through the house at one Mr Prestons at Broadoak End farm near Goldings in the parish of Bramfield for 2 days together, 2 foot deepe and from thence into the Bramfield Road near Goldings and washed the road away so deep near the entrance of the North Road that it was unpassable to Bramfield till it was filled up which cost the parish £10. I was surveyor.

Page 136:
The very remarkable mild, open winter 1789. No frost, some wet & warm like sum[m]er wather it took up to be dry the 28 of January 1790 and held dry

tell the 15 of April and this day a great deal of snow, the wind blew from the East. Dry summer 1792, and dryer spring then 1793, and dry summer 1796, and dry summer 1794.

The dry summer 1793 and the fine open winter and forward spring 1794. And we all where in expetation of having the greatest plenty as supposed ever was known. But it sudingly changed and took up to be dry about the middle of May and so continued excessive hott and dry till the 5th day of September following which is and has been a dryer sumer then last, onley there was moore wet in this spring then last. Our harvest was brought forward, begun about 25 July, all fine hay time and fine harvest. Grass all barnt up, no turnops, peas all burnt up, we mowd them to make hay of in generall and they now sell at our Hertford market Sepr 6th at 40 shillings per load and tears (*tares*) at £5 per load, wheat at 32s per load, barley at 36 per quarter, oates at 27 d[itt]o.

Page 137:
In the year 1795 begining of the same, an Act was passed for all countys through out England and Wales to send a sertaine number of men for his Majesty's service in the Navey as sea men.[29] 116 was alloted for this county of Hartford and other countys in proportion. And they where to be raised according to the number of taxed houses in each parrish. 67 of those houses that paid window and door and house tax were to find one man. Therefore a meeting of the Justices for this County was held at the Town Hall at Hartford on the 23 March this spring to alott the parishes quota of men according to their assessed houses. In my division as follows, 5 parishes 2 men, 3 d[itt]o 1 man and so on through the county more or less. Codicote, Sandradge, Hexton, Sheephall, Bramfield 2 men, Pauls Walden, Norton, Newnham 1 man. The officers of each parish met together at the Bell at Codicote in April 1795 and agreed to hier (*hire*) men according to their allotment, which wee did at £24 & £25 per man and each parish paid his quota accordingly. I was there as they was assed (*assessed*) to the taxes. Therefore Codicote, Pauls Walden & Sandredge payd the most.

Page 138: (Printed plate: *'TABLES OF PRACTICE For THE MORE Compendious way OF Casting up All Sorts of MERCHANDIZE'*)

---

[29] Act of Parliament 35 Geo 3 c9.

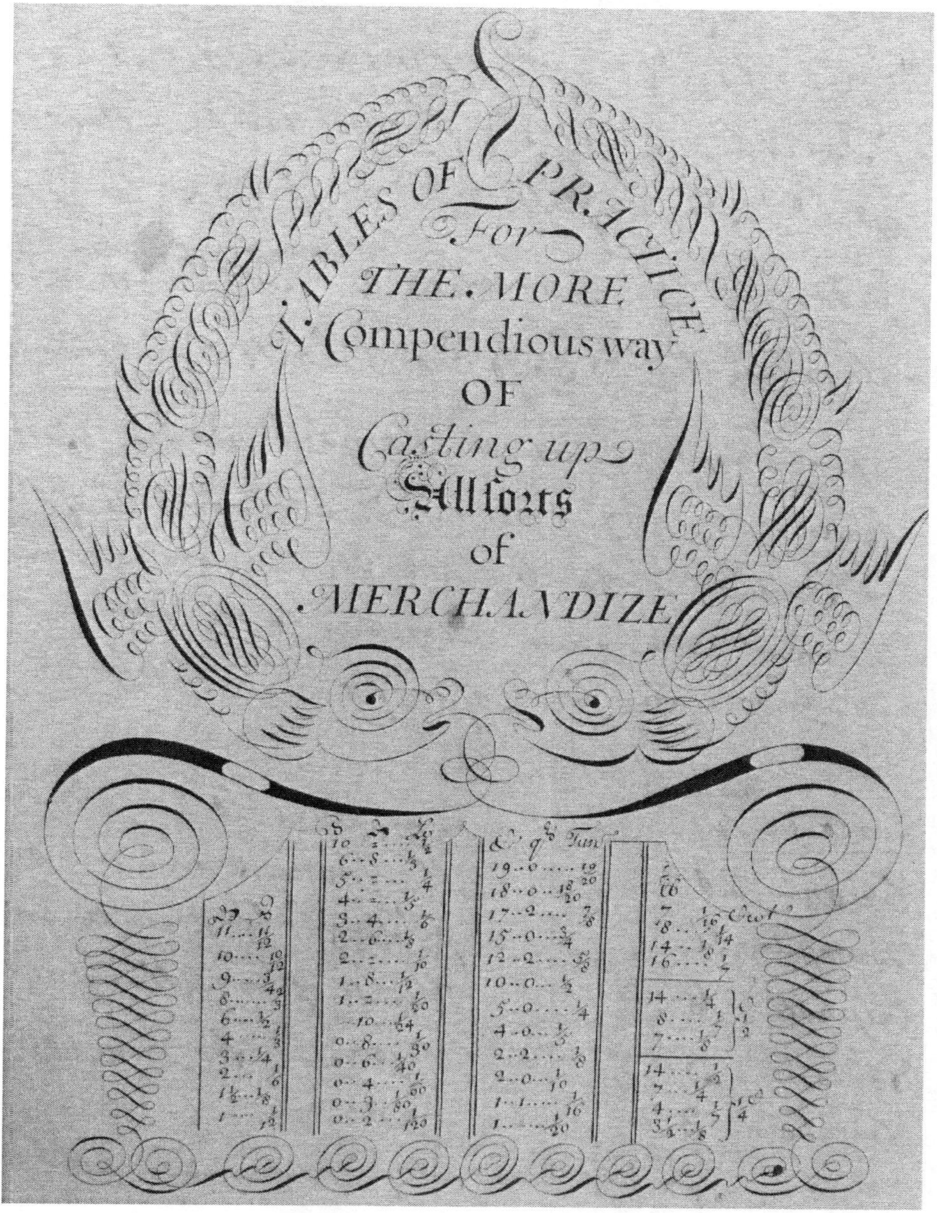

Arithmetic Book: printed plate on page 138 (*HALS: DE/X3/15*)

APPENDIX ONE

Page 139:
Memorandom. Harmergreen Farme in the parish of Wellwin now in occipation of Mr Ed Pennyfather pays £60 per anam to the poor of the parishes of Bookham & Fetcham in Surrey.[30] That is £36 to one & £24 to the other Sepr 1795.

Memorandom. Met at Mr Morgans at the Bell at Codicote this January 27 1797 with Henry Hunsdon overseer of Bramfield and Mr Preston of d[itt]o to settle their quota of money for each parish under mentioned according to the taxed houses of each parish for paying for 2 men for his Majestys Navey or Armey. Taxt houses: Codicote 47, Hexton 20, Bramfield 11, Sheephall 6, Norton 5, Newnham 3, [total] 92. The sum to pay by order of the Justices in lew or of not finding the 2 men into the hands of Mr Allington of Hartford treasure[r] for this County was £52 10s 0d, other expences in all by the differant overseers £8 4s 6d. Totall expence £60 14s 6d. So each parish paid 13s 2½d per house.

Codicote	£31 0s 9½d
Hexton	£13 2s 8½d
Bramfield	£ 7 5s 3½d
Shephal	£ 3 19s 3d
Norton	£ 3 6s 0½d
Newnham	£ 1 19s 7½d
	£60 13s 8½d

Pages 140-144: (*Mathematical calculations*)

Page 145: (*Mathematical calculations*)
Tusday Octr 25th 1796 went to Hollords Farme near Codicote to attend the funorl (*funeral*) of my old neighbour Mr Wm Hunsdon formerly of Bramfield West End Farme. He was over at Bramfield Fryday the afternoon the 7th of this month harty and well, the next morning was found both sence less and speech less and remaind so for 8 or 10 days and then departed. Buried at Great Amwell a herce & coach with 2 horses each. I and Mr Randall, Mr Basset, Mr Richardson, Mr Burges, Mr Stratton and Thorowgood rode behind with cloaks and silk bands & gloves.

---

[30] Harmer Green Farm is actually in the parish of Digswell [Gover, Mawer and Stenton, *The Place Names of Hertfordshire*, p125].

APPENDIX ONE

Page 146: (*Mathematical calculations*)

Page 147: (*Mathematical calculations*)
Dementions of a vatt or great vessell built by Mr Maux (*Meux*) brewer in Liquerburn Street, London, diameter 65 feet, hith (*height*) 25 feet, 313 staves, 60 hoops. The least ways (*weighs*) 1 tone, the largest 5 tone. Containes to hold 20,000 barrels. Cost £10,000 building. It was finished in May 1795. I saw it & others that held 10,000 barels.[31]

Pages 148-152: (*Mathematical calculations*)

Page 153:
Calculation of the number of inhabitants existing on the earth, 1792.

Great Britain	7,500,000
Ireland	2,600,000
France	18,400,000
Spain	7,400,000
Portigal	3,600,000
Meditteranin Isles	2,700,000
Germany	20,600,000
Holland &c	3,200,000
Austrian & Netherlands	1,500,000
Switserland & Geneva Republic	3,100,000
Sweeden	3,300,000
Norway	1,600,000
Hungary	5,000,000
Prusia	17,000,000
Poland	5,000,000
Turkey in Europe & Rusia	18,000,000

[31] This was the Griffin Brewery in Liquorpond Street, now Clerkenwell Road, London trading as Reid, Meux & Co. By 1787, under Richard Meux it was producing close on 50,000 barrels of porter a year. For the first time, in 1795, the brewery's output exceeded 100,000 barrels, clearly placing it among the capital's half dozen market leaders. Meux had a good eye for publicity and in 1790 he had constructed a vat sixty feet across and over twenty feet high. On its completion 200 people dined inside it with a similar number standing around to toast its builder. Five years later he was constructing one designed to hold 20,000 barrels and costing £10,000 (equivalent to the cost of a large country house) [R G Wilson, 'Meux family', *ODNB*, Jan 2008].

APPENDIX ONE

Totall in Europe	120,500,000
Asia is supposed at	450,000,000
Africa at	150,000,000
America at	160,000,000
In the whole world	880,500,000

Page 154: (Printed plate: *'The Rule of Three Reverse'*)

Page 155:
Account of Land Tax paid by the differant parishes in the Division of John Carrington at 4s for this year 1793:

Pauls Walden	John Hill, colle[c]tor	£218 0s 0d
Coddicote	Edw Pierce	£214 4s 0d
Hexton	Wm Carter	£124 9s 0d
Norton	Wm Harmer	£124 18s 0d
Sheephall	Jos Parker	£106 5s 0d
Newnham	Wm Simkings	£ 80 0s 0d
Bramfield	John Carrington	£ 92 16s 0d
	July 14 1793	£960 12s 0d

Lieutenant Robt Cowill and his wife left Hertford Saturday morning 7 clock July 6th 1793. Sudingly called to go to Montrille (*Montreal*) in North America.

Pages 156-part 165: (*Essay: 'Of the Nature & use of Logarithms'*)

Pages 165 (continued):
On Saturday the 28 of December 1782 about 6 o clock in the evening was shott dead Old Walter Clibbon and one of his sons taken about 30 pole from Okenvaley Bottom toward Bulls Green in the parish of Tewin. This said Clibbon was a labouring man & when this happned lived at Babbs Green nere Ware, Wareside and used to go a robing with his sons as they grew upp as foot padds every winter season, for he kept them at home for that purpose. And had done maney great and abusive

Page 166
robreys and one Kent, farmer of Beningon, they killed and throwd him into his cart and the horses brought him home as was confessed by his son when taken, which was as follows. They came to a wood nere Bools (*Bulls*) Green erley this Saturday morning and there stayd till evening with intent to robb

homewords. They robed in smock frocks with their faces blacked, the first they stoped was Whittingbury's son, of Datchworth, in a little cart and instead of his going on to Datchworth after being robbed, turns on the left first opening and came to Quino (*Queen Hoo*) Hall to tell his uncle Benj[ami]n Whittenbury w[ha]t had happned. The uncle told him he had just parted from his father and his other uncle as they came home togather, therefore he called his man Geo[rge] North & bid North take the gunn and called his son Thos & he took his stick & dogg & theese 3 went to the Bottom but before they came there they [Clibbon and sons] had stopped the 2 brothers, one they robbed, the other run away. When they come to the Bottom, Mr Ben Whittenbury told his man & son theyd walk up the hill & go home, but they came out of the wood & attacked them thinking they was others coming from market, they atacted without speaking and knocked Mr Whittingbury down & Mr Whittenbury knocked the old Clibbon down & a great battle for some time till they overpowerd Mr Whittenbury & he called for his man to shoot, which he did & killed the old roogue on the spott, he shoot him in the brest for his gun allmost touched him. After this one son run away, the other was taken and hanged at the Lent Assize following.

Page 167:
And a corraner (*coroner*) came on the Monday following and Jury met and they found he met his death as he deserved & they buried him by the road side where he was shott dead.[32]

(*Essay: 'Of proportion'*)

Pages 168-part 172: (*Essay: 'Of Proportion'*)

Page 172 (continued):
Mr Noon of Wing in Buckinghamshire near Tring its said will cure the bite of a mad dogg on a person when they are taken with madness, or the Hydrophobia is on them, Tewin May 16, 1794.[33]

Page 173: (*Mathematical calculations*)

[32] Walter Clibbon of Babbs Green, near Ware, and his wife Elizabeth had six children. The eldest, Joseph was born in 1764, the next Samuel in 1766.
[33] Numerous 'cures' were circulating by this time. On p166 of *The Art of Cookery, made Plain & Easy* (London, 1747), Hannah Glasse reproduced two such cures, 'A certain cure for the Bite of a Mad Dog' by D Mead and 'Another for the Bite of a Mad dog'.

APPENDIX ONE

Page 174:
The first manner (*manor*) court for Tewin hild by Lord Cowper at Tewin Berrey (*Bury*) was this 21st Day of Decbr 1789 on Monday when Esqr Schrybear of Tewin House took up that estate bought of Esqr Mackey. The fine paid was £185. I and Mr Hunsdon signed and that was the w[h]ole buisness that day. Mr Neall of Hartford atturney was stewrd, & Counciller or Henery Cowper was there.

Mr John Aldredge of Hayley Hall was buried at Amwell church Sunday the 10th of March 1793 aged about 64. I was there & Mr B Whittenbury and my son John & Mr Henery Hunsdon carried on men sholders, a walking buring. No age nor naile on coffen.

Page 175: (Printed plate: *'INTEREST is either Simple or Compound'*)

Page 176:
The first charity sermon preached at Tewin church for the benefitt of the Sunday Schools at Tewin, which had being established there from Mix (*Michaelmas*) 1792 by order of the parish, but it was begun 2 years before by Mr Strutt and Mr Gass at their own expence. The sermon was preached Oct 27, 1793 by Mr Grayham, curat[e] of Hardfordingbury (*Hertingfordbury*). They church wardens & overseer collectted £21 15s 0d. Lord Cowper & family was there for the first time.
The 2d charity sermon preached by the Revd Mr Lloyd, minister of Bramfield in Octr 1794. Collected about £22 0s 0d.
The 3 d[itt]o by the Revd Mr May, minister of Diggswell on Sunday Octr 25, 1795 collected about £21 0s 0d.

Page 177-part 178: (*Mathematical calculations*)

Page 178 (continued):
The first Lord Mayor of London was one Henery Fitz-Alwin, draper appointed by King Richard the first on the first year of his reign in ye year 1189. And continued mayor untill the 15 year of King John which was 24 years and some w[ha]t more. The 2d mayor was Roger Fitz Alwin, the 3 d[itt]o Robt Serle, mercer, 4 d[itt]o Wilm Hordel &c.[34]

---

[34] Henry Fitz-Ailwyn, 1189-1211; Roger Fitz-Alan, 1212-1214; Seriole Mercer, 1215; William Hardel, 1215 [List of Lord Mayors of London on www.cityoflondon.gov.uk].

APPENDIX ONE

Pages 179-188: (*Mathematical calculations*)
To measure timber by the pen – suppose a timber tree is 18 foot long & 14 inches girt, tell me how maney solid foot of timber it doth contain, square the girt by the same & multiply the length by it & devide by 144.
(*Calculation follows*)

Page 190:
Sepr 9, 1791 Mett my constables by appointment at the Robin Hood & Little John at Robley Heath at the house of Underwood Maleses, in the parish of Codicote. Mr Strutt & his son Joseph went with me. I walked from the mount on the s[ai]d heath to my sons at the Roase & Crown, Tewin Lower Geen in 40 minuetts and measured Ninns Wood as I walked through which is 800 hundred & 20 steps long.

Bacons the 9th Novemr 1791 sold Mr Macky of Marden a hay rick for fifty two guineas to be taken away at his pleasure, to be paid for in the course of six months.

Page 191: (Printed plate: *'Rebate or Discount'*)

Page 192:
Account of the prises of corne at Hartford market this year 1795 after the hard frost and flood this spring.
February: wheat £1 15s 0d per load, barley £2 0s 0d per quater, oates £1 10s 0d d[itt]o, peas £1 15s 0d per load.
March: rather dearer.
April: wheat £2 0s 0d d[itt]o, barley £2 0s 0d qr, oates £1 8s 0d d[itt]o.
May: wheat £2 5s 0d, oats and barley abot the same.
June: wheat £2 10s per load, no peas but little barley & oates dearer.
July the 4th wheat £2 15s per load, d[itt]o the 11th wheat £3 5s 0d per load, d[itt]o the 18th wheat £3 10s 0d per load, d[itt]o the 25 wheat as they could git it, there was but one load pitched in the market and sold and the may[o]r had but 1 pt tole (*toll*).

Page 193: (*Mathematical calculations*)
1795 acpt (*account*) of markets further:
August 1 not one sack in market to day, mealman bought the wheat as they could git it at £4 or 4 ginnes (*guineas*) per load, 16s or 18s per bushell, barley 52s quater, oates 40 d[itt]o, rye 50s per load.

Saturday Augst 8 no wheat in market againe to day, mealmen got it as they could at £4 etc per load.
Saturday 15 no wheat in market & much the same, 9 load of new rye 48s per load.
Saturday 22 some new wheat at market but not dry, sold at 60s per load as was good.
Saturday 29 severall parcells of new wheat, som[e] sold at 60s per load as was good. I sold 3 load at 57s 6 pence per load
Sept Saturday 5th marketts at 50s per load, I sold 4 load at 50s.
Coming cheeper.

Pages 194-part 199: (*Mathematical calculations*)

Page 199 (continued):
It is said that wheare weevils are in graniers (*granaries*) amongst wheat or malt &c put some live lobsters in the binns of corne and let them stay 3 or 4 days and it will drive them away and destroy them.[35]

Pages 200-201: (*Mathematical calculations*)

Page 202: (*Mathematical calculations*)
Mr Harrington's fiest at sisters. I was there, Mr Thos Maw, Mr Mason, Mr Lawrance painter, the he[a]d groom of the Marquis of Salsbury. It was on Munday 15th February 1790.
(*Pinned to this page: newspaper cutting dated in Carrington's hand '1788', title of newspaper unknown. Article entitled 'Extract of a letter from Doncaster, Yorkshire, dated July 23rd' concerning a riot at an inn following an argument about a lady, during which several people were killed.*)

Page 203:
George Clavering Cowper was born at London Aug[u]st 1738, the 3rd Earl Cowper, brought up at Cole Green till 16 years of age and then went abroad to Ittiley (*Italy*) at this age and did not return, though very much desired so to do by his father in his life time. Till July 1786 he came to England over to Cole

[35] *Gentleman's Magazine*, vol 60, part II, 1790, 'Means of destroying insects or preventing their increase', pp880-885: 'It is an observation of the Romans, that weevils, and other creatures of that kind, have a great aversion to river crawfish. In France, they throw live lobsters on wheat in granaries when infested with them; and in a few hours the weevils will come from all parts, dispersing themselves on the walls, and thus are easily destroyed'.

Green House and stayd about 3 months & returned againe to Florance, but he was brought back to Cole Green House to be buried on Tusday the 16th of February and lay in state that night at Cole Green and was buried the next day Wednesday the 17th 1790, which was this year Ash Wednesday, at the familey vault Hardfoardingbury (*Hertingfordbury*) church about 12 clock noon. Herce with 6 horses, 4 coaches with 6 horses, all scutchings (*escutcheons*) & his corrinett (*coronet*) carried on horseback on a velvet cushen, the man bear headed before the herce & about 20 of his tenants road before with silk bands & sashes, aged 52.[36] A great number of people there. Very cold day.

Page 204: (*Flowing design in ink surrounding the word 'Finis'*)

Page 205: (*Mathematical calculations*)
The great storme and tempest wch happned on the Thursday morning about 3 & 4 clock the 23 of Decbr great thunder & lightning & high wind wch did great damage. Very shocking, dredfull it came SW and went over NE. Great damage at London as blowing down chimneys, roofs of houses & sheets of led etc.

Page 206:
At the Quarter Sesions held at the Town Hall, St Albans on Thursday the 12th day of July 1787. Charles De Late Esqr chairman of that court.[37] An appeal was brought by the constable for the parish of Aldenham that the s[ai]d parish of Aldenham refused to pay his bill at their Easter settlement last on account of 13 presepts being paid to the Chieff Constable. It was then orderd by that court for the parish to pay his bill and that the Chieff Constable hath a rite to a shilling for each presept so deliverd and if they should refuse to pay againe the Justices would grant him a rate on the said parish for his money. At this said sessions a poor person was robed at Barnet of a tea chest and a few shillings in it and a crown piece. The person was sespeted (*suspected*) and a

---

[36] George Augustus Clavering Cowper, 3rd earl Cowper (1738-1790) left England in 1757 for the Grand Tour. He never returned during his father's lifetime (the 2nd earl died in 1764). He settled in Florence and became a leader of society and a patron of art, science, literature and the opera. A long epitaph was published in *The Gentleman's Magazine*, Feb 1799, reproduced in Jones, *Hertfordshire 1731-1800,* p250.

[37] Charles De Late (Laet) of Poterells, North Mimms. His death is recorded in *The Gentleman's Magazine*, July 1792, reproduced in Jones, *Hertfordshire 1731-1800,* p228.

warrant was fitched to take the person which wass done & brought to tryall at this sessions and found gilty. The person that was robed craved her expences which was granted and in the bill was 18d for the warrant which was told her she must take that againe from the Justice for no Justice must take for worants granted for felloney.

Page 207:
The w[eigh]t of St Pauls great bell, London as Mr Phelps the founder assured me is 5 tun 2 hundred one ¼ 21 pound. 1750

Pages 207 (part)-210 *upside down*: (*Essay: 'Of the Nature & Extraction of the Square Root'*)

Page 211:
On the 20th of June 1787 on Wednesday abot 11 in the foorenon the terable fire happned at Swangleys Farme near Datchworth church in this county of Hartford suposed to be set on fire which burnt 4 large barnes, stables & other offices, 1 fatt calf, 3 hoggs, 2 doggs w[hic]h was tied up in the stable, 1 rick of hay, cart harness, sacks & barne utincels, the horses being out at plow, corne & straw in the barns &c &c. Young Mr Chounds & his sister lived there, sun & daughter of Mr Chounds of Welches Farme. I was there & saw the same. Everything being very dry was all down by 2 clock. The house was saft (*saved*) though grately damaged. Great loss and spoyle in remooveing goods. The farme belongs to Knaboth (*Knebworth*) Estate, neighther part[i]es inshured.

Page 212: (*Doodles and calculations including several J or John Carrington signatures, one being dated 'July 16th 1788'*)

Page 213: (*upside down*)
Mr Coate left Bacons June 27 1789 to go to his father's comr of Wicklow, Iarland.
Esq Seamor came to Pansanger & Esq Law left this March 7th 1790.
The 2 Mrs Becks left Bacons July 27th 1792 as being w[i]th us 9 days with little Jack.
Thos Cradock, baker near Shorditch church London throwd him self of the Monement, London about the year 1790.
Neatsfood oyle rubb well on hoggs, calves or cows or other cattle that are lowsey is a sertaine cure.

APPENDIX ONE

(The following items were published by Branch Johnson in 'Memorandoms For…' (pp22-4). They were written on separate scraps of paper and enclosed within a transcript of the Arithmetic Book lent to Branch Johnson by Mrs Ekins. Neither the Ekins' transcript nor the loose papers were deposited at HALS.)

May 2nd 1754 was the day that the County Election was held at Hertford, when Hale of Kings Walden and Gore of Thring (*Tring*) was chosen againe. But let not brave [Edward] Gardner be forgot, Bishopbury (*Pishobury, Sawbridgeworth*) near Bishop Stortford, for opposing of them bothe and causeing of treats and money to be spent plentifuly in every parish, but haveing only six gentlemen on his side as stood as real friends for him was so judged to be wrongfully throwd up.[38]

September 5 1757 was the day and date when the gentlemen & Lord Leftenant and Deputy Leftenant for this county of Hertford met at Hertford to chuse and raise a Millitia first for this county, when John Squire and John Brazer was drawn for this parish of Tewin. But it did not take place this year for the county people would not submit but thretned mischieff wher of some was put into Hertford Geoall, but the year 1758 they brought it to bear and John Crawley and Rich[ar]d Cutt for Tewin went, being chosen.

Son of Judge Lee of London came into Hartford to offer himself a member for the Borrough of Hartford Feby 1st 1758,[39] but after spending £800 and upwards he gave it up before the election for there was a club that used him ill. This was the Red Herring club.

One Alderman or Sir William Baker from London a building a new house in the parish of Bayford a little above the Bury Farm and inclosing a park now this year 1760, now caled Bayford Bury Place.[40]

---

[38] Paggen Hale of Kings Walden (1715-55) MP for Hertfordshire, 1747-55. This was a contested election and Hale stood on a joint interest with Charles Gore (1711-68) of Tring, MP for Hertfordshire 1741-61, and came out head of the poll [L Namier and J Brooke, *The House of Commons, 1757-1790*, 2 vols (1964)].

[39] William Lee (c1726-78) of Totteridge Park, the only son of Sir Willam Lee, Lord Chief Justice of the Kings bench, 1737-54 [Namier and Brooke, *The House of Commons, 1757-1790*].

[40] William Baker (1705-70), alderman of London and MP for Plympton Erle, Devon, 1747-68, purchased the Bayfordbury estate in 1757 [Namier and Brooke, *The House of Commons, 1757-1790*; *VCH Hertfordshire,* vol 3, p419].

APPENDIX ONE

On Sunday 20th September went to London in Mr Warrens shaisse to the coronation when George the 3rd and Princess Chorlotte of Mecklenburgh in Germany was crowned the 22nd 1761 King & Queen of England, expenses 10s. A platform was bilt for them to walk on from Westminster Hall north door to the west end of Westminster Abbey door, about 3 qrs of a mile and scaffolds wass built all along the side of it by the houses for the publick to see, which I believe there wass one million of peaple there that day.

June 28 1762 the Hartfordshire Millitia came upp from the City of Woster (*Worcester*) & Lord Cowper gave them all a breakfast at Cole Green, which they went to campp at Brentwood, Es[s]ex.

April 14 1766 was the last day when Dr Vangables men mounted stage at Tewin in the yard at Browns the ale house at Tewin Upper Green.[41] They gave away 1p[in]t silver cupp & buckells and ring, 2 spoons & tea kettle, I throwed upp 2 but got nothing.

April 2nd 1768 at 10 clock at night died my good old master Richard Warren of Marden of a kind of dropsey and gout, lying ill about six weeks, was buried on the 10th at Tewin church in the vault. Carried in his own charrott, the coffin put into the charrott end ways through the doors.

The new Sheare (*Shire*) House at Hertford, or County Hall, finished in the year 1771, being new built from the ground, the old one was pulled down.[42] The olde Sheare House or County Hall was bilt on stout wooden pillers so that you might walk under & the market kept under & the Court of Justice above.

October 12 1771 on Saturday morning about 2 clock begun the great fire at Watton Woodhall & in about 4 or five hours more than half that great house was burnt down. I was there and saw it with all the rich furnitur as far as the fire went. The remainder part of the house is now puld down and a new house is now building about 40 pole further in the park by Esqre Rumbold, October 1777.

---

[41] These men were probably travelling players. A stage was erected in the yard at the Feathers Inn for their use.

[42] Hertford Shire Hall, completed in 1771, was built to plans of James and Robert Adam at a total cost of about £5,700. An assembly room was added to the design paid for by public subscription. However considerable repairs became necessary to the structure some 15 years later [The plans dated 1767-8 are HALS: DE/P/P11 and see *HCR* vol VIII ppxv-xix for more details of the building].

APPENDIX ONE

June 1766 was the month that Lady Cathcart or Macquire returnd to England from Scotland and being gone 20 years about the middle of September mext to come. The affaire wass as follows: she was a brewer's daughter neare London at Battersea, 2nd daughter of Thomas Maylin. Her maiden name was Maylin, of no fortun but a great beauty, which Esqre Fleet, a gentlemen of great fortun, fell in love with her & married her. They came to live at Tewin Water house (about the year 1714) which estate belonged to Esquire Fleet, he died in the year 1733 & left her in possession of his estate for her life. She soon married againe to one Collonel Sabine, a gentleman of small fortune. He died soon, she married againe to one Lord Cathcart a Scotch Lord which gave her the title of Lady, but he died about the year 1740, which is now a widow the 3rd time. I went to live with her as under gardiner about 15 years of age in 1743 and lived with her until [she was] taken away to Irland. She was a brisk lively woman about 57 yeares of age when she was taken away. She used to say to her maides she should never marry againe, but she went down to Bath in 1744-5 and came home againe with a new husband, one Coll Macquire an Irishman of no fortun, about 40 years of age. He lived at Tewin Water about a year with her & then one day in September 1746 he persuaded her to take a ride in a coach to Brocket Hall as an airing with some more, his brother & another Captaine an Irishman, to the water at Brocket Hall and ordered two geese for dinner at home, at 2 precisely, to be ready. But instead of comming home to diner he gave the coochman orders to drive on for the west road and so kidnabed her away to Irland in a hurry & left us servants to eat the diner, which we did. But in about 3 ours after they were gone he sent two of his servants back in a great hurry to stripp the house of plate, chane (*china*), best furniture and naggs and chaisses and every thing that was good and they told us that they met an express on the road neare Lempstead (*Lemsford*) Mills that the Colls mother was dying at Oxford and that my Lady gave consent to drive down there & sent them back for their goods for she thought of staying some time. So he stript us of our Mistress and the home of the goods in a few ours & hurried all to Ireland where he kept her under confinment in his house nor alowed her to rite or receeve a friend till this June 1766 which is now 20 years. He dying, she now returnd to old England againe in as much hurry as she was carrid away, quite brisk, hearty and well onley twenty years older, and come to Tewin Water, her seat as she was taken from, which was inhabited by one Squire Steel whom she gave warning to quit, for he had taken the place on lease for 21 years of the Coll Macquire, he was obligd to quit as the lease was void at his death. She bought a great maney things at Steel's sale to help furnish her house with. She came to live at Tewin Water againe in about eleven months after her return to England. One man & woman she brought from Iarland with her, Mr & Mrs Colley, other servants she hired here and she lived in great carrecter and keep a good house and was very charitable and good to the poor for 23 years after her return and in good state of helth and retained her senses considering her great age and receeve company & ride out in her cariage till within one month of her death which happned as thus on Fryday morning folowing the 3rd day of August 1789, aged 98 years. Buried in Tewin church in a vault there which was made in the year 33 for her first husband and only him & her aunt Thornbury and herself in the said vault. She had the said vault opend about two months before her death to see if it wanted any repairs and cleand and closed up again. She was charitable at her burial as before for an invitation was given to all her neighbours, which was on Wednsday 12 August following, upwards of 100 silk hat bands & gloves was given.

Arithmetic Book: design in ink on page 204 (*HALS: DE/X3/15*)

APPENDIX TWO

Hertfordshire Inns

BENGEO:
Reindeer, Port Hill. In 1740 was the 'Running Deer' under the proprietorship of Edward George and owned by the Dunster family of Jenningsbury. Richard Flower bought it in 1792 on the death of Henry Dunster. Richard Gear was the landlord at least from 1801, Jonathan Neal in 1806.

Windmill, Waterford. William and Ann Gear ran this house until 1804. Subsequently Ann, as a widow continued there until at least 1817. Later Robert Smith of Goldings, turned it into a Coffee Tavern until 1908 when it became a grocery shop and Post Office. Now a private house.

BRAMFIELD:
Grandison Arms. A seventeenth century building with later frontage and probably an inn from this time when George Villiers, Viscount Grandison, became Lord of the Manor. Also had a forge and wheelwrights shop next door. Kept by the Widow Deards after her husband William died in July 1792. It was John Carrington's 'local' and he could take a short cut through Bury Lane from Bacons. The Bramfield Easter Vestry was held here.

DIGSWELL:
Cowper Arms, Digswell Water. A map c1799 marks a 'Cowper Arms' at Digswell Water (*HALS: DE/P/P14*) and the Cowper estate survey of 1810 names the 'Fordwich Arms' in the same place (*HALS: DE/P/P38*). John Elsom or Elston(e) was the landlord at least until 1806. The present Cowper Arms at Welwyn North railway station was built in 1850 by Benjamin Young, brewer of Hertford (*HALS: DE/P/E296*). Not to be confused with the Cowper Arms at Birch Green (*see below under Hertingfordbury*).

HATFIELD:
The Horse and Groom, Stanborough. Known as the Horse and Groom by 1756, Carrington often stopped here on his frequent journeys to St Albans. He names the landlord as Jonas Langton but the victuallers' recognizances list Joseph Langton at this inn until 1827, and Sarah Langton thereafter. It stood a little to the north of the present Bull Inn but when the Great North Road was improved, c1845 it was demolished and rebuilt on the west side of the road at the junction of the Great North Road and Brocket Road leading to Wheathampstead. By the mid nineteenth century it was known as the Bull

and in the 1930s it moved to its present site on the east of the Great North Road. It is now a Chinese restaurant.

HERTFORD:
Bell, Fore Street. Was formerly the 'Bell & Three Cranes', and from 1820 the 'Salisbury Arms'. Records from as early as 1431 show the premises as an inn. John Beecroft was landlord from 1774-1801 and then his widow, Sarah, until 1808.

Blackbirds, Castle Street (now Parliament Square). George Richardson, also Bramfield Parish clerk, took the premises in 1808 when he married for the second time. Variously known in the past as the 'Three Magpies' and the 'Pye'. Formerly very large, it stretched to present No. 2 Fore Street.

Bull, Bull Plain. Was the 'Prince's Arms' until the Commonwealth. Its galleried yard was the subject of a painting by Thomas Rowlandson about 1800. In 1832 the 'Zephir' coach departed for London 6 days a week and the 'Express' to Hull and Lincoln. In 1848 Catholic Mass was celebrated in its theatre. It was demolished in 1857 but its tap was retained as the 'Bull' public house. The building remains as Nos. 13 & 15 Bull Plain.

Bull's Head, Market Place. Proprietor, George Richardson, Bramfield Parish clerk, had been at the 'Rose & Crown', Aston, and was later to go on to the 'Blackbirds'. George married Rebecca Hornet at Bramfield in 1801 and then Martha Hale at Tewin in 1808. It was next to the White Hart and possibly extended around the corner into Fore Street.

Cold Bath, North Road. First mentioned in 1731. From 1775 to 1802 Richard Griffiths was licensee, followed by the Winters family. The inn was situated on the north side of North road, opposite the end of Cross Lane until circa 1822 when it moved to the end of St Andrew Street. Francis' Nursery took over the old premises.

Falcon, Fore Street. This inn was old in 1620. Rebuilt in 1858 as Sharples Bank to designs by William Wilds of 25 St Andrew Street, the site can be found at 72-74 Fore Street (now Baroosh Bar, formerly Barclays Bank). By the 1770s John Ramsey was proprietor. The 'Favourite' coach used to run from here to the 'Boar & Castle', Oxford Street, leaving Hertford at 2.30 pm via Hertingfordbury, Essendon & Potters Bar. Fares 5s inside and 3s outside. In 1805 another route was started via the 'Spread Eagle' at Ware, 'Bull' at

Hoddesdon and 'Four Swans' at Waltham Cross to the 'Bull Inn' at Bishopsgate. In 1756 there were 16 beds at the Falcon and stabling for 46 horses. Carrington attended bell-ringing feasts here and at the Shire Hall with the Ramseys supplying the food.

Green Dragon, Maidenhead Street. Established there in 1620. Later in the seventeenth century Henry Sweeting paid for a block in the street from which customers could mount their horses. In 1724 there was mention of a 'great parlour' and bonded vaults for spirits. In 1805, at least, there was a theatre at the Green Dragon. Richard Griffiths was proprietor 1773-7 (apparently managing two hostelries – see Cold Bath), followed by Matthew Campbell 1794, Francis Baxter 1802, and George Webster in 1805. It was rebuilt in 1858, destroyed by fire in 1902 and again rebuilt, this time by McMullens. Discontinued as an inn in 1952. The building is now shop premises with accommodation above. Carrington was a member of its Sick Benefit Club.

White Swan, Fore Street. On the Church Street corner, now a newsagent. In 1620 it was the 'Bull' and later, in 1719, the 'Church House', then the 'Swan'. Originally stretched from present-day No. 42 Fore Street.

World's End, Ware Road. Later known as the 'Plough'. Its sign showed a globe on fire. Earliest records are from 1691. Frequently the resort of All Saints' Vestry. Towards the end of the eighteenth century it was the meeting place of the Hertford College Youths Change Ringers of which John Carrington and landlord Thomas North were members. Mr Onwin was landlord in 1801.

HERTINGFORDBURY:
Cowper Arms, Birch Green was kept by Samuel Janes or James until his death in Dec 1804. His son Charles became Earl Cowper's gamekeeper. The building still exists as cottages. A fire in 1854 destroyed the brewery and stables after which the licence was transferred to Cole Green when the railway was built.

Crown. Now the Dell, or Dell cottage. In Carrington's day it was run by an elderly man, Thomas Wells, who died in 1803.

White Horse. Began in some cottages next to the mill and known initially as The Nags Head. Transferred across the road to Place Farm, the old home farm of Panshanger, in 1808. This is the present building, a half timbered manor house dating from c1557 with a fine Jacobean staircase. The 1810 Panshanger estate survey mentions a 'magistrates room' (*HALS: DE/P/P38*).

ST ALBANS:
Angel. This was probably in Fishpool Street and traded until at least 1826.

Red House. An alehouse from circa 1760 to 1826. It stood in Market Place across the old north entrance to Chequer Street. It was run by Carrington's cousin Thomas Piggot and his son Isaac from circa 1780 to Thomas' death in January 1802. Carrington relates that it was then taken over by Grubb and later in 1804 Plumer.

White Hart, Holywell Hill, the earliest know reference is 1535. In the 1750s it was the largest inn in St Albans with beds for 26 guests and stabling for 50 horses. Carrington records that there was a great fire there on 12 Oct 1802.

TEWIN:
Rose & Crown. Jack Carrington was landlord from 1791 to 1820. He also worked Crown Farm, behind. A newly-invented beer engine was installed in 1806 to draw beer up from the cellar. Moses Gillman of Hertford supplied the beer. A building to the rear of the pub housed a skittle alley. Earl Cowper purchased the Rose and Crown together with Bacons Farm in 1801. During 1817-18 a dispute arose between Jack Carrington and the Cowper estate about the supply of beer (*HALS: DE/P/T24-25 and DE/P/E301*).

Plume of Feathers. An early seventeenth century building known as the Plume of Feathers from the 1750s. Joseph Whittenbury was landlord until at least 1817.

WARE:
Spread Eagle, Amwell End. Stood where the level crossing is now, until 1843. The premises were owned by John Carrington and let to his in-laws the Haslers or Heaslers. In his will he bequeathed it to his daughter Mary Ann. During a flood in March 1824, it is said the water stood 6 feet high in the tap room. The Haslers were landlords until at least 1828.

WATTON AT STONE:
Bull. The earliest reference to this house is in 1704 when it was mortgaged by the Boteler family, lords of the Manor of Watton. On the sale of the Benfield estates in 1801 it was part of the property sold to Samuel Smith.

White Horse. Known as The White Horse at least from 1767 abutting south on Watton Street. The licensee was Daniel Crawley in 1806. Meetings of the Watton Vestry and the Turnpike Trustees were held here. In Nov 1831 'Watton House, formerly the White Horse' was sold to Samuel Smith (*HALS: DE/AS/3518-3549*).

George and Dragon. An inn at least from 1619 when it was licensed to Thomas Diason. In 1806 the licensee was John Woolfe.

WELWYN:

Chequers, Woolmer Green. An early seventeenth century building. Run by James Waller, 1803-1828.

Red Lion, Woolmer Green. An inn at least from 1780. John Carrington owned this house and it was run by the widow Crow (Alice Crow in the victuallers recognizances from 1806-1828). By his will Carrington bequeathed it to his eldest son John. In 1818 it was purchased by Henry Crabb, brewer of Hitchin. Rebuilt in 1927.

White Hart. One of the leading coaching inns along the Great North Road with extensive stabling. Established circa 1675, the present frontage dates from around 1760. It housed an assembly room in the eastern end. Abraham Batten was the landlord from around 1799 to at least 1806.

LONDON:

Angel, Islington. A coach terminus, dating from at least 1665, demolished 1819 and rebuilt. The original, which Carrington knew, was a galleried inn and in early times a first stop-over for travellers from London.

Bear & Ragged Staff, east corner of Smithfield. The sign was taken from the arms of the Earls of Warwick.

Black Bear, Piccadilly. Mr Buttery, a friend of John Carrington was landlord.

Hole in the Wall, Kirby Street, Hatton Garden. This was Joseph Strutt's 'local' where he met Carrington on the latter's visits to London. Strutt lived and died in Charles Street, nearby. A former lodger at Bacons, Strutt was the author of several works including *The Sports & Pastimes of the People of England* and *Queen Hoo Hall, a Romance*. Strutt died in 1802, aged 52, and was buried in the churchyard of St Andrew's Holborn. The 'Hole in the Wall' can be a name taken from a local compter or debtors' prison where it is the least comfortable accommodation, or, can refer to a hole through which the prisoner communicates. Alternatively it can be a premises reached through a narrow passage or with a concealed entrance. Mr Vaughan was the landlord in Carrington's time.

Salopian Coffee House 18 Spring Gardens, Charing Cross. In 1749 when a chess club started there it was referred to as being 'near the Admiralty, Whitehall'. In Carrington's time, 1793, Roach's *London Pocket Pilot* describes it as snug rather than elegant, and used by military heroes who barter commissions via Little Whiting, a broker. By 1803 it was famed for its good dinners and wines. Proprietor Thomas Follit. From 1818 to 1830s it was a resort for engineers, including Thomas Telford. Its name may have indicated that it also sold 'Saloop' a 'beverage made from Sassafras chips' [*OED*]. This was a popular eighteenth century drink particularly with those who were less well-off.

APPENDIX THREE

Selected biographies of people that John Carrington knew or mentioned in his Diary

FRIENDS and FAMILY:

Stephen Austin I set up as a printer in Hertford in 1768. He remained Bramfield vestry clerk until his death in 1818. His son, Stephen Austin II (d 1845) became official bookseller to the East India Company's college at Haileybury, Hertford Heath. His grandson, Stephen Austin III (1804-1892) developed the printing of Oriental texts. Messrs Stephen Austin also published the *Hertford Mercury* newspaper from 1772, which under various titles has continued to the present day.

The Beck family from Long Lane, London were the children and grandchildren of Carrington's eldest sister Mary (died 1750), who had married Simon Beck of Hertford (died 1776).

The Cooks, fishmongers in Billingsgate, were relatives of Carrington's wife Elizabeth.

William Deards of Bramfield, licensee of the Grandison Arms public house, Bury Lane, Bramfield. His widow continued to keep the house after his death in 1792. Carrington was a frequent guest.

The Heaslers (or Haslers) were also relatives of Elizabeth Carrington. Her sister Anne had married William Heasler in 1779. They kept the Spread Eagle at Amwell End, Ware, of which Carrington owned the freehold, bequeathing it to his daughter Mary Ann (Pol).

William Hunsdon was at Hollards Farm, Codicote, from 1791 until his death in 1796, his widow until 1803. Their son Henry farmed at West End Farm, Bramfield, adjacent to Bacons. He was appointed overseer of the poor for Bramfield 11 Apr 1801. He died on 13 July 1803 and was buried at Great Amwell. His widow continued there until her own death in Sep 1805. He was the last of three generations of tenant farmers at West End (349 acres in the survey of 1804). The farm buildings were demolished in 1969.

The Pearce or Pierce family were cousins of Carrington's wife Elizabeth, whose mother was a Pearce before her marriage.

APPENDIX THREE

The Piggotts were relatives of Carrington's mother Mary (née Piggott, died 1747). Thomas Piggott, a cousin, kept the Red House Inn, St Albans, until his death in January 1802.

Bryand or Bryant Preston of Broad Oak End Farm, Bramfield. He was overseer of the poor 1799-1801. He and Carrington carried out the first census in Bramfield 1801.

John Randall, tenant farmer of Place Farm, Bramfield. A churchwarden and overseer of Bramfield. He left the farm in November 1801 and settled in Brighton and became a coal merchant there. Carrington visited him in July 1804.

George Richardson, church clerk of Bramfield, licensee of the Rose and Crown, Aston; then the Bulls Head, Hertford; then the Blackbirds in Parliament Square, Hertford.

Joseph Strutt (1748-1802), antiquary and engraver, was born at Springfield Mill near Chelmsford, Essex, the son of Thomas Strutt, a prosperous miller. After his education at the King Edward VI School at Chelmsford, in 1764 he was apprenticed to the engraver William Wynne Ryland. He moved to London in 1771. During the 1780s he won the Royal Academy gold medal for two oil paintings and exhibited at the Academy on several occasions. He married Ann Blower of Bocking, Essex, on 16 Aug 1774 by whom he had two surviving sons. The couple settled in a house in Duke Street, Portland Place, London. He lodged at Bacons Farm from 1790-94 and established a day school and Sunday school at Tewin. After returning to London he lived in Charles Street, Hatton Garden. He was the author of several antiquarian books, the most well known being *The Sports and Pastimes of the People of England* first published in 1801. He included many Hertfordshire examples in his work. A medieval romance, *Queen Hoo Hall*, was completed by Sir Walter Scott and published after his death. Joseph's son William Thomas (1777-1850) held a position in the Bank of England but was also a miniature painter of some repute – he painted the only known view of Bacons Farm aged 13. Two of William's sons, Arthur and William, were also painters.

John Vaux, tenant of Greenhall Farm, Bramfield and from 1802 Bramfield Place Farm (234 acres in the 1804 Survey). He was overseer of the poor in 1802/1803.

APPENDIX THREE

LOCAL CLERGY:

The Revd Edward Bourchier (1776-1840) was the third of that name to be rector of Bramfield, though not in succession. He held the living from 1801 until 1840. His grandfather from 1740 to 1775 and father from 1775 to his death in 1785. He married Harriet Jenner in London on 7 Feb 1804. The ceremony was conducted by the Revd Thomas Lloyd (qv). After their marriage the couple made extensive alterations to Bramfield Rectory. Harriet died on 18 Jan 1864, aged 62. There are monumental inscriptions to all three Edwards and their families on the south chancel wall of Bramfield church.

Revd Robert Cholmondley was both rector of Hertingfordbury, 1755-1804 and Hertford St Andrew 1755-1804. He died at Bath in June 1804. A nephew of Horace Walpole, he married Mary Woffington, sister of the actress Peg in 1746.

Revd James Hook (1771-1828) was both rector of Hertingfordbury 1804-1817 and Hertford St Andrew 1805-1817. Later Dean of Worcester and chaplain to the Prince of Wales. His father James was a composer and conductor and his brother Theodore a wit and dramatist.

Charles Woolsey Johnson was rector of Datchworth for 43 years from 1785 until his death on 30 Nov 1828. He was one of the subscribers who contributed to the building of Datchworth School in 1820.

Revd William Lloyd, rector of Bramfield from 1786 to 1800. The Revd Thomas Lloyd, his son (1772-1851), was rector of both Sacombe, Hertfordshire, 1807-51 and Fordwich, Kent, 1802-1851, and domestic chaplain to Earl Cowper.

Thomas Newton, son of Thomas, the Assistant Master of Knaresborough Grammar School, Yorkshire. He was appointed to the rectory of Tewin on 25 Feb 1797 and held the living until his death in 1843. He was also a JP for the North Riding of Yorkshire. Carrington records Newton's wife residing in Yorkshire as she was 'out of her mind' Apr 1803.

Revd Thomas Nicholson (c1750-1832) curate of Hertford St Andrew from 1791 until his death. One of his sons, George, a solicitor, founded the well known Hertford firm of Longmores and another son Thomas, also a solicitor, built Wallfields, now adjacent to County Hall, Hertford.

APPENDIX THREE

LOCAL LANDOWNERS:

William Baker (1743-1824) of Bayfordbury served as MP for the Borough of Hertford 1780-1784 and for the county 1790-1802, and 1805-1807. He had been critical of the introduction of the Income Tax and opposed the Treaty of Amiens as being too lenient to France. However Carrington declared that it was very much a local issue which lost him his seat – see diary entry for 12 July 1802. He was an officer of the Herts yeomanry until 1810. He married Juliana Penn in 1771 by whom he had a daughter, Juliana, born in 1772. His wife died very shortly after the birth and in 1775 he married secondly Sophia Conyers of Stoke Park, Buckinghamshire, by whom he had a further six daughters and nine sons. It was his grandson, also called William, who inherited Bayfordbury in 1824. Bayfordbury had been purchased by his father William (1705-70) in 1757 and rebuilt. The Baker family sold the estate in 1945 and Bayfordbury has recently been split into several houses. His brother Samuel lived at Hertingfordbury Park until his death in 1804. (A long series of Baker family correspondence is held at HALS Reference: *DE/Bk*).

Thomas Hope Byde, son of Thomas Plumer Byde of Ware Park, was Receiver General of Taxes for the area. Carrington frequently went to Ware Park or into the town to give him the land and income taxes collected. The Bydes were lords of the manor of Ware from 1668 until 1829.

George Caswall (1762-1825) inherited the Manor of Sacombe from his father Timothy, who had died in Aug 1802. He served as a Justice of the Peace from 1806-12 and 1819-20. In 1803, he began to build a new house near the site of the former demolished mansion house. In the same year he also sold 'the great fall of timber' from the park described by Carrington. Sacombe House, surrounded by a park of 150 acres, lies south-east from the parish church. It was sold to the Smith family of Watton Woodhall on George's death in 1825. It was severely damaged by fire in 1911-12.

Timothy Caswall (1733-1802), MP for Hertford, 1761-1768, and MP for Brackley, 1771-1789, a Commissioner of Excise, 1789-1802. He was a personal friend of William Pitt who visited him at Sacombe Park. Timothy acquired the Sacombe estate on his marriage to Mary Constantia Rolt.

Lady Elizabeth Cathcart of Tewin Water (1691-1789) second daughter of Thomas Maylin, a London brewer. She married first James Fleet (died 1733) and came to Tewin Water. Her second husband was Colonel William Sabine, and her third Charles, 8th Baron Cathcart. Fourthly she married in May 1745 the Irishman Hugh Macquire, who kept her confined in Ireland until his death in 1766, when she returned to Tewin Water. She died aged 98 in 1789 and is buried at Tewin. Carrington, aged 15, was employed as her gardener in 1743 but by 1750 he was working for Richard Warren of Marden Hill.

James Cecil, 7th Earl and 1st Marquess of Salisbury of Hatfield (1748-1823). On 13 June 1800 the Grand Review by George III in Hatfield Park was attended by most of the Royal Family. This a spectacular military parade by almost 1,600 troops was witnessed by Carrington. War with France was declared at the end of May 1803 after the uneasy Peace of Amiens.

Edward Spencer Cowper (1779-1823), younger brother of the 4th and 5th Earls, was born in Florence. He married Catherine, the youngest daughter of Thomas March Phillips of Garendon Park, Leicestershire, in May 1808. He was MP for the Borough of Hertford 1802-Jan 1817. He demolished the old medieval manor house at Digswell and rebuilt it partly on the same site. Known as Digswell Park, the house was the headquarters of the Digswell Arts Trust for many years and is now divided into apartments.

George Augustus Clavering Cowper, 3rd Earl Cowper (1738-1789) left England in 1757 for the Grand Tour and never returned during his father's lifetime. Carrington relates that he returned to Cole Green House for only a few months in 1786. He remained in Florence becoming a leader of society and a patron of art, science, literature and the opera.

George Augustus Cowper, 4th Earl Cowper (1776-1799) died unmarried, aged 22. A newspaper cutting amongst Carrington's papers reports that he died of a 'severe cold caught while doing duty with the Hertfordshire Regiment of Militia' (*HALS: DE/X3/14*). He was succeeded by his brother Peter Leopold Louis Francis Nassau Clavering-Cowper, 5th Earl Cowper (1778-1837). The 5th Earl demolished Cole Green House in 1801 and began to build a new house on the site of a farm at Panshanger on the opposite side of the Mimram valley. He married Emily Lamb, sister of Peniston Lamb of Brocket Hall; through her, the Brocket estate came to the Cowpers. He purchased Bacons Farm and the Rose and Crown, Tewin, in 1801.

Henry Cowper (died 1841) was a descendent of Spencer Cowper, the brother of William, 1st Earl Cowper, and was therefore a distant cousin of the 4th and 5th Earls. Together with his father Lt-General Spencer Cowper (1726-1797) he acted as guardian to the young sons of the 3rd Earl when they were sent to England in 1781 from their home in Florence. He leased Tewin Water from the Cowper estate from 1791, rebuilding the house and making many improvements to the park. He was chairman of the Hertfordshire Quarter Sessions, a position he resigned in 1821, and clerk to the House of Lords.

William Cowper (1665-1723), Lord Chancellor, 1707, and created 1st Earl Cowper in 1718. He began to build Cole Green House in 1704 and commissioned Louis Laguerre in 1716 to paint the ceiling of 'the great room' (*HALS: DE/P/E1*).

William Cowper, 2nd Earl Cowper (1709-1764). He was a Lord of the Bedchamber from 1733 to 1747, became lord lieutenant and custos rotulorum for Hertfordshire in 1744, and was a Fellow of the Royal Society. He died at Cole Green in 1764.

Dr Thomas Dimsdale (1712-1800) and his second son, Nathaniel (1748-1811), also a doctor, had both been created Barons of the Russian Empire by the Empress Catherine the Great for inoculating her and her court against smallpox. Thomas made two visits to Russia, the first in 1768-9 together with Nathaniel. He was made a Fellow of the Royal Society in 1769. The second in 1781 with his wife Elizabeth. On their return they lived mostly at Cowbridge House, Hertford, with occasional visits to Bath and London. Thomas was MP for Hertford from 1780 to 1790; Nathaniel from 1790 to 1802.

Francis Egerton, Baron Ellesmere, Marquis of Brackley, 8th Earl and 3rd and last Duke of Bridgewater (1736-1803) of Ashridge, Little Gaddesden, purchased Woolmers Park, Essendon from the brewer Samuel Whitbread in 1801 for £16,502 10s. He then commissioned the architect James Lewis to alter the house. The Duke died 8 March 1803 at his London house and was buried at Little Gaddesden, Hertfordshire. Remembered as the builder of the Worsley Basin and canals to Manchester and Runcorn on the River Mersey assisted by the engineer James Brindley, 1761-1776.

Richard Emmott of Goldings, Waterford, near Hertford (1747-1820). In 1811 he sold the Goldings estate to Samuel Smith of Watton Woodhall. In 1803 he demolished Bulls Mill House to Carrington's dismay. He is buried at St Leonard's church, Bengeo.

APPENDIX THREE

James Bucknall Grimston, 3rd Viscount Grimston of Gorhambury, St.Albans (1747-1806) and builder of the present Gorhambury (architect Sir Robert Taylor), MP for the borough of St Albans 1783-1784, MP for Hertfordshire 1784-1790.

James Walter Grimston (1775-1845), son of the above, created 1st Earl of Verulam, MP for the borough of St Albans 1802-1808.

Peniston Lamb (1770-1805), MP for Hertfordshire 1802-1805. Eldest son of Sir Peniston Lamb, 1st Viscount Melbourne of Brocket Hall, and brother of William Lamb later Queen Victoria's Prime Minister 1834-1841. Captain Herts Yeomanry Cavalry from 1794.

William Plumer of Gilston, near Sawbridgeworth (1736-1822) was MP for the county 1768-1807. His family originated from Blakesware, near Widford, but he abandoned that estate in favour of New Place, Gilston. Blakesware was demolished in 1823, although rebuilt in 1852. New Place was rebuilt in 1878 and renamed Gilston Park.

Sir Thomas Rumbold, baronet (1736-1791) served the East India Company and was Governor of Madras from 1777. Purchased the Watton Woodhall estate in 1777 from the Botelers (who were related to the Botelers of Bramfield). He commissioned Thomas Leverton to build a new mansion house. Carrington describes the destruction by fire of the Tudor house in October 1771. On his death Watton Woodhall was sold to Paul Benfield also of the East India Company, who, becoming bankrupt, sold the property to Samuel Smith in 1801. The remainder of his estate he bequeathed to the children of his second wife Joanna, daughter of Revd Dr Law, Lord Bishop of Carlisle.

Sir John Saunders Sebright of Beechwood Park, Flamstead, 7th Baronet (1767-1846) was a notable agriculturalist and naturalist and generous to the poor. Sheriff of Hertfordshire in 1797-8, Captain of the Herts Yeomanry Cavalry in 1798 and MP for Hertfordshire 1807-1834. The house at Beechwood is now a school.

Lord John Townshend (1757-1832) was the second son of the 1st Marquess Townshend of Raynham Hall, Norfolk. The Townshend family acquired Balls Park, Hertford, through the marriage in 1723 of Etheldreda or Audrey Harrison, daughter of Edward Harrison of Balls Park, with Charles

Townshend of Kings Lynn (1700-1764). Also owned Datchworthbury and Jenningsbury.

George Mason Villiers, 1st Earl of Grandison (1751-1800) was lord of the manor of Bramfield. His daughter and sole heir, Lady Gertrude Villiers (1778-1809), married in 1802, Lord Henry Stuart, younger son of the 1st Marquess of Bute of Luton Hoo, Bedfordshire. Their son Henry, who took the name Villiers-Stuart, sold the manor of Bramfield in 1825. The Grandisons came from Dromana in Ireland so were absentee landlords but gave their name to the Bramfield public house frequented by Carrington and his friends. Carrington visits Luton Hoo in July 1802. The old Tudor manor house in Bramfield became Place Farm and was leased to farming tenants.

Richard Warren of Marden in the parish of Tewin was John Carrington's 'good old master', who died in April 1768. Carrington probably began to work for him after Lady Cathcart was taken from Tewin Water in 1746. After Richard Warren's death his son Arthur returned to live at Marden but sold the house *c*1785 for £7,500 to Robert Mackey of Tewin House, who proceeded to rebuild it. According to Carrington, Arthur then moved to Charlton near Hitchin, then later to Graveley, where he died in April 1804. Mackey sold Marden to Richard Flower in 1808, who sold in 1817 to Claude George Thornton. Thornton then asked the architect Sir John Soane to redesign the house. It is now divided into apartments.

Glossary

acre: the area that could be ploughed by a team of eight oxen in one day; standardized by Edward I (1272-1307) as a plot of land measuring 4,840 square yards and traditionally 40 poles long by 4 poles wide (220 yards x 22 yards; 0.4047 hectares).

Assizes: criminal courts, presided over by a judge, which tried capital and other serious offences. Hertfordshire was in the Home Circuit led by judges from London. The court sat in Hertford, the visits of the judges being amongst the social highlights of the year and brought in much business to the town.

bling: blind.

bloat: a disease affecting cows. On eating clover cows' stomachs react badly and expand very quickly; if not treated immediately the cows literally burst.

bran(n): the husk of wheat, barley, oats or other grain separated from the flour after grinding. The coarsest portion of the ground husk.

brasier: one who works in brass.

bread (bred): trained for.

brief: briefs were royal mandates for collections of money towards some supposedly deserving object, such as for the victims of a fire. They were read from the pulpit to appeal to the charity of the congregation.

broker: a retail dealer, one who bought to sell over again

bush fair: a fair held on open ground usually in a village, 'in the bush', rather than a market place in a town.

bushel: the Imperial bushel was not established in Great Britain until 1824; prior to that it could be smaller and could vary in local use according to the kind or quality of goods in question. 4 pecks or 8 gallons (56 lbs; approx 27kg).

butt: a cask for wine or ale of varying capacity from 108 to 140 gallons. Arithmetic Book says: 84 gallons = 1 pipe or butt.

chaff: a collective term for the husks of corn or other grain separated by threshing or winnowing. Also the cut hay or straw used for cattle feed.

chaise: a light, open carriage for one or two persons.

chalk drawer: one who digs chalk.

chalking: the manuring, or marling, of land with chalk. Hertfordshire farmers dug pits through the heavy surface clay into the underlying chalk, which was then scattered over the fields [Young, p164]. Chalk was also burnt to make lime mortar for building.

churchwarden: two churchwardens, appointed annually at the Easter Vestry (qv), were responsible for the maintenance of the parish church and provision of services. Until 1868 they were allowed to levy a rate on all parishioners.
'cockt up hat': a hat or cap turned up in front.
collarmaker: one who makes collars especially for horses and other draught animals. The collar was a leather covered roll made to fit over the lower part of the neck of a horse forming part of the harness.
coppses (copse): a U-shaped iron, which by means of a pin passing through the ends can be fixed on a pole or beam to provide an attachment for something. Used in agricultural implements or harness etc.
cow leases: cow pasture.
cuppel (couple): a pair of sheep, one of each sex.
ditchen (ditching): the digging or repairing of ditches.
dray plough: a plough made without either wheel or foot.
dring: drink
faggotting: making into faggots or binding up into faggots.
farrier: one who shoes horses but also one who may treat diseases in horses.
flurey: fight, argument, a sudden confusion or excitement.
Four Corners: 'Is so called from four large pins which are placed singly at each angle of a square frame. The Players stand at a distance, which may be varied by joint consent, and throw at the pins a large heavy bowl, which sometimes weighs six or eight pounds. The excellency of the game consist in beating them down in the fewest casts of the bowl' [J Strutt, *The Sports and Pastimes of the People of England* (1845 edition), p273].
gring: appears to be part of the process of making malt.
griseled (grizzled): speckled, grey (of horses).
grist: corn which is to be ground or that has been ground. Also malt crushed or ground for brewing.
Half-bowl: see Roley-poley
hand post: a direction sign or guide post placed at the parting of roads. Often shaped like the fingers of a hand at the end of the arm.
harrow: heavy frame of timber or iron set with iron teeth. It is dragged over ploughed land to break up clods, turn the soil, root up weeds or cover the seed.
higler: an itinerant dealer.
homage: the jurors of a manor court.
horn: about half a pint of beer, which may have been served in a cup made of horn.

hostler: see ostler.
hovel(l): an open shed or lean-to building; an outhouse used as a shelter for cattle, a receptacle for grain or tools.
hoy: a small, rigged ship for conveying passengers and goods along a coast.
Hundred: an administrative division of a county and area of jurisdiction for taxation purposes etc.
hurdlemaker: one who makes hurdles chiefly used to form temporary fences, sheep pens etc. They are made from interwoven withes of hazel, willow etc over a portable, rectangular frame.
illuminations: fireworks.
jog(g): a small cart load [Yaxley, *Researcher's Glossary*, p112].
journeyman: one who having served his apprenticeship to a handicraft or trade, is qualified to work at it for day wages. A qualified artisan who works for another.
Justice of the Peace: established by 1361 when a statute gave them the right to try minor offenders. They were appointed by the Crown from the major landowners of a county who received no payment for their duties. In addition the Justices were responsible for the regulation of trade, including licencing the sale of alcohol and the checking of weights and measures, overseeing the operation of the Poor Law, and the upkeep of roads and bridges.
kitt: a straw or rush basket for fish.
larges (largesse): hospitality.
Lent: the first day of Lent, Ash Wednesday, traditionally began a period of fasting and penitence in commemoration of Christ's 40 days in the wilderness, culminating in the Christian festival of Easter four weeks later.
load: a unit of capacity or weight that can vary by locality and substance. Carrington states that in Hertfordshire a load is 5 bushels [Feb 1801].
malt dust: refuse which falls from the grain in the process of malting. In Hertfordshire this is used as manure. [Young, *Agriculture of Hertfordshire* p170].
meal: the finer part of the ground grain, as opposed to the bran (qv).
meal man: one who deals in meal.
Michaelmas: 29 September; one of the 'quarter' days when traditionally tenants paid their rent. The Quarter Sessions held around this date was known as the Michaelmas Sessions.
mock turtle: cooked dish made from the head of a calf which is stuffed with various ingredients.

mountane (mountain) wine: a type of wine formerly produced in Malaga, Spain [*OED*].

neatsfood oyle (neat's-foot oil): oil made from boiled cow heel, especially used to dress leather. Here used to treat animals infected with lice or the like.

oyle (oil) mill: perhaps where cow heel etc is ground to make oil as above.

ostler/hostler: a man who attends to horses at an inn, a stableman, a groom.

overseer: parish officer chosen at the Easter Vestry to administer the Poor Law for the ensuing year. Their names were then submitted to the Justices of the Peace for approval. Funds were raised in the parish in the form of a rate assessment to meet the demands of poor relief and the maintenance of the parish workhouse.

peck: a measure of capacity used for dry goods - a quarter of a bushel; a liquid measure of two gallons.

Petty Sessions: a court of summary jurisdiction, held by two or more Justices of the Peace for trying lesser offences, or to enquire into the more serious cases to be tried at Quarter Sessions (qv) or the Assizes (qv).

phosphorus man: a person who sells phosphorus. Phosphorus is a non-metallic element, yellowish and resembling wax, extremely inflammable and hence appears luminous in the dark. A small quantity dissolved in oil emits a light if uncorked in the dark and a paste containing phosphorus was used to kill vermin.

pightle: a small enclosed field, usually irregular in shape.

pipe of port: 84 gallons.

pocket(t): a bag or sack used as a measure of quantity, chiefly hops or wool – can vary in capacity according to the commodity and locality. A pocket of hops was about 168 lbs.

poiner: dialect form of 'pioneer', a labourer in the militia.

pole: linear measurement of 5½ yards; 4 poles = 22 yards; 40 poles = one furlong.

pollard: the bran sifted from the flour; also, relating to a tree, cut back or lopped.

presentment: a statement made on oath at a court of any kind.

Quarter Sessions: quarterly meetings of the Justices of the Peace for each county and county borough at which criminals were tried for minor offences.

quartern: a quarter.

quick: live slips or cuttings of plants, set in the ground to grow especially those of whitethorn or other shrub of which hedges are made.

Raising feast: a celebration similar to the laying of a foundation stone or topping out ceremony held to mark the beginning or various stages of building a new house eg at Tewin Water.

reek: (hay) rick.

Rogation: a perambulation of the parish boundaries was traditionally undertaken at Rogationtide (near the 5th Sunday after Easter) and was meant to ensure the community knew where the boundaries were and maintained them. Carrington describes the Bramfield parish boundaries in detail in his entry for 30 May 1803. At Bramfield the children joined the walk and plenty of food was provided along the way.

Roley-poley or Half-bowl: Joseph Strutt describes this in detail and specifically cites Hertfordshire as a location where it is still played: 'This is one of the games prohibited by Edward IV and received its denomination from being played with one half of a sphere of wood. Half-bowl is practised to this day in Hertfordshire, where it is commonly called rolly-polly; and it is best performed upon the floor of a room, especially if it be smooth and level. There are fifteen small pins of a conical form required for this pastime; twelve of which are placed at equal distances upon the circumference of a circle of about two feet and a half diameter; one of the three remaining pins occupies the centre; and the other two are placed without the circle at the back part of it, and parallel with the bowling-place, but so as to be in a line with the middle pin; forming a row of five pins, including two of those upon the circumference. In playing this game, the bowl, when delivered, must pass above the pins, and round the end-pin, without the circle, before it beats any of them down; if not, the cast is forfeited: and, owing to the great bias of the bowl, this task is not very readily performed by such as have not made themselves perfect by practice. The middle pin is distinguished by four balls at the top; and, if thrown down, is reckoned for four towards the game; the intermediate pin upon the circle, in the row of five, has three balls, and is reckoned for three; the first pin without the circle has two balls, and is counted for two; and the value of all the others singly is but one. Thirty-one chalks complete the game; which he who first obtains is the conqueror. If this number be exceeded, it is a matter of no consequence: the game is equally won.' [J Strutt, *The Sports and Pastimes of the People of England* (1845 edition), p274].

rood: a unit of land area equal to 40 square rods (a quarter of an acre, approx. 0.1012 hectare), but varying locally.

rough music: the making of a rude cacophony of sound and simple dramatic performance, was used to ridicule or express hostility towards those who had offended against communal values and moral standards.
sack carrier: a man buying, selling or carting on commission and as a part-time job. The term is also used in Bedfordshire.
score: twenty.
seedsman: a sower or dealer in seed.
shell coffin: a plain wooden coffin with no lining.
Shuffell half: 'Among the domestic pastimes, playing at shovel-board claims a principal place. In former times the residences of the nobility, or the mansions of the opulent, were not thought to be complete without a shovel-board table; and this fashionable piece of furniture was usually stationed in the great hall. The tables for this diversion were sometimes very expensive, owing to the great pains and labour bestowed upon their construction. In the hall at Chartley, Staffordshire the shuffle-board table, is ten yards one foot and an inch long. The length of these tables, if they be perfectly smooth and level, adds to their value, in proportion to its increase; but they rarely exceed three feet, or three feet and a half, in width. At one end of the shovel-board there is a line drawn across, parallel with the edge, and about three or four inches from it; at four feet distance from this line another is made, over which it is necessary for the weight to pass when it is thrown by the player, otherwise the go is not reckoned. The players stand at the end of the table, opposite the two marks above mentioned, each of them having four flat weights of metal, which they shove from them, one at a time, alternately: and the judgment of the play is, to give sufficient impetus to the weight to carry it beyond the mark nearest to the edge of the board, which requires great nicety, for if it be too strongly impelled, so as to fall from the table, and there is nothing to prevent it, into a trough placed underneath for its reception, the throw is not counted; if it hangs over the edge, without falling, three are reckoned towards the player's game; if it lie between the line and the edge, without hanging over, it tells for two; if on the line, and not up to it, but over the first line, it counts for one. The game, when two play, is generally eleven; but the number is extended when four, or more, are jointly concerned' [J Strutt, *The Sports and Pastimes of the People of England* (2nd edition, 1810), pp263-4].
small beer: beer of a weak, poor or inferior quality.
Statute fair: Statute fairs were hiring fairs so called because an Act of Parliament of 1677 (29 Cha 2 c3) endorsed the yearly bonds made between

farmers and their servants. Traditionally these would have expired at Martinmas (11 Nov) but certainly after the harvest was over at the end of the farming year.

strange: exceptional.

swath: Carrington uses this term to mean the growing crop ready for reaping.

tears (tares): common cultivated vetch grown as a natural manure and for the feeding of livestock. In Hertfordshire most farmers 'have tares for soiling their horses' [Young, *Agriculture of Hertfordshire*, pp125-6].

todd: weight of wool, roughly 28 lbs.

tole: market toll payable to the mayor and aldermen of the Borough of Hertford

town crier: the town crier or bellman was an officer of the court who made public pronouncements whenever required.

understrapper: an underling; a subordinate agent; an assistant (in common use from *c*1710 [*OED*]).

vestry: a room attached to the chancel of a church used for the keeping of vestments, also used for parish meetings. The meeting itself, attended by the minister, churchwardens, overseers, parish constable and leading parishioners, became known as the 'Vestry'. In Bramfield the Easter Vestry, at which the new officials for the coming year were elected, was held in the Grandison Arms.

vitriol: a metal sulphate; oil of vitriol is concentrated sulphuric acid; spirit of vitriol is a much watered version used in medicine.

wether sheep: a castrated ram.

wheeler, wheelwrite (wheelwright): one whose trade was to make or repair wheels, wheeled carriages etc.

white oats: any variety of oats having light-coloured grains.

whitesmith: person who makes articles from tin-plated iron or from tin or other white metal; also, person who makes iron tools with a sharp edge, or other iron articles with a polished surface [*OED*].

wiggs: sweet buns flavoured with ale and caraway seeds.

wiskey (whiskey/whisky): type of light two-wheeled one-horse carriage, used in England and America in the late 18th and early 19th century [*OED*].

woodward: the keeper of a wood; an officer of a wood or forest, having charge of the growing timber.

Bibliography

Manuscripts
Hertfordshire Archives and Local Studies:
DE/Jn/Z58-59: Transcript by W Branch Johnson of the Carrington diaries, 1798-1810, typed by Miss Eileen Lynch
DE/P: Panshanger Estate collection
DE/X3/1-14: The diaries of John Carrington of Bacons Farm, Bramfield, 1798-1810, and miscellaneous papers
DE/X3/17-23: The diaries of Jack Carrington of the Rose and Crown, Tewin, 1810-1812
DE/X3/15: The Arithmetic Book
DP: Hertfordshire Parish Registers
DP22/12/2: Bramfield vestry minutes and overseers' accounts, 1803-1818
DP22/29/2: Draft survey of the Manors of Bramfield and Queen Hoo, 1804
DP48/29/14: Hertford College Youths, annual lists of members, 1786-1924
NQ1/5D/1: Hertfordshire and Bedfordshire Quaker Quarterly Meeting burial digest, 1656-1838
NQ2/1A/21: Hertford Quakers Monthly Mens Meeting minute book, 1787-1804
QS and LS: Quarter Sessions records for both the County and Liberty Sessions including Victuallers' Recognizances (QSVR and LSVR)
TP8/2: Watton Turnpike Trust minutes, 1778-1819

Printed primary Sources
Branch Johnson, W, '*Memorandoms For…' The Diary between 1798 and 1810 of John Carrington Farmer, Chief Constable, Tax Assessor, Surveyor of Highways and Overseer of the Poor, of Bramfield in Hertfordshire* (Chichester, 1973)
Falvey, H, ed, *The Receipt Book of Baroness Elizabeth Dimsdale, c1800*, HRS, vol XXVIII (Hertford, 2013)
Falvey, H, & Hindle, S, eds, *'This little commonwealth': Layston parish memorandum book, 1607-c1650 & 1704-c1747*, HRS vol XIX (Hertford, 2003)
Gibbs, A E, *The Corporation Records of St Albans* (St Albans, 1890)
Hardy, W J, *Notes and Extracts from the Sessions Rolls, 1699-1850*, vol II, Hertfordshire County Records (Hertford, 1905)

Le Hardy, W, *Notes and Extracts from the Sessions Records of the Liberty of St Alban Division, 1770-1840*, vol IV, Hertfordshire County Records (Hertford, 1923)
Le Hardy, W, *Calendar to the Sessions Books and other Sessions Records, 1752-1799,* vol VIII, Hertfordshire County Records (Hertford, 1935)
Le Hardy, W, ed, *Quarter Sessions and Other Records in the Custody of the Officials of the County,* Guide to the Hertfordshire Record Office, part 1 (Hertford, 1961)
Le Hardy, W and Reckitt, G Ll, *Calendar to the Sessions Books and other Sessions Records, 1799-1833,* vol IX, Hertfordshire County Records (Hertford, 1939)
Sheldrick, G, ed, *The Accounts of Thomas Green, 1742-1790*, HRS vol VIII (Hertford, 1992)

Secondary Sources

Austin, Stephen pub, *List of Sheriffs of the County of Hertford from the Accession of William the Conqueror to the present time* (Hertford, 1947)
Bagenal, P, *Hertingfordbury Park and its links with the Bayfordbury Estate* (Hertfordshire Gardens Trust, 2000)
Baines, D C, *'Two Coats Colder', Chronicles of Offley in Hertfordshire* (Offley, 1994)
Birley, D, *A Social History of Cricket* (1999)
Bowyer, N, *A Short History of Bramfield* (Hertford, 1970)
Branch Johnson, W, *The Carrington Diary, 1797-1810* (Letchworth, 1956)
Branch Johnson, W, *Hertfordshire Inns*, part 1, *East Herts* (Letchworth, 1962)
Branch Johnson, W, *Welwyn, By & Large, Historical Gossip from a Hertfordshire Village* (Welwyn, 1967)
Branch Johnson, W, *The Hertfordshire Pepys, John Carrington of Bramfield and his Diary from 1797-1810* (Letchworth, 1970)
Briggs, A, *How They Lived*, Vol III, *1700-1815* (Oxford, 1969)
Broad, J, 'John Carrington and the Crisis of 1800-01: ambiguity in the face of the "moral economy"' (paper given in Glasgow Apr 2012)
Broad, J, 'Farmers and Improvement, 1780-1840', in R W Hoyle, ed, *The Farmer in England, 1650-1980* (Farnham, 2013)
Burke, J, *Genealogical and Heraldic Dictionary of the Peerage and Baronetage of the British Empire*, 6th edn (1839)
Butler, D M, *The Quaker Meeting Houses of Britain*, vol 1 (1999)
Cecil, D, *The Cecils of Hatfield House, A Portrait of an English Ruling Family* (1973)

Clutterbuck, R, *The History and Antiquities of the County of Hertford*, 3 vols (1815-27)
Cokayne, G E et al, eds, *The Complete Peerage of England, Scotland, Ireland, Great Britain and the United Kingdom, Extant, Extinct or Dormant, new edn,* 13 vols (1910-1959)
Colvin, H, *A Biographical Dictionary of British Architects, 1600-1840* (1978)
Cussans, J E, *History of Hertfordshire,* 3 vols (1870-1878)
Dimsdale, R, 'The Old Poor Law and medicine in and around Hertford, 1700-1834', in Steven King and Gillian Gear, eds, *Social welfare in Hertfordshire from 1600. A Caring County?* (Hatfield, 2013)
Dodds, G, *The Church Bells of Hertfordshire* (Welwyn Garden City, 1994)
Dodds, J, *Hertfordshire Bellfounders* (Hatfield, 2003)
Fellowes, E H, *The military knights of Windsor, 1352-1944* (Windsor, 1944)
Foster J, ed, *Alumni Oxonienses; The members of the University of Oxford 1500-1714*, 4 vols (Oxford, 1891-2)
Fraser, M, *History of Slough* (Slough, 1973, 2nd edn 1980)
Gander, R, *Richard Hale School* (Tewin, 2008)
Gover, J E B, Mawer, A, and Stenton, F M, *The Place-Names of Hertfordshire* (Cambridge, 1938)
HALS, *Tracing Your Family History in Hertfordshire* (Hatfield, 2003)
Heath, C, *The Book of Hertford* (Chesham, 1975)
Hey, D, *The Oxford Companion to Local and Family History* (Oxford, 1996)
Hindle, S, 'Beating the Bounds of the Parish: Order, Memory, and Identity in the English Local Community, c1500-1700', in M Halvorson and K E Spierling, eds, *Defining community in early modern Europe* (Aldershot, 2008)
Hope-Jones, A, *Income Tax in the Napoleonic Wars* (1939)
Hughes, P G, *Wales and the Drovers* (1943, reprinted 1988)
Hutton, R, *The Stations of the Sun, A History of the Ritual Year in Britain* (Oxford, 1996)
Jones, A, ed, *Hertfordshire 1731-1800 as recorded in the Gentleman's Magazine* (Hatfield, 1993)
Kennedy, W, *English Taxation* (1964)
Lysons, D, *An Historical Account of those parishes in the County of Middlesex which are not described in the Environs of London* (1800)
Malet, H, *Bridgewater, The Canal Duke, 1736-1803* (Manchester, 1977)
Mathias, P, *The Brewing Industry in England, 1700-1830* (Cambridge, 1959)
Moran, J, *Stephen Austin of Hertford* (Hertford, 1968)
Namier, L and Brooke, J, *The House of Commons, 1757-1790*, 2 vols (1964)

Newcome, P, *The History of the Ancient and Royal Foundation called the Abbey of St Alban* (1795)

Osborn, N, *The Story of Hertfordshire Police* (Letchworth, 1969)

Page, W, ed, *The Victoria History of the Counties of England: A History of Hertfordshire*, 4 vols (1902-14)

Parker, J, *'Nothing for Nothing for Nobody' A History of Hertfordshire Banks and Banking* (Hatfield, 1986)

Partington, A, ed, *Oxford Dictionary of Quotations* (Oxford, 1941, and revised 4th edn, 1996)

Perman, D, *Scott of Amwell, Dr Johnson's Quaker Critic* (Ware, 2001)

Prince, H, *Parks in Hertfordshire since 1500* (Hatfield, 2008)

Sainsbury, J, *Hertfordshire's Soldiers from 1757* (Hatfield, 1969)

Sainsbury, J, 'Local Volunteers during the Napoleonic Wars' in D Short, ed, *An Historical Atlas of Hertfordshire* (Hatfield, 2011) pp176-7

Smith, J T, *Hertfordshire Houses Selective Inventory* (RCHM, 1993)

Southerden Burn, J, *The History of Parish Registers in England* (first pub 1829; reprint 1976)

Strutt, J, *The Sports and Pastimes of the People of England; including the rural and domestic recreations, May-games, mummeries, pageants, processions, and pompous spectacles, from the earliest period to the present time* (first pub 1801; 1845 edition)

Thorne, R G, *The House of Commons, 1790-1820,* History of Parliament, 5 vols (1986)

Tregelles, J A, *A History of Hoddesdon* (Hertford, 1908)

Turnor, L, *History of the Ancient Town & Borough of Hertford* (Hertford, 1830)

Venn, J A, *Alumni Cantabrigiensis*, part 2, *1752-1900*, 6 vols (Cambridge, 1940-1951)

Weinreb B, Hibbert C, Keay, J and Keay, J, *The London Encyclopaedia* (3rd edn, 2008)

Western, J R, *The English Militia in the 18th century, The Story of a Political Issue, 1660-1805* (1965)

Whitaker, A, *Brewers in Hertfordshire A Historical Gazetteer* (Hatfield, 2006)

Woodruff, P, *The Men who Ruled India*, 2 vols (1953-54)

Yaxley, D, *A Researcher's Glossary of words found in historical documents of East Anglia* (Dereham, 2003)

Young, A, *General View of the Agriculture of Hertfordshire* (1804; reprint 1971)

The Hertfordshire Record Society

The Hertfordshire Record Society exists to make Hertfordshire's historical records of all kinds more readily available to the general reader. Since 1985 a regular series of texts has been published.

Membership enquiries and orders for previous publications to the Hon Treasurer, 2 Fairview Cottages, Amwell Hill, Great Amwell, Nr Ware, SG12 9RA.

Annual Subscription (2015-16) £17.50

Previous publications:

I *Tudor Churchwardens' Accounts*. Edited by Anthony Palmer (1985) O/P

II *Early Stuart Household Accounts*. Edited by Lionel M Munby (1986) O/P

III *'A Professional Hertfordshire Tramp' John Edwin Cussans, Historian of Hertfordshire*. Edited by Audrey Deacon and Peter Walne (1987) O/P

IV *The Salisbury-Balfour Correspondence, 1869-1892*. Edited by Robin *Harcourt* Williams (1988) O/P

V *The Parish Register & Tithing Book of Thomas Hassall of Amwell* [Registers, 1599-1657; Tithing Book, 1633-35]. Edited by Stephen G Doree (1989). Price £6.00

VI *Cheshunt College: The Early Years*. Edited by Edwin Welch (1990) O/P

VII *St Albans Quarter Sessions Rolls, 1784-1820*. Edited by David Dean (1991) O/P

VIII *The Accounts of Thomas Green, 1742-1790*. Edited by Gillian *Sheldrick* (1992) O/P

IX *St Albans Wills, 1471-1500.* Edited by Susan Flood (1993) O/P

X *Early Churchwardens' Accounts of Bishops Stortford, 1431-1538.* Edited by Stephen G Doree (1994). Price £6.00

XI *Religion in Hertfordshire, 1847-1851.* Edited by Judith Burg (1995). Price £6.00

XII *Muster Books for North & East Hertfordshire, 1580-1605.* Edited by Ann J King (1996). Price £6.00

XIII *Lifestyle & Culture in Hertford: Wills and Inventories, 1660-1725.* Edited by Beverly Adams (1997). Price £6.00

XIV *Hertfordshire Lay Subsidy Rolls, 1307 and 1334.* Edited by Janice Brooker and Susan Flood, with an Introduction by Dr Mark Bailey (1998). Price £6.00

XV *'Observations of Weather': The Weather Diary of Sir John Wittewronge of Rothamsted, 1684-1689.* Edited by Margaret Harcourt Williams and John Stevenson (1999). Price £19.00 (members £15.00)

XVI *Survey* of *the Royal Manor of Hitchin, c1676.* Edited by Bridget Howlett (2000). Price £6.00

XVII *Garden-Making and the Freeman family A Memoir of Hamels, 1713-1733.* Edited by Anne Rowe (2001). Price £18.50 (members £15.00)

XVIII *Two Nineteenth Century Hertfordshire Diaries, 1822-1849.* Edited by Judith Knight and Susan Flood (2002). Price £6.00

XIX *"This little commonwealth": Layston parish memorandum book, 1607-c1650 & 1704-c1747.* Edited by Heather Falvey and Steve Hindle (2003). Price £21.00 (members £15.00)

XX *Julian Grenfell, soldier and poet: letters and diaries, 1910-1915.* Edited by Kate Thompson (2004). Price £20.00 (members £15.00)

XXI *The Hellard Almshouses and other Stevenage Charities, 1482-2005.* Edited by Margaret Ashby (2005). Price £21.00 (members £15.00)

XXII *A Victorian Teenager's Diary: the Diary of Lady Adela Capel of Cassiobury, 1841-1842.* Edited by Marian Strachan (2006). Price paperback £9.99

XXIII *The Impact of the First Civil War on Hertfordshire, 1642-1647.* Edited by Alan Thomson (2007). Price £22.00 (members £17.50)

XXIV *The Diary of Benjamin Woodcock Master of the Barnet Union Workhouse, 1836-1838.* Edited by Gillian Gear (2008). Price £22.00 (members £17.50)

XXV *Datchworth Tithe Accounts, 1711-1747.* Edited by Jane Walker (2009). Price £22.00 (members £17.50)

XXVI *The Diary of John Carrington, Farmer of Bramfield, 1798-1810 Volume I (1798-1804).* Edited and with an Introduction by Susan Flood (2015). Price £22.00 (members £17.50)

XXVII *Humphry Repton's Red Books of Panshanger and Tewin Water, 1799-1800.* With an Introduction by Twigs Way (2011). Price £30.00 (members £17.50)

XXVIII *The Receipt Book of Baroness Elizabeth Dimsdale, c1800.* Edited and with an Introduction by Heather Falvey. Price £22.00 (members £17.50)

XXIX *Records of the Manor of Norton in the Liberty of St Albans, 1244-1539.* Translated by Peter Foden. Edited and with an Introduction by the Norton Community Archaeology Group. Price £22.00 (members £17.50)

XXX *Weston School Logbooks, 1876-1914.* Transcribed by Joan Amis, Margaret Bowyer and Janet Gunn; edited and with an Introduction by Margaret Ashby. Price £22.00 (members £17.50)

The County of Hertford From Actual Survey by A Bryant In the Years 1820 and 1821 (2003; reprinted 2012). Price £8.50 (members £5.00)

A Topographical Map of Hartford-Shire by Andrew Dury and John Andrews, 1766 (2004; reprinted 2013). Price £9.50 (members £8.50)

For more information visit www.hrsociety.org.uk

Index of Names

The following abbreviations have been used:
bro, brother; bur, buried; d, died; dau, daughter; dec, deceased; gent, gentleman; mar, married; s, son; sis, sister; w, wife; wid, widow.
Eliz, Elizabeth; Geo, George; Richd, Richard; Robt, Robert; Tim, Timothy; Thos, Thomas; Wm, William.

INDEX OF NAMES

INDEX OF NAMES

INDEX OF NAMES

INDEX OF NAMES

Index of Places

Places are in Hertfordshire unless otherwise stated. The place name spellings used are those given in J E B Gover, A Mawer, and F M Stenton, *The Place-Names of Hertfordshire* (Cambridge, 1938).

INDEX OF PLACES

INDEX OF PLACES

INDEX OF PLACES

Index of Subjects

INDEX OF SUBJECTS

INDEX OF SUBJECTS

Walden
Langley
Sheephall
Sheephall HUND.
Broad Water
Bury
Dishland
Russell End
Whitwell Street
Hoo Far.
Knebworth Bury
Dades Green
The Holt
The Hoo
Three Houses
Hoo End
Tags End
Knebworth Green
Bragbury
West End
Ansels End
Kimpton
Rye End
HUND.
Rabley
Swordley
Head
Coddicot
Datchworth
Kimpton Hall
Woolmer Gr.
Coddicot Street
Mardley Heath
Potters Heath
Mardley Bury
Ayot Lawrence
Wellwyn
Lockleys
Harmer Green
Tewin
Bride Hall
Ayot St. Peters
Wheathamsted
Digswell House
Cobble End
Lea R.
Water End
Ayot Green
Digswell Water
Black Fan
Digswell
Brocket Hall
Brickwall House
Digswell Lodge
H U N D.
Grubs Bushes
Beech Hide
Harside
Cromer Hide
Hornby Hall
Lemsford Mills
Grubs Barn
Tower Hill
Symonds Hide
Ludwick Hide
Sandridge
Stanbrough
Wood Hall
Pidgeon Hall
Coopers
Astwick
Green Lane
Bush H.
Holywell
Hatfield Mill
Ash Farm
Bullocks Gr.
HATFIELD
Essendon
Newgate Fa.
Harpsfield Hall
Popesfield
Riddells
Hatfield House
Esfen
3 Houses
Nut Hide
West End
Birds Pl.
Row
Green
Popes